The Constitution
Evolution of a Government

ఴఴ

Teachers Guide

A Supplemental Teaching Unit from the Records of the National Archives

NATIONAL
ARCHIVES

National Archives Trust Fund Board
National Archives and Records Administration

A B C ⬥ C L I O

ABC – CLIO, Inc
130 Cremona Drive, P.O. Box 1911
Santa Barbara, CA 93116-1911
ISBN 1-57607-778-0

Photographs used as illustrations on the cover and throughout this book are held in the National Archives and Records Administration. To access these and thousands more like them, visit the National Archives Web site at **www.nara.gov.**

Table of Contents

Foreword

In its efforts to make the historical records of the federal government available nationally, the National Archives began in 1970 a program to introduce these vast resources to secondary school students. School classes visiting the National Archives in Washington were given the opportunity to examine and interpret original sources as historians use them. Teachers and students responded enthusiastically and encouraged the development of a series of supplemental teaching units.

The Constitution: Evolution of a Government is the seventh in that series. It celebrates two special occasions for us and for the public. First, 1985 marks the reestablishment of the National Archives as an independent agency of the federal government, a position it held from its founding in 1934 until 1949, when it became part of the General Services Administration. We are confident that this change in our status will strengthen our role as public custodian of the records that document the history of the federal government and its relation to the American people since 1774.

Second, we will soon mark the 200th anniversary of the creation of the Constitution of the United States, a document that began an experiment in government that continues to this day. The Declaration of Independence, the Constitution, and the Bill of Rights form the core of the National Archives' vast holdings, which it is our mission to make accessible to the public nationwide. Through this unit, we hope to bring you and your students a sense of the origins of these great documents, their evolution, and their meaning.

ROBERT M. WARNER
Archivist of the United States
1985

...to bring you and your students the excitement and satisfaction of working with primary sources and to enhance your instructional program.

Preface

As the repository of many documents produced during the formative years of the United States, the National Archives has a mission, as the 1987 bicentennial of the Constitution approaches, to disseminate these materials more widely. *The Constitution: Evolution of a Government* is a teaching unit designed to supplement your students' study of the constitutional period and constitutional issues. The unit is made up of 20 exercises that illuminate three processes: The Making of the Constitution (exercises 1-10), The Beginning of a Government (exercises 11-16), and The Evolution of a Constitutional Issue (exercises 17-20). Each exercise includes reproductions of documents from the National Archives and suggests classroom activities based on these documents. The documents include official correspondence, documents-in-process, petitions, legislative proceedings, government bonds, maps, and court decisions. Students practice the historian's skills as they complete exercises, using these documents to gather information, identify points of view, evaluate evidence, form hypotheses, and draw conclusions.

The documents in this unit do not reflect every topic usually included in a history textbook. In some instances, the federal government had no interest in or authority over a given event and therefore compiled no records on it. In other cases, documents in the National Archives on several historic topics proved to be limited or difficult to use in the classroom – mainly due to crabbed lettering and the fading of two-century-old inks. However, the documents included do reflect historical, political, economic, and social aspects of our blueprint for an ideal government, the Constitution.

The documents in this unit are organized under three broad categories. "The Making of the Constitution," documents 1-10, provides a historical sequence toward the modern Constitution, commencing with the Articles of Association and concluding with one of the most recent amendments to the Constitution, the Twenty-sixth. "The Beginning of a Government" includes three subsections: Organizing the New Government (documents 11-16), Problems Confronting the New Government (documents 17-19), and Challenges to the New Government (documents 20-26). "The Evolution of a Constitutional Issue" examines the relationship of church and state. Study of the religion clause of the First Amendment is divided into three sub-sections: Emergence of the First Amendment (document 27), Issues Raised by the First Amendment (documents 28-34), and Case Study in Church-State Relations (document 34).

National Archives education specialists Wynell Burroughs Schamel, Jean M. West, and Walter Bodle and education branch chief Elsie Freeman developed this publication. We are pleased to issue a revised and updated set of these documentary teaching materials.

WYNELL B. SCHAMEL
LEE ANN POTTER
Education Specialists
2001

> *The Constitution: Evolution of a Government* is a teaching unit designed to supplement your students' study of the constitutional period and constitutional issues.

$\mathcal{A}$cknowledgments

Many people helped in the original production of this unit. They included National Archives staff members Mary Alexander, Susan Cooper, John Dwyer, Dane Hartgrove, David Kepley, Eva Krusten, Sally Marks, R. Michael McReynolds, Heather Paisley-Jones, David Paynter, George Perros, Leonard Rapport, Linda Simmons, Christina Rudy Smith, Edward Schamel, and William Sherman.

Joseph Onofrey and other social studies teachers in Montgomery County, MD, reviewed elements of this unit. Their reactions and comments have shaped and improved the document selection and the teaching exercises.

Edd Doerr, Executive Director of Americans for Religious Freedom; J. Dane Hartgrove, archivist in the Legislative and Diplomatic Branch; Edith James; Director of the Exhibits and Educational Programs Division; and R. Michael McReynolds, archivist in the Judicial, Fiscal, and Social Branch, reviewed the unit for historical content. [Positions held at the time of original publication.]

During the republication process, we were ably assisted by George Mason University intern Adam Jevec; volunteers Elizabeth S. Lourie, Jane Douma Pearson and Donald Alderson; and National Archives staff members Michael Hussey, A.J. Daverede, Patrick Osborn, Amy Patterson, Kate Flaherty, Donald Roe, and Charles Mayn.

Publisher's Note

Primary source documents have long been a cornerstone of ABC-CLIO's commitment to producing high-quality, learner-centered history and social studies resources. When our nation's students have the opportunity to interact with the undiluted artifacts of the past, they can better understand the breadth of the human experience and the present state of affairs.

It is with great enthusiasm that we celebrate the release of this series of teaching units designed in partnership with the National Archives—materials that we hope will bring historical context and deeper knowledge to U.S. middle and high school students. Each unit has been revised and updated, including new bibliographic references. Each teaching unit has been correlated to the curriculum standards for the teaching of social studies and history developed by the National Council for the Social Studies and the National Center for History in the Schools.

For more effective use of these teaching units in the classroom, each booklet is accompanied by an interactive CD-ROM which includes exercise worksheets, digital images of original documents, and, for four titles, sound recordings. A videocassette of motion pictures accompanies the teaching unit *The United States At War: 1944*. For those who would like to order facsimiles of primary source documents in their original sizes, or additional titles in this series, we have included an order form to make it easy for you to do so.

The mission of the National Archives is "to ensure ready access to the essential evidence that documents the rights of American citizens, the actions of Federal officials, and the national experience."

These units go a long way toward fulfilling that mission, helping the next generation of American citizens develop a clear understanding of the nation's past and a firm grasp of the role of the individual in guiding the nation's future. ABC-CLIO is honored to be part of this process.

BECKY SNYDER
Publisher & Vice President
ABC-CLIO Schools

> The mission of the National Archives is "to ensure ready access to the essential evidence that documents the rights of American citizens, the actions of Federal officials, and the national experience."

Teaching With Documents Curriculum Standards Correlations

The National Council for the Social Studies and the National Center for History in the Schools have developed a set of comprehensive curriculum standards for the teaching of social studies and history. Take a look at how thoroughly the Teaching With Documents series supports the curriculum.

	The Constitution: Evolution of a Government	The Bill of Rights: Evolution of Personal Liberties	The United States Expands West: 1785–1842	Westward Expansion: 1842–1912	The Civil War: Soldiers and Civilians	The Progressive Years: 1898–1917	World War I: The Home Front	The 1920's	The Great Depression and The New Deal World	War II: The Home Front	The United States At War: 1944	The Truman Years: 1945–1953	Peace and Prosperity: 1953–1961
National Council for the Social Studies													
CULTURE—should provide for the study of culture and cultural diversity	●		●	●				●		●			●
TIME, CONTINUITY & CHANGE—should provide for the study of the ways people view themselves in and over time	●	●	●			●	●	●	●	●	●		
PEOPLE, PLACES & ENVIRONMENT—should provide for the study of people, places, and environments	●	●	●	●				●	●				
INDIVIDUAL DEVELOPMENT & IDENTITY—should provide for the study of individual development and identity	●	●	●	●	●	●	●	●	●				●
INDIVIDUALS, GROUPS & INSTITUTIONS—should provide for the study of interactions among individuals, groups, and institutions	●	●	●	●	●	●		●	●		●	●	●
POWER, AUTHORITY & GOVERNANCE—should provide for the study of how structures of power are created and changed	●	●	●	●	●	●	●	●				●	●
PRODUCTION, DISTRIBUTION & CONSUMPTION—should provide for the study of the usage of goods and services	●		●	●	●	●		●	●			●	
SCIENCE, TECHNOLOGY & SOCIETY—should provide for the study of relationships among science, technology, and society				●		●		●	●		●	●	●
GLOBAL CONNECTIONS—should provide for the study of global connections and interdependence	●		●			●					●	●	●
CIVIC IDEALS & PRACTICES—should provide for the study of the ideals, principles, and practices of citizenship	●	●						●			●		
National Center for History in the Schools													
CHRONOLOGICAL THINKING	●	●	●	●	●	●	●	●	●	●	●	●	●
HISTORICAL COMPREHENSION	●	●	●	●	●	●	●	●	●	●	●	●	●
HISTORICAL ANALYSIS & INTERPRETATION	●	●	●	●	◻	●	◻	◻	◻	◻	◻	●	◻
HISTORICAL RESEARCH CAPABILITIES													
HISTORICAL ISSUES-ANALYSIS & DECISION-MAKING						●							

Introduction

This unit contains two elements: 1) a book, which contains a teachers guide and a set of reproductions of print documents, and 2) a CD-ROM, which contains the exercise worksheets from the teachers guide and a set of reproductions of documents in electronic format. In selecting the documents, we applied three standards. First, the documents must be entirely from the holdings of the National Archives and must reflect the actions of the federal government or citizens' responses to those actions. Second, each document must illuminate the evolutionary nature of the Constitution. Third, the documents must be legible and potentially useful for vocabulary development. In selecting documents we attempted to choose those having appeal to young people.

There are physical problems with many of the documents that have survived. Some documents are badly faded. Others, on which both sides of the paper were written, are illegible due to ink staining through both sides of the paper. Some of the documents' authors had poor handwriting and others spelled and used grammar whimsically, at best. At times we could avoid using such documents but a few were too important to omit. We decided that, when a document that was marginally legible was selected, a transcription would be made for inclusion in the Teachers Guide.

UNIT CONTAINS:

◆ **1)** a book, which contains a teachers guide and a set of reproductions of print documents, and

◆ **2)** a CD-ROM, which contains the exercise worksheets from the teachers guide and a set of reproductions of documents in electronic format.

Objectives

We have provided an outline of the general objectives for the unit. You will be able to achieve these objectives by completing several, if not all, of the exercises in the unit. Because each exercise aims to develop skills defined in the general objectives, you may be selective and still develop those skills. In addition, each exercise has its own specific objectives.

Outline

This unit on the evolution of the Constitution is structured in three sections. The first section examines the making of the Constitution, the second the beginning of a government, and the third the evolution of a constitutional issue, religious freedom. The structure and the relation of the exercises and documents to these sections are presented in an outline.

List of Documents

The list of documents gives specific information (e.g. date and name of author) and record group number for each document. Records in the National Archives are arranged in record groups. A typical record group (RG) consists of the records created or accumulated by a department, agency, bureau, or other administrative unit of the federal government. Each record group is identified for retrieval purposes by a record group number; for example, RG 58 (Internal Revenue Service) or RG 267 (Supreme Court). Complete archival citations of all documents are listed in the appendix, p. 90.

Exercise Summary Chart

The chart shows the organization of exercises 1-20. For each exercise, the chart outlines the materials needed, the document content, the student activities that are emphasized, and the number of class periods needed. Review the chart carefully and decide which exercises to use based on your objectives for the students, their ability levels, and the content you wish to teach. The exercises may be adapted to fit your objectives and teaching style.

Introductory Exercises

Before starting exercises 1-20, it is important to familiarize students with documents and their importance to the historian who interprets them and writes history from them. We suggest that you direct students to do one or both of the introductory exercises: Written Document Analysis, p. 12 and The Historian's Tools, p. 13. The first exercise is designed to help students systematically analyze any written document in this unit. The second exercise is designed to increase student awareness of the process of analyzing historical information on the constitutional era without using documents. It is most appropriate for students working at or above ninth grade reading level.

Classroom Exercises

This unit contains 20 suggested exercises on constitutional topics. Within the explanatory material for each of the exercises, you will find the following information:

➤ Note to the teacher   ➤ Materials needed

➤ Classroom time required   ➤ Procedures

➤ Objectives (specific)   ➤ Student worksheets

You may choose to combine several exercises on a topic within the unit. In some instances a document is used in more than one exercise when it is appropriate to the skill or content objectives of several exercises. We encourage you to select and adapt the exercises and documents that best suit your own teaching style.

Ability Levels

As in our other units, we developed exercises for students of different abilities. For some topics, we designed two procedures, tailored to different student needs. Throughout the unit we have made an effort to provide exercises in which students utilize a variety of skills, including reading for understanding, interpreting maps and ledgers, and analyzing petitions and court cases. All lessons have procedures for ability levels one, two, and three. Procedures begin with strategies designed for level three students, continue with level two strategies, and conclude with level one strategies. Our definition of each ability level is as follows:

Level One: Good reading skills, minimal direction needed from teacher to organize and interpret information from several sources, and ability to complete assignments independently;

Level Two: Average reading skills, general direction needed from teacher to organize and interpret information from several sources, and ability to complete assignments with some assistance from teacher;

Level Three: Limited reading skills, step-by-step direction needed from teacher to organize and interpret information from several sources, and ability to complete assignments with close supervision from teacher.

These ability levels are merely guides. We recognize that you will adapt the exercises to suit your students' needs and your own teaching style.

Time Line

A time line is included for use by your students. You may want to reproduce it for each student or display it.

Bibliography

As students work with the constitutional documents, they should be assigned appropriate readings from their text and other secondary sources. They should also be encouraged to use the resources of school and public libraries. To guide them, an annotated bibliography appears at the end of the Teachers Guide.

General Objectives

Upon successfully completing the exercises in this unit, students should be able to demonstrate the following skills using a single document:

➤ Identify factual evidence

➤ Identify points of view (bias and/or prejudice)

➤ Collect, reorder, and weigh the significance of evidence

➤ Develop defensible inferences, conclusions, and generalizations from factual information

Using several documents from this unit, students should be able to:

➤ Analyze the documents to compare and contrast evidence

➤ Evaluate and interpret evidence drawn from the documents

Outline of Classroom Exercises

The Constitution: Evolution of a Government

List of Documents

Following the identifying information for each document reproduced in the unit, we have given the record group (RG) number in which the original can be found. Should you want copies of these documents or, for other reasons, wish to refer to them in correspondence with us, give the complete archival citation, which is found in the appendix on page 90. **You may duplicate any documents in this unit for use with your students.**

Documents in *The Constitution: Evolution of a Government* are taken from the following record groups: Bureau of Land Management (RG 49), Bureau of Public Debt (RG 53), Continental and Confederation Congresses and the Constitutional Convention (RG 360), Department of State (RG 59), Internal Revenue Service (RG 58), John F. Kennedy Presidential Library (Papers of John F. Kennedy), Supreme Court of the United States (RG 267), United States Government (RG 11), United States House of Representatives (RG 233), and United States Senate (RG 46).

1.   Articles of Association, October 20, 1774 (RG 360).

2.   Lee Resolution showing congressional vote, July 2, 1776 (RG 360).

3.   Engrossed copy of the Declaration of Independence, August 2, 1776 (RG 360).

4.   Printed and corrected draft of the Articles of Confederation, showing amendments adopted, November 15, 1777 (RG 360).

5.   Northwest Ordinance, July 13, 1787 (RG 360).

6.   Resolution to convene the Philadelphia Convention, February 21, 1787 (RG 360).

7.   Minutes of the Congress showing vote on the Great Compromise, July 16, 1787 (RG 360).

8.   George Washington's copy of the Constitution, August 6, 1787 (RG 360).

9.   Senate's draft of 17 amendments for a bill of rights, August 24, 1789 (RG 46).

10. Twenty-sixth Amendment to the Constitution, March 23, 1971 (RG 11).

11. Minutes of the Senate describing George Washington's oath of office ceremony, April 30, 1789 (RG 46).

12. Bradhead's letter to George Washington congratulating him and asking for a job, April 4, 1789 (RG 360).

13. Jefferson's letter to President Washington accepting nomination, February 1, 1790 (RG 59).

14. Jay's letter to U.S. agent at Morocco, December 1, 1789 (RG 59).

15. Petition to make the Kentucky District a state, July 28, 1790 (RG 46).

16. Plea to the Court of Impeachment in defense of William Blount, December 24, 1798 (RG 46).

17. Petition for Lancaster to be the capital, March 17, 1789 (RG 46).

18. Franklin's petition to abolish slavery, February 3, 1790 (RG 46).

19. Paine's petition to be informed of charges, January 7, 1779 (RG 360).

20. Broadside asking for money, October 12, 1785 (RG 360).

21. Jay's letter to John Adams about Shays' Rebellion, February 21, 1787 (RG 360).

22. Map made in accordance with the 1785 Land Ordinance, 1786 (RG 49).

23. U.S. loan certificate, December 16, 1790 (RG 53).

24. Pages from the government Loan Office ledger, January 1, 1788 (RG 53).

25. Annals of Congress entry containing House debate on Hamilton's financial plan, February 19, 1790 (RG 233).

26. Supervisor Carrington's letter to U.S. Revenue Inspector Smith about the Whiskey Rebellion, August 13, 1794 (RG 58).

27. Senate debate on the wording of the First Amendment, September 3, 1789 (RG 46).

28. Bill amending the Pledge of Allegiance, June 14, 1954 (RG 11).

29. *Minersville v. Gobitis* letter, March 7, 1940 (RG 267).

30. *Engel v. Vitale* opinion, June 25, 1962 (RG 267).

31. Women of Utah petition, December 17, 1875 (RG 233).

32. *Reynolds v. United States* decision, May 5, 1879 (RG 267).

33. Campbell's letter to a Salt Lake City newspaper about B. H. Roberts' expulsion from the House of Representatives, October 7, 1899 (RG 233).

34. Pope John XXIII's Christmas greetings to President Kennedy, December 31, 1961 (John F. Kennedy Presidential Library).

Exercise Summary Chart

EXERCISE	NUMBER OF DOCUMENTS	CONTENT	STUDENT ACTIVITIES	NUMBER OF CLASS PERIODS
1. The Articles of Association Document 1 Transcription, Document 1	1	Colonial protests	Analyzing documents and drawing conclusions Working in groups Role-playing Using creative writing skills to editorialize	2
2. The Lee Resolution Document 2 Written Document Analysis worksheet Additional Material: The Lee Resolution	1	Steps toward American independence	Analyzing documents Role-playing Letter writing Comparing and contrasting early and final versions of a document	1
3. The Declaration of Independence Document 3 Additional Materials: Deleted sections of Jefferson's draft and Declaration of Sentiments and Resolutions, Seneca Falls	1	The substance of the Declaration of Independence Democratic values	Reading critically Comparing and contrasting original draft with the adopted Declaration of Independence Comparing and contrasting the Declaration of Independence and the Seneca Falls Declaration	2-6
4. The Articles of Confederation Document 4 Worksheet 1	1	Purposes of government Differences between a confederation and a federal republic	Analyzing documents Brainstorming Gathering information Evaluating the successes and failures of the Articles of Confederation	1-2
5. The Northwest Ordinance Document 5 Worksheet 2	1	Actions of the Confederation Procedure for statehood	Gathering information Summarizing main ideas Tracing territorial expansion over time	1 or 2
6. Resolution to Convene the Philadelphia Convention Document 6 Worksheet 3 Transcription, Document 6	1	Steps toward the Constitutional Convention	Gathering information Analyzing and drawing conclusions from documents Researching from contemporary sources	1

EXERCISE	NUMBER OF DOCUMENTS	CONTENT	STUDENT ACTIVITIES	NUMBER OF CLASS PERIODS
7. The Great Compromise Document 7 Worksheet 4 Transcription, Document 7	1	The Constitutional Convention "One man, one vote," rule Compromise in a democratic society	Analyzing and drawing conclusions from documents Examining and comparing historic conflicting views Debating points of view Researching "one man, one vote" rule Graphing information found in a document	1-2
8. Washington's Copy of the Constitution Document 8	1	The Constitution as drafted and approved	Examining the process of writing the Constitution Examining the content of the Constitution Drawing conclusions about the process of composing a constitution	2
9. Working Draft of the Bill of Rights Document 9	1	The amendment process The Bill of Rights	Analyzing the documents and coming to conclusions Role-playing Paraphrasing documents Conducting a public opinion poll	2
10. The 26th Amendment Document 10	1	The 18-year-old vote The amendment process	Analyzing documents Examining the amendment process Drafting amendments Researching related topics	2
11. Starting a New Government Documents 11-16 Worksheet 5 Transcriptions, Documents 12, 15	6	Establishing the government: executive, foreign policy, territorial growth, impeachment	Brainstorming Gathering information Analyzing documents and drawing conclusions Working in small groups	1 or 2
12. Jay's letter to the U.S. Agent at Morocco Document 14 Worksheet 6 Transcription, Document 14	1	Establishing the government and foreign policy	Analyzing documents and drawing conclusions Comparing and contrasting conduct of foreign relations between the 18th and 20th centuries	1

EXERCISE	NUMBER OF DOCUMENTS	CONTENT	STUDENT ACTIVITIES	NUMBER OF CLASS PERIODS
13. Issues Facing the New Government Documents 17-19 Written Document Analysis worksheet Worksheet 7 Transcription, Document 19	3	Issues of concern: trial rights, locating the capital, abolition of slavery	Gathering information Analyzing documents Researching from community sources Petition writing Comparing and contrasting communications between the 18th and 20th centuries	1 or 2
14. The National Debt Documents 20-26 Worksheet 8 Transcription, Document 26	7	Economic recovery plan of Hamilton	Analyzing documents and drawing conclusions Comparing and contrasting government finances between the 18th and 20th centuries	1 or 2
15. Survey Map of Ohio's Seven Ranges Documents 5, 22	2	Territorial expansion Federal land policy	Interpreting a map Gathering information Evaluating the impact of Federal land policies Researching from community sources Role-playing	2-3
16. Summary Exercise: Federalism and the Constitution Documents 8, 11-16 Worksheet 9	17	Federalism and the purposes of the national government	Memorizing the Preamble Paraphrasing Gathering information Categorizing information Debating points of view	2-4
17. Background of the First Amendment Document 5 Document 27	2	Evolution of the First Amendment	Analyzing documents Comparing and contrasting points of view Gathering information Tracing the growth of influence of the First Amendment	1-2

EXERCISE	NUMBER OF DOCUMENTS	CONTENT	STUDENT ACTIVITIES	NUMBER OF CLASS PERIODS
18. The Establishment of Religion Documents 28-30 Worksheet 10	3	"Anti-establishment" clause of the First Amendment	Analyzing documents Gathering information Comparing and contrasting points of view Tracing the growth of influence of the First Amendment	1-3
19. The Free Exercise of Religion Documents 31-33 Worksheet 11	3	Case study of the Mormon Church and the "free exercise" clause of the First Amendment	Debating points of view Tracing the evolution of judicial interpretation of the "free exercise" clause Identifying persuasive techniques in writing and methods for influencing public opinion and policy	1-2
20. The Constitution and the Roman Catholic Church Document 34 Written Document Analysis worksheet	1	Case study of the Catholic Church and the Constitution	Analyzing documents Interpreting political cartoons Brainstorming Gathering information Formulating and evaluation hypotheses Comparing and contrasting points of view	1-4

Introductory Exercises

These two exercises introduce students to the general objectives of the unit. They focus students' attention on documents and their importance to the historian who interprets and records the past. They serve as valuable opening exercises for this unit.

Written Document Analysis

The Written Document Analysis worksheet helps students to analyze systematically any written document in this unit. In sections 1-5 of the worksheet, students locate basic details within the document. In section 6, students analyze the document more critically as they complete items A-E. There are many possible correct answers to section 6, A-E. We suggest you use documents 2, 10, 18, or 34 with this worksheet.

The Historian's Tools

The Historian's Tools worksheet is designed to increase students' awareness of the process of analyzing historical information. It focuses on both the nature of historical sources and those factors that influence the historian's analysis of evidence. The worksheet includes specific questions on distinctions between primary and secondary sources, the reliability of those sources, and the influence of bias, point of view, and perspective on the historian's interpretation.

Unlike other exercises in this unit, students do not analyze documents to complete this worksheet. Class discussion is essential to helping students understand the issues raised by the worksheet because there are many ways to answer the questions. You may wish to assign the worksheet as homework and discuss it with students in class.

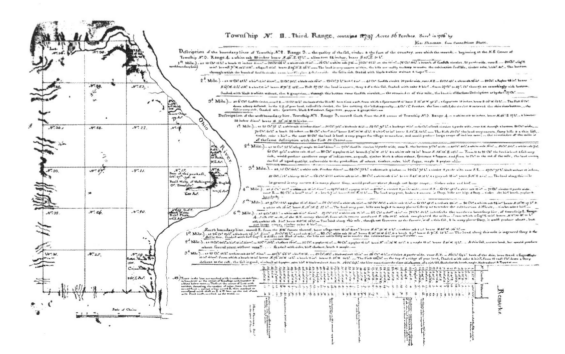

Written Document Analysis

Worksheet

1. Type of Document (Check one):

_____ Newspaper	_____ Map	_____ Advertisement
_____ Letter	_____ Telegram	_____ Congressional record
_____ Patent	_____ Press release	_____ Census report
_____ Memorandum	_____ Report	_____ Other

2. Unique Physical Qualities of the Document (check one or more):

_____ Interesting letterhead	_____ Notations
_____ Handwritten	_____ "RECEIVED" stamp
_____ Typed	_____ Other
_____ Seals	

3. Date(s) of Document: _____

4. Author (or creator) of the Document: _____

   Position (Title): _____

5. For What Audience was the Document Written? _____

6. Document Information (There are many possible ways to answer A-E.)

   A. List three things the author said that you think are important:

      1. _____

      2. _____

      3. _____

   B. Why do you think this document was written?

      _____

      _____

   C. What evidence in the document helps you to know why it was written?
      Quote from the document.

      _____

      _____

   D. List two things the document tells you about life in the United States
      at the time it was written:

      1. _____

      2. _____

   E. Write a question to the author that is left unanswered by the document:

      _____

      _____

Designed and developed by the education staff of the National Archives and Records Administration, Washington, DC 20408.

The Historian's Tools

Worksheet

1. If you were writing a chapter in your textbook on the constitutional period, list three things you would like to know about that period.

   1. _____

   2. _____

   3. _____

2. Where might you look to find information about the three topics you listed in #1?

Topic	Source of Information
_____	_____
_____	_____
_____	_____

3. Historians classify sources of information as **PRIMARY** or **SECONDARY**. Primary sources are those created by people who actually saw or participated in an event, while secondary sources are those that were created by someone either not present when that event occurred or removed from it by time. Classify the sources of information you listed in #2 as either primary or secondary by placing a **P** or **S** next to your answers in #2. Reconsider the sources you would use to find information about the Constitutional period; list three more here.

   1. _____

   2. _____

   3. _____

4. Some sources of historical information are viewed as more **RELIABLE** than others, though all of them may be useful. Factors such as bias, self-interest, distance, and faulty memory affect the reliability of a source. Below is a list of sources of information on the inauguration of President Washington in 1789. Rate the reliability of each source on a numerical scale in which 1 is reliable and 5 is very unreliable. Be able to support your ratings.

   A. A committee plan for the
   conduct of the inauguration.   1   2   3   4   5

   B. The journal of the secretary of the Senate
   describing the inaugural ceremony.   1   2   3   4   5

   C. A newspaper article written the day after
   President Washington's inauguration.   1   2   3   4   5

D. A transcript of an interview conducted with an eyewitness eight years after the first inauguration of Washington.   1   2   3   4   5

E. A high school U.S. history textbook description of President Washington's inauguration.   1   2   3   4   5

F. A description of Washington's inauguration in an encyclopedia.   1   2   3   4   5

5. What personal and social factors might influence historians as they write about people and events of the past?

_____

_____

_____

6. What personal and social factors influence *you* as you read historical accounts of people and events?

_____

_____

_____

Designed and developed by the education staff of the National Archives and Records Administration, Washington, DC 20408.

Exercise I
The Articles of Association

Note to the Teacher:

Meeting in Carpenter's Hall in Philadelphia, PA, the First Continental Congress passed in the fall of 1774 resolutions that had been drafted to force Great Britain to change its policy toward its American colonies. These resolutions, known as the Articles of Association, were an extension of the petitions, declarations, and policies of the Stamp Act Congress.

The preamble to the Articles declares that "We, his Majesty's most loyal subjects . . . affected with the deepest anxiety and most alarming apprehensions . . . find, that the present unhappy situation of our affairs is occasioned by a ruinous System of colony administration . . . evidently calculated for enslaving these colonies and with them the British Empire."

Fourteen articles list the grievances of the colonists and outline action to be taken by the colonies, including nonimportation of British goods, nonconsumption of British goods, and nonexportation of merchandise or commodities to Great Britain.

The Articles also provided for committees to be ". . . chosen in every county, city and town . . . to observe the conduct of all persons touching this association . ." and for committees of correspondence in each colony to inspect the customhouses and ". . . to inform each other, from time to time, of the true state thereof . . ."

The document concluded with a pledge binding the members to the Articles and a recommendation that the various colonies establish regulations to carry out the plan of the association.

Signed by delegates from 12 colonies (only Georgia was not represented), the Articles of Association was the earliest document in the papers of the Continental Congress that bears the signature of most of its members. This united action was signed on October 20, 1774, with the effective date for operation of nonimportation set for December I, 1774, and of nonexportation set for September 10, 1775.

In these exercises, students examine **document 1**, the Articles of Association, as approved by the Continental Congress in 1774.

Time: 2 class periods

Objectives:

* To examine the early colonial protests against England.

* To introduce original documents and document analysis.

Materials Needed:

Document 1
Transcription of document 1, p. 71

I

Procedures:

Some documents are very difficult to read. This document contains several important historical actions and requires careful reading.

1. Distribute copies of the document to the students. Read aloud the transcription in this guide as the students follow. The students should become accustomed to reading a handwritten document by following the teacher's oral reading.

2. Discuss the following questions with the students:
   a. Is this a document that shows the colonies to be on the road to revolution?
   b. What degree of loyalty to the King is expressed?
   c. Does the document sound sincere?
   d. Which actions are primarily political, primarily economic, and primarily social?
   e. Which statements indicate that some colonists will not agree to the sanctions?
   f. How does the Congress expect to enforce the "rules"?
   g. Do the enforcement procedures seem realistic?
   h. Is the tone of the document strong or weak?

3. Ask the students to summarize in writing the purpose of the document, the methods of protest, and the means of enforcement.

4. Extended Activity: Divide the class into three groups for editorial writing. Explain that an editorial expresses an opinion or takes a position on an issue. Assign each group a point of view: (a) British journalist, (b) colonial journalist loyal to the King, and (c) colonial journalist revolutionary in attitude. Each group should write an editorial for the newspaper of a colonial city addressing the following points:
   a. General reaction to the Articles of Association
   b. Real effects of the restrictions on exports and imports
   c. Role of the committees of correspondence
   d. Effect of the embargo
   e. Prohibition of the slave trade
   f. Hypothetical support or rejection of the restrictions on mourning dress

Exercise 2
The Lee Resolution

Note to the Teacher:

Acting under the instruction of the Virginia Convention, Richard Henry Lee on June 7, 1776, introduced a resolution in the Second Continental Congress proposing independence for the colonies. The Lee Resolution contained three parts: a declaration of independence, a call to form foreign alliances, and "a plan for confederation." The document that is included on page 18 is the complete resolution in Richard Henry Lee's handwriting.

On June 11, 1776, the Congress appointed three concurrent committees in response to the Lee Resolution: one to draft a declaration of independence, a second to draw up a plan "for forming foreign alliances," and a third to "prepare and digest the form of a confederation."

Because many members of the Congress believed action such as Lee proposed to be premature or wanted instructions from their colonies before voting, approval was deferred until July 2. On that date, Congress adopted the first part (the declaration). **Document 2** of this exercise is the favorable report of the committee of the whole. The affirmative votes of 12 colonies are listed at the right. New York cast no vote until the newly elected New York Convention upheld the Declaration of Independence on July 9, 1776.

The plan for making treaties was not approved until September of 1776; the plan of confederation was delayed until November of 1777.

Time: 1 class period

Objectives:

- To analyze a written document.
- To identify a preliminary step in America's seeking independence.
- To compare and contrast several original and final versions of an official document.

Materials Needed:

Document 2
Written Document Analysis worksheet, p. 12
The Lee Resolution, p. 18

Procedures:

1. Duplicate document 2 and the Written Document Analysis worksheet and distribute them to the students. Ask one student to read aloud while the others follow. (Explain that the handwritten "t" is not crossed and the "s" has two forms, *f* and s.)

2. Direct the students to complete the Written Document Analysis worksheet. All questions can be answered, including item 4. (Q. Author of the document? A. A delegate or the secretary of the Congress.) The students and teacher should share and discuss their answers.

3. Describe the historical background to the class. Be certain to distinguish between document 2 and the complete Lee Resolution pictured below.

4. Compare the content of the enclosed document with the Lee resolution in the Teachers Guide. Discuss the following questions:

   a. What advantages were gained when Congress adopted the measure for forming foreign alliances?

   b. What might have been disadvantages?

   c. Why would it be necessary to call for a plan of confederation for the colonies?

   d. Is the Lee Resolution a revolutionary act?

   e. Compare the significance of the Lee Resolution with other revolutionary acts for independence in modern times. What can you conclude about methods of revolution?

5. Extended activity: Assign a letter-writing exercise giving the following directions: Imagine that you are a true loyalist, supporting the King and Great Britain. Write to your friend and state your opposition to your friend's intentions to support the Lee Resolution. Try to convince your friend that he or she is wrong by listing your reasons for loyalty and your objections to his or her views.

   — or —

   Imagine that you give full support to independence. Write a letter to your friend, a loyalist, and explain your reasons for such views. Try to change your friend's mind and seek support.

Resolved

That these United Colonies are, and of right ought to be, free and independent States, that they are absolved from all allegiance to the British Crown; and that all political connection between them and the State of Great Britain is, and ought to be, totally dissolved.

That it is expedient forthwith to take the most effectual measures for forming foreign Alliances.

That a plan of confederation be prepared and transmitted to the respective Colonies for their consideration and approbation.

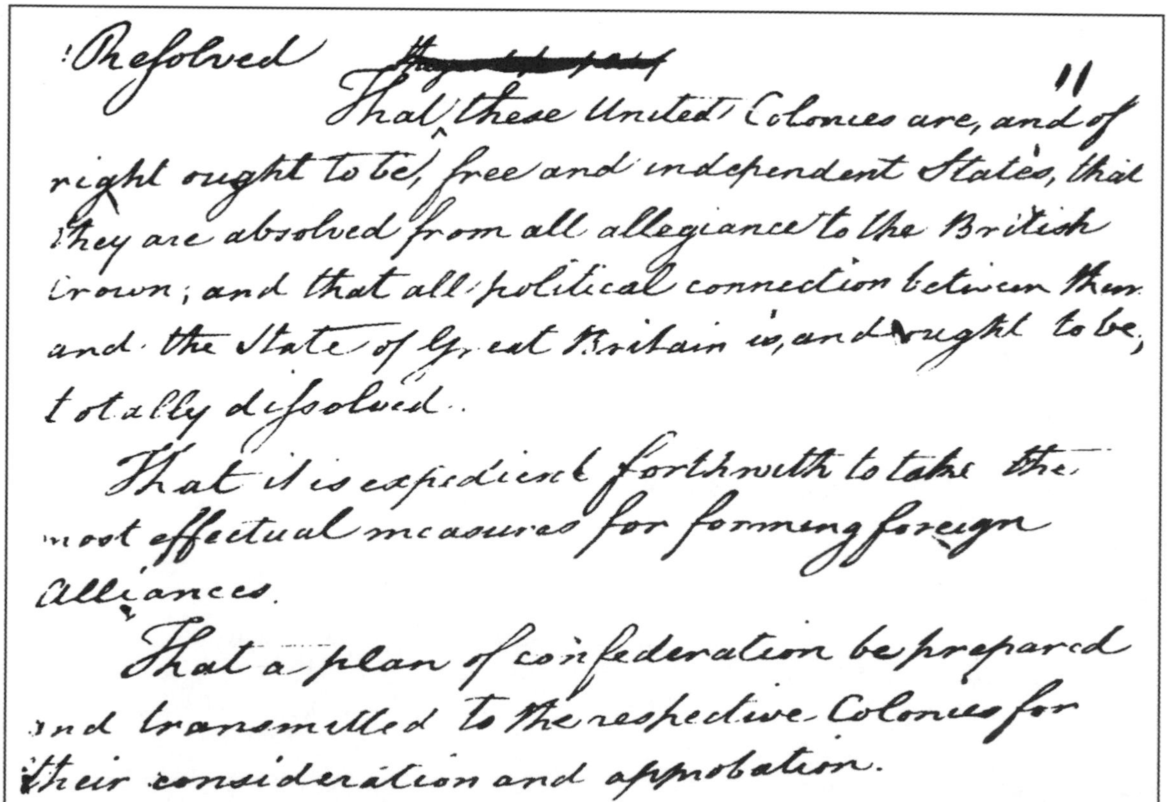

Exercise 3
The Declaration of Independence

Note to the Teacher:

Although the section of the Lee Resolution dealing with independence was not adopted until July 2, Congress appointed on June 10 a committee of five to draft a statement of independence for the colonies. The committee included Thomas Jefferson, John Adams, Benjamin Franklin, Robert R. Livingston, and Roger Sherman, with the actual writing delegated to Jefferson.

Jefferson drafted the statement between June 11 and 28, submitted drafts to Adams and Franklin who made some changes, and then presented the draft to the Congress following the July 2nd adoption of the independence section of the Lee Resolution. The congressional revision process took all of July 3rd and most of July 4th. Finally, in the afternoon of July 4th, the Declaration (**document 3**) was adopted.

Under the supervision of the Jefferson committee, the approved Declaration was printed on July 5th and a copy was attached to the "rough journal of the Continental Congress for July 4th." These printed copies, bearing only the names of John Hancock, President, and Charles Thomson, secretary, were distributed to state assemblies, conventions, committees of safety, and commanding officers of the Continental troops.

On July 19th, Congress ordered that the Declaration be engrossed on parchment with a new title, "the unanimous declaration of the thirteen united states of America," and "that the same, when engrossed, be signed by every member of Congress." Engrossing is the process of copying an official document in a large hand. The engrosser of the Declaration was probably Timothy Matlock, an assistant to Charles Thomson, secretary to the Congress.

On August 2nd John Hancock, the President of the Congress, signed the engrossed copy with a bold signature. The other delegates, following custom, signed beginning at the right with the signatures arranged by states from northernmost New Hampshire to southernmost Georgia. Although all delegates were not present on August 2nd, 56 delegates eventually signed the document. Late signers were Elbridge Gerry, Oliver Wolcott, Lewis Morris, Thomas McKean, and Matthew Thornton, who was unable to place his signature with the other New Hampshire delegates due to a lack of space. Some delegates, including Robert R. Livingston of New York, a member of the drafting committee, never signed the Declaration.

The Declaration of Independence receives the scholarly attention it deserves as a milestone document in the history of democracy. The following activities will focus students' attention on its contents.

Time: 2 to 6 class periods

Objectives:

- To read critically the contents of the Declaration of Independence.
- To review the substance of the document.
- To discuss omissions and deletions from the document in terms of modern views and values.

3

Materials Needed:

Document 3
Deleted Sections of Jefferson's Draft, p. 21
Declaration of Sentiments and Resolutions, Seneca Falls Convention, p. 22
U.S. history or government textbooks

Procedures:

1. Circulate the enclosed copy of the Declaration of Independence (document 3) so that students may compare it with the copy in their textbooks. Discuss the following questions, which are related to their study of contrasts and comparisons:

   a. Does the textbook version indicate that it is a "unanimous" declaration?

   b. Is the textbook version accurate?

   c. Is the textbook version complete?

   d. Is the textbook version a primary or secondary source?

   e. Does the textbook show the names of the signers?

   f. Are there any other differences between the textbook version and the one shown here?

2. Read the text aloud while the students read silently. (A recording may be available in your library.) Discuss the following questions during a second reading:

   a. Related to paragraph 1: What laws of nature and of nature's God entitle one people to a separate and equal station?

   b. Related to paragraph 2: In what way are all men created equal? What are unalienable rights? How can life, liberty, and the pursuit of happiness be unalienable? If a person does not believe in God, are his or her rights also unalienable?

   c. Do the two references to "men" imply that women are not created equal, do not have certain unalienable rights, or have no say in the formation and operations of government? Were women, in fact, omitted from the Declaration and Constitution?

   d. Where does government get its power? According to the Declaration, when is it necessary for the people to change a government? Is there any indication in the preamble that this is only a warning to Great Britain?

   e. Related to paragraphs 3 through 31 (Charges against King George III):

   While reading the charges against the King, find specific examples of rights that are mentioned in our Constitution and its amendments. Make a list of those specific items identified, e.g.—

King's Offense	Constitution
(a) "quartering large bodies of armed troops"	Third Amendment
(b) "He has refused his Assent to Laws"	Article 2, section 7, paragraph 2
(c) "He has dissolved Representative Houses repeatedly"	Amendment 20, section 2

f.   Related to the final paragraph: Is this a form of declaration of war against Great Britain?

3.   The text of a deleted section of Thomas Jefferson's draft is included on the bottom of this page. Present this deletion to the class and discuss the following:

a.   Who are the distant people?

b.   What are infidel powers?

c.   What reasons might Jefferson have for underlining the word "Christian" in the phrase "The Christian king of Great Britain"?

d.   According to this statement, what does Jefferson suggest that the King is trying to encourage these people to do?

e.   Why was Jefferson reluctant to use the words "slave" or "slavery"?

f.   Why, do you suppose, were the ideas of this complete section deleted from the Declaration of Independence?

g.   What elements of the political process are suggested by this deletion?

4.   Extended Activity: A copy of the Declaration of Sentiments and Resolutions, Seneca Falls Convention (1848), is also included in the guide. Ask a student to read it aloud. Other students should listen to and compare the two declarations and make note of the Seneca Falls issues that are unresolved today. A student may wish to make an "engrossed" copy of the resolution for class display. Underline or highlight the complaints that remain unanswered today.

Deleted Sections of Jefferson's Draft

[he has incited treasonable insurrections of our fellow-citizens, with the allurements of forfeiture & confiscation of our property.

he has waged cruel war against human nature itself, violating it's most sacred rights of life and liberty in the persons of a distant people who never offended him, captivating & carrying them into slavery in another hemisphere or to incur miserable death in their transportation thither. this piratical warfare, the opprobrium of *infidel* powers, is the warfare of the *Christian* king of Great Britain. determined to keep open a market where *Men* should be bought & sold, he has prostituted his negative for suppressing every legislative attempt to prohibit or to restrain this execrable commerce. and that this assemblage of horrors might want no fact of distinguished die, he is now exciting those very people to rise in arms among us, and to purchase that liberty of which he has deprived them, by murdering the people on whom he also obtruded them: thus paying off former crimes committed against the *Liberties* of one people, with crimes which he urges them to commit against the *lives* of another.]

Source: Boyd, Julian P. (Ed.), *The Papers of Thomas Jefferson*,
Princeton: Princeton University Press, 1950. pp. 317-318.

Declaration of Sentiments and Resolutions

When, in the course of human events, it becomes necessary for one portion of the family of man to assume among the people of the earth a position different from that which they have hitherto occupied, but one to which the laws of nature and of nature's God entitle them, a decent respect to the opinions of mankind requires that they should declare the causes that impel them to such a course.

We hold these truths to be self-evident: that all men and women are created equal; that they are endowed by their Creator with certain inalienable rights; that among these are life, liberty, and the pursuit of happiness; that to secure these rights governments are instituted, deriving their just powers from the consent of the governed. Whenever any form of government becomes destructive of these ends, it is the right of those who suffer from it to refuse allegiance to it, and to insist upon the institution of a new government, laying its foundation on such principles, and organizing its powers in such form, as to them shall seem most likely to effect their safety and happiness. Prudence, indeed, will dictate that governments long established should not be changed for light and transient causes; and accordingly all experience hath shown that mankind are more disposed to suffer, while evils are sufferable, than to right themselves by abolishing the forms to which they were accustomed. But when a long train of abuses and usurpations, pursuing invariably the same object evinces a design to reduce them under absolute despotism, it is their duty to throw off such government, and to provide new guards for their future security. Such has been the patient sufferance of the women under this government, and such is now the necessity which constrains them to demand the equal station to which they are entitled.

The history of mankind is a history of repeated injuries and usurpations on the part of man toward woman, having in direct object the establishment of an absolute tyranny over her. To prove this, let facts be submitted to a candid world.

He has never permitted her to exercise her inalienable right to the elective franchise.

He has compelled her to submit to laws, in the formation of which she had no voice.

He has withheld from her rights which are given to the most ignorant and degraded men—both natives and foreigners.

Having deprived her of this first right of a citizen, the elective franchise, thereby leaving her without representation in the halls of legislation, he has oppressed her on all sides.

He has made her, if married, in the eye of the law, civilly dead.

He has taken from her all right in property, even to the wages she earns.

He has made her, morally, an irresponsible being, as she can commit many crimes with impunity, provided they be done in the presence of her husband. In the covenant of marriage, she is compelled to promise obedience to her husband, he becoming, to all intents and purposes, her master – the law giving him power to deprive her of her liberty, and to administer chastisement.

He has so framed the laws of divorce, as to what shall be the proper causes, and in case of separation, to whom the guardianship of the children shall be given, as to be wholly regardless of the happiness of women – the law, in all cases, going upon a false supposition of the supremacy of man, and giving all power into his hands.

After depriving her of all rights as a married woman, if single, and the owner of property, he has taxed her to support a government which recognizes her only when her property can be made profitable to it.

He has monopolized nearly all the profitable employments, and from those she is permitted to follow, she receives but a scanty remuneration. He closes against her all the avenues to wealth and distinction which he considers most honorable to himself. As a teacher of theology, medicine, or law, she is not known.

He has denied her the facilities for obtaining a thorough education, all colleges being closed against her.

He allows her in Church, as well as State, but a subordinate position, claiming Apostolic authority for her exclusion from the ministry, and, with some exceptions, from any public participation in the affairs of the Church.

He has created a false public sentiment by giving to the world a different code of morals for men and women, by which moral delinquencies which exclude women from society, are not only tolerated, but deemed of little account in man.

He has usurped the prerogative of Jehovah himself, claiming it as his right to assign for her a sphere of action, when that belongs to her conscience and to her God.

He has endeavored, in every way that he could, to destroy her confidence in her own powers, to lessen her self-respect, and to make her willing to lead a dependent and abject life.

Now, in view of this entire disfranchisement of one-half the people of this country, their social and religious degradation – in view of the unjust laws above mentioned, and because women do feel themselves aggrieved, oppressed, and fraudulently deprived of their most sacred rights, we insist that they have immediate admission to all the rights and privileges which belong to them as citizens of the United States.

In entering upon the great work before us, we anticipate no small amount of misconception, misrepresentation, and ridicule; but we shall use every instrumentality within our power to effect our object. We shall employ agents, circulate tracts, petition the State and National legislatures, and endeavor to enlist the pulpit and the press in our behalf. We hope this Convention will be followed by a series of Conventions embracing every part of the country.

WHEREAS, The great precept of nature is conceded to be, that "man shall pursue his own true and substantial happiness." Blackstone in his Commentaries remarks, that this law of Nature being coeval with mankind, and dictated by God himself, is of course superior in obligation to any other. It is binding over all the globe, in all countries and at all times; no human laws are of any validity if contrary to this, and such of them as are valid, derive all their force, and all their validity, and all their authority, mediately and immediately, from this original; therefore,

Resolved, That such laws as conflict, in any way, with the true and substantial happiness of woman, are contrary to the great precept of nature and of no validity, for this is "superior in obligation to any other."

Resolved, That all laws which prevent woman from occupying such a station in society as her conscience shall dictate, or which place her in a position inferior to that of man, are contrary to the great precept of nature, and therefore of no force or authority.

Resolved, That woman is man's equal – was intended to be so by the Creator, and the highest good of the race demands that she should be recognized as such.

Resolved, That the women of this country ought to be enlightened in regard to the laws under which they live, that they may no longer publish their degradation by declaring themselves satisfied with their present position, nor their ignorance, by asserting that they have all the rights they want.

Resolved, That inasmuch as man, while claiming for himself intellectual superiority, does accord to woman moral superiority, it is pre-eminently his duty to encourage her to speak and teach, as she has an opportunity, in all religious assemblies.

Resolved, That the same amount of virtue, delicacy, and refinement of behavior that is required of woman in the social state, should also be required of man, and the same transgressions should be visited with equal severity on both man and woman.

Resolved, That the objection of indelicacy and impropriety, which is so often brought against woman when she addresses a public audience, comes with a very ill-grace from those who encourage, by their attendance, her appearance on the stage, in the concert, or in feats of the circus.

Resolved, That woman has too long rested satisfied in the circumscribed limits which corrupt customs and a perverted application of the Scriptures have marked out for her, and that it is time she should move in the enlarged sphere which her great Creator has assigned her.

Resolved, That it is the duty of the women of this country to secure to themselves their sacred right to the elective franchise.

Resolved, That the equality of human rights results necessarily from the fact of the identity of the race in capabilities and responsibilities.

Resolved, therefore, That, being invested by the Creator with the same capabilities, and the same consciousness of responsibility for their exercise, it is demonstrably the right and duty of woman, equally with man, to promote every righteous cause by every righteous means; and especially in regard to the great subjects of morals and religion, it is self-evidently her right to participate with her brother in teaching them, both in private and in public, by writing and by speaking, by any instrumentalities proper to be used, and in any assemblies proper to be held; and this being a self-evident truth growing out of the divinely implanted principles of human nature, any custom or authority adverse to it, whether modern or wearing the hoary sanction of antiquity, is to be regarded as a self-evident falsehood, and at war with mankind.

Resolved, That the speedy success of our cause depends upon the zealous and untiring efforts of both men and women, for the overthrow of the monopoly of the pulpit, and for the securing to woman an equal participation with men in the various trades, professions, and commerce.

Source: Stanton, Elizabeth Cady; Anthony, Susan B., and Gage, Matilda Joslyn (Eds.), *History of Woman Suffrage,* Vol. 1, New York, Fowler and Wells, 1881. pp. 70-73. Also online in The Library of Congress' American Memory collection at **lcweb2.loc.gov**.

Exercise 4
The Articles of Confederation

Note to the Teacher:

On June 11, 1776, the Second Continental Congress appointed three committees in response to the Lee Resolution. One of these committees, created to determine the form of a confederation of the colonies, was composed of one representative from each colony with John Dickinson, a delegate from Delaware, as the principal writer.

The Dickinson Draft of the Articles of Confederation named the Confederation "the United States of America," provided for a Congress with representation based on population, and gave to the national government all powers not designated to the states. After considerable debate and alteration, the Articles of Confederation were adopted by Congress on November 15, 1777. In this "first constitution of the United States" each state retained "every Power . . . which is not by this confederation expressly delegated to the United States," and each state had one vote in Congress. Instead of forming a strong national government, the states entered into " . . . a firm league of friendship with each other . . . ."

Ratification by all 13 states was necessary to set the Confederation into motion. Because of disputes over representation, voting, and the western lands claimed by some states, ratification was delayed until Maryland ratified on March 1, 1781, and the Congress of the Confederation came into being.

Document 4 included is the corrected copy of the Articles used by Charles Thomson, secretary of the Continental Congress. The amendment process for each section was completed in October 1777. The printed and corrected version was adopted on November 15, 1777.

Time: 1 or 2 class periods

Objectives:

- To determine the purpose of government.
- To appraise the document in terms of the government it was intended to provide.
- To distinguish between a confederation and a federal system.

Materials Needed:

Document 4
U.S. history or government textbooks
Worksheet 1

Procedures:

1. Introduce the students to the Articles of Confederation by discussing these questions concerning the structure and function of a national government:

   a. Why does a nation have a government?

4

b. What are the advantages and disadvantages of a union of states?

c. Why is a written plan for government desirable?

d. What disadvantages might there be in a written plan?

e. What is the disadvantage of having a government that reacts to a given situation without reference to a written law?

f. What are the elements of a good government?

g. How often should the elected officials of government be accountable to the people?

h. Is it necessary to have a "head" of government?

i. How much power should a government have?

j. How should the power be controlled?

k. How can the framers of a constitution ensure freedoms for the people?

l. Who should be excluded/included in the decision-making process concerning the writing of a constitution or the formation of a government?

2. On the chalkboard make a list with the students of general qualifications for decision-makers. Discuss these qualifications. Discuss characteristics that would generally disqualify persons from participation.

3. Summarize the discussion with an explanation of the complexities of forming a governmental structure, considering the possibilities for such questions as the following:

a. Who governs? (a direct democracy, a form of representative-governed democracy, an elite group, a single person, or some combination?)

b. What structure is used (unitary, federal, or confederate)?

c. Who determines the answers to questions a and b?

4. Assign for homework the reading of the textbook's section dealing with the Articles of Confederation. Students should read to understand the major concepts of the Articles and then make a written list of the main features, the strengths, and the weaknesses of the Articles of Confederation, according to the textbook authors.

5. Following the completion of the homework assignment, distribute copies of the document and the worksheet to the students. Ask students to examine the document and complete the worksheet.

6. After the worksheets are completed, discuss with the students the weaknesses of the Articles.

7. The Articles are often considered a failure by modern historians. Consider with the students what the government accomplished under the Articles of Confederation. After reading the Articles, ask the students the following questions:

a. What kind of government did the writers want?

b. Did the Articles provide that kind of government?

c. What was accomplished during the period of the Articles?

d. Were the Articles a failure?

Exercise 4: The Articles of Confederation

Worksheet 1

Directions: Check either "True" or "False" in the column to the left of each statement.

True   **False**

_____ _____   1. The document is printed.

_____ _____   2. The handwritten notes are only someone's doodling.

_____ _____   3. The dates in the margin indicate the time each section was agreed to.

_____ _____   4. The dates are in chronological order.

_____ _____   5. The earliest date is April 21, 1777.

_____ _____   6. The latest date is October 27, 1777.

_____ _____   7. The addition of article 2 reserved states' rights.

_____ _____   8. The document is undoubtedly the final draft.

_____ _____   9. Article 8 gave each state one vote.

_____ _____   10. The Articles of Confederation required a simple majority vote for ratification.

Exercise 5
The Northwest Ordinance

Note to the Teacher:

The Northwest Ordinance, adopted July 13, 1787, by the Second Continental Congress, chartered a government for the Northwest Territory, provided a method for admitting new states to the Union from the territory, and listed a bill of rights guaranteed in the territory. Following the principles outlined by Thomas Jefferson in the Ordinance of 1784, the authors of the Northwest Ordinance (probably Nathan Dane and Rufus King) spelled out a plan that was subsequently used as the country expanded to the Pacific.

The following three principal provisions were ordained in the document: (1) a division of the Northwest Territory into "not less than three nor more than five States"; (2) a three-stage method for admitting a new state to the Union – with a congressionally appointed governor, secretary, and three judges to rule in the first phase; an elected assembly and one nonvoting delegate to Congress to be elected in the second phase, when the population of the territory reached "five thousand free male inhabitants of full age"; and a state constitution to be drafted and membership to the Union to be requested in the third phase when the population reached 60,000; and (3) a bill of rights protecting religious freedom, the right to a writ of habeas corpus, the benefit of trial by jury, and other individual rights. In addition the ordinance encouraged education and forbade slavery.

The copy of the ordinance included in the packet **(document 5)** is a printed document, dated in the last paragraph and signed by the secretary of Congress, Charles Thomson. A transcription of the document may be found in *Documents of American History*, volume 1, edited by Henry Steele Commager.

Time: 1 or 2 class periods

Objectives:

- To read for facts and general content.

- To develop skills in summarizing main ideas.

Materials needed:

Document 5
Worksheet 2

Procedures:

1. Distribute copies of the document to the students. Explain the three general purposes of the Northwest Ordinance:

   (a) to provide temporary government in the territory

   (b) to establish statehood procedures for the territories

   (c) to protect individuals' rights in the territory

2. Distribute the worksheet to the students and ask them to read the document to find the answers to the questions.

3. After the students have completed the worksheet, review and discuss their answers.

4. Ask the students to write a short essay answering the question: What was the general purpose of the Northwest Ordinance in terms of the formation of a new nation?

5. Extended activity: Ask a student or group of students to prepare a large map of the Northwest Territory as described in the document under "Article the Fifth." The students might indicate the state boundaries of that territory as they exist today.

6. Ask a team of students to research and report on the following:

    a. What are the current territorial possessions of the United States?

    b. How did they become our territories?

    c. Do the people of those territories want to become states, to become independent nations, or to remain territories?

    d. Is there any current movement or desire for any of the territories to seek statehood or become independent nations?

    e. Do you think there could ever be justification for the United States to acquire or dominate other lands in the future?

Exercise 5: The Northwest Ordinance
Worksheet 2

Directions: The three principle elements of the Northwest Ordinance were (a) a division of the Northwest Territory into "not less than five states," (b) a three-stage method for admitting a new state, and (c) a bill of rights. Read the document and write answers to the following questions:

1. List the duties and powers of the governor of the territory.

    _____

    _____

2. When would a district (territory) be able to establish a general assembly?

    _____

    _____

3. How was the number of representatives in the assembly determined?

    _____

    _____

4. Who was eligible to act as a representative?

    _____

    _____

5. Who was eligible to act as an elector (to vote)?

    _____

    _____

6. What restriction was placed on a territory's delegate to Congress?

    _____

    _____

7. List the inhabitants' rights protected by the ordinance.

    _____

    _____

8. What consideration was given to the Indians?

    _____

    _____

9. When would a territory be eligible to become a state?

    _____

    _____

10. What statement was made about slavery?

    _____

    _____

11. Would you consider the Northwest Ordinance to be a democratic achievement? Explain.

    _____

    _____

Exercise 6
Resolution to Convene the Philadelphia Convention

Note to the Teacher:

Following the Mt. Vernon Conference and the Annapolis Convention, a resolution was passed in the Second Continental Congress for delegates (to be appointed by the states) to convene in Philadelphia in May 1787 "for the sole and express purpose of revising the Articles of Confederation." Contrary to plan, when the convention assembled, the 55 delegates from 12 states formulated a greater work – the Constitution of the United States.

Document 6 is two pages of Secretary Charles Thomson's official journal of the Congress, containing the resolution, dated February 21, 1787. A transcription of the document is included in this guide.

Time: 1 class period

Objectives:

- To refine skills in working with original documents.

- To develop critical thinking skills.

- To appreciate the deliberate and orderly change in government that followed a revolutionary change.

Materials Needed:

Document 6
Worksheet 3
Transcription of document 6, p. 74

Procedures:

1. Before you use this document, assign for homework the historical background of the Annapolis Convention. Students should determine the cause, date, purpose, and result of the meeting. If possible, students should determine if the convention was a success or failure, stating their standards for each. Review and discuss their understanding of the issues surrounding the convention.

2. Distribute copies of the document and the worksheet. Read aloud the first two paragraphs of the transcription as the students read the document silently. Alert the students to certain penmanship characteristics of the author: e.g., the letters s, t, and d. Ask the students to complete the transcription of the document and to answer the questions on the worksheet.

3. Verify their answers and then identify the source of the document. Then ask the question: Why was this resolution necessary?

4. Extended activity: Through research in periodicals or through a letter to their representatives in Congress, the students should determine if there is any serious consideration of a convention for the purpose of amending the Constitution. The report and subsequent discussion should consider the several viewpoints concerning the merits of this type of convention.

Exercise 6: Resolution to Convene the Philadelphia Convention

Worksheet 3

Directions: Using the copy of the original document, complete the following transcription:

_____that in the opinion of _____it is

expedient that on the _____Monday in _____

next a _____of _____ who shall have been

appointed by the _____ states be _____at Philadelphia

for the sole and express _____of _____ the Articles of

Confederation and _____ to Congress and the several

legislatures _____alterations and provisions _____ as

shall when agreed _____ in _____ and

_____ by the states render the _____ constitution

_____ to the exigencies of Government & the preservation of the _____.

Answer the following questions related to the content of the above transcription:

1. Who is to meet? _____

2. When? _____

3. Where? _____

4. Why? _____

5. What is the date of the original document? _____

Exercise 7
The Great Compromise

Note to the Teacher:

On May 25, 1787, "one of the greatest sessions of wise men in the history of the world" began in Philadelphia's Independence Hall. The assembled delegates were in unanimous agreement in choosing George Washington as President of the Constitutional Convention, but in controversy about everything else. Fierce debate raged between large and small state delegations and between northern and southern.

The Great Compromise, devised by a committee of 11 moderates and introduced by Roger Sherman of Connecticut, resolved a major conflict over representation in Congress. The committee recommended that in the lower house each state be apportioned representatives according to population, that a census be taken every ten years, that bills for raising or appropriating money originate in the lower house, and that each state have an equal vote in the upper house.

This and other compromises were necessary to establish a constitution for all the people. Many disputes – including the counting of slaves, the structure of the executive, and the control of commerce – were settled through compromise.

Because of the delegates' pledge to secrecy, only a list of motions and the official votes were kept on record. The entry known as the Great Compromise is logged in July 16, 1787, in William Jackson's formal Journal of the Federal Convention and is included with this exercise as **document 7**.

> **Time:** Procedure 1: 1 class period
> Procedure 2: 2 class periods

Objectives:

- To recognize the importance of the concept and reality of compromise in the democratic process.

- To realize the significance of the "one man, one vote" rule in a republican form of government.

- To examine and compare historically conflicting views.

- To practice debating skills.

Materials Needed:

Document 7
Worksheet 4
Transcription of document 7, p. 74
U.S. history or government textbook

7

Procedure 1:

1. Assign for homework the reading of textbook sections dealing with the Virginia Plan and the New Jersey Plan. Students should list for comparison the features of each plan.

2. Distribute copies of the document to the students. Ask several students to read the document aloud. Use the transcription to verify their efforts.

3. Distribute the worksheet and ask the students to answer the questions using the document for reference.

– or –

Distribute graph paper to students. Ask the students to construct a bar graph to illustrate voting power of each state as listed in the document. (Usually 1/4-inch graph paper using two squares per vote is a good format.) Ask the students to separate the southern "slave" states from the northern "free" states. Discuss the differences in voting power in both houses.

Procedure 2:

1. Assign as homework the reading of textbook sections dealing with the Virginia Plan and the New Jersey Plan. Students should list the features of each plan in their notes.

2. Divide the class into four groups:

    (a) **Debating Group:** (3-5 students) Students are to make an in-depth study of the issues related to the above plans and prepare a debate on the issues. One student should act as a moderator, with one or two students arguing the pro side and one or two the con side of the issue, "Resolved: The New Jersey Plan for legislative structure is the best plan to strengthen the United States." At the conclusion of the argument, the audience should be asked to vote their agreement or disagreement to the resolution.

    (b) **Law Group:** (3-5 students) Ask the students of this group to read and outline the appropriate sections of their textbooks for the above plans. They should also read and outline the section that deals with the "one man, one vote" principle. If possible, their report should include a brief case study of four historical Supreme Court cases: *Colegrove v. Green* (1946), *Baker v. Carr* (1962), *Wesberry v. Sanders* (1964), and *Reynolds v. Simms* (1964).

    Members of the group should make oral reports to the class to explain:

    1. The principle of "one man, one vote"

    2. How the principle relates to the Virginia Plan and the New Jersey Plan

    3. The reasons why the representation in the U.S. Senate challenges the principle

    4. Why the courts cannot apply the principle to the U.S. Senate

    (c) **Compromise Group:** (2-3 students) Ask the members of this group to examine the other issues of major conflict; e.g., the "three-fifths compromise," the selection of the chief executive, and the slave trade issue. Oral reports should be prepared and presented to the class.

(d) **Voting Power Group:** (2-3 students) Direct these students in the making of a bar graph based on the document.

- vertical axis represents the size of the vote
- horizontal axis has each state represented with a separate bar
- slave states and non-slave states are represented in different colors

(The group report will be made after completion of step 3.)

3. After the debate and the reports from the Law and Compromise Groups have been made, distribute copies of the document to the students. Ask a student to read aloud the document. Direct other students to use the transcription on page 74 to verify the oral reading.

4. The Voting Power Group should display and explain their graph. They should be able to illustrate the significance of block voting (a) large state v. small state and (b) slave state v. nonslave state.

5. Ask the students to summarize orally or in writing (a) the importance of these compromises, (b) the general importance of compromise in a democratic society, and (c) the possible situation(s) when compromise should not be accepted in the legislative process.

7

Exercise 7: The Great Compromise

Worksheet 4

Directions: Answer the following questions from the information in document 7.

1. What was the total number of members in the original House of Representatives ("... the first Branch")?

   _____

2. Which state had the largest delegation? _____

   Which two states had the smallest? _____

3. What was the main factor that would change the appropriation of the number of representatives? Name other factors that would affect the number of representatives.

   _____

   _____

   _____

   _____

   _____

4. What government function would also be concerned with population?

   _____

5. In which house would bills for raising money originate?

   _____

6. How many votes did each state have in the Senate ("...the Second Branch")?

   _____

7. If a vote were taken on a question dealing with a trade issue, what would be the result if the states voted:
   a. Slave state v. nonslave state? _____

   b. Large state v. small state? _____

8. Which five of the large states could control the House if they always agreed on the issues?

   _____

9. If the above states conspired to control the House, what could the other states do to oppose that power?

   _____

10. When was the first census to be taken?

   _____

Exercise 8
Washington's Copy of the Constitution

Note to the Teacher:

On August 6, 1787, the Philadelphia Convention accepted the first draft of the Constitution. The notes, additions, corrections, and rewordings of George Washington's copy of the draft **(document 8)** reveal the arduous process by which the final document evolved. For 5 weeks the delegates examined, argued, and voted, article by article, on the draft. The most serious issues of controversy were the regulation of commerce, slavery, and the method of electing the executive.

By September 8, the Constitution was given to a Committee of Style and Arrangement with committee member Gouverneur Morris responsible for the final wording. The completed historic document was accepted by the Convention on September 15, 1787.

Time: 2 class periods

Objectives:

- To examine the process of writing and approving the Constitution.

- To examine the elements of the constitutional draft that were eliminated.

- To define the strengths of the final document.

Materials Needed:

Document 8
A copy of the U.S. Constitution
Overhead projector

Procedures:

Note: The document is the one used by George Washington at the Constitutional Convention. His notations reflect the degree of debate and compromise. You may have the students examine the total document and compare it to the finished product. The following exercise points out *some* "interesting" features of the Washington draft and suggests questions for discussion.

1. Duplicate and distribute enough copies of pages 1 through 6 of the document to allow at least two pages per student. (Or use a clear duplicated transparency on an overhead projector.)

2. Ask a student with page one to read the following sections. Discuss each section, using the related questions:

Page One

Preamble: Read the preambles to the draft and to today's Constitution.
Discuss the following:

   a. Why is the original preamble inadequate for today's Constitution?

   b. How did the elimination of the states' names change the nature of the document?

Article IV, Section 5: Read the section and discuss the following:

    a.   What was proposed in this section?

    b.   Why was the section "struck out" of the Constitution?

    c.   Why would the smaller states object to this section?

3.   Continue to read and discuss the designated section on a page-by-page basis.

Page Two

Article V, Section 1: Read the section and discuss the following:

    a.   How were the members of the Senate originally selected?

    b.   Why would such a proposal be considered a reasonable procedure?

    c.   Why is the word "member" underlined in the last sentence?

Article VI, Section 2 and 3: Read the sections and discuss the following:

    a.   What objections to section 2 could result in disagreement?

    b.   Why was there an addition to section 3?

Page Three

Article VI, Section 10: Read the original and the amended version and discuss the following: What was accomplished by the change in the section?

Article VI, Section 13: Read the section and discuss the effect of changing the two-thirds vote to three-fourths. What is the final fraction of the vote needed to override a veto?

Article VII, Section 1 (lines 17 and 18): Read the list of legislative powers through line 18, "To raise armies." Discuss the following questions:

    a.   (line 17) What is the difference in stating the congressional power as "To make war" or "to declare war"?

    b.   (line 18) "To raise and support armies." What historical event might have prompted the inclusion of the words "and support"? What did the words add to the powers of the article?

Page Four to Five

Article VIIII, Section 2: Read the complete section, which continues on page 5.
Ask the students to explain what purpose the long section served and why there was such a long procedure for settlement of disputes.

Page Five

Article X, Section 1: Read the section and discuss the following:

    a.   What was the original title for the President?

    b.   How was the President to be elected?

    c.   How long was his term?

    d.   How many terms of office did the President have?

Article X, Section 2: Read the section labeled "postponed Aug. 27."
Discuss the following questions:

a. What government body was originally capable of impeaching the President?

b. What possible reason could be given for the change?

Page Six

Article XV (Washington's notes above Article XVII):
Read the notes and answer the following:

a. What does the article provide?

b. What happened to the article according to Washington's notes?

4. Give the document to a student for a tally of the following:

a. Total sections marked "agreed"

b. Total sections marked "disagreed"

c. Total sections marked "struck out"

d. Total sections disposed of in other manners
Report the findings to the class.

5. Ask the students to summarize orally or in writing the process of writing the Constitution.

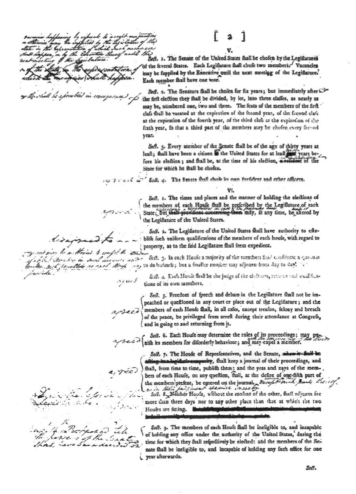

Exercise 9
Working Draft of the Bill of Rights

Note to the Teacher:

The omission of a list of individual rights in the Constitution hindered ratification by the states. Specific citizen rights were guaranteed in state constitutions and in the Northwest Ordinance but left out of the federal Constitution. The states of Massachusetts, South Carolina, New Hampshire, Virginia, and New York submitted proposed amendments for individual freedoms with their resolutions for ratification. North Carolina and Rhode Island ratified the Constitution only after a bill of rights was adopted by the new Congress.

James Madison, Virginia representative to the first federal Congress, responded to the popular demands for constitutional guarantees to individuals. From a host of suggested amendments, Madison offered 17, which were passed by the House of Representatives. The Senate cut the 17 amendments to 12 by combining and deleting items. On October 2, 1789, President Washington sent copies of the approved 12 amendments to the states. By December 15, 1791, three-fourths of the states had ratified 10, known thereafter as the Bill of Rights **(document 9)**.

Time: 1 class period

Objectives:

- To examine the constitutional amendment process.

- To read and discuss the principles of the Bill of Rights.

- To discuss the values of certain rights and liberties enumerated in the Bill of Rights.

Materials Needed:

Document 9

Procedures:

1. Duplicate 17 copies of the document. Distribute the copies to students working in pairs if the class size permits. Assign each student or pair of students a single article from the document. Instruct the students to read the article and to prepare an oral report to the class. The oral report should describe the contents of the article, the changes made (if any), and the disposition of the article (i.e., approved or not approved).

2. This particular document lends itself to a role-playing situation if the teacher thinks it to be appropriate: Assign students a senatorial role of approving or rejecting the proposed Bill of Rights as sent from the House. Group students in a workable manner and distribute copies of the document. Each group should examine one or two articles for content. On

the basis of the content and the obvious changes, they should report to the "floor" the content of that article and their recommended changes. They should be ready to justify their recommendations. At the conclusion of the role-playing, the students should be asked to consider the following three questions:

a. Were any items eliminated from the final Bill of Rights that would be appropriate today?

b. Are there any items in the Senate version that would be obsolete today?

c. Were any important individual rights and liberties overlooked in the Bill of Rights?

3. Students should rewrite the approved amendments in contemporary language, decide on one amended version, and type it in petition form. Duplicate and distribute copies to teams of students for polling. Instruct students to take the petitions to a public area (neighborhood, mall, downtown) and ask for signatures of support for the petition. Give the students some guidelines in conducting a poll. Caution them not to identify the articles as the Bill of Rights.

Following the completion of this task, conduct a discussion of the results. Ask about successes, refusals, comments, and reactions they experienced. Ask the students to reflect and then write an essay on the question "Does the Bill of Rights allow too many liberties?"

Exercise 10
The 26th Amendment

Note to the Teacher:

During the years since the Constitution was written, changes have been made through Supreme Court interpretation and amendment additions. Only 27 amendments have been added to the Constitution; the 26th, passed in the midst of the Vietnam War, lowered the voting age to 18 years.

Introduced by Senator Jennings Randolph of West Virginia, the amendment was proposed by a joint resolution of Congress on March 23, 1971 **(document 10)**. Ratified more quickly than any other amendment, the Twenty-sixth Amendment was approved by three-fourths of the state legislatures within 100 days after it was proposed. The Amendment became part of the Constitution when the Administrator of the General Services Administration, Robert L. Kunzig, certified the document on July 5, 1971.

In a ceremonial signing, President Richard Nixon invited three 18-year-olds to add their signatures along with his to the certification.

Time: 2 class periods

Objectives:

- To discuss the amendment process.
- To identify amendment issues.

Materials Needed:

Document 10
Overhead projector
U.S. history or government textbook

Procedures:

1. Display a transparency of document 10 on the overhead projector for students to read. Ask the questions from the Written Document Analysis worksheet, p. 12, for class discussion.

2. Using textbooks, review sections on the amendment procedures.

3. Ask teams of students to draft proposals for amendments to the Constitution to be considered by the class. Students should write the drafts using the language and style of the document as a model. Post the drafts in the room, allow time for students to study them, and then present the drafts for a vote of the class.

4. Extended activity: Ask students to prepare research reports that include the history of voting rights, voting patterns of youth, laws related to 18-year-olds, and minority rights.

Exercise II
Starting A New Government

Note to the Teacher:

Following the ratification of the Constitution, the Continental Congress established a timetable to begin the operation of the new government. According to schedule, the states chose electors of the President on the first Wednesday in January of 1789, the electors chose George Washington President and John Adams Vice President on the first Wednesday in February, and the new Congress organized and began functioning in New York City on the first Wednesday in March.

While most of the documents (11-16) used in this exercise demonstrate the process of organizing and starting the new government, **document 16** illustrates an unfamiliar episode that requires background information. Document 16 is part of the file on the impeachment of William Blount. Blount was one of the signers of the Constitution from the state of North Carolina. In 1790 he moved to Tennessee and became a leader in its transition from territory to statehood. He was elected to serve as one of the first U.S. senators from Tennessee. Blount became involved with intrigues to expel the Spanish from Louisiana and Florida. A letter referring to the plan was turned over to President Adams, who transmitted it to the Senate for action. On July 8, 1797, the Senate voted to expel Blount. Subsequently, the House of Representatives impeached him. Plans were made for his trial by the Senate. However, the Senate dropped the charges in 1799 because expulsion was the full extent of actions that could legally be taken to punish Blount.

Time: 1 or 2 class periods

Objectives:

- To examine the transition period between the Articles of Confederation and the Constitution.

- To identify the procedure for addition of new states to the original thirteen United States.

Materials Needed:

Documents 11-16
Worksheet 5
Transcriptions of documents 12 and 15, pp. 75 and 77

Procedures:

1. Divide the class into groups. Ask each group to develop a list of 10 actions that needed to be taken to translate the written constitutional framework into a functioning government. Direct students to arrange their ideas in order of priority. Ask groups to share their lists by recording them on either a chalkboard, overhead transparencies, or newsprint.

2. Duplicate a copy of the set of six documents for each group and a worksheet for each student. Direct students to circulate the documents within the group as they each complete the worksheet.

3. After the worksheets are complete, review each document with the students. Compare and contrast the students' recommendations with actions revealed in the documents.

4. Choose a culminating activity from the following:

   a. Ask students to write an essay identifying the actions that were most crucial to starting the operation of the new government and explaining why.

   b. Allow students to respond to one of the letters from these authors: Bradhead, Jay, or Ingersoll and Dallas in the character of the original recipient of the letter.

   c. Ask students to do additional research and write a paragraph explaining whether the Congress had jurisdiction in William Blount's case.

186.

Oath administered to the President of the U. States.

April 30th 1789.

The Vice Presidents chair was fixed on right of the Presidents, Speaker's the left. The Senate did not adjourn— The House did— came up headed by their Speaker and followed by the clerk. The President seated himself, and being informed by the Vice President that the two Houses were ready to attend him to take the oath, The Secretary of the Senate whose seat was inclined to the right of the Vice—President carrying a bible on a cushion, The Chancellor of the State administer-ed the oath. The President laying his hand on the bible and repeating the oath—after which the President of the United States kissed the book, and the Chancel-lor proclaimed him President of the United States— The President of the United States returning, and reposing a few minutes on his chair, arose and addressed the two Houses of Congress (as by

Exercise 11: Starting a New Government

Worksheet 5

Directions: Use information from documents 11-16 to complete the worksheet.

1. Compare and contrast the description of the first inauguration of George Washington with the most recent inauguration of a President.

    _____

    _____

2. What evidence is there in the documents that transportation and communication were slow?

    _____

    _____

    How did that slowness impede the government?

    _____

    _____

3. What reasons are given by the representatives of the District of Kentucky for petitioning to be separated from the jurisdiction of Virginia and to be established as an independent state?

    _____

    _____

4. In reference to document 12, what is the purpose of this letter?

    _____

    How might responding to requests of this sort affect the performance of the Executive?

    _____

    How could the President-elect deal with this request?

    _____

    _____

5. Which branch of the government appears to be the primary interpreter of the meaning of the Constitution at this time? Give examples.

    _____

    _____

Exercise 12
Jay's Letter to the U.S. Agent at Morocco

Note to the Teacher:

Document 14, which was used in the previous lesson, is singled out for study in this lesson.

John Jay was one of the outstanding early diplomats of the United States. In the final years of the American Revolution, he led a diplomatic mission to Spain as Minister Plenipotentiary. He served on the U.S. delegation that negotiated the Paris Peace Treaty in 1783. As Minister of Foreign Affairs from 1784 to 1790, Jay worked out an agreement (1785) to settle differences between Spain and the United States.

In 1789, in the midst of organizing the government under the Constitution, he wrote this letter to the U.S. agent explaining the delay in communication with foreign nations and the absence of Thomas Jefferson, who had been appointed Secretary of State. He explained to the agent the steps that were being taken to set up and activate the new government.

Time: 1 class period

Objectives:

- To examine the transition period between the Articles of Confederation and the Constitution.

- To describe the process of initiating the federal government.

Materials Needed:

Document 14
Worksheet 6
Transcription of document 14, p. 76

Procedures:

1. Duplicate and distribute copies of document 14 and worksheet 6 to each student.

2. Direct students to read the document and complete the worksheet.

3. Review the worksheet with students.

4. Ask students to compare and contrast the conduct of foreign relations during the 18th century and the 20th century, noting the slow pace of the past and jet/TV/computer diplomacy of today.

Exercise 12: Jay's Letter to the U.S. Agent at Morocco

Worksheet 6

Directions: Use information from the document to complete the worksheet.

1. In John Jay's words, "The new Government has been organized and peaceably established." List examples from his letter to show what has been done or is scheduled to be done in starting up the following offices of government:

    a. the executive branch

    _____

    _____

    _____

    b. the legislative branch

    _____

    _____

    _____

    c. the Department of State

    _____

    _____

    _____

2. How long was the time between Don Francisco's letter and Jay's reply? _____

    To what do you attribute this delay?

    _____

    _____

    _____

3. Why hasn't Jefferson taken over as Secretary of State?
   (You may want to refer to document 13.)

    _____

    _____

    _____

4. Why do you think Jay doesn't send the enclosed letter to Don Guiseppe directly instead of via Don Francisco?

    _____

    _____

    _____

5. How does the slow communication of the late 18th century affect the conduct of foreign relations?

    _____

    _____

    _____

Exercise 13
Issues Facing the Government

Note to the Teacher:

The ratification of the Constitution did not answer all questions or resolve all issues facing the United States. While the Constitution could serve as a framework for principles and forms of the new government, some matters required further clarification and others demanded continued debate. Private citizens could use the traditional form of petition to request government action.

The practical necessity of finding a location for the seat of government of the United States preoccupied many people in the new government. **Document 17** reveals that Lancaster, PA, was one of several cities that sought the honor of becoming the nation's capital. In July of 1790, at the same time that the selection of the capital was under consideration, another issue emerged: the question of whether the federal government should assume the $25 million debt of the states. During congressional debates over the proposed assumption bill, representatives of the southern states that had reduced many of their debts opposed the assumption of state debts. Secretary of the Treasury Hamilton met with Thomas Jefferson and worked out a compromise with him. Jefferson agreed to push support for the assumption bill by southern representatives in exchange for Hamilton's commitment to deliver northern support for situating the new capital city in the South. By a 13 to 12 vote, the Senate approved an undeveloped site along the Potomac River for the capital city.

As the institution of slavery expanded, the abolition movement emerged. In the late 17th century, the Mennonite and Quaker churches led the fight against slavery. Other denominations and associations of concerned individuals joined the antislavery movement as the 18th century progressed. Belief in humanity's natural rights was not strong enough to permit inclusion of a denunciation of slavery in the Declaration of Independence, as originally written by Jefferson. Yet, the gallant service of black soldiers in the Revolution weighed heavily on people of conscience, including Franklin, Jay, and Washington. Even before the end of the Revolution, Pennsylvania enacted a law to abolish slavery gradually in the state. During the years of the Confederation, other northern states followed suit and even the southern state of Virginia relaxed manumission laws and freed slaves who served in the Revolution. Slavery was prohibited in the northwest territories by the Northwest Ordinance of 1787. The Constitutional Convention did not provide for the abolition of slavery in the Constitution, but included a clause that restricted Congress from prohibiting the importation of slaves before 1808. However, at the convention a number of southern delegates voiced their belief that the southern states would end slavery of their own volition. There was a movement in the South at the time to manumit (free) slaves by will or deed; George Washington's slaves were freed in this manner. **Document 18** is a petition to the Congress on the subject of abolition of slavery.

In the newspaper *Pennsylvania Packet*, Thomas Paine published information pertaining to secret aid that the United States had received from France. As a result of this indiscretion, Congress initiated an inquiry into Paine's conduct. **Document 19** comes from a file of letters received by Congress from Paine in 1779 regarding their proceedings against him.

The documents (17-19) in the exercise are representative of the issues under consideration by the new government.

Time: 1 or 2 class periods

Objectives:

- To identify issues that posed special problems to the new nation.

- To compare and contrast the impact of the speed of communications between the 18th century and the 20th century.

- To conduct research into regional resources.

Materials Needed:

Documents 17-19
Written Document Analysis worksheet, p. 12
Worksheet 7
Transcription of document 19, p. 78

Procedures:

1. Review the content of the documents using the Written Document Analysis worksheet.

2. Duplicate documents 17-19 and worksheet 7 for each student and direct students to complete the puzzle.

3. Ask students to do research to determine what actions Congress took in response to the following issues raised in these documents:

   a. Location of the capital

   b. Slavery

   c. Right to be informed of criminal charges

4. Ask students to research the resources of their region, then write a letter detailing why the U.S. capital should be relocated from Washington, DC, to their area. Sources of information for the students might include: the local Chamber of Commerce, city hall, county courthouse, local historical society, board of tourism and information, local libraries, and the U.S. Department of Commerce.

5. Ask students to write a petition on a subject of personal concern. Suggest that students send the petition to the authority who seems most responsible and able to act upon their concern.

Worksheet 7 Answers
1. slavery 2. Benjamin Franklin 3. House of Representatives 4. Liberty 5. memorialists
6. Senate 7. inconsistency 8. color 9. President

Exercise 13: Issues Facing the Government

Worksheet 7

Directions: Use information from document 18 to complete the worksheet.

1. What condition does the Pennsylvania Society seek to abolish?

   _____

2. Who is the person who sent this document?

   _____

3. Who received this document?

   _____

4. What birthright does the Constitution attempt to secure for all citizens?

   _____

5. The petitioners of the Pennsylvania Society are referred to as

   _____

6. Who else received this document?

   _____

7. Considering American character, the writer of this document finds slavery to be

   _____

8. What distinction caused the bondage of the enslaved people referred to in this document?

   _____

9. What position in the Pennsylvania Society does the writer of this document hold?

   _____

10. (Vertical) To end slavery

Exercise 14
The National Debt

Note to the Teacher:

The failure of the Congress of the Confederation to meet the daily challenges and expectations of a government eroded its credibility and resulted in its replacement by the federal government under the Constitution. This new government inherited all the problems that were unresolved under the Articles, some of which had been exacerbated by neglect over the years. Particularly crucial to the success or failure of the new government were challenges arising from the public debt. In 1785, under the Articles of Confederation, Massachusetts' attempts to raise revenues to pay Revolutionary debts led to the insurrection referred to in **document 21**, Shays' Rebellion. The early government grappled over methods for repayment of loans to creditors, generation of revenues, and encouragement of agriculture, manufacture, and trade. The account of the debates over public credit was printed in 1834 in *Annals of Congress*, on the basis of contemporary newspaper reports **(document 25)**. Pivotal for the future of the federal government was the Whiskey Rebellion of 1794 with its familiar refrain of revolutionary resistance to taxation. For the first and last time in U.S. history, a President took the field as commander in chief. Washington led the army of 15,000 militiamen to Pennsylvania, where Henry Lee took over command with Secretary of the Treasury Alexander Hamilton in accompaniment. The insurrection was crushed, and the federal government sustained its authority to levy taxes.

The **documents (20-26)** in this exercise illustrate the difficulties to be overcome by the new government lest it be overwhelmed by those very problems.

Time: 1 or 2 class periods

Objectives:

- To explain why the national debt posed such grave problems to the new nation.

- To identify the issues involved in the repayment of loans.

- To identify measures taken to generate revenues to pay off the national debt.

Materials Needed:

Documents 20-26
Worksheet 8
Transcription of document 26, p. 79

Procedures:

1. Divide the class into groups. Duplicate a set of the seven documents for each group and a worksheet for each student. Direct students to circulate the documents within the group as they each complete the worksheet.

2. After the worksheets are complete, review each document with the students and discuss their reactions to the government's financial plan.

3. Direct one student to find out the interest rate on U.S. Savings Bonds today. Compare rates from 1790 with the present.

4. As a culminating activity, ask students to investigate what measures are being taken to ensure the financial security of the Unites States. Compare the measures of the early Republic with contemporary approaches to the debt.

---

be appointed, not only in different States, but in different places of the same State. If commissioners are appointed, for instance, in Charleston, the citizens must attend from the remotest parts of the State, and be worried in travelling backwards and forwards to seek for witnesses, many of whom may be dead, or removed into other countries—not to mention the length of time and the enormous expense which so complicated a business must occasion. He concluded, by declaring it to be his opinion, that the proposition, if agreed to, would throw things into confusion and perplexity, which he could not see the extent of; he should, therefore oppose it.

Mr. MADISON.—If paper, or the honor of statues or medals, can discharge the debts of justice, payable in gold or silver, we cannot only exonerate ourselves from those due to the original holders, but from those of the assignees; so far as paper goes the latter have received the compensation. If honor can discharge the debt, they have received civil honors; look round to the officers of every Government in the Union, and you find them sharing equal honors with those bestowed on the original creditors. But, sir, the debt due in gold and silver is not payable either in honor, appointments, or in paper.

Gentlemen say it will work injustice; but are we not as much bound to repair the injustice done by the United States? Yet I do not believe the assertion has been established by any thing that has been urged in its support. The gentleman from Maryland, (Mr. STONE,) acknowledges that there is a moral obligation to compensate the original holders; how will they get what he admits is their due? He is willing to make an effort by applying the resources of the country to that purpose; but if we are to judge by the sentiments of other gentlemen who have spoken on this occasion, we have little to expect from that quarter. Suppose the debt had depreciated to a mere trifle, and suppose the sale of the Western Territory had extinguished the certificates, let me ask, whether, if the United States had thus exonerated themselves from the obligation to the assignee, whether the claim of the original holder would not still remain in its full force in a moral view? But believing the point of justice to be exhausted, I will just add one remark upon the practicability. The transferred certificates, generally, will show the names of the original holders, and here there is no difficulty. With respect to those granted to the heads of either of the five great departments, the books of the Treasurer of Loans, as well as the accounts of those departments now in the Treasury, will designate with a great degree of accuracy, and this may be followed up by the usual mode of obtaining evidence; and I believe, every security may be provided against fraud in this case that was provided in the case of the commissioners who were sent into the respective States for ascertaining and liquidating the claims of individuals. That there will be some difficulty I admit, but it is enough for me that it is not insuperable; and I trust, with the assistance which the cause of equity and justice will ever obtain

from the members of the National Legislature, they will easily be surmounted.

Mr. WHITE wished to ascertain a fact which had been mentioned. He did not mean to infer that gentlemen had related a fact they did not believe; but supposed they might have been misinformed. He asked, whether foreigners had been induced to purchase in our funds by assurances from the ministers of the United States, residing at Foreign Courts, that no variation would be made in the domestic debt.

Mr. BLAND asked his colleague, (Mr. MADISON,) how long he supposed the settlement which he contemplated would take in its completion? For his part he supposed two or three generations might pass away before that object could be accomplished, considering the dispersed situation of the claimants through America, Europe, Asia, and Africa.

Mr. MADISON said, the claims of individuals were presented and liquidated by the Commissioners throughout the United States in nine months; that was the period fixed for that purpose by Congress; he would not say but it was too short, yet he thought this experiment fairly inferred that the ascertainment he contended for could be effected in a short time.

Mr. BOUDINOT had seen an authentic letter, in which the writer mentioned that the opinion of Mr. JEFFERSON was asked, and obtained. He also had reason to believe the sentiments of the President of the late Congress were given to the same effect.

The committee now rose, and the House adjourned.

MONDAY, February 22.

The House proceeded to consider the amendments of the Senate to the bill providing for the enumeration of the inhabitants of the United States, and agreeing to a part and disagreeing to other parts; a message was sent to the Senate informing them thereof.

PUBLIC CREDIT.

The House then resolved itself into a Committee on the Report of the Secretary of the Treasury, Mr. BALDWIN in the Chair.

Mr. MADISON's proposition still under consideration.

Mr. PAGE.—As the worthy and eloquent member who replied to me did not answer the questions I put to the committee, I suppose he either did not hear them, did not understand me, or could not answer them. I hope, before the committee decide, they will attempt at least to resolve them. I asked, where is the injustice of the States complying with its engagements made to the first holders of certificates, as far as the case admits? Where is the justice of doing more for the assignee than he or his assignor expected could or would be done? Where is the breach of faith in Government, if it paid its whole debt with justice blended with mercy? Where is the interference in contracts, when the proposition is to comply sacredly, as far as the case will admit,

Exercise 14: The National Debt

Worksheet 8

Directions: Use information from documents 20-26 to complete the worksheet.

1. List two reasons suggested in the documents for the emptiness of the U.S. Treasury.

   _____

   _____

2. List three reasons why the national debt posed such a problem to the new nation.

   _____

   _____

3. List three ideas for generating revenues that are indicated in the documents.

   _____

   _____

4. Why does Madison believe the original holders of government bonds should be compensated?

   _____

   What difficulties might repayment of original purchasers present?

   _____

   _____

5. Refer to document 24

   a. In what years were the bonds originally issued?

      _____

      In what year were they paid?

      _____

   b. Why is the original dollar amount undergoing a rate of exchange to fix the amount due for payment?

      _____

   c. Which holder is primarily cashing in his own loan certificates?

      _____

   d. Which holders are cashing the certificates of others?

      _____

      Why might they be doing this?

      _____

6. List at least three effects the finance program had on U.S. citizens.

   _____

   _____

   _____

Exercise 15
Survey Map of Ohio's Seven Ranges

Note to the Teacher:

By 1784, Congress began considering plans for surveying the public lands of the United States. Virtually all the States under the Articles had experienced problems due to indiscriminate land allotment. To avoid future difficulties, various plans, including Thomas Jefferson's, were reviewed and debated. On May 20, 1785, a national rectangular system was adopted, providing for division of the public domain. The first area to be surveyed under this innovative system was the Ohio River Valley. The Geographer's Line (along the Pennsylvania border) served as the meridian and the Ohio River as the base line for dividing the public domain into townships six miles square.

Congress projected that sales of surveyed lands would help to generate revenues for the government. However, the sale of public lands did little to diminish the national debt. The initial purchasers often used depreciated paper money ("continentals") for payment. The selling price was only about one dollar per acre. Also, certain townships were excluded from public sale. In each 36 section township, Congress first reserved sections 8, 11, 26, and 29 for future disposal. In 1796, the reservations were changed to sections 15, 16, 21, and 22. Mineral reservations were also made, although they proved to be of little significance. The most important of the reservations was that of section 16, which, under the provisions of the Land Ordinance of 1785, was designated for school purposes. By the 1980s approximately 80 million acres of U.S. lands have been granted in support of education.

The **documents (5 and 22)** in this exercise provide information on the disposition of public lands.

Time: 2 to 3 class periods

Objectives:

- To illustrate how the provisions of the Land Ordinance of 1785 and the Northwest Ordinance of 1787 facilitated orderly settlement of the western territories.

- To interpret information from a map and surveyor's field notes.

Materials Needed:

Documents 5 and 22
Worksheet 9

Procedures:

1. Ask students to review information in their textbooks on the Land Ordinances of 1785 and 1787. Share with the students additional background information found in the Note to the Teacher and in document 5.

2. Distribute copies of document 22 to the students.

3. Distribute the worksheet to the students and ask them to examine the document to find answers to the questions. After the students have completed the worksheet, review and discuss their answers.

4. Ask students to research and determine the impact of the American colonial system's state-making procedure on the following:

    a. Land speculators

    b. States with large claims in the territories that became the public domain of the United States, especially Virginia

    c. Land-poor states with no claims in the territories

    d. Territorial governments

    e. Settlers of the Ohio territory

   Students may wish to act "in character" as they present their findings to the class.

5. If you have a student who is a hiking enthusiast, ask that pupil to compare and contrast Isaac Sherman's blazing marks with modern trail blazes. The findings might be displayed on a bulletin board. Also, to help students visualize what an acre of land looks like, ask an interested student to find out the acreage of the school campus, football field, or a local shopping center. Another project might be to ask students to study a map of the town and to see if the oldest section was laid out in a rectangular or grid pattern. Students might determine the pattern of settlement and perhaps, with a science teacher, do a botanical study such as Isaac Sherman did in 1786.

6. Discuss with students alternatives to distributing land in the manner selected by the Congress. What assumptions about human nature and the functions of government motivated the government to act as it did?

15

Exercise 15: Survey Map of Ohio's Seven Ranges

Worksheet 9

Directions: Study the map and write answers to the questions below.

1. Examine the map title to determine the following:

   a. When the territory was surveyed _____

   b. Who the surveyor was and where he came from _____

   c. What the size of the area was that he surveyed _____

   _____

2. Examine the field notes:

   a. List the categories of information that can be determined from this map:

   _____

   _____

   b. Determine what types of trees appeared most frequently in this township in 1786

   _____

   _____

3. Examine the map and decide the following:

   a. Which lands were sold first _____

   b. On what dates land was sold _____

   c. What was the attraction of sections 19, 14, 9, 15, 11 and 24

   _____

   d. What topographic features are shown on this map _____

4. Why does this township have only 24 sections rather than the customary 36?

   _____

5. What value would positive knowledge of the boundaries of a tract of land have for settlers?

   _____

6. Imagine that you are a farmer living in 1787 and you have a chance to move west to Ohio.

   a. What features of Township 2 in the Third Range would be attractive to you and why?

   _____

   _____

   b. Which section of those still available would you want to purchase and why?

   _____

   _____

Exercise 16
Summary Exercise: Federalism and the Constitution

Note to the Teacher:

Federalism is the division of power between the national government and the state governments. The Constitution delegates powers to the national government whether the power is expressed, inherent, or implied. Yet also, under the Constitution the existence of state governments and the exercise of their powers (whether concurrent with the national government or reserved to the state) is guaranteed. This constitutional division of powers is, nonetheless, imprecise. Throughout American history the balance between national and state power has shifted back and forth. One of the still unresolved questions about federalism is whether this division of power is rational or effective. The **documents (8, 11-26)** in this exercise demonstrate the relationship between national and state power.

Time: 2 to 4 class periods

Objectives:

- To describe the major purposes of the government assigned to it in the preamble to the Constitution.

- To examine the relationship between national and state powers in the federal government.

Materials needed:

Documents 8, 11-26
Preamble to the Constitution

Procedures:

NOTE: These exercises are progressively more difficult.

1. In preparation for study of the preamble, you may wish to require students to memorize it so that confusion with the Declaration of Independence is reduced and familiarity with the Constitution is enhanced.

2. Ask students to paraphrase the preamble to the Constitution of the United States. Emphasize that this is not to be a summary but should be roughly the same length and contain all the main ideas of the original.

16

3. Divide the class into six groups and

   a. Assign to each group one of the following categories of federal power: Form a More Perfect Union, Establish Justice, Ensure Domestic Tranquillity, Provide for the Common Defense, Promote General Welfare, Secure Blessings of Liberty.

   b. Ask students to examine documents 11-26 for examples of the exercise of the federal government's power that has been assigned to their group. Each group should list the documents and cite illustrative passages.

   c. Give each group time to share its findings with the entire class. Note documents that overlap categories.

4. Select four students who would be willing to conduct research and present in the format of a debate their positions regarding the following topic: Resolved, that the Constitution fails to maintain an efficient and realistic balance between national and state power and that a Constitutional Convention should be called to remedy this problem.

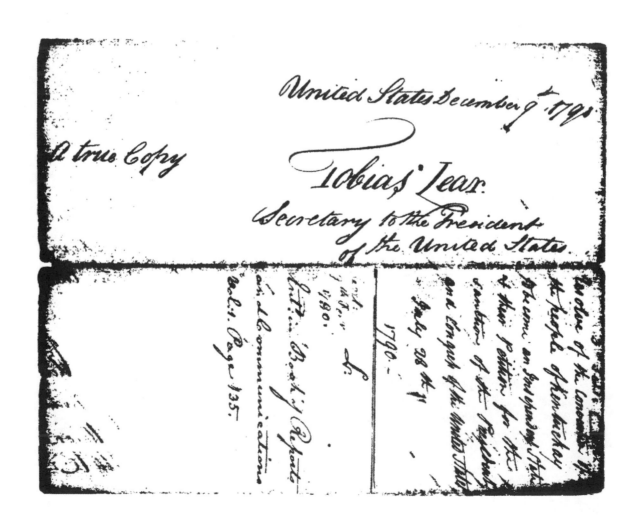

Exercise 17
Background of the First Amendment

Note to the Teacher:

"Congress shall make no law respecting an establishment of religion, or prohibiting the free exercise thereof . . ."

Although the British colonies of North America were populated by many immigrants seeking a haven from religious persecution, on the eve of the American Revolution state-established religions appeared quite secure. However, a logical extension of the social contract theory that dominated 18th-century American political thought is that religious freedom is a natural right. John Locke's *Two Treatises of Government* and his first *Letter Concerning Toleration* set forth the argument that a commonwealth is created to advance only civil interests and that, accordingly, religion, whose authority is derived from God, is outside the jurisdiction of government. In 1776, the Virginia Convention adopted a new state constitution and a bill of rights, which included an article written by George Mason and amended by James Madison guaranteeing the free exercise of religion. In the years following the Revolution, under the Articles of Confederation, many states adopted constitutions or acts of toleration that moved to separate church from state and guarantee some measure of religious toleration among Christians. Of the 13 original states, only Virginia and Rhode Island moved beyond toleration of dissenting churches to guarantee religious freedom. When the Northwest Ordinance of 1787 was adopted, however, a bill of rights was included that proclaimed religious freedom in the territories.

At the Constitutional Convention, no statement was made concerning religious freedom. The only time the subject of religion specifically arises in the Constitution is in article VI. In setting qualifications for federal office, the representatives determined that "no religious test shall ever be required as a qualification to any office or public trust under the United States." The omission of a bill of rights nearly prevented ratification of the Constitution.

To remedy the shortcoming, James Madison drafted a bill of rights for consideration by the first U.S. Congress. His original amendment pertaining to religion read: "The civil rights of none shall be abridged on account of religious belief, nor shall any national religion be established, nor shall the full and equal rights of conscience in any manner or on any pretext be infringed." The amendment that emerged clearly prohibited Congress from making laws respecting the establishment of religion or to interfere with free exercise of religion. What was not clear, however, was whether the executive or judicial branches, or the states, were bound by the First Amendment. It was not until the adoption of the Fourteenth Amendment in 1868 that the Bill of Rights could be interpreted as binding upon the states under the clause "nor shall any State deprive any person of life, liberty, or property without due process of the laws; nor deny to any person within its jurisdiction the equal protection of the laws."

Document 27, notes from the debate on the First Amendment, called article three, is from *Journal of Proceedings of the U.S. Senate, First Session, First Congress*, which was printed in 1820 by Gales and Seaton in Washington and was based on the original minutes of the clerk of the Senate.

The documents (5, 27) used in this exercise illustrate the principle of the separation of church and state.

Time: 1 or 2 class periods

17

Objective:

- To trace the evolution of the principles of separation of church and state and religious freedom in the United States.

Materials Needed:

Documents 5, 27
A copy of the Constitution and Amendments to the Constitution.

Procedures:

1. Ask students to review the Northwest Ordinance; the Constitution, section VI, clause 3; and the First and Fourteenth Amendments to the Constitution. Share with students additional background information found in the Note to the Teacher.

2. Duplicate and distribute copies of document 27 to the students. Direct students' attention to the section beginning "On motion to amend article third . . ." Ask students to write the First Amendment as it would have been worded if any of the three alternative wordings had been adopted. Discuss what the reasons may have been for rejection of the alternative wordings and the pros and cons of the various wordings. Ask for a show of hands for the wording that the students favor.

3. Ask students to define religious toleration and religious freedom and to distinguish the difference between them. Direct students to research and present in class the ideas about the government's role vis à vis religion expressed by the following:
   John Locke
   Sir Henry Vane, the Younger
   George Mason
   James Madison
   Thomas Jefferson
   Thomas Paine
   John Adams
   George Washington

   Discuss the similarities and differences between each man's opinion and the position of the present administration as to the role of government and religion.

4. As a culminating activity, ask selected students to research the Supreme Court case *Barron v. Baltimore* (1833) and relate how, in 1868, Representatives John A. Bingham and Thaddeus Stevens and Senator J. M. Howard managed the Fourteenth Amendment in Congress, in part to reverse *Barron v. Baltimore*. Students may present their findings in the form of an essay or an oral report. (The ruling in the case of *Barron v. Baltimore* was that the Bill of Rights was not binding upon the states.)

Exercise 18
The Establishment of Religion

Note to the Teacher:

The documents (28-30) in this lesson reflect the many facets of the issue of establishment of religion. A narrow construction of the establishment clause of the First Amendment would restrict its meaning to prohibiting establishment of a state church. However, in the first major establishment case brought before the Supreme Court, *Everson v. Board of Education*, in 1947, the justices interpreted the clause in a broad manner. Justice Hugo Black's opinion in the case enunciates this construction with clarity:

> The 'establishment of religion' clause of the First Amendment means at least this: Neither a state nor the Federal Government can set up a church. Neither can pass laws which aid one religion, aid all religions, or prefer one religion over another. Neither can force nor influence a person to go to or to remain away from church against his will or force him to profess a belief or disbelief in any religion. No person can be punished for entertaining or professing religious beliefs or disbeliefs, for church attendance or non-attendance. No tax in any amount, large or small, can be levied to support any religious activities or institutions, whatever they may be called, or whatever form they may adopt to teach or practice religion. Neither a state nor the Federal Government can, openly or secretly, participate in the affairs of any religious organizations or groups and vice versa. In the words of Jefferson, the clause against establishment of religion by law was intended to erect, 'a wall of separation between church and State.'

A wide variety of issues has been considered by the federal courts on the basis of their relationship to the establishment clause. These include state aid to religion, church intervention in state affairs, state intervention in church affairs, religion in public schools, and state aid to denominational schools. Some of the cases raised by the state aid to religion have included public financial grants to religious bodies and sectarian social welfare organizations, equal access to public facilities, and tax exemptions to churches. The government sanctions several exceptions to intervention of churches in state affairs, including paid legislative and military chaplains, chapel attendance at military academies, and "In God We Trust" on U.S. currency. The state also intervenes in some church affairs; for example, presidential proclamations of Thanksgiving, fasting, and prayer, and ambassadorial representation to the Holy See.

The issue of religion in public schools is of particular interest to educators, pupils, and parents. Topics that have emerged include Bible-reading and prayer in schools, teaching of evolution v. creationism, released time, and observation of holy days by schools. State aid to church-related schools by tuition tax credits and vouchers to parents of students in private sectarian schools, is also an issue of great continuing interest.

All of the documents in this lesson relate to the establishment of religion and have particular relevance to public school teachers and students. **Document 28** is the bill passed by Congress in 1954 inserting "under God" in the Pledge of Allegiance. **Document 29** is from the support files of *Minersville v. Gobitis*, 1940, the compulsory flag salute case. **Document 30** comes from the support files of *Engel v. Vitale*, 1962, the case by which the New York Regents prayer in public schools was ruled in violation of the First Amendment.

Time: 1 to 3 class periods

18

Objectives:

- To identify and examine issues related to the establishment clause of the First Amendment.

- To consider the arguments and take a position on an issue.

- To trace the history of the interpretation of the establishment clause.

Materials Needed:

Documents 28, 29, and 30
Worksheet 10

Procedures:

1. Duplicate the three documents and the worksheet for each student.

   a. Ask students to complete the chart, beginning in class and continuing outside of class. Allow 2 periods for this assignment because the students will need to consult reference material.

   b. When the charts are completed, review the findings, emphasizing the history of the issue in each document.

2. Divide the class into groups of 5 to 6 students.

   a. The question of state-mandated, sponsored, or ritualized group prayer came before the Supreme Court in the New York Regents school prayer case (*Engel v. Vitale*, 1962). Below is a summation of the major arguments pro and con, extracted from the judicial record of the case. Give each group a copy of the arguments, which are related to document 30.

Pro Prayer in Public Schools

- Recognition of Almighty God in public prayer is an integral part of our national heritage.

- The Constitution of the U.S. is incapable of being so interpreted as to require that the wall of separation of church and state become an iron curtain.

- Judicial, legislative, administrative, and textual writers have agreed that what the framers of the First Amendment had in mind did not project the idea of a wall of separation between church and state into a "government hostility to religion" which would be "at war with our national tradition."

- A few seconds of voluntary prayer in schools acknowledging dependence on Almighty God is consistent with our heritage of "securing the blessing of freedom" which are recognized in both the Federal and states constitutions as having emanated from Almighty God.

Con Prayer in Public Schools

- Use of public schools and the time and efforts of teachers and staff of the schools violates the establishment clause.

- Saying prayer as teaching of religion and religious practices is contrary to the belief of the petitioners and is offensive to the petitioners and their children.

- Saying prayers results in exercise of coercion by school officials.

- Saying of prayers as a sectarian or denominational practice favors one or more religions or religious practices over others and religion over nonbelief.

- Saying of prayers results in divisiveness.

- Saying of prayers is contrary to the prohibition against establishment, and the right to free exercise and the exercise of religion without discrimination or preference.

- Saying of prayers exceeds the statutory authority of the schools and is in violation of their statutory duties.

b. Ask students to discuss each argument thoroughly and then take a position, pro or con. Encourage the group to reach a consensus rather than take a vote. A recorder from each group should report to the class the group's position and the reasons for taking that position.

3. A similar exercise would be appropriate for the issues in document 29 (compulsory flag salute), in document 28 (reference to God in the Pledge of Allegiance), or in the list of issues in Note to the Teacher.

4. Extended Activity: For additional research, students can consider the changes in the interpretation of the establishment clause over time. Ask your most capable students to trace the history of the interpretation of the clause, both broad and narrow, including the interpretations of the Court in the Everson case, the McCollum Case, the Zorach case, the McGowan case, the Torcaso case, and the Schempp-Murray cases. The students could chart a time line in the classroom showing the changes that have taken place in the interpretation. Ask one student to explain the events and changes to the class.

ECONOMY STORES

WALTER GOBITAS

Produce, Meats and Groceries

15-17 SUNBURY STREET

MINERSVILLE, PA.

March 7, 1940   *(stamp: OFFICE OF THE CLERK — MAR 9 1940 — SUPREME COURT U.S.)*

Clerk of the Supreme Court
 of the United States
Washington, D.C.

Dear Sir:

In Re: Case of Minersville School District, Appellants,
        vs. Walter Gobitis and others, Plaintiff Appellees

        My chief counsel in this case is

Joseph F. Rutherford of 124 Columbia Heights,

Brooklyn, New York, whom I have substituted in

the place of O. R. Moyle. I will also be rep-

resented in the case by Mr. H. M. McCaughey of

Philadelphia who is the Attorney of record and

Mr. Hayden C. Covington of Brooklyn, New York.

        Respectfully yours,

        Walter Gobitas

WG*lq

18

Exercise 18: The Establishment of Religion

Worksheet 10

Directions: Use the documents and references to complete the following chart.

	Document 28	Document 29	Document 30
Document type, date, and author (creator)			
Central issue of each document			
Purpose of document (why written)			
Circumstances surrounding the issue			
Legal position, then and now			
Popular feeling, then and now			
How do you account for changes in legal and/or popular positions?			

Exercise 19
Free Exercise of Religion

Note to the Teacher:

The documents (31-33) used in this exercise provide a case study of the issue of free exercise of religion. Since 1659, when Quakers William Robinson and Marmaduke Stevenson were hanged by the Puritans of Massachusetts, religious minorities have been misunderstood and frequently persecuted by religious majorities in this country. Since the inception of the federal government, many religious groups have found themselves at odds with the government when their religious practices impeded, or were perceived to impede, the orderly functioning of society, particularly as they were thought to affect national defense, public health, and peaceful moral conduct. Notable cases have involved Jehovah's Witnesses, Seventh Day Adventists, Amish, Quakers, Black Muslims, and Christian Scientists.

The first major case involving the free exercise clause to be heard by the Supreme Court was *Reynolds v. United States* in 1878, in which the plural marriages of Mormon George Reynolds were seen to be in conflict with federal antipolygamy law. The decision in that case is used in this exercise. Because of its salient position in constitutional law, the Church of Jesus Christ of Latter-Day Saints (the Mormon Church) will be our case study in free exercise and the First Amendment.

The Church of Jesus Christ of Latter-Day Saints was established by Joseph Smith in 1830. Based on divine revelation, Smith endorsed the practice of polygamy by church members. This expression of religious belief provoked non-Mormons, called "gentiles" by Mormons, to a violent persecution of the church. In 1847, led by Brigham Young, thousands of Mormons emigrated to Mexican territories where they could worship and live freely. With the Mexican War and cession of the territories to the United States, the Mormons' settlement near the Great Salt Lake fell under the authority of the United States. In 1849, a convention was held, the State of Deseret was organized, and the Mormons applied for statehood and were rejected. In 1850, Utah was organized by congressional compromise as a U.S. territory, in part due to objections in Congress to polygamy. In 1852, Brigham Young, who was governor of the Territory of Utah, proclaimed polygamy to be an official tenet of the church. Suspicions and tensions increased until, in May 1857, 2,500 U.S. troops were sent to march against Utah. In defiance, Brigham Young ordered "scorched earth" guerrilla-style resistance. In September a band of Indians with Mormons present killed 131 emigrants from Arkansas on their way to California in the Mountain Meadows Massacre. The crisis was resolved in 1858 as U.S. troops withdrew from Salt Lake City and pardons were issued to Mormons who submitted to the authority of the United States. Opposition to the Mormons continued, and, in 1862, the Morrill Act was passed by Congress prohibiting and punishing polygamy in the territories, a move reinforced in 1882 by the Edmunds Act, which defined and punished polygamy, polygamous cohabitation, and bigamy. But Mormon evasion of these laws was widespread, and Utah's admission as a state was therefore delayed by Congress. Finally, in 1890, President Woodruff of the Mormon Church issued a manifesto pronouncing a church ban on the practice of polygamy. As a result, on January 4, 1896, Utah was admitted as a state under a constitution that specifically prohibited polygamy.

Document 31 is a petition of the women of Utah requesting repeal of the 1862 Morrill Act, enactment of a homesteading bill for women, and admission of Utah as a state. **Document 32** is the 1879 decision from *Reynolds v. United States*, in which the Supreme Court sustained the conviction of George Reynolds (private secretary to Brigham Young) of practicing polygamy in violation of the Morrill Act. In this decision the First Amendment was not seen as applying to religious practices. As Chief Justice Waite wrote in his opinion, "Laws are made for the government of actions, and while they cannot interfere with mere religious beliefs and opinions, they may with practices . . . To permit this would be to make the professed doctrines of religious belief superior to the law of the land and in effect to permit every citizen to become a law unto himself." **Document 33** is from the records of the House of Representatives, 56th Congress. It is in the file of the case of Brigham H. Roberts, a polygamist with three wives, who was elected to the U.S. House of Representatives from Utah but was refused his seat in 1899.

Time: 1 or 2 class periods

Objectives:

- To trace the evolution of the Supreme Court's interpretation of the free exercise clause of the First Amendment.

- To examine a case involving conflict over the free exercise of religion.

- To study techniques of persuasion and other methods for influencing public opinion and policy.

Materials needed:

Documents 31, 32, and 33
Worksheet 11

Procedures:

1. Share with students the background information from the Note to the Teacher and ask students to review what their textbooks say about the Mormon case.

2. Ask students to discuss whether, in the realm of protecting public morals, the common good takes precedence over individual conscience. What are the proper limits on public good and on individual exercise of conscience? Is this a resolvable question? How can the common good be determined and by whom? Ask students to identify what constituted the common good in *Reynolds v. United States*, document 32, and what constitutes the common good today. Ask for volunteers to trace the interpretation of free exercise, including the following cases, and to share their findings with the class.

   a. *Reynolds v. United States* (1878)

   b. *Davis v. Beason* (1890)

   c. *Minersville v. Gobitis* (1940)

   d. *Cantwell v. Connecticut* (1940)

   e. *Murdock v. Pennsylvania* (1943)

   f. *West Virginia State Board of Education v. Barnette* (1943)

   g. *Sherbert v. Verner* (1963)

   h. *Wisconsin v. Yoder* (1972)

3. Duplicate and distribute copies of documents 31 and 33 to each student. Ask students to read the two documents, then discuss the contents of the documents as a group. Divide the class into groups of 3 to 4 students. Duplicate and distribute worksheet 11 and direct students to reread the two documents and then complete the worksheet cooperatively. Go over any persuasive terms that the students are unfamiliar with.

4. Review with the whole class their responses to worksheet 11. Refer back to documents 17, 18, and 19 and compare and contrast document 31 with those earlier petitions. Ask students for examples from current local, state, and national events of lobbying efforts made to promote public morality.

| 44TH CONGRESS, | HOUSE OF REPRESENTATIVES. | MIS. DOC. |
| 1st Session. | | No. 42. |

PETITION OF WOMEN OF UTAH.

A PETITION

OF

22,626 WOMEN OF UTAH

ASKING FOR

The repeal of certain laws, the enactment of others, and the admission of the Territory of Utah as a State.

JANUARY 13, 1876.—Referred to the Committee on the Judiciary and ordered to be printed without the names.

MEMORIAL OF THE WOMEN OF UTAH TO THE CONGRESS OF THE UNITED STATES.

To the Senate and House of Representatives of the United States of America in Congress assembled :

We, your memorialists, women of Utah, prompted by a due sense of justice, and in consideration of those equal rights so long the proud boast of American citizens, hereby appeal to your honorable body, praying you to grant our petition as shall be herein specified.

We, as a people, are willing to submit to, and do strictly obey, the Constitution and laws of these United States as handed down to us by the fathers of our country ; and we do earnestly pray that you will repeal the anti-polygamy law of 1862 ; also the bill known as the Poland bill ; both being special and unconstitutional measures directed against the people of Utah, holding the peace and happiness of our lives in constant jeopardy by imperiling the safety of our husbands and fathers, by daily and hourly subjecting them to danger of arrest and imprisonment, which would not only deprive us of their society, but also of their support and protection. To you, the executives of a great and powerful nation, we appeal for protection against these cruel and oppressive measures, which have shorn our glorious Constitution of its efficacy and us of every protection but the overruling power of God.

We ask to be relieved from the unjust and law-breaking officials forced upon us by the Government, and that we may have the jurisdiction of our own courts and the selection of our own officers, as we had in the past, when our cities were free from dram-shops, gambling-dens, and houses of infamy. As mothers and sisters, we earnestly appeal to you

19

Exercise 19: Free Exercise of Religion

Worksheet 11

Directions: Please refer to your copy of the documents to complete the following questions.

Document 31: Petition of Women of Utah

1. What are the three major requests made by the women of Utah?

   _____

   _____

2. According to the women of Utah, what evils did the antipolygamy law unleash upon Utah? (Name at least three.)

   _____

   _____

3. What is the legal basis for their appeal?

   _____

   _____

4. What would have been the economic impact if Congress had endorsed both homesteading privileges for married women of Utah and polygamy?

   _____

   What were the prevailing laws relating to married women's property rights?

   _____

5. a. Underline the adjectives in this petition. What is the tone associated with the U.S. government? What is the tone of references to the effects of the antipolygamy law?

   _____

   _____

   b. List emotionally charged words or expressions that the women of Utah use to try to persuade the reader that polygamy supports public morality and that the antipolygamy law undermines morality.

   _____

   _____

Document 33: Letter of Reverend William R. Campbell

1. Locate and quote examples of Campbell's use of the following persuasive techniques: straw man, "right is on our side," loaded words, name calling, cause and effect, repetition.

   _____

   _____

2. What two actions does Campbell see as necessary to prevent the spread of polygamy?

   _____

   _____

3. List the steps to organize the campaign against Roberts that Campbell outlines in his postscript.

   _____

   _____

Exercise 20
The Constitution and the Roman Catholic Church

Note to the Teacher:

For our case study of church-state relations over the course of the history of the United States, we have selected the Roman Catholic Church. From the inception of the Constitution, questions have arisen about the relation of the Catholic Church to religious tests, free exercise, and establishment.

Article VI, clause 3 proscribes religious tests for qualification to federal office, yet the American electorate historically has restricted, informally, adherents of a number of religions from public service by declining to nominate them or by voting against candidates on the basis of their religion. The informal exclusion of Catholics from high elective office ended on November 8, 1960. John F. Kennedy's victory marked the first time that American voters had elected a member of the Roman Catholic Church to the office of President of the United States. During the campaign, Kennedy stressed the absence of conflict between his duty as a congressman and his loyalty to his faith and convinced the American people of the sincerity of his submission to the primacy of the Constitution. He also benefited from the ecumenical spirit within Christianity, which had reduced Protestant-Catholic hostility. The conciliatory, liberal measures of the charismatic Pope John XXIII (1958-1963) further defused anti-Catholicism as a political force in the 1960 election. The landmark election of John F. Kennedy may have resolved doubts about whether a Catholic could perform as President, but there continue to be constitutional complications in other aspects of this church-state relationship between the Roman Catholic Church and the United States.

Document 34 can either serve only as data in the study of Kennedy's election and term of office, or it may be used as a springboard to examine larger issues such as anti-Catholicism in the United States (from the Know-Nothings to the Ku Klux Klan), the appointment of an ambassador to the Vatican, or the Catholic Church as a lobbying group.

Time: 1 to 4 class periods

Objectives:

- To trace the attitudes toward Catholics over the course of American history.

- To interpret political cartoons.

- To identify the contradictions in constitutional interpretations that can be used both to justify and to invalidate diplomatic recognition of the Vatican.

- To examine the process of forming public opinion.

Materials needed:

Document 34
Written Document Analysis worksheet

20 Procedures:

1. Duplicate and distribute copies of document 34 and the Written Document Analysis worksheet to each student. Direct pupils to study the document and complete the worksheet. Discuss the worksheet questions and the reasons why document 34 might be of historical interest.

2. Ask students to refer to the Constitution and to list the formal qualifications of the office of President. Have students brainstorm the informal qualifications of the first 10 Presidents. Then take the first twenty and list the informal qualifications for them. Then take the first thirty and, finally, take all Presidents to the present and list informal qualifications. (The list should shrink over four examinations.) Ask students to hypothesize reasons for former attitudes that Catholics were not suited for civil office. Assign to a pair of students a project for researching the "Catholic issue" in the campaigns of Al Smith and John F. Kennedy. Ask students to account for differences and similarities between the two campaigns.

3. A study of American minorities and changing attitudes toward minorities might focus on the Catholics in American society. Exercises that might be used include the following:

   a. Show copies or transparencies of some Thomas Nast cartoons on the topic of the Catholic Church and public education. (Suitable collections for use in the classroom are found in *Thomas Nast: Cartoons and Illustrations* by Thomas Nast St. Hill, published by Dover Publications, Inc., in New York in 1974 or online at **www.harpweek.com**.) Analyze the symbols in the cartoons and ask students to explain Nast's position regarding the Catholic Church and public education.

   b. Ask students to research how Bible reading, reciting prayers, and religious observances in the early 1800s prompted the creation of a separate Catholic school system in the United States.

   c. Ask students to research anti-Catholicism in America. Anti-Catholic groups that have been particularly active include the Know-Nothing Party and the Ku Klux Klan. Legal measures ranging from court decisions involving Catholic school children to discriminatory immigration and naturalization laws may be cited. Discuss in class the larger issue of how individual freedom of conscience of minorities can be balanced against the majority's interpretation of the common good.

4. The issue of diplomatic relations with the Vatican has been debated since the government under the Constitution began. Before examining this issue, direct students to define and distinguish between Vatican City and the Holy See. Also ask students to distinguish the differences in the diplomatic roles of consul, personal representative of the President, and ambassador. Have students compare and contrast the means of appointment to the different positions. Direct two motivated students to locate the constitutional arguments for and against diplomatic recognition of the Vatican and present them to the class. Ask students to locate the reasons why President Reagan appointed, and Congress confirmed, an ambassador to the Vatican in 1984.

5. The Catholic Church is one of many churches that have lobbied for or against selected government policies. The teacher may wish to suggest to students that they investigate the stand of the Catholic Church and/or other churches on such historic or current issues as abortion, aid to the poverty-stricken, civil disobedience, prayer in school, slavery, temperance, tuition tax credits, U.S. military aid or intervention, and women's rights.

Transcription of Document 1

We, his majesty's most loyal subjects, the delegates of the several colonies of New-Hampshire, Massachusetts-Bay, Rhode-Island, Connecticut, New-York, New-Jersey, Pennsylvania, the three lower counties of Newcastle, Kent and Sussex on Delaware, Maryland, Virginia, North-Carolina, and South-Carolina, deputed to represent them in a continental Congress, held in the city of Philadelphia, on the 5th day of September, 1774, avowing our allegiance to his majesty, our affection and regard for our fellow-subjects in Great-Britain and elsewhere, affected with the deepest anxiety, and most alarming apprehensions, at those grievances and distresses, with which his Majesty's American subjects are oppressed; and having taken under our most serious deliberation, the state of the whole continent, find, that the present unhappy situation of our affairs is occasioned by a ruinous system of colony administration, adopted by the British ministry about the year 1763, evidently calculated for enslaving these colonies, and, with them, the British Empire. In prosecution of which system, various acts of parliament have been passed, for raising a revenue in America, for depriving the American subjects, in many instances, of the constitutional trial by jury, exposing their lives to danger, by direction a new and illegal trial beyond the seas, for crimes alleged to have been committed in America: And in prosecution of the same system, several late, cruel, and oppressive acts have been passed, respecting the town of Boston and the Massachusetts-Bay, and also an act for extending the province of Quebec, so as to border on the western frontiers of these colonies, establishing an arbitrary government therein, and discouraging the settlement of British subjects in that wide extended country; thus, by the influence of civil principles and ancient prejudices, to dispose the inhabitants to act with hostility against the free Protestant colonies, whenever a wicked ministry shall chose so to direct them.

To obtain redress of these grievances, which threaten destruction to the lives, liberty, and property of his majesty's subjects, in North-America, we are of opinion, that a non-importation, non-consumption, and non-exportation agreement, faithfully adhered to, will prove the most speedy, effectual, and peaceable measure: And, therefore, we do, for ourselves, and the inhabitants of the several colonies, whom we represent, firmly agree and associate, under the sacred ties of virtue, honour and love of our country, as follows:

1. That from and after the first day of December next, we will not import, into British America, from Great-Britain or Ireland, any goods, wares, or merchandize whatsoever, or from any other place, any such goods, wares, or merchandize, as shall have been exported from Great-Britain or Ireland; nor will we, after that day, import any East-India tea from any any part of the world; nor any molasses, syrups, paneles, coffee, or pimento, from the British plantations or from Dominica; nor wines from Madeira, or the Western Islands; nor foreign indigo.

2. We will neither import nor purchase, any slave imported after the first day of December next; after which time, we will wholly discontinue the slave trade, and will neither be concerned in it ourselves, nor will we hire our vessels, nor sell our commodities or manufactures to those who are concerned in it.

3. As a non-consumption agreement, strictly adhered to, will be an effectual security for the observation of the non-importation, we, as above, solemnly agree and associate, that from this day, we will not purchase or use any tea, imported on account of the East-India company, or any on which a duty hath been or shall be paid; and from and after the first day of March next, we will not purchase or use any East-India tea whatever; nor will we, nor shall any person for or under us, purchase or use any of those goods, wares, or merchandize, we have agreed not to import, which we shall know, or have cause to suspect, were imported

after the first day of December, except such as come under the rules and directions of the tenth article hereafter mentioned.

4. The earnest desire we have not to injure our fellow-subjects in Great-Britain, Ireland, or the West-Indies, induces us to suspend a nonexportation, until the tenth day of September, 1775; at which time, if the said acts and parts of acts of the British parliament herein after mentioned, are not repealed, we will not directly or indirectly, export any merchandize or commodity whatsoever to Great-Britain, Ireland, or the West-Indies, except rice to Europe.

5. Such as are merchants, and use the British and Irish trade, will give orders, as soon as possible, to their factors, agents and correspondents, in Great-Britain and Ireland, not to ship any goods to them, on any pretence whatsoever, as they cannot be received in America; and if any merchant, residing in Great-Britain or Ireland, shall directly or indirectly ship any goods, wares or merchandize, for America, in order to break the said non-importation agreement, or in any manner contravene the same, on such unworthy conduct being well attested, it ought to be made public; and, on the same being so done, we will not, from thenceforth, have any commercial connection with such merchant.

6. That such as are owners of vessels will give positive orders to their captains, or masters, not to receive on board their vessels any goods prohibited by the said non-importation agreement, on pain of immediate dismission from their service.

7. We will use our utmost endeavours to improve the breed of sheep, and increase their number to the greatest extent; and to that end, we will kill them as seldom as may be, especially those of the most profitable kind; nor will we export any to the West-Indies or elsewhere; and those of us, who are or may become overstocked with, or can conveniently spare any sheep, will dispose of them to our neighbours, especially to the poorer sort, on moderate terms.

8. We will, in our several stations, encourage frugality, economy, and industry, and promote agriculture, arts and the manufactures of this country, especially that of wool; and will discountenance and discourage every species of extravagance and dissipation, especially all horse-racing and all kinds of gaming, cock fighting, exhibitions of shews, plays, and other expensive diversions and entertainments; and on the death of any relation or friend, none of us, or any of our families will go into any further mourning-dress, than a black crape or ribbon on the arm or hat, for gentlemen, and a black ribbon and necklace for ladies, and we will discontinue the giving of gloves and scarves at funerals.

9. Such as are venders of goods or merchandize will not take advantage of the scarcity of goods, that may be occasioned by this association, but will sell the same at the rates we have been respectively accustomed to do, for twelve months last past,— And if any vender of goods or merchandize shall sell such goods on higher terms, or shall, in any manner, or by any device whatsoever, violate or depart from this agreement, no person ought, nor will any of us deal with any such person, or his or her factor or agent, at any time thereafter, for any commodity whatever.

10. In case any merchant, trader, or other person, shall import any goods or merchandize, after the first day of December, and before the first day of February next, the same ought forthwith, at the election of the owner, to be either re-shipped or delivered up to the committee of the country or town, wherein they shall be imported, to be stored at the risque of the importer, until the non-importation agreement shall cease, or be sold under the direction of the committee aforesaid; and in the last-mentioned case, the owner or owners of such goods shall be reimbursed out of the sales, the first cost and charges, the profit, if any, to be

applied towards relieving and employing such poor inhabitants of the town of Boston, as are immediate sufferers by the Boston port-bill; and a particular account of all goods so returned, stored, or sold, to be inserted in the public papers; and if any goods or merchandizes shall be imported after the said first day of February, the same ought forthwith to be sent back again, without breaking any of the packages thereof.

11. That a committee be chosen in every county, city, and town, by those who are qualified to vote for representatives in the legislature, whose business it shall be attentively to observe the conduct of all persons touching this association; and when it shall be made to appear, to the satisfaction of a majority of any such committee, that any person within the limits of their appointment has violated this association, that such majority do forthwith cause the truth of the case to be published in the gazette; to the end, that all such foes to the rights of British-America may be publicly known, and universally condemned as the enemies of American liberty; and thenceforth we respectively will break off all dealings with him or her.

12. That the committee of correspondence, in the respective colonies, do frequently inspect the entries of their customhouses, and inform each other, from time to time, of the true state thereof, and of every other material circumstance that may occur relative to this association.

13. That all manufactures of this country be sold at reasonable prices, so that no undue advantage be taken of a future scarcity of goods.

14. And we do further agree and resolve, that we will have no trade, commerce, dealings or intercourse whatsoever, with any colony or province, in North-America, which shall not accede to, or which shall hereafter violate this association, but will hold them as unworthy of the rights of freemen, and as inimical to the liberties of their country.

And we do solemnly bind ourselves and our constituents, under the ties aforesaid, to adhere to this association, until such parts of the several acts of parliament passed since the close of the last war, as impose or continue duties on tea, wine, molasses, syrups, paneles, coffee, sugar, pimento, indigo, foreign paper, glass, and painters' colours, imported into America, and extend the powers of the admiralty courts beyond their ancient limits, deprive the American subject of trial by jury, authorize the judge's certificate to indemnify the prosecutor from damages, that he might otherwise be liable to from a trial by his peers, require oppressive security from a claimant of ships or goods seized, before he shall be allowed to defend his property, are repealed. – And until that part of the act of the 12 G. 3. ch. 24, entitled "An act for the better securing his majesty's dock-yards, magazines, ships, ammunition, and stores," by which any persons charged with committing any of the offenses therein described, in America, may be tried in any shire or county within the realm, is repealed — and until the four acts, passed the last session of parliament, viz. that for stopping the port and blocking up the harbour of Boston – that for altering the charter and government of the Massachusetts-Bay – and that which is entitled "An act for the better administration of justice, &c." – and that "for extending the limits of Quebec, &c." are repealed. And we recommend it to the provincial conventions, and to the committees in the respective colonies, to establish such farther regulations as they may think proper, for carrying into execution this association.

The foregoing association being determined upon by the Congress, was ordered to be subscribed by the several members thereof; and thereupon, we have hereunto set our respective names accordingly.

In CONGRESS, PHILADELPHIA, October 20, 1774.
[Signed] PEYTON RANDOLPH, President

Transcription of Document 6

A motion was then made by the delegates for nays and ayes to postpone the further consideration of the report in order to take into consideration a motion which they read in their place, this being agreed to, the motion of the delegates for Massachusetts was taken up and being amended was agreed to as follows

Whereas there is provision in the Articles of Confederation of perpetual Union for making alterations therein by the assent of a Congress of the United States and of the legislatures of the several States; and whereas experience hath evinced that there are defects in the present Confederation, as a mean to remedy which several of the States and particularly the State of New York by express instructions to their delegates in Congress have suggested a convention for the purpose expressed in the following resolution and such Convention appearing to be the most probable mean of establishing in these states a firm national government.

Resolved that in the opinion of Congress it is expedient that on the second Monday in May next a Convention of delegates who shall have been appointed by the several states be held at Philadelphia for the sole and express purpose of revising the Articles of Confederation and reporting to Congress and the several legislatures such alterations and provisions therein as shall when agreed to in Congress and confirmed by the states render the federal constitution adequate to the exigencies of Government & the preservation of the Union.

Transcription of Document 7

Journal of the Federal Convention Monday, July 16, 1787

The question being taken on the whole of the report from the grand Committee as amended it passed in the affirmative and is as follows, namely,

Resolved – That in the original formation of the Legislature of the United States the first Branch hereof shall consist of sixty five members of which number

New Hampshire shall send	Three	Delaware	One
Massachusetts	Eight	Maryland	Six
Rhode Island	One	Virginia	Ten
Connecticut	Five	North Carolina	Five
New York	Six	South Carolina	Five
New Jersey	Four	Georgia	Three
Pennsylvania	Eight		

But as the present situation of the States may probably alter in the number of their inhabitants, the Legislature of the United States shall be authorized from time to time to apportion the number of representatives: and in case any of the States shall hereafter be divided, or enlarged by addition of territory, or any two or more States united, or any new States created within the limits of the United States the Legislature of the United States shall possess authority to regulate the number of representatives: in any of the foregoing cases upon the principle of their number of inhabitants, according

Journal of the Federal Convention Monday July 16, 1787 to the provisions hereafter mentioned, namely,

Provided always that representation ought to be proportioned according to the direct Taxation, and in order to ascertain the alteration in the direct Taxation, which may be required from time to time by the changes in the relative circumstances of the States. Resolved that a Census be taken within six years from the first meeting of the Legislature of the United States, and once within the term of every ten years afterwards of all the inhabitants of the United States in the manner and according to the ratio recommended by Congress in their resolution of April 18, 1783 – and that the Legislature of the United States shall proportion the direct Taxation accordingly. Resolved That all Bills for raising or appropriating money, and for fixing the salaries of the Officers of the Government of the United States Shall originate in the First Branch of the Legislature of the United States, and shall not be altered or amended by the Second Branch – and that no money shall be drawn from the Public Treasury but in pursuance of appropriations to be originated by the First Branch.

Resolved That in the Second Branch of the Legislature of the United States each State shall have an equal vote.

It was moved and seconded to agree to the first clause of the sixth resolution reported from the Committee of the whole House, namely,

That the national Legislature ought to possess the legislative rights vested in Congress by the confederation which passed unanimously in the affirmative,

It was moved and seconded to commit the second clause of the sixth resolution reported from the Committee of the whole House which passed in the negative and then the House adjourned till tomorrow at 11 o'clock A.M.

Transcription of Document 12

Philadelphia, April 4th, 1789

Dear General,

I most sincerely congratulate you upon your election to the most dignified station in the Nation and I pray God to continue your services to your Country for many years.

As you will soon be involved in a multiplicity of Business, I take the liberty to beg this favor of such testimonial of my services in the late army as you may think me entitled to. I have with reluctance made this application, but as circumstances may render it necessary, trust I shall be excused.

With most respectful compliments to your lady I have the honor to be with this most perfect attachment & respect.

Dear General your most
Obedient Servant
David Bradhead

Transcription of Document 14

To Senr Don Francisco Chiappe, Agent of the
United States at Morocco

New York 1st Decr 1789

Sir,

Both before and since the arrival of your letter of 20th August 1789 to the President of the late Congress, the Government of the United States has been in a state so deranged by the Measures preparatory to the Change which has lately taken place, that proper attention could not be paid to our foreign, and indeed to many other important affairs.

It gives me Pleasure to inform you that these Embarrassments diminish daily. The new Government has been organized and peaceably established, agreeably to the Constitution of which for your Information, I herewith enclose a copy.

General Washington, who so gloriously and successfully commanded our military operations during the late war, has, by the unanimous Votes of the States been appointed to the supreme executive authority by the Title of President of the United States. The two Houses of the national legislature have been elected, and have been assembled, but their first Session was wholly employed in passing such Laws and domestic Regulations as the State of the Nation rendered indispensable, and would not admit of any Delay. They are soon to assemble again, and then their attention will be extended to such objects as the Situation of our foreign affairs may point out, for without their Consent no Monies can be raised or appropriated.

The President has appointed Mr. Jefferson to the office of Secretary of State, which now includes the Department of foreign affairs, but he being still absent, though daily expected, the President has been pleased to direct me to write to you on these Subjects, and to explain to you the Reasons why you have not received more frequent and regular advices from this Country.

The President has been informed how well you and your Brothers deserve of the United States, and I am persuaded that due Attention will be paid to your and their Services.

I have now the Honor of transmitting to you a Letter from the President to his Imperial Majesty, with a Copy of it for your Information. I also enclose a Letter for your Brother Giuseppe, which I request the Favor of you to forward to him.

I have the Honor to be, sc
[signed]
John Jay

Transcription of Document 15

Copy No. 2
District of Kentucky (to wit)

In Convention July 28th 1790

Resolved, That it is expedient for, and the will of, the good people of the District of Kentucky that the same be erected into an Independent State on the terms and conditions specified in an Act of the Virginia assembly passed the 18th day of December 1789 entitled an Act concerning the erection of the District of Kentucky into an Independent State.

Resolved, That We the Representatives of the people of Kentucky duly elected in pursuance of an Act of the Legislature of Virginia passed the 18th day of December 1789 entitled an Act concerning the erection of the District of Kentucky into an Independent State, and now met in Convention having with full powers maturely investigated the expediency of the proposed seperation on the terms and conditions, specified in the above recited Act; do by these presents and in behalf of the people of Kentucky accept the terms and conditions, and do declare that on the first day of June 1792 the said District of Kentucky shall become a State separate from and independent of the Government of Virginia, and that the said Articles become a solemn compact binding on the said People.

To the President and the Honble the
Congress of the United States of America

The Memorial of the Representatives of the people of Kentucky in Convention assembled pursuant to an Act of the Legislature of Virginia passed the 18th day of December 1789, entitled an Act concerning the erection of the District of Kentucky into an Independent State.

Humbly Sheweth, That the Inhabitants of this Country are as warmly devoted to the American Union and as firmly attached to the present happy establishment of the Federal Government as any of the Citizens of the United States.

That migrating from thence, they have with great hazard and difficulty effected their present settlements. The hope of increasing numbers could alone have supported the early adventurers under those arduous exertions; they have the satisfaction to find that hope verified. At this day, the population, and strength of this Country, render it fully able, in the opinion of your Memorialists, to form and support an efficient Domestic Government.

The inconveniences resulting from its local situation as a part of Virginia at first but little felt, have for some time been objects of their most serious attention; which occasioned application to the Legislature of Virginia for redress.

Here your Memorialists would acknowledge with peculiar pleasure the benevolence of Virginia in permitting them to remove the evils arising from that source by assuming upon themselves a State of Independence.

This they have thought expedient to do on the terms and conditions stipulated in the above recited

Act; and have fixed on the first day of June 1792 as the period when the said Independence shall commence.

It now remains with the President and the Congress of the United States to sanction these proceedings, by an Act of their Honble Legislature prior to the first day of November 1791 for the purpose of receiving in the federal Union the people of Kentucky by the name of, The State of Kentucky.

Should this determination of your Memorialists meet the approbation of the General Government, they have to call a Convention to form a Constitution, subsequent to the Act of Congress and prior to the day fixed for the Independence of this Country.

When your Memorialists reflect on the present comprehensive system of Federal Government, and when they also recollect the determination of a former Congress on this subject, they are left without a doubt that the object of their wishes will be accomplished.

And your Memorialists as in duty
bound shall forever pray

attest
Thomas Todd Clk. C.

(Signed) George Muter Pr.

Transcription of Document 19

Honorable Sirs,

From the manner in which I was called before this House yesterday, I have reason to suspect an unfavorable disposition in them towards some parts in my late publications. What the parts are against which they object or what these objections are are wholly unknown to me. If any Gentleman has presented any Memorial to this House, which contains any charge against me, or any ways allude in a censurable manner to my character or interest, so as to become the ground of any such charge, I request, as a Servant under your authority, an attested copy of that charge, and in my personal character as a freeman of this country, I demand it. I attended the bar of this House yesterday as their Servant, tho' the warrant did not express my official station which I conceive it ought to have done otherwise it could not be compulsive unless backed by a Magistrate. My hopes were that I should be made acquainted with the charges and admitted to my defence which I am all times ready to make either in writing or personally.

I cannot in duty to my character as a human, submit to be censured unheard. I have evidence which I presume will justify me. And I entreat this House to consider how great their reproach will be should it be told, that they passed a sentence upon me without hearing me and that a copy of the charge against me was refused to me; and likewise, how much that reproach will be aggravated should I afterwards prove the censure of this House to be a Libel found upon a mistake which they refused to enquire fully into.

I make my application to the heart of every Gentleman in this House, that he, before he decides in a point that may affect my reputation, will duly consider his own. Did I covet popular praise I should not send this letter. My wish is, that by thus Stating my Situation to the House, that they may not commit an Act they cannot Justify.

I have obtained Fame Honor and Credit in this Country. I am Proud of those honors and as they can be taken from me by any unjust Censure, grounded in a concealed charge, therefore it will become my duty afterwards to do justice to myself. I have no favor to ask more than to be candidly and honorably dealt by, and such being my right, I ought to have no doubt but this House will proceed accordingly. Should Congress be disposed to hear me, I have to request that they will give me sufficient time to prepare.

Philadelphia
Janry 7th 1779

I am Honorable Sirs
Your honors most obt
and dutiful Humble Servant

Thos. Paine

Transcription of Document 26

Richmond, Supervisors Office, Aug. 13th 1794

Sir,

Having necessarily been absent from Town for two mails past yours of the 2d inst. did not fall into my hands until this morning on my return.

The Copy of your letter to the Commissioner of the Revenue as founded upon the intelligence of Mr. Wells and which you enclosed in the above, communicates your intended conduct when you arrive at Morgan Town on your journey towards Ohio. I feel it my duty to relieve you from the necessity of resting upon a future approbation in a case whose personal danger stands in competition with a duty of Office, and have therefore determined to send this immediately by Express to Morgan Town, where I expect you will be found.

The late acts of the people of the Country which you must pass to get to Ohio rendered it certain that you could not pass in safety, even had you no public money with you, but as you are charged with a considerable Sum, that circumstance adds to the necessity for caution. It is also certain that while so extensive an insurrection continues unsuppressed in the powerful Counties of Pensylvania which, in a manner, envelope Ohio, it would be folly to attempt measures for executing the laws in the latter, where, even should the people be disposed to comply, their more numerous neighbours would awe them into disobedience, this appearing to be the Spirit which actuates this Lawless people with regards to the well disposed, who live amongst, or near them. an attempt to enforce the laws in Ohio, while the influence of the insurgents is preponderant over that of the Government, could have no probable tendency but to infest the people of that County, in the cause of foment, and must render the evil greater than it now is.

This Rebellion against Government has now arrived at that degree of atrocity that admits of no longer continuance of that forbearance on the part of Government, which has been practiced. decisive measures must, and certainly will, be taken, for apprehending & bringing to condign punishment, the persons who can be ascertained as actors in the late high Treasons which have been committed, and for Securing to the Offices of Revenue, the necessary protection in their future operations.

Pending this insurgency in Pensylvania, it behoves the officers employed in Virginia, to be vigilant, and as active as possible, to prevent its introduction there. it is not impossible that emissaries will be sent into our Counties of Monogalia, Harrison & Randolph for this purpose, with a view to this circumstance, your remaining at Morgan Town will be extremely proper, and of great public utility. in that situation you will, from time to time, discover whether from any source mischief is to be apprehended and can take the necessary Steps for suppressing the evil. It is unnecessary to mention to you that according to the degree of support which upon any occasion is required in our business, we are to call in the magistrates and Militia Officers.

How long you shall remain at Morgan Town with a view to the subjects which I have presented, will depend on your own judgement, & your proceeding or not proceeding to Ohio, must also depend on your intelligence, as to the reestablishment of Government in the Counties of Pensylvania which join it. in the meantime you will hold such communications with Mr. Riggs as you shall judge discreet & proper. write us fully by return of the Express as to such matters as may be passing, and particularly as to the temper of the People in that part of Virginia.

The People of the Monongalia District, even in Ohio, have never shown any great fondness for joining in the licentious spirit of their Neighbours in Pensylvania, and I trust, indeed doubt not, that the very unprincipled & base rebellion now raging there, will meet with their decided censure & counteraction.

P.S. Herewith you will receive a letter of advice from
Mr. Campbell the attorney for the District how you
are to act in case of discovery of any emissary from
the Insurgents.

> I am very respectfully
> Sir
> Your Most Obt.
> E. Carrington
> Supt. O. T.

David Smith Esq.
Inspector of Revenue
now on his way to Morgan Town

a copy
E. Carrington

Time Line

1774	**September 5–October 26**	The first Continental Congress meets in Philadelphia. Each of the 13 colonies except Georgia sends delegates.
	October 18	The Continental Association resolves to end all trade with England by September 9, 1775, if the Intolerable Acts are not repealed by the Crown. The resolution provides that the colonies unite and act against all violators.
1775	**February 9**	Act of Parliament declares that a state of rebellion exists in Massachusetts and that additional troops should be sent to Boston.
	April 19	Paul Revere's midnight ride alerts Minutemen of British troops advancing on colonists' stores of weapons at Lexington and Concord. Later that day "the shot heard 'round the world" is fired, signaling the beginning of armed conflict between the colonies and the Crown.
	May 10	The Second Continental Congress convenes in Philadelphia.
	June 15	George Washington of Virginia becomes Commander in Chief of the Continental Army.
1776	**January 9**	Thomas Paine's pro-independence pamphlet, *Common Sense*, is published in Philadelphia.
	June 7	Delegate Richard Henry Lee of Virginia introduces a resolution calling for independence, the formation of foreign alliances, and the creation of a plan of confederation after independence is achieved.
	July 2	Congress adopts the Lee Resolution for independence.
	July 4	Thomas Jefferson's Declaration of Independence as amended by Congress is approved and signed by John Hancock.
	July 12	A draft of the Articles of Confederation is submitted to the Congress and after much debate is adopted on November 15, 1777.
	December 12	As British successes in the New Jersey campaign threaten Philadelphia, Congress flees to the safety of Baltimore where they meet in a private home until March 4, 1777.
	December 25–26	General Washington crosses the Delaware River from Pennsylvania to Trenton, NJ, and defeats the Hessians in a surprise attack.
1777	**October 17**	British Major General John Burgoyne surrenders 5,700 troops at Saratoga, NY. The British defeat prompts France to recognize American independence and render the new nation valuable aid.
1781	**March 2**	The Continental Congress is succeeded by "The United States Congress Assembled" as empowered by the ratified Articles of Confederation.
	October 19	British General Cornwallis surrenders to General George Washington and the French Commander Comte de Rochambeau at Yorktown, VA.
1783	**September 3**	The Treaty of Paris, formally ending the Revolutionary War, is signed by John Adams, Benjamin Franklin, and John Jay. It is ratified by Congress on January 14, 1784.
1784	**April 23**	Congress establishes a system to divide western lands and admit them as states on equal footing with the original 13 states. This plan will serve as the basis for the Northwest Ordinance of 1787.

	December 23	Congress designates New York City the temporary national capital.
1785	July-November	Foreign ministers encounter difficulty negotiating with Spain and Great Britain. Difficulties with Spain concern the boundary of Florida and the right to passage on the Mississippi River. Great Britain continues to occupy western forts in violation of the Treaty of Paris.
1786	January 16	The Virginia legislature adopts Thomas Jefferson's Statute for Religious Freedom. It will serve as a model for the First Amendment to the Constitution.
	August 7	In Congress, Charles Pinckey of South Carolina moves for a revision of the Articles of Confederation, but the motions that are suggested are never submitted to the states.
	September 11-14	Members of five states meeting in Annapolis, MD, call a convention to meet in Philadelphia in May of 1787 for the purpose of revising the Articles of Confederation.
	August 1786-February 1787	Massachusetts farmer Daniel Shays leads a mob action, which becomes known as Shays' Rebellion. Shays and his followers demand more paper money, tax relief, relief for debtors, and an end to imprisonment for debt.
1787	May 25	The Constitutional Convention opens in Philadelphia. Eventually all states but Rhode Island attend. George Washington is elected President of the Convention.
	May 29	The Virginia Plan, proposed by Edmund Randolph, goes beyond revising the Articles and calls for a new national government.
	June 15	William Paterson's New Jersey Plan revises the Articles of Confederation and maintains state supremacy. The plan is turned down by the convention, which votes to work toward a national government based on the Virginia Plan.
	July 13	Congress passes the Northwest Ordinance providing for the admission of new states on an equal footing with the original 13 colonies.
	July 16	The Connecticut or Great Compromise resolves the convention's deadlock over representation in the new Congress. With the removal of this obstacle, the convention writes a rough draft of a constitution.
	September 17	Debate in the Constitutional Convention ends. The Constitution is adopted by that body and is submitted to Congress.
	October 27	Seeking to persuade New Yorkers to ratify the Constitution, Alexander Hamilton, James Madison, and John Jay begin to publish their 85 carefully crafted essays, which will later be published as *The Federalist Papers*.
1788	June 21	With ratification by New Hampshire, the ninth state, the Constitution becomes effective and thereby replaces the Articles of Confederation.
	September 13	Congress sets dates for the election of the President and Vice President and for the convening of the first Congress in New York City.
	December 23	Maryland offers Congress 100 square miles of land along the Potomac River for the site of the future capital city.
1789	March 4	Under the authority of the Constitution, the first session of the first Congress gathers.
	April 6	George Washington is elected President by a unanimous vote of the electors.
	April 30	George Washington and John Adams are inaugurated in New York City as the first President and Vice President of the United States.

	August 7	The War Department is established. Henry Knox is the first secretary.
	September 2	Department of the Treasury, with Alexander Hamilton as the first secretary, is established.
	September 9	The House of Representatives recommends 12 amendments to the Constitution. The 10 that are ratified in 1791 will become the Bill of Rights.
	September 24	Congress passes the Federal Judiciary Act organizing the Supreme Court and the federal judiciary system.
	September 26	George Washington appoints John Jay the first Chief Justice of the Supreme Court.
1790	**March 22**	Thomas Jefferson is sworn in as the first Secretary of State.

Sir   Monticello Feb. 14. 1790   136

I have duly received the letter of the 21st of January
with which you have honored me, and no longer hesitate to
undertake the office to which you are pleased to call me. your
desire that I should come on as quickly as possible is a sufficient reason for me to postpone every matter of business, however
pressing, which admits postponement. still it will be the close
of the ensuing week before I can get away, & then I shall have
to go by the way of Richmond, which will lengthen my road.
I shall not fail however to go on with all the dispatch possible
nor to satisfy you, I hope, when I shall have the honor of seeing
you at New York, that the circumstances which prevent my
immediate departure, are not under my controul. I have
now that of being with sentiments of the most perfect res—
pect & attachment, Sir
           Your most obedient & most humble servant

                              Th Jefferson

The President of the U.S.

Annotated Bibliography

This select bibliography includes books readily available in basic library collections. For more extensive references, see Stephen Millet's *A Selected Bibliography of American Constitutional History*, Paul Leicester Ford's classic *Bibliography and Reference List of the History and Literature relating to the Adoption of the Constitution of the United States*, and the indispensable *Harvard Guide to American History*, edited by Frank Freidel.

I. Convention and Ratification

Bowen, Catherine D. *Miracle at Philadelphia: The Story of the Constitutional Convention, May to September 1787*. Boston: Little, Brown & Co., 1986.

> This narrative-style history, based on extensive original sources, traces the convention delegates' evolution from conflict to consensus. While Bowen's work is especially useful for raising interest, the frankly admiring tone of her work also makes it a good tool for introducing questions of historical objectivity and critical use of sources. For students.

Burns, James MacGregor. *The Vineyard of Liberty*. New York: Vintage Books, 1983.

> Burns provides a traditional narrative but emphasizes what he describes as a "think cadre" of those persons who failed to make major biographical dictionaries, especially women. Useful for a wide audience, particularly to capture interest.

Chidsey, Donald Barr. *The Birth of the Constitution: An Informal History*. New York: Crown Publishers, 1964.

> The clear, direct language of this history from Shays' Rebellion through ratification makes the brief popular account useful for junior and senior high school students with average reading skills.

Elliot, Jonathan, ed. *The Debates in the Several State Conventions on the Adoption of the Federal Constitution, as Recommended by the General Convention at Philadelphia in 1787*. 2d ed. Buffalo, NY: William S. Hein, 1996.

> This is the indispensable source on the ratification struggles within the states. Since the 1950s, increasing attention has been given to the states' arguments. For advanced students and teachers.

Farrand, Max, ed. *The Records of the Federal Convention of 1787*. 4 vols. New Haven: Yale University Press, 1986.

> This comprehensive work is an essential source, probably the best available source for the Constitution itself. It categorizes all available materials, for example, proceedings of convention and committees and plans considered. Useful for students beginning to deal with original sources in the study of the Constitution; essential for more advanced pupils.

Findley, Bruce Allyn, and Esther Blair Findley. *Your Rugged Constitution: How America's House of Freedom is Planned and Built*. 2d rev. ed. Palo Alto, CA: Stanford University Press, Books on Demand, 1969.

> This basic introduction for the uninitiated features left-hand pages citing constitutional clauses or sections that authors explain on right-hand and subsequent pages. They fill pages with illustrations and notes of powers we give, get, and deny. Note: Unabashedly patriotic. For average or below-average students.

Hamilton, Alexander; Madison, James; and Jay, John. *The Federalist Papers*. (Various editions.)

> Hamilton, Jay, and Madison collaborated on these 85 essays written to urge the Constitution's ratification. Since then, courts have cited their explanations as authoritative comments. For high school students and teachers.

Jensen, Merrill. *The New Nation: A History of the United States during the Confederation, 1781-1789.* Boston: Northeastern University Press, 1981.

> Jensen's book provides a classic treatment of the 1780s. See also The Documentary History of the Ratification of the Constitution, 2 vols, State Historical Society of Wisconsin, 1976. For advanced students and teachers.

Madison, James. *Notes of Debates in the Federal Convention of 1787.* New York: Norton, 1987.

> These records, kept by one of the founding fathers, provide the daily debates of the delegates at Philadelphia in 1787. For advanced students and teachers.

Middlekauff, Robert. *The Glorious Cause: The American Revolution 1763-1789.* Oxford History of the United States, edited by C. Vann Woodward. New York: Oxford University Press, 1982.

> Middlekauff concludes his volume with four chapters on the move to ratify and ratification of the Constitution. This is a well-written, narrative approach that serves as a fine introduction to a study of the Constitution. Other series volumes touch on later constitutional developments. For teachers and students.

Rossiter, Clinton. *1787: The Grand Convention.* New York: W.W. Norton, 1987.

> While Rossiter emphasizes the convention as a case study in the political process of constitutional democracy, his anecdotes and personality sketches enliven the book for student use.

Van Doren, Carl. *The Great Rehearsal: The Story of the Making and Ratifying of the Constitution of the United States.* New York: Penguin Books, 1986.

> Using federal and state convention records as well as press and diary accounts, Van Doren traces step by step the conflicts of personalities and ideas that were reconciled by 1789. Details of personal eccentricities will intrigue students.

II. Growth and Development

Beth, Loren P. *The Development of the American Constitution 1877-1917. The New American Nation,* edited by Henry Steele Commager and Richard B. Morris. New York: Harper and Row, 1971.

> Beth's volume traces the Constitution's adaptation to late 19th-century changes: industrialization, immigration, labor unions, trusts, imperialism, expanding federal responsibilities. For average readers.

Boorstin, Daniel J., ed. *An American Primer.* Chicago: The University of Chicago Press, 1966.

> Boorstin devotes a section to the Constitution, its preamble, each article, the Bill of Rights, and the Civil War amendments. Each author's work is edited to a minimal length; the collection provides a handy treatment of these parts of the Constitution. For average students.

Corwin, Edward S. *The Constitution and What It Means Today.* Princeton: Princeton University Press, 1979.

> Corwin's work provides a clause-by-clause contrast between what the Constitution meant in 1787 and what it meant as of 1979. The book provides a general evolutionary pattern and includes margin labels for easy use as well as tables of cases. For teachers and high school students.

Cushman, Robert F., ed. *Leading Constitutional Decisions.* Englewood Cliffs, NJ: Prentice Hall, 1992.

> In this edition, Cushman provides a useful, extensive introduction for Supreme Court cases representing the evolution of ideas pertaining to the three federal branches, nationalization of the Bill of Rights, First Amendment rights, rights of the accused, and equal protection of rights. The editor's aim, to give "ammunition with which to do intellectual battle," meets high school or college needs in U.S. government and history classes.

Garraty, John A., ed. *Quarrels That Have Shaped the Constitution*. Rev. ed. New York: Perennial Library, 1987.

> This Harper Torchbook contains 16 historians' essays on Supreme Court decisions from the Marshall to Warren benches. The style and scope recommend it for all students above junior high.

Kelly, Alfred H.; Harbison, Winfred A.; and Belz, Herman. *The American Constitution: Its Origins and Development*. 7th ed. New York: Norton, 1991.

> This book provides an introductory text on American constitutionalism from 17th-century English colonial origins through Richard Nixon's impeachment crisis. Its glossary of legal terms makes it useful for advanced secondary or college students.

Mitchell, Broadus, and Mitchell, Louise P. *A Biography of the Constitution of the United States; Its Origin, Formation, Adoption and Interpretation*. 2d ed. New York: Oxford University Press, 1975.

> This text, in a popular style, traces the Constitution from its inception through 1970. Rather than following a general chronology, the Mitchells cite representative votes on ratification and cases, especially in Massachusetts, Virginia, New York, and provide thumbnail sketches of participants. This book is suitable for use by high school students.

National Archives Trust Fund Board. *A More Perfect Union: The Creation of the United States Constitution*. Washington, DC: General Services Administration, 1978.

> This brief, heavily illustrated story of the Constitution as a document traces it from origin to enshrinement at the Archives. A longer version based upon an exhibit, with photographic reproductions of many handwritten documents, appeared in *The Formation of the Union* (1970). For all students.

Seckler-Hudson, Catheryn. *Federal Textbook on Citizenship: Our Constitution and* Government. Lessons on the Constitution and Government of the United States for Use in Public Schools by Candidates for Citizenship. Washington, DC: U.S. Government Printing Office, 1971.

> This official Immigration and Naturalization Service handbook, complete with sample test booklet, is designed for the use of foreign-born persons preparing to become U.S. citizens. Since each chapter has questions and vocabulary, it's especially useful for students who need those aids.

III. Legal and Historiographic Interpretations

Aptheker, Herbert. *Early Years of the Republic: From the End of the Revolution to the First Administration of Washington, 1783-1793. A History of the American People*. New York: International Publishers, 1976.

> Aptheker's Marxist interpretation includes a "Basic Facts" useful for introducing historiography to the college bound class. He defends the Constitution as originally intended to be a "bourgeois democratic document for the governing of a slaveholding-capitalist republic" that was "essentially progressive in its time." It is useful for discussing the ideas and values of the founding fathers and of historians. For advanced students and teachers.

Beard, Charles A. *An Economic Interpretation of the Constitution*. Union, NJ: Lawbook Exchange, 2000.

> Beard's study produced critical rethinking about the founders' motivations in rejecting the Articles of Confederation. His economic interpretation of the background and motives of Constitutional Convention participants, largely rejected today, remains valuable for its impact on historical processes and thought. For advanced students and teachers.

Brown, Robert. *Charles Beard and the Constitution: A Critical Analysis of "An Economic Interpretation of the Constitution."* Westport, CT: Greenwood Press, 1979.

> Published a half-century after Beard, Brown's 14 summary points demolish Beard's economic interpretation. Instead, Brown finds the Constitution a document adopted by an essentially democratic society and by a basically middle class and propertied population. Brown also contributes a *Reinterpretation of the Formation of the American Constitution* (Boston University Press, 1936), a compilation of his Gaspar G. Bacon lectures on the Constitution. For advanced students.

Elkins, Stanley, and McKitrick, Eric. *The Founding Fathers: Young Men of the Revolution.* Washington, DC: American Historical Association, 1963.

> Teachers or secondary students beginning historiographical studies should welcome this AHS bibliographical essay covering interpretations from Beard through Merrill Jensen.

Friendly, Fred W., and Elliott, Martha J. H. *The Constitution: That Delicate Balance.* New York: Random House, 1984.

> This book focuses on landmark cases that have shaped the Constitution. Chapter 7, "God and the Classroom – Free Exercise of Religion v. Establishment of Religion," is a valuable aid to study of the First Amendment. Good for secondary students.

Jones, Robert F., ed. *The Formation of the Constitution.* Huntington, NY: R. E. Krieger Pub. Co., 1978.

> In his volume of this series, Jones introduces students to historical interpretation by abstracting representative economic, political, social, and consensus views. His preface defends the notion of interpretation, arguing that students should learn that "disagreement is the normal condition for historians." For high school or college students.

Koch, Adrienne. *Power, Morals and the Founding Fathers: Essays in the Interpretation of the American Enlightenment.* Ithaca, NY: Cornell University Press, 1961.

> Koch's sketches depict Franklin, Jefferson, Hamilton, Adams, and Madison as creatures of the Enlightenment who borrowed its ideals and combined them with pragmatism to mold 18th-century political thought. Good for the college-bound student.

Latham, Earl. *The Declaration of Independence and the Constitution. Problems of American Civilization.* 3d ed. Lexington, MA: Heath, 1976.

> In his volume, Latham employs excerpts from major interpretations. This approach serves high school or college students well in their initial attempts to deal with historiography. To update, pair with Aptheker or Jones.

U.S. Library of Congress Legislative Reference Service. *The Constitution of the United States of America; Analysis and Interpretation, Annotations of cases decided by the Supreme Court of the United States.* Washington, DC: U.S. Government Printing Office, 1996.

> This decennial publication with biennial supplements presents the Constitution with citations to cases and includes a section on laws declared unconstitutional. Often cited as *Annotated Constitution*. Useful to teachers of government.

Wills, Garry. *Explaining America: The Federalist.* Garden City: Doubleday, 1981.

> Wills contends that both Madison and Hamilton's political thought owed a great debt to 18th century Scottish thought, especially Hume's political essays. For Wills, Madison "explains America," for he represents Enlightenment values and the concept of public duty that produced the republic. For teachers.

IV. Church and State

Brant, Irving. *The Bill of Rights: Its Origin and Meaning.* Indianapolis: The Bobbs-Merrill Co., 1965.

> Particularly helpful for research into the passage and meaning of the Bill of Rights and the Fourteenth Amendment (includes discussion of *Barron v. Baltimore.*) For students.

Buckley, Thomas E., S.J. *Church and State in Revolutionary Virginia, 1776-1787.* Charlottesville: University Press of Virginia, 1977.

> This is a comprehensive study of the evolution of the concept of religious freedom in Virginia, encompassing the views of George Mason, Patrick Henry, Thomas Jefferson, and James Madison. For teachers and advanced students.

McCarthy, Martha M. *A Delicate Balance: Church, State, and the Schools.* Bloomington, IN: Phi Delta Kappan Educational Foundation, 1983.

> Examines closely the role of schools in the church-state controversy. Particularly interesting to teachers of advanced students.

Miller, Robert T., and Flowers, Ronald B. *Toward Benevolent Neutrality: Church, State, and the Supreme Court.* 5th ed. Waco, TX: Markham Press Fund of Baylor University Press, 1996.

> A chronological account that examines the major issues emerging from the First Amendment and the Supreme Court cases pertaining to those issues. A handy reference for both teachers and advanced pupils.

Pfeffer, Leo. *Church, State, and Freedom.* Rev. ed. Boston: Beacon Press, 1967.

> This single volume provides a comprehensive study of the origins and history of church-state relations in the United States with references to state and federal cases. A superb reference and text for both teachers and advanced students.

Pfeffer, Leo. *Religion, State, and the Burger Court.* Buffalo: Prometheus Books, 1985.

> An excellent book that covers every possible issue. For all students.

V. Biographies

Brant, Irving. *The Fourth President: A Life of James Madison.* Indianapolis and New York: The Bobbs-Merrill Company, 1970.

> This is Brant's conversion of his earlier six-volume life of Madison to a more accessible one volume work. The period up to and including the writing of the Constitution accounts for one-third of the 681-page volume. For all students.

Burns, Edward McNall. *James Madison: Philosopher of the Constitution.* New York: Octagon Books, 1973.

> This edition of Burns' work, originally published in 1938, has a new chapter on republicanism, written to emphasize the mixture of conservatism and liberalism in the philosophy of the founding fathers. As the title suggests, this is an examination of Madison's ideas and theories of government. Burns shows the concern of the times for establishing a correct balance between the executive and legislative branches, and the impact of the ideas of others, such as Montesquieu, Locke, and Jefferson, on Madison's thinking. Primarily for reference.

Flexner, James Thomas. *Washington: The Indispensable Man.* Plume ed. New York: New American Library, 1984.

> Between 1965 and 1972, Flexner wrote a four-volume life of Washington, and he subsequently prepared this one-volume biography for a wider public. The book is also available in paperback editions. For all students.

McGee, Dorothy Horton. *Framers of the Constitution*. New York: Dodd, Mead, 1987.

> This work covers the major figures of the Constitutional Convention in short biographies arranged by state. Within this format is also a good presentation of the process by which the Constitution was framed. For all students.

Miller, Helen Hill. *George Mason, Gentleman Revolutionary*. Chapel Hill: The University of North Carolina Press, 1975.

> This readable text includes good background on the Mason family, the history of Virginia, and the architecture and customs of the period, all woven into an account of Mason's life and his contributions to Virginia and the nation. Appendixes include the text of the first draft of the Virginia Declaration of Rights, the printed "Committee Draft of the Virginia Declaration," and the final version. Mason refused to sign the Constitution; this book helps to show why. For all students.

Mintz, Max M. *Gouverneur Morris and the American Revolution*. Norman: The University of Oklahoma Press, 1970.

> Good biography of this important figure, who wrote the final draft of the Constitution. It emphasizes the Continental Congress, the writing of the Constitution, and Morris' later career in Europe. Well-written and lively. For all students.

Rutland, Robert A. *James Madison and the Search for Nationhood*. Washington, DC: Library of Congress, 1981.

> Heavily illustrated, attractive account, with reproductions of many portraits, documents, and maps of the period. For all students.

From the *Founding Fathers* Series, published by Newsweek, Inc., and distributed by Harper & Row Publishers.

> For all students.

Mary Jo Kline, ed. *Alexander Hamilton: A Biography in His Own Words*. New York, 1973.

Editors unlisted. *Thomas Jefferson: A Biography in His Own Words*. New York, 1974.

Merrill D. Peterson, ed. *James Madison: A Biography in His Own Words*. New York, 1974.

Ralph K. Andrist, ed. *George Washington: A Biography in His Own Words*. New York, 1972.

The Constitution: Evolution of a Government
Archival Citations of Documents

1. Articles of Association, October 20, 1774; (National Archives Microfilm Publication M332, roll 10); Miscellaneous Papers of the Continental Congress, 1774-1789; Records of the Continental and Confederation Congresses and the Constitutional Convention, 1774-1789, Record Group 360; National Archives Building, Washington, DC.

2. Lee Resolution showing congressional vote, July 2, 1776; Volume 1, p. 17 of item 23 (National Archives Microfilm Publication M247, roll 31); Papers of the Continental Congress, 1774-1783; Records of the Continental and Confederation Congresses and the Constitutional Convention, 1774-1789, Record Group 360; National Archives Building, Washington, DC.

3. Engrossed copy of the Declaration of Independence, August 2, 1776; (National Archives Microfilm Publication M332, roll 10); Miscellaneous Papers of the Continental Congress, 1774-1789; Records of the Continental and Confederation Congresses and the Constitutional Convention, 1774-1789, Record Group 360; National Archives Building, Washington, DC.

4. Printed and corrected copy of the Articles of Confederation, showing amendments adopted, November 15, 1777; pp. 69-76 of item 47; (National Archives Microfilm Publication M247, roll 61); Papers of the Continental Congress, 1774-1789; Records of the Continental and Confederation Congresses and the Constitutional Convention, 1774-1789, Record Group 360; National Archives Building, Washington, DC.

5. Northwest Ordinance, July 13, 1787; (National Archives Microfilm Publication M332, roll 9); Miscellaneous Papers of the Continental Congress, 1774-1789; Records of the Continental and Confederation Congresses and the Constitutional Convention, 1774-1789, Record Group 360; National Archives Building, Washington, DC.

6. Resolution to convene the Philadelphia Convention, February 21, 1787; Volume 38; (National Archives Microfilm Publication M247, roll 14); Journal of the Constitutional Congress, 1786-1788; Papers of the Continental Congress, 1774-1789; Records of the Continental and Confederation Congresses and the Constitutional Convention, 1774-1789, Record Group 360; National Archives Building, Washington, DC.

7. Minutes of the Congress showing vote on the Great Compromise, July 16, 1787; (National Archives Microfilm Publication M866, roll 1); Formal Journal of the Proceedings of the Convention; Official Records of the Constitutional Convention; Records of the Continental and Confederation Congresses and the Constitutional Convention, 1774-1789, Record Group 360; National Archives Building, Washington, DC.

8. George Washington's copy of the Constitution, August 6, 1787; (National Archives Microfilm Publication M866, roll 1); Formal Journal of the Proceedings of the Convention; Official Records of the Constitutional Convention; Records of the Continental and Confederation Congresses and the Constitutional Convention, 1774-1789, Record Group 360; National Archives Building, Washington, DC.

9. Senate's draft of 17 amendments for a bill of rights, August 24, 1789; (SEN1A-G3); 1st Congress; Records of the U.S. Senate, Record Group 46; National Archives Building, Washington, DC.

10. 26th Amendment to the Constitution, March 23, 1971; (National Archives Microfilm Publication M1518, roll 15); Ratified Amendments XI-XXVI to the United States Constitution; General Records of the U.S. Government, Record Group 11; National Archives Building, Washington, DC.

11. Minutes of the Senate describing George Washington's oath of office ceremony, April 30, 1789; (National Archives Microfilm Publication M1251, roll 1), Journal of Legislative Proceedings of the U. S. Senate, 1789-1817; Records of the U.S. Senate, Record Group 46; National Archives Building, Washington, DC.

12. Bradhead's letter to George Washington congratulating him and asking for a job, April 4, 1789; Volume IV, Item 78, p. 577; (National Archives Microfilm Publication M247, roll 92); Papers of the Continental Congress, 1774-1789; Records of the Continental and Confederation Congresses and the Constitutional Convention, 1774-1789, Record Group 360; National Archives Building, Washington, DC.

13. Jefferson's letter to President Washington accepting nomination, February 1, 1790; (National Archives Microfilm Publication M179, roll 3); Letters Received, Miscellaneous Letters of the Department of State, 1789-1906; General Records of the Department of State, Record Group 59; National Archives at College Park, College Park, MD.

14. John Jay's letter to the U.S. agent in Morocco, December 1, 1789; (National Archives Microfilm Publication M61, roll 1); Foreign Letters of the Continental Congress and the Department of State, 1785-1790; General Records of the Department of State, Record Group 59; National Archives Building, Washington, DC.

15. Petition to make the Kentucky District a state, July 28, 1790; (SEN1A-G3); 1st Congress; Records of the U.S. Senate, Record Group 46; National Archives Building, Washington, DC.

16. Plea to the Court of Impeachment in defense of William Blount, December 24, 1798; (SEN5C-A3); 5th Congress; Records of the U.S. Senate, Record Group 46; National Archives Building, Washington, DC.

17. Petition by Edward Hand for Lancaster, Pennsylvania to be the nation's capital, March 17, 1789; (SEN1A-G3); 1st Congress; Records of the U.S. Senate, Record Group 46; National Archives Building, Washington, DC.

18. Benjamin Franklin's petition to abolish slavery, February 3, 1790; (SEN1A-G3); 1st Congress; Records of the U.S. Senate, Record Group 46; National Archives Building, Washington, DC.

19. Thomas Paine's petition to be informed of charges, January 7, 1779; (National Archives Microfilm Publication M247, roll 68); Letters and Papers of Thomas Paine, 1779-1785; Papers of the Continental Congress, 1774-1789; Records of the Continental and Confederation Congresses and the Constitutional Convention, 1774-1789, Record Group 360; National Archives Building, Washington, DC.

20. Broadside asking for money, October 12, 1785; (National Archives Microfilm Publication M332, roll 9); Miscellaneous Papers of the Continental Congress; Records of the Continental and Confederation Congresses and the Constitutional Convention, 1774-1789, Record Group 360; National Archives Building, Washington, DC.

21. John Jay's letter to John Adams about Shays' Rebellion, February 21, 1787; (National Archives Microfilm Publication M61, roll 1); Foreign Letters of the Continental Congress and Department of State, 1785-1790; Records of the Continental and Confederation Congresses and the Constitutional Convention, 1774-1789, Record Group 360; National Archives Building, Washington, DC.

22. Map made in accordance with the 1785 Land Ordinance; Plat of Township No. II in the Third Range, Old Seven Ranges, Ohio, surveyed by Isaac Sherman, 1786; Miscellaneous Headquarters Plats with Field Notes; Records of the Bureau of Land Management, Record Group 49; National Archives at College Park, College Park, MD.

23. U.S. loan certificate, December 16, 1790; Samples of Redeemed Securities, 1790-1833; Division of Management Analysis; Records of the Office of Administration; Records of the Bureau of Public Debt, Record Group 53; National Archives at College Park, College Park, MD.

24. Pages from the government Loan Office ledger, January 1, 1788; Volume 266, p. 46; (National Archives Microfilm Publication M925, roll 1); Records of the Massachusetts Continental Loan Office, 1777-1791; Records of the Bureau of Public Debt, Record Group 53; National Archives at College Park, College Park, MD.

25. Annals of Congress entry containing House debate on Alexander Hamilton's financial plan, February 19, 1790; Annals of Congress, Volume 2, pp. 1295-1296, 1st Congress; Records of the U. S. House of Representatives, Record Group 233; National Archives Building, Washington, DC.

26. Supervisor Carrington's letter to U. S. Revenue Inspector Smith about the Whiskey Rebellion, August 14, 1794; Correspondence Concerning the Whiskey Rebellion; Records for the Period 1790-1803; Records of the Internal Revenue Service, Record Group 58; National Archives at College Park, College Park, MD.

27. Senate debate on the wording of the first amendment, September 3, 1789; Senate Journal, p. 69, 1st Session, 1st Congress; Records of the U.S. Senate, Record Group 46; National Archives Building, Washington, DC.

28. Bill amending the Pledge of Allegiance, June 14, 1954; Public Law 396, 83rd Congress, 2nd Session, Part 2; General Records of the U.S. Government, Record Group 11; National Archives Building, Washington, DC.

29. *Minersville* v. *Gobitis* letter, March 7, 1940; Case File 690, *Minersville* v. *Gobitis*; Appellate Jurisdiction Case Files, 1792-; O. T. 1939; Records of the Supreme Court of the United States, Record Group 267; National Archives Building, Washington, DC.

30. *Engel* v. *Vitale* opinion, June 25, 1962; Case File 468, *Engel* v. *Vitale*; Appellate Jurisdiction Case Files, 1792- ; O. T. 1961; Records of the Supreme Court of the United States, Record Group 267; National Archives Building, Washington, DC.

31. Women of Utah petition, December 17, 1875; Interior and Insular Affairs Committee (HR45A-H23.3); 45th Congress; Records of the U. S. House of Representatives, Record Group 233; National Archives Building, Washington, DC.

32. *Reynolds* v. *United States* decision, May 5, 1879; Case File 7811, Appellate Jurisdiction Case Files, 1792-1984; Records of the Supreme Court of the United States, Record Group 267; National Archives Building, Washington, DC.

33. Campbell's letter to a Salt Lake City newspaper about B. H. Roberts' expulsion from the House, October 7, 1899; Committee on Elections; (HR55A-H31.1); 55th Congress; Records of the U. S. House of Representatives, Record Group 233; National Archives Building, Washington, DC.

34. Pope John XXIII's Christmas greetings to President Kennedy, December 31, 1961; File PP 2-3/CO thru (Executive), White House Central Subject File; White House Central Files; John F. Kennedy Presidential Library, Boston, MA.

His Excellency
John Fitzgerald Kennedy
President of the United States of America

On the occasion of the Feast of Christmas, Your Excellency and your gracious wife have thoughtfully sent Us greetings and good wishes, and We acknowledge this kind gesture with warm appreciation and gratitude.

We invoke the choicest blessings of the Infant Saviour upon Your Excellency, upon Mrs Kennedy, your children and family, and upon the people of the United States of America, praying that the New Year may bring true peace and lasting joy to your noble nation and to the world.

From the Vatican, December 31, 1961

Joannes XXIII

About the National Archives:
A Word to Educators

The National Archives and Records Administration (NARA) is responsible for the preservation and use of the permanently valuable records of the federal government. These materials provide evidence of the activities of the government from 1774 to the present in the form of written and printed documents, maps and posters, sound recordings, photographs, films, computer tapes, and other media. These rich archival sources are useful to everyone: federal officials seeking information on past government activities, citizens needing data for use in legal matters, historians, social scientists and public policy planners, environmentalists, historic preservationists, medical researchers, architects and engineers, novelists and playwrights, journalists researching stories, students preparing papers, and persons tracing their ancestry or satisfying their curiosity about particular historical events. These records are useful to you as educators either in preparing your own instructional materials or pursuing your own research.

The National Archives records are organized by the governmental body that created them rather than under a library's subject/author/title categories. There is no Dewey decimal or Library of Congress designation; each departmental bureau or collection of agency's records is assigned a record group number. In lieu of a card catalog, inventories and other finding aids assist the researcher in locating material in records not originally created for research purposes, often consisting of thousands of cubic feet of documentation.

The National Archives is a public institution whose records and research facilities nationwide are open to anyone 14 years of age and over. These facilities are found in the Washington, DC, metropolitan area, in the 11 Presidential libraries, the Nixon Presidential Materials Project, and in 16 regional archives across the nation. Whether you are pursuing broad historical questions or are interested in the history of your family, admittance to the research room at each location requires only that you fill out a simple form stating your name, address, and research interest. A staff member then issues an identification card, which is good for two years.

If you come to do research, you will be offered an initial interview with a reference archivist. You will also be able to talk with archivists who have custody of the records. If you have a clear definition of your questions and have prepared in advance by reading as many of the secondary sources as possible, you will find that these interviews can be very helpful in guiding you to the research material you need.

The best printed source of information about the overall holdings of the National Archives is the *Guide to the National Archives of the United States* (issued in 1974, reprinted in 1988), which is available in university libraries and many public libraries and online at **www.nara.gov**. The *Guide* describes in very general terms the records in the National Archives, gives the background and history of each agency represented by those records, and provides useful information about access to the records. To accommodate users outside of Washington, DC, the regional archives hold microfilm copies of much that is found in Washington. In addition, the regional archives contain records created by field offices of the federal government, including district and federal appellate court records, records of the Bureau of Indian Affairs, National Park Service, Bureau of Land Management, Forest Service, Bureau of the Census, and others. These records are particularly useful for local and regional history studies and in linking local with national historical events.

For more information about the National Archives and its educational and cultural programs, visit NARA's Web site at **www.nara.gov**.

Presidential Libraries

Herbert Hoover Library
210 Parkside Drive
West Branch, IA 52358-0488
319-643-5301

Franklin D. Roosevelt Library
511 Albany Post Road
Hyde Park, NY 12538-1999
914-229-8114

Harry S. Truman Library
500 West U.S. Highway 24
Independence, MO 64050-1798
816-833-1400

Dwight D. Eisenhower Library
200 Southeast Fourth Street
Abilene, KS 67410-2900
785-263-4751

John Fitzgerald Kennedy Library
Columbia Point
Boston, MA 02125-3398
617-929-4500

Lyndon Baines Johnson Library
2313 Red River Street
Austin, TX 78705-5702
512-916-5137

Gerald R. Ford Library
1000 Beal Avenue
Ann Arbor, MI 48109-2114
734-741-2218

Jimmy Carter Library
441 Freedom Parkway
Atlanta, GA 30307-1498
404-331-3942

Ronald Reagan Library
40 Presidential Drive
Simi Valley, CA 93065-0600
805-522-8444/800-410-8354

George Bush Library
1000 George Bush Drive
P.O. Box 10410
College Station, TX 77842-0410
409-260-9552

Clinton Presidential Materials Project
1000 LaHarpe Boulevard
Little Rock, AR 72201
501-254-6866

National Archives Regional Archives

NARA-Northeast Region
380 Trapelo Road
Waltham, MA 02452-6399
781-647-8104

NARA-Northeast Region
10 Conte Drive
Pittsfield, MA 01201-8230
413-445-6885

NARA-Northeast Region
201 Varick Street, 12th Floor
New York, NY 10014-4811
212-337-1300

NARA-Mid Atlantic Region
900 Market Street
Philadelphia, PA 19107-4292
215-597-3000

NARA-Mid Atlantic Region
14700 Townsend Road
Philadelphia, PA 19154-1096
215-671-9027

NARA-Southeast Region
1557 St. Joseph Avenue
East Point, GA 30344-2593
404-763-7474

NARA-Great Lakes Region
7358 South Pulaski Road
Chicago, IL 60629-5898
773-581-7816

NARA-Great Lakes Region
3150 Springboro Road
Dayton, OH 45439-1883
937-225-2852

NARA-Central Plains Region
2312 East Bannister Road
Kansas City, MO 64131-3011
816-926-6272

NARA-Central Plains Region
200 Space Center Drive
Lee's Summit, MO 64064-1182
816-478-7079

NARA-Southwest Region
501 West Felix Street
P.O. Box 6216
Fort Worth, TX 76115-0216
817-334-5525

NARA-Rocky Mountain Region
Denver Federal Center, Building 48
P.O. Box 25307
Denver, CO 80225-0307
303-236-0804

NARA-Pacific Region
24000 Avila Road
P.O. Box 6719
Laguna Niguel, CA 92607-6719
949-360-2641

NARA-Pacific Region
1000 Commodore Drive
San Bruno, CA 94066-2350
650-876-9009

NARA-Pacific Alaska Region
6125 Sand Point Way, NE
Seattle, WA 98115-7999
206-526-6507

NARA-Pacific Alaska Region
654 West Third Avenue
Anchorage, AK 99501-2145
907-271-2443

Reproductions of Documents

Reproductions of the oversized print documents included in these units are available in their original size by special order from Graphic Visions.

We, his Majesty's most loyal subjects the Delegates of the several Colonies of New Hampshire, Massachusetts-Bay, Rhode Island, Connecticut, New York, New Jersey, Pennsylvania, The three lower counties of Newcastle, Kent and Sussex on Delaware, Maryland, Virginia, North-Carolina and South-Carolina deputed to represent them in a continental Congress held in the city of Philadelphia on the fifth day of September 1774, avowing our allegiance to his Majesty, our affection and regard for our fellow subjects in Great-Britain and elsewhere, affected with the deepest anxiety and most alarming apprehensions at those grievances and distresses, with which his Majesty's American subjects are oppressed, and having taken under our most serious deliberation the state of the whole continent find, that the present unhappy situation of our affairs is occasioned by a ruinous system of colony administration adopted by the British Ministry about the year 1763 evidently calculated for enslaving these colonies and with them the British Empire. In prosecution of which system, various acts of parliament have been passed, for raising a revenue in America, for depriving the American subjects in many instances of the constitutional trial by jury, imposing ... by directing a new and illegal trial beyond the seas, for crimes alleged to have been committed in America: And in prosecution of the same system, several late cruel and oppressive acts have been passed respecting the town of Boston and the Massachusetts-Bay, and also an act for extending the province of Quebec so as to border on the western frontiers of these colonies, establishing an arbitrary government therein and discouraging the settlement of British subjects in that wide extended country; thus by the influence of civil principles and ancient prejudices to dispose the inhabitants to act with hostility against the free protestant colonies, whenever a wicked Ministry shall choose so to direct them. —

To obtain redress of these grievances, which threaten destruction to the lives, liberty and property of his Majesty's subjects in North-America we are of opinion, that a non-importation, non-consumption and non-exportation agreement faithfully adhered to will prove the most speedy, effectual and peaceable measure: And therefore we do for ourselves and the inhabitants of the several colonies whom we represent firmly agree and associate under the sacred ties of virtue, honour and love of our country as follows.

1. That from and after the first day of December next we will not import into British America from Great-Britain or Ireland, any goods, wares or merchandize whatsoever or from any other place any such goods, wares or merchandize as shall have been exported from Great-Britain or Ireland; nor will we after that day import any East-India Tea from any part of the World, nor any Molasses, Syrups, paneles, coffee or pimento from the British Plantations or from Dominica, nor Wines from Madeira or the Western Islands nor foreign Indigo. —

2. That we will neither import nor purchase any Slave imported after the first day of December next, and after which time we will wholly discontinue the slave trade, and will neither be concerned in it ourselves, nor will we hire our vessels nor sell our commodities or manufactures to those who are concerned in it. —

3. As a non-consumption agreement strictly adhered to will be an effectual security for the observation of the non-importation we as above solemnly agree and associate, that from this day we will not purchase or use any Tea imported on account of the East-India Company, or any on which a duty hath or shall be paid; and from and after the first day of March next we will not purchase or use any East-India tea whatever, nor will we nor any person for or under us purchase or use any of those goods, wares or merchandize we have agreed not to import, which we shall know or have cause to suspect were imported after the first day of December except such as come under the rules and directions of the tenth article hereafter mentioned.

4. The earnest desire we have not to injure our fellow subjects in Great-Britain, Ireland or the West-Indies induces us to suspend a non-exportation until the tenth day of September 1775, at which time if the said acts and parts of acts of the British Parliament are not repealed we will not directly or indirectly export any merchandize or commodity whatsoever to Great-Britain, Ireland or the West-Indies, except Rice to Europe.

5. Such as are merchants and use the British and Irish trade will give orders as soon as possible to their factors, agents and correspondents in Great-Britain and Ireland not to ship any goods to them on any pretence whatsoever as they cannot be received in America; And if any merchant residing in Great-Britain or Ireland shall directly or indirectly ship any goods, wares or merchandize for America in order to break the said non-importation agreement or in any manner ... the

---

Document 1a. Articles of Association, October 20, 1774. [National Archives]

same, on such unworthy conduct being well attested it ought to be made public, and on the same being so done, we will not from thence forth have any commercial connexion with such merchant.

6. That such as are owners of vessels will give positive orders to their captains or masters not to receive on board their vessels any goods prohibited by the said non-importation agreement on pain of immediate dismission from their service.

7. We will use our utmost endeavours to improve the breed of sheep and increase their number to the greatest extent, and to that end we will kill them as seldom as may be especially those of the most profitable kind nor will we export any to the West Indies or elsewhere and those of us who are or may become overstocked with or can conveniently spare any sheep will dispose of them to our neighbours especially to the poorer sort upon moderate terms.

8. That we will in our several stations encourage frugality, œconomy and industry and promote agriculture, arts and the manufactures of this country, especially that of wool, and will discountenance and discourage every species of extravagance and dissipation especially all horse racing and all kinds of gaming, cock fighting, exhibitions of plays, shows and other expensive diversions and entertainments — And on the death of any relation or friend none of us or any of our families will go into any further mourning dress than a black crape or ribbon on the arm or hat for Gentlemen, and a black ribbon & necklace for Ladies, and we will discontinue the giving of gloves and scarfs at funerals.

9. That such as are venders of goods or merchandize will not take advantage of the scarcity of goods that may be occasioned by this association but will sell the same at the rates we have been respectively accustomed to do for twelve months last past — And if any vender of goods or merchandize shall sell any such goods higher terms or shall in any manner or by any device whatsoever violate or depart from this agreement no person ought nor will any of us deal with any such person or his or her factor or agent at any time thereafter for any commodity whatever.

10. In case any merchant, trader or other person shall import any goods or merchandize after the first day of December and before the first day of February next the same ought forthwith at the election of the owner to be either reshipped or delivered up to the committee of the county, or town wherein they shall be imported, to be stored at the risque of the ~~importer~~ until the non-importation agreement shall cease, or be sold under the direction of the committee aforesaid and in the last mentioned case the owner or owners of such goods shall be reimbursed out of the sales the first cost and charges, the profit if any to be applied towards relieving and employing such poor inhabitants of the town of Boston as are immediate sufferers by the Boston port Bill, and a particular account of all goods so returned, stored, or sold to be inserted in the public papers; And if any goods or merchandize shall be imported after the said first day of February the same ought forthwith to be sent back again without breaking any of the packages thereof.

11. That a committee be chosen in every county, city and town by those who are qualified to vote for representatives in the legislature, whose business it shall be attentively to observe the conduct of all persons touching this association and when it shall be made to appear to the satisfaction of a majority of any such committee that any person within the limits of their appointment has violated this association that such majority do forthwith cause the truth of the case to be published in the Gazette to the end that all such foes to the rights of British America may be publickly known and universally contemned as the enemies of American liberty and thenceforth we respectively will break off all dealings with him or her.

12. That the committees of correspondence in the respective colonies do frequently inspect the entries of their Custom House and inform each other from time to time of the true state thereof and of every other material circumstance that may occur relative to this association.

13. That all manufactures of this country be sold at reasonable prices so that no undue advantage be taken of a future scarcity of goods.

14. And we do further agree and resolve, that we will have no trade, commerce, dealings or intercourse whatsoever, with any colony or province in North America which shall not accede to, or which shall thereafter violate this association, but will hold them as unworthy of the rights of freemen, and as inimical to the liberties of their country.

And we do solemnly bind ourselves and ~~those~~ under the ties aforesaid to adhere to this association until such parts of the several acts of parliament passed since the ~~year~~ as impose or continue duties on tea, wine, molasses, syrups, paneles, coffee, sugar, pimento, Indigo, foreign

foreign paper, glass and painters colours imported into America; and extend the powers of the admiralty courts beyond their ancient limits, deprive the American subject of trial by jury, authorize the judges certificate to indemnify the prosecutor from damages, that he might otherwise be liable to from a trial by his peers, require oppressive security from a claimant of ships or goods seized, before he shall be allowed to defend his property, are repealed — And until that part of the Act of the 12 G. 3. ch. 24 entitled "an Act for the better securing his Majesty's dock yards, magazines, ships, ammunition and stores" by which any person charged with committing any of the offences therein described, in America, may be tried in any shire or county within the realm, is repealed. And until the several acts passed in the last session of Parliament, viz.: that for stopping the port and blocking up the harbour of Boston — that for altering the charter and government of the Massachusetts Bay — and that which is entitled "an act for the better administration of justice &c, and that for extending the limits of Quebec &c are repealed. And we recommend it to the provincial conventions, and to the committees in the respective colonies to establish such farther regulations as they may think proper for carrying into execution this association. ————

The foregoing association being determined upon by the Congress, was ordered to be subscribed by the several members thereof and thereupon we have hereunto set our respective names accordingly.

In Congress, Philadelphia October 20th 1774. —

Peyton Randolph President

Jno Sullivan
Natht Folsom
Thomas Cushing
Saml Adams
John Adams
Robt Treat Paine
Stephen Hopkins
Sam: Ward

Elipht Dyer
Roger Sherman
Silas Deane

Isaac Low
John Alsop
John Jay
Jas Duane
Phil. Livingston
Wm Floyd
Henry Wisner
S Boerum

J. Kinsey
Wil: Livingston
Stepn Crane
Richd Smith
John DeHart

Jos. Galloway
John Dickinson
Cha Humphreys
Thomas Mifflin
E Biddle
John Morton
Geo: Ross

Caesar Rodney
Tho M'Kean
Geo Read

Mat Tilghman
Ths Johnson Junr
Wm Paca
Samuel Chase
Richard Henry Lee
G Washington
P. Henry Junr
Richard Bland
Benj Harrison
Edmd Pendleton

Will Hooper
Joseph Hewes
R Caswell

Henry Middleton
Thos Lynch
Christ Gadsden
J Rutledge
Edward Rutledge

New Hamp.
Massachusetts
Connecticut
New York
New Jersey
Pennsylvania
The Lower Counties New Castle &c
Maryland
Virginia
North Carolina
South Carolina

The Com.ee of the whole Congress to whom was referred the resolution and also the *Declaration* respecting independence. —— 17

Resolved   That these united colonies are and of right

ought to be free and independant states;

that they are absolved from all allegiance

to the british crown and that all political

connection between them and the state of

great Britain is and ought to be totally

dissolved

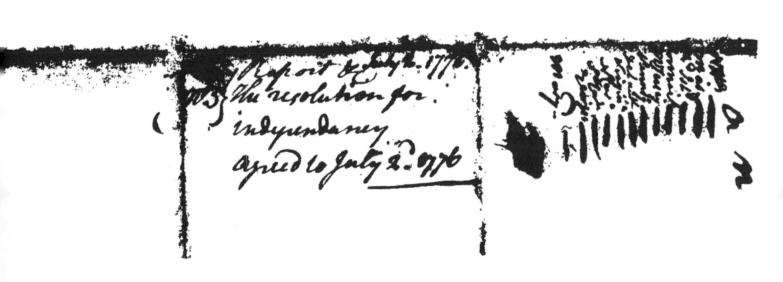

Report of July 2. 1776.
on the resolution for
independency
agreed to July 2. 1776

Document 2. Lee Resolution showing congressional vote, July 2, 1776. [National Archives]

IN CONGRESS, JULY 4, 1776.

The unanimous Declaration of the thirteen united States of America,

When in the Course of human events, it becomes necessary for one people to dissolve the political bands which have connected them with another, and to assume among the powers of the earth, the separate and equal station to which the Laws of Nature and of Nature's God entitle them, a decent respect to the opinions of mankind requires that they should declare the causes which impel them to the separation. — We hold these truths to be self-evident, that all men are created equal, that they are endowed by their Creator with certain unalienable Rights, that among these are Life, Liberty and the pursuit of Happiness. — That to secure these rights, Governments are instituted among Men, deriving their just powers from the consent of the governed, — That whenever any Form of Government becomes destructive of these ends, it is the Right of the People to alter or to abolish it, and to institute new Government, laying its foundation on such principles and organizing its powers in such form, as to them shall seem most likely to effect their Safety and Happiness. Prudence, indeed, will dictate that Governments long established should not be changed for light and transient causes; and accordingly all experience hath shewn, that mankind are more disposed to suffer, while evils are sufferable, than to right themselves by abolishing the forms to which they are accustomed. But when a long train of abuses and usurpations, pursuing invariably the same Object evinces a design to reduce them under absolute Despotism, it is their right, it is their duty, to throw off such Government, and to provide new Guards for their future security. — Such has been the patient sufferance of these Colonies; and such is now the necessity which constrains them to alter their former Systems of Government. The history of the present King of Great Britain is a history of repeated injuries and usurpations, all having in direct object the establishment of an absolute Tyranny over these States. To prove this, let Facts be submitted to a candid world.

He has refused his Assent to Laws, the most wholesome and necessary for the public good.
He has forbidden his Governors to pass Laws of immediate and pressing importance, unless suspended in their operation till his Assent should be obtained; and when so suspended, he has utterly neglected to attend to them.
He has refused to pass other Laws for the accommodation of large districts of people, unless those people would relinquish the right of Representation in the Legislature, a right inestimable to them and formidable to tyrants only.
He has called together legislative bodies at places unusual, uncomfortable, and distant from the depository of their public Records, for the sole purpose of fatiguing them into compliance with his measures.
He has dissolved Representative Houses repeatedly, for opposing with manly firmness his invasions on the rights of the people.
He has refused for a long time, after such dissolutions, to cause others to be elected; whereby the Legislative powers, incapable of Annihilation, have returned to the People at large for their exercise; the State remaining in the mean time exposed to all the dangers of invasion from without, and convulsions within.
He has endeavoured to prevent the population of these States; for that purpose obstructing the Laws for Naturalization of Foreigners; refusing to pass others to encourage their migrations hither, and raising the conditions of new Appropriations of Lands.
He has obstructed the Administration of Justice, by refusing his Assent to Laws for establishing Judiciary powers.
He has made Judges dependent on his Will alone, for the tenure of their offices, and the amount and payment of their salaries.
He has erected a multitude of New Offices, and sent hither swarms of Officers to harrass our people, and eat out their substance.
He has kept among us, in times of peace, Standing Armies without the Consent of our legislatures.
He has affected to render the Military independent of and superior to the Civil power.
He has combined with others to subject us to a jurisdiction foreign to our constitution, and unacknowledged by our laws; giving his Assent to their Acts of pretended Legislation:
For Quartering large bodies of armed troops among us: — For protecting them, by a mock Trial, from punishment for any Murders which they should commit on the Inhabitants of these States: — For cutting off our Trade with all parts of the world: — For imposing Taxes on us without our Consent: — For depriving us in many cases, of the benefits of Trial by Jury: — For transporting us beyond Seas to be tried for pretended offences — For abolishing the free System of English Laws in a neighbouring Province, establishing therein an Arbitrary government, and enlarging its Boundaries so as to render it at once an example and fit instrument for introducing the same absolute rule into these Colonies: — For taking away our Charters, abolishing our most valuable Laws, and altering fundamentally the Forms of our Governments: — For suspending our own Legislatures, and declaring themselves invested with power to legislate for us in all cases whatsoever.
He has abdicated Government here, by declaring us out of his Protection and waging War against us.
He has plundered our seas, ravaged our Coasts, burnt our towns, and destroyed the lives of our people.
He is at this time transporting large Armies of foreign Mercenaries to compleat the works of death, desolation and tyranny, already begun with circumstances of Cruelty & perfidy scarcely paralleled in the most barbarous ages, and totally unworthy the Head of a civilized nation.
He has constrained our fellow Citizens taken Captive on the high Seas to bear Arms against their Country, to become the executioners of their friends and Brethren, or to fall themselves by their Hands.
He has excited domestic insurrections amongst us, and has endeavoured to bring on the inhabitants of our frontiers, the merciless Indian Savages, whose known rule of warfare, is an undistinguished destruction of all ages, sexes and conditions. In every stage of these Oppressions We have Petitioned for Redress in the most humble terms: Our repeated Petitions have been answered only by repeated injury. A Prince, whose character is thus marked by every act which may define a Tyrant, is unfit to be the ruler of a free people. Nor have We been wanting in attentions to our British brethren. We have warned them from time to time of attempts by their legislature to extend an unwarrantable jurisdiction over us. We have reminded them of the circumstances of our emigration and settlement here. We have appealed to their native justice and magnanimity, and we have conjured them by the ties of our common kindred to disavow these usurpations, which, would inevitably interrupt our connections and correspondence. They too have been deaf to the voice of justice and of consanguinity. We must, therefore, acquiesce in the necessity, which denounces our Separation, and hold them, as we hold the rest of mankind, Enemies in War, in Peace Friends.

We, therefore, the Representatives of the united States of America, in General Congress, Assembled, appealing to the Supreme Judge of the world for the rectitude of our intentions, do, in the Name, and by Authority of the good People of these Colonies, solemnly publish and declare, That these United Colonies are, and of Right ought to be Free and Independent States; that they are Absolved from all Allegiance to the British Crown, and that all political connection between them and the State of Great Britain, is and ought to be totally dissolved; and that as Free and Independent States, they have full Power to levy War, conclude Peace, contract Alliances, establish Commerce, and to do all other Acts and Things which Independent States may of right do. — And for the support of this Declaration, with a firm reliance on the protection of divine Providence, we mutually pledge to each other our Lives, our Fortunes and our sacred Honor.

John Hancock

Button Gwinnett
Lyman Hall
Geo Walton.

Wm Hooper
Joseph Hewes,
John Penn

Edward Rutledge.
Thos Heyward Junr.
Thomas Lynch Junr.
Arthur Middleton

Samuel Chase
Wm Paca
Thos Stone
Charles Carroll of Carrollton
George Wythe
Richard Henry Lee
Th Jefferson
Benja Harrison
Thos Nelson jr.
Francis Lightfoot Lee
Carter Braxton

Robt Morris
Benjamin Rush
Benja Franklin
John Morton
Geo Clymer
Jas Smith
Geo Taylor
James Wilson
Geo Ross
Caesar Rodney
Geo Read
Tho M:Kean

Roger Sherman
Samel Huntington
Wm Williams
Oliver Wolcott
Matthew Thornton

Fras Lewis
Lewis Morris
Richd Stockton
Jno Witherspoon
Fras Hopkinson
John Hart
Abra Clark

Josiah Bartlett
Wm Whipple
Saml Adams
John Adams
Robt Treat Paine
Elbridge Gerry
Step Hopkins
William Ellery
Roger Sherman
Saml Huntington
Wm Williams
Oliver Wolcott

Floyd
Phil Livingston

ARTICLES

OF

CONFEDERATION AND PERPETUAL UNION,

BETWEEN THE STATES OF

1777
Monday April 21

NEW-HAMPSHIRE,   ~~The Counties of NEW-CASTLE~~
MASSACHUSETTS-BAY,   ~~KENT AND SUSSEX of~~ DELAWARE,
RHODE-ISLAND,   MARYLAND,
CONNECTICUT,   VIRGINIA,
NEW-YORK,   NORTH-CAROLINA,
NEW-JERSEY,   SOUTH-CAROLINA, AND
PENNSYLVANIA,   GEORGIA.

april 25

Art. 2 Each state retains its so-
vereignty, freedom & independance *agreed —*
and every power, jurisdiction and
right, which is not by this Confederation
expressly delegated to the united states
in Congress assembled.
Art 3. agreed to. — —

ART. I. THE name of this Confederacy shall be "THE UNITED STATES OF AMERICA."

ART. II. *3* The said States hereby severally enter into a firm league of friendship with each other, for their common defence, the security of their liberties, and their mutual and general welfare, binding themselves to assist each other against all force offered to or attacks made upon them or any of them, on account of religion, sovereignty, trade, or any other pretence whatever.

ART. III. Each State reserves to itself the sole and exclusive regulation and government of its internal police in all matters that shall not interfere with the articles of this Confederation.

Agreed
"21" Octo 1777

ART. IV. No State, without the consent of the United States in Congress Assembled, shall send any Embassy to or receive any embassy from, or enter into any conference, agreement, alliance or treaty with any King, Prince or State; nor shall any person holding any office of profit or trust under the United States or any of them, accept of any present, emolument, office or title of any kind whatever from any King, Prince or foreign State; nor shall the United States Assembled, or any of them, grant any title of nobility.

agreed
21 Octob. 1777.

ART. V. No two or more States shall enter into any treaty, confederation or alliance whatever between them, without the consent of the United States in Congress Assembled, specifying accurately the purposes for which the same is to be entered into, and how long it shall continue.

agreed
Sept 23 1777

ART. VI. No State shall lay any imposts or duties which may interfere with any stipulations in treaties ~~hereafter entered into by~~ the United States Assembled with any King, Prince or State. *in pursuance of any treaties already proposed by Congress to the courts of France and Spain*

agreed
Octr ~~Sept. 2 3. 177~~

ART. VII. No veffels of war fhall be kept up in time of peace by any State, except fuch number only as fhall be deemed neceffary by the United States Affembled for the defence of fuch ftate or its trade, nor fhall any body of forces be kept up by any State in time of peace, except fuch number only as in the judgment of the United States in Congrefs Affembled fhall be deemed requifite to garrifon the forts neceffary for the defence of fuch State, but every State fhall always keep up a well regulated and difciplined Militia, fufficiently armed and accoutred, and fhall provide and conftantly have ready for ufe in public ftores a due number of field pieces and tents and a proper quantity of *arm* ammunition and camp equipage.

agreed
Octr ~~Sept~~. 23 1777

ART. VIII. When land forces are raifed by any State for the common defence, all officers of or under the rank of Colonel fhall be appointed by the legiflatures of each State refpectively by whom fuch forces fhall be raifed, or in fuch manner as fuch State fhall direct, and all vacancies fhall be filled up by the State which firft made the appointment.

amended Octr 14. 1777

ART. IX. All charges of war and all other expences that fhall be incurred for the common defence or general welfare, and allowed by the United States Affembled, fhall be defrayed out of a common treafury, which fhall be fupplied by the feveral States in proportion to the number of inhabitants of every age, fex and quality, except Indians not paying taxes in each State; a true account of which, diftinguifhing the white inhabitants, fhall be triennially taken and tranfmitted to the Affembly of the United States. The taxes for paying that proportion fhall be laid and levied by the authority and direction of the legiflatures of the feveral States within the time agreed upon by the United States Affembled.

agreed
Octr ~~Sept~~. 2 3 1777

agreed ~~Sept~~. *Octr* 23 1777

ART. X. Every State fhall abide by the determinations of the United States in Congrefs Affembled, on all queftions which by this Confederation are fubmitted to them.

Amended & agreed
to ~~Sept~~. *Octr* 23 1777

ART. XI. No State fhall engage in any war without the confent of the United States in Congrefs Affembled, unlefs fuch State be actually invaded by enemies or fhall have received certain advice of a refolution being formed by fome nation of Indians to invade fuch State, and the danger is fo imminent as not to admit of a delay till the other States can be confulted; nor fhall any State grant commiffions to any fhips or veffels of war, nor letters of marque or reprifal, except it be after a declaration of war by the United States Affembled, and then only againft the Kingdom or State and the subjects thereof against which war has been so declared, and under such regulations as shall be established by the United States Assembled.

ART. ~~XII.~~ For the more convenient management of the general interests of the United States, Delegates shall be annually appointed in such manner as the legislature of each State shall direct, to meet ~~at the city of Philadelphia in Pennsylvania, until otherwise directed by the United States in Congress Assembled, which meeting shall~~ be on the first Monday in November in every year, with a power reserved to each State to recal its Delegates or any of them at any time within the year, and to send others in their stead for the remainder of the year. Each State shall support its own Delegates in a meeting of the States, and while they act as ~~members~~ mentioned.

ART. XIII. In determining questions each State shall have one vote.

ART. XIV. The United States Assembled shall have the sole and exclusive right and power of determining on peace and war, except in the cases mentioned in the eleventh article—of establishing rules for deciding in all cases what captures on land or water shall be legal—in what manner prizes taken by land or naval forces in the service of the United States shall be divided or appropriated—granting letters of marque and reprisal in times of peace—appointing Courts for the trial of piracies and felonies committed on the high seas—establishing Courts for receiving and determining finally appeals in all cases of captures—sending and receiving Ambassadors—entering into treaties and ~~alliances—deciding all disputes and differences now subsisting or that hereafter may arise between two or more States, concerning boundaries, jurisdiction~~

fixing the standard of weights and measures throughout the United States—regulating the trade and managing all affairs with the Indians, not members of any of the States—Establishing and regulating Post-Offices from one State to another throughout all the United States, and exacting such postage on the papers passing through the same as may be requisite to defray the expences of said office —appointing all the officers of the land forces in the service of the United States

appointing all the officers of the naval forces in the service of the United States—making rules for the government and regulation of the said land and naval forces, and directing their operations.

THE United States in Congress Assembled shall have authority to appoint a Council of State and such Committees and Civil Officers as may be necessary for managing the general affairs of the United States, under their direction while assembled and in their recess under that of the Council of State—to appoint one of their number to preside and a suitable person for Secretary, and to adjourn to any time within the year and to any place within the United States—to agree upon and fix the necessary sums and expences—to borrow money or emit bills on the credit of the United States—to build and equip a navy—to agree upon the number of land forces, and to make requisitions from each State for its quota in proportion to the number of white inhabitants in such State, which requisitions shall be binding, and thereupon the legislature of each State shall appoint the regimental officers, raise the men, and arm and equip them in a soldier-like manner, and the officers and men so armed and equipped shall march to the place appointed and within the time agreed on by the United States Assembled.

BUT if the United States in Congress Assembled shall on consideration of circumstances judge proper that any State or States should not raise men, or should raise a smaller number than the quota or quotas of such State or States, and that any other State or States should raise a greater number of men than the quota or quotas thereof, such extra numbers shall be raised, officered, armed and equipped in the same manner as the quota or quotas of such State or States, unless the legislature of such State or States respectively shall judge that such extra-numbers cannot be safely spared out of the same, in which case they shall raise officer, arm and equip as many of such extra-numbers as they judge can be safely spared. And the officers and men so armed and equipped shall march to the place appointed and within the time agreed on by the United States Assembled.

THE United States in Congress Assembled shall never engage in a war, nor grant letters of marque and reprisal in time of peace, nor enter into any treaties or alliances, except for peace, nor coin money, nor regulate the value thereof, nor agree upon the sums and expences necessary for the defence and welfare of the United States, or any of them, nor emit bills, nor borrow money on the credit of the United States, nor appropriate money, nor agree upon the number of vessels of war to be built or purchased, or the number of land or sea forces to be raised, nor appoint a Commander in Chief of the army or navy unless nine States assent to the same; nor shall a question on any other point, except for adjourning from day to day be determined, unless by the votes of a majority of the United States.

no State shall be represented in Congress by less than two nor by more than seven members

No person shall be capable of being a Delegate for more than three years in any term of six years.

Being a Delegate shall be capable of

No person holding any office under the United States for which he, or another for his benefit, receives any salary, fees or emolument of any kind, ~~shall be capable of being a Delegate~~.

THE Assembly of the United States to publish the Journal of their Proceedings monthly, except such parts thereof relating to treaties, alliances, or military operations, as in their judgment require secrecy, the yeas and nays of the Delegates of each State on any question to be entered on the Journal when it is desired by any Delegate; and the Delegates of a State or any of them, at his or their request, to be furnished with a transcript of the said Journal, except such parts as are above excepted, to lay before the legislatures of the several States.

ART. XV. ~~THE committee~~ Delegate from each State, to be named annually by the Delegates of each State, and where they cannot agree, ~~by the legislatures~~

The committee ~~to sit in the recess of Congress~~ *of the states*

shall have power to receive and open all letters directed to the United States, and to return proper answers, ~~but~~ not to make any engagements that shall be binding on the United States.—To correspond with the legislature of every State, and all persons acting under the authority of the United States, or of the said legislatures —To apply to such legislatures, or to the Officers in the several States who are entrusted with the executive powers of government, for occasional aid whenever and wherever necessary.—To give counsel to the Commanding Officers, and to direct military operations by sea and land, not changing any objects or expeditions determined on by the United States Assembled, unless an alteration of circumstances which shall come to the knowledge of the Council after the recess of the States, shall make such change absolutely necessary—To attend to the defence and preservation of forts and strong posts—To procure intelligence of the condition and designs of the enemy—To expedite the execution of such measures as may be resolved on by the United States Assembled, in pursuance of the powers hereby given to them—To draw upon the Treasury for such sums as may be appropriated by the United States Assembled, and for the payment of such sums as are

The committee shall be authorised to execute such of the powers of Congress as the United States in Congress assembled by the consent of nine states shall from time to time think expedient to vest them with provided that they delegate to the said committee no power for the exercise of which by the articles of confederation the voice of nine states in the Congress of the states assembled is requisite.—

Document 4e. Printed and corrected draft of the Articles of Confederation, showing amendments adopted, November 15, 1777. [National Archives]

said Council may make in pursuance of the powers hereby given to them—To superintend and controul or suspend all Officers civil and military, acting under the authority of the United States—In case of the death or removal of any Officer within the appointment of the United States Assembled, to employ a person to fulfill the Duties of such Office until the Assembly of the States meet—To publish and disperse authentic accounts of military operations—To summon an Assembly of the States at an earlier day than that appointed for their next meeting, if any great and unexpected emergency should render it necessary for the safety or welfare of the United States or any of them—To prepare matters for the consideration of the United States, and to lay before them at their next meeting all letters and advices received by the Council, with a report of their proceedings—To appoint a proper person for their Clerk, who shall take an oath of secrecy and fidelity before he enters on the exercise of his office—seven Members shall have power to act—In case of the death of any Member, the Council shall immediately apply to his surviving colleagues to appoint some one of themselves to be a Member thereof till the meeting of the States, and if only one survives, they shall give immediate notice, that he may take his seat as a Councillor till such meeting.

ART. XVI. Canada acceding to this Confederation, and ~~entirely~~ joining in the measures of the United States, shall be admitted into and entitled to all the advantages of this Union: But no other Colony shall be admitted into the same unless such admission be agreed to by nine States.

agreed

THESE Articles shall be proposed to the legislatures of all the United States, to be by them considered, and if approved by them, they are advised to authorise their Delegates to ratify the same in the Assembly of the United States, which being done, the Articles of this Confederation shall inviolably be observed by every State, and the Union is to be perpetual: Nor shall any alteration at any time hereafter be made in these Articles or any of them, unless such alteration be agreed to in an Assembly of the United States, and be afterwards confirmed by the legislatures of every State.

An ORDINANCE for the GOVERNMENT of the TERRITORY of the UNITED STATES, North-West of the RIVER OHIO.

BE IT ORDAINED by the United States in Congrefs affembled, That the faid territory, for the purpofes of temporary government, be one diftrict; fubject, however, to be divided into two diftricts, as future circumftances may, in the opinion of Congrefs, make it expedient.

Be it ordained by the authority aforefaid, That the eftates both of refident and non-refident proprietors in the faid territory, dying inteftate, fhall defcend to, and be diftributed among their children, and the defcendants of a deceafed child in equal parts; the defcendants of a deceafed child or grand-child, to take the fhare of their deceafed parent in equal parts among them: And where there fhall be no children or defcendants, then in equal parts to the next of kin, in equal degree; and among collaterals, the children of a deceafed brother or fifter of the inteftate, fhall have in equal parts among them their deceafed parents fhare; and there fhall in no cafe be a diftinction between kindred of the whole and half blood; faving in all cafes to the widow of the inteftate, her third part of the real eftate for life, and one third part of the perfonal eftate; and this law relative to defcents and dower, fhall remain in full force until altered by the legiflature of the diftrict. —— And until the governor and judges fhall adopt laws as herein after mentioned, eftates in the faid territory may be devifed or bequeathed by wills in writing, figned and fealed by him or her, in whom the eftate may be, (being of full age) and attefted by three witneffes; —— and real eftates may be conveyed by leafe and releafe, or bargain and fale, figned, fealed, and delivered by the perfon being of full age, in whom the eftate may be, and attefted by two witneffes, provided fuch wills be duly proved, and fuch conveyances be acknowledged, or the execution thereof duly proved, and be recorded within one year after proper magiftrates, courts, and regifters fhall be appointed for that purpofe; and perfonal property may be transferred by delivery, faving, however, to the French and Canadian inhabitants, and other fettlers of the Kaskaskies, Saint Vincent's, and the neighbouring villages, who have heretofore profeffed themfelves citizens of Virginia, their laws and cuftoms now in force among them, relative to the defcent and conveyance of property.

Be it ordained by the authority aforefaid, That there fhall be appointed from time to time, by Congrefs, a governor, whofe commiffion fhall continue in force for the term of three years, unlefs fooner revoked by Congrefs; he fhall refide in the diftrict, and have a freehold eftate therein, in one thoufand acres of land, while in the exercife of his office.

There fhall be appointed from time to time, by Congrefs, a fecretary, whofe commiffion fhall continue in force for four years, unlefs fooner revoked, he fhall refide in the diftrict, and have a freehold eftate therein, in five hundred acres of land, while in the exercife of his office; it fhall be his duty to keep and preferve the acts and laws paffed by the legiflature, and the public records of the diftrict, and the proceedings of the governor in his executive department; and tranfmit authentic copies of fuch acts and proceedings, every fix months, to the fecretary of Congrefs: There fhall alfo be appointed a court to confift of three judges, any two of whom to form a court, who fhall have a common law jurifdiction, and refide in the diftrict, and have each therein a freehold eftate in five hundred acres of land, while in the exercife of their offices; and their commiffions fhall continue in force during good behaviour.

The governor and judges, or a majority of them, fhall adopt and publifh in the diftrict, fuch laws of the original ftates, criminal and civil, as may be neceffary, and beft fuited to the circumftances of the diftrict, and report them to Congrefs, from time to time, which laws fhall be in force in the diftrict until the organization of the general affembly therein, unlefs difapproved of by Congrefs; but afterwards the legiflature fhall have authority to alter them as they fhall think fit.

The governor for the time being, fhall be commander in chief of the militia, appoint and commiffion all officers in the fame, below the rank of general officers; all general officers fhall be appointed and commiffioned by Congrefs.

Previous to the organization of the general affembly, the governor fhall appoint fuch magiftrates and other civil officers, in each county or townfhip, as he fhall find neceffary for the prefervation of the peace and good order in the fame: After the general affembly fhall be organized, the powers and duties of magiftrates and other civil officers fhall be regulated and defined by the faid affembly; but all magiftrates and other civil officers, not herein otherwife directed, fhall, during the continuance of this temporary government, be appointed by the governor.

For the prevention of crimes and injuries, the laws to be adopted or made fhall have force in all parts of the diftrict, and for the execution of procefs, criminal and civil, the governor fhall make proper divifions thereof—and he fhall proceed from time to time, as circumftances may require, to lay out the parts of the diftrict in which the Indian titles fhall have been extinguifhed, into counties and townfhips, fubject, however, to fuch alterations as may thereafter be made by the legiflature.

So foon as there fhall be five thoufand free male inhabitants, of full age, in the diftrict, upon giving proof thereof to the governor, they fhall receive authority, with time and place, to elect reprefentatives from their counties or townfhips, to reprefent them in the general affembly; provided that for every five hundred free male inhabitants there fhall be one reprefentative, and fo on progreffively with the number of free male inhabitants, fhall the right of reprefentation increafe, until the number of reprefentatives fhall amount to twenty-five, after which the number and proportion of reprefentatives fhall be regulated by the legiflature; provided that no perfon be eligible or qualified to act as a reprefentative, unlefs he fhall have been a citizen of one of the United States three years and be a refident in the diftrict, or unlefs he fhall have refided in the diftrict three years, and in either cafe fhall likewife hold in his own right, in fee fimple, two hundred acres of land within the fame:—Provided alfo, that a freehold in fifty acres of land in the diftrict, having been a citizen of one of the ftates, and being refident in the diftrict; or the like freehold and two years refidence in the diftrict fhall be neceffary to qualify a man as an elector of a reprefentative.

The reprefentatives thus elected, fhall ferve for the term of two years, and in cafe of the death of a reprefentative, or removal from office, the governor fhall iffue a writ to the county or townfhip for which he was a member, to elect another in his ftead, to ferve for the refidue of the term.

The general affembly, or legiflature, fhall confift of the governor, legiflative council, and a houfe of reprefentatives. The legiflative council fhall confift of five members, to continue in office five years, unlefs fooner removed by Congrefs, any three of whom to be a quorum, and the members of the council fhall be nominated and appointed in the following manner, to wit: As foon as reprefentatives fhall be elected, the governor fhall appoint a time and place for them to meet together, and, when met, they fhall nominate ten perfons, refidents in the diftrict, and each poffeffed of a freehold in five hundred acres of land, and return their names to Congrefs; five of whom Congrefs fhall appoint and commiffion to ferve as aforefaid; and whenever a vacancy fhall happen in the council, by death or removal from office, the houfe of reprefentatives fhall nominate two perfons, qualified as aforefaid, for each vacancy, and return their names to Congrefs; one of whom Congrefs fhall appoint and commiffion for the refidue of the term; and every five years, four months at leaft before the expiration of the time of fervice of the members of council, the faid houfe fhall nominate ten perfons, qualified as aforefaid, and return their names to Congrefs, five of whom Congrefs fhall appoint and commiffion to ferve as members of the council five years, unlefs fooner removed. And the governor, legiflative council, and houfe of representatives, shall have authority to make laws in all cases for the good government of the district, not repugnant to the principles and articles in this ordinance established and declared. And all bills having passed by a majority in the house, and by a majority in the council, shall be referred to the governor for his assent; but no bill or legislative act whatever, shall be of any force without his assent. The governor shall have power to convene, prorogue and dissolve the general assembly, when in his opinion it shall be expedient.

The governor, judges, legislative council, secretary, and such other officers as Congress shall appoint in the district, shall take an oath or affirmation of fidelity, and of office, the governor before the president of Congress, and all other officers before the governor. As soon as a legislature shall be formed in the district, the council and house, assembled in one room, shall have authority by joint ballot to elect a delegate to Congress, who shall have a seat in Congress, with a right of debating, but not of voting, during this temporary government.

And for extending the fundamental principles of civil and religious liberty, which form the basis whereon these republics, their laws and constitutions are erected; to fix and establish those principles as the basis of all laws, constitutions and governments, which forever hereafter shall be formed in the said territory;—to provide also for the establishment of states, and permanent government therein, and for their admission to a share in the federal councils on an equal footing with the original states, at as early periods as may be consistent with the general interest:

It is hereby ordained and declared by the authority aforesaid, That the following articles shall be considered as articles of compact between the original states and the people and states in the said territory, and forever remain unalterable, unless by common consent, to wit:

Article the First. No person, demeaning himself in a peaceable and orderly manner, shall ever be molested on account of his mode of worship or religious sentiments in the said territory.

Article the Second. The inhabitants of the said territory shall always be entitled to the benefits of the writ of habeas corpus, and of the trial by jury; of a proportionate representation of the people in the legislature, and of judicial proceedings according to the course of the common law; all persons shall be bailable unless for capital offences, where the proof shall be evident, or the presumption great; all fines shall be moderate, and no cruel or unusual punishments shall be inflicted; no man shall be deprived of his liberty or property but by the judgment of his peers, or the law of the land; and should the public exigencies make it necessary for the common preservation to take any person's property, or to demand his particular services, full compensation shall be made for the same;— and in the just preservation of rights and property it is understood and declared, that no law ought ever to be made, or have force in the said territory, that shall in any manner whatever interfere with, or affect private contracts or engagements, bona fide and without fraud previously formed.

Article the Third. Religion, morality and knowledge, being necessary to good government and the happiness of mankind, schools and the means of education shall forever be encouraged. The utmost good faith shall always be observed towards the Indians; their lands and property shall never be taken from them without their consent; and in their property, rights and liberty, they never shall be invaded or disturbed, unless in just and lawful wars authorised by Congress; but laws founded in justice and humanity shall from time to time be made, for preventing wrongs being done to them, and for preserving peace and friendship with them.

Article the Fourth. The said territory, and the states which may be formed therein, shall forever remain a part of this confederacy of the United States of America, subject to the articles of confederation, and to such alterations therein as shall be constitutionally made; and to all the acts and ordinances of the United states in Congress assembled, conformable thereto. The inhabitants and settlers in the said territory, shall be subject to pay a part of the federal debts contracted or to be contracted, and a proportional part of the expences of government, to be apportioned on them by Congress, according to the same common rule and measure by which apportionments thereof shall be made on the other states; and the taxes for paying their proportion, shall be laid and levied by the authority and direction of the legislatures of the district or districts or new states, as in the original states, within the time agreed upon by the United States in Congress assembled. The legislatures of those districts, or new states, shall never interfere with the primary disposal of the soil by the United States in Congress assembled, nor with any regulations Congress may find necessary for securing the title in such soil to the bona fide purchasers. No tax shall be imposed on lands the property of the United States; and in no case shall non-resident proprietors be taxed higher than residents. The navigable waters leading into the Mississippi and St. Lawrence, and the carrying places between the same shall be common highways, and forever free, as well to the inhabitants of the said territory, as to the citizens of the United States, and those of any other states that may be admitted into the confederacy, without any tax, impost or duty therefor.

Article the Fifth. There shall be formed in the said territory, not less than three nor more than five states; and the boundaries of the states, as soon as Virginia shall alter her act of cession and consent to the same, shall become fixed and established as follows, to wit: The western state in the said territory, shall be bounded by the Mississippi, the Ohio and Wabash rivers; a direct line drawn from the Wabash and Post Vincent's due north to the territorial line between the United States and Canada, and by the said territorial line to the lake of the Woods and Mississippi. The middle state shall be bounded by the said direct line, the Wabash from Post Vincent's to the Ohio; by the Ohio, by a direct line drawn due north from the mouth of the Great Miami to the said territorial line, and by the said territorial line. The eastern state shall be bounded by the last mentioned direct line, the Ohio, Pennsylvania, and the said territorial line: Provided however, and it is further understood and declared, that the boundaries of these three states, shall be subject so far to be altered, that if Congress shall hereafter find it expedient, they shall have authority to form one or two states in that part of the said territory which lies north of an east and west line drawn through the southerly bend or extreme of lake Michigan: and whenever any of the said states shall have sixty thousand free inhabitants therein, such state shall be admitted by its delegates into the Congress of the United States, on an equal footing with the original states in all respects whatever; and shall be at liberty to form a permanent constitution and state government: Provided the constitution and government so to be formed, shall be republican, and in conformity to the principles contained in these articles; and so far as it can be consistent with the general interest of the confederacy, such admission shall be allowed at an earlier period, and when there may be a less number of free inhabitants in the state than sixty thousand.

Article the Sixth. There shall be neither slavery nor involuntary servitude in the said territory, otherwise than in punishment of crimes whereof the party shall have been duly convicted: Provided always, that any person escaping into the same, from whom labor or service is lawfully claimed in any one of the original states, such fugitive may be lawfully reclaimed and conveyed to the person claiming his or her labor or service as aforesaid.

Be it ordained by the authority aforesaid, That the resolutions of the 23d of April, 1784, relative to the subject of this ordinance, be, and the same are hereby repealed and declared null and void.

DONE by the UNITED STATES in CONGRESS assembled, the 13th day of July, in the year of our Lord 1787, and of their sovereignty and independence the 12th.

Cha² Thomson sec²

Georgia M Few ay ?
~ M Pierce no }
So the question was lost. —

A motion was then made by the delegates for Massachusetts to postpone the farther consideration of the report in order to take into consideration a motion which they read in their place, this being agreed to, the motion of the delegates for Massachusetts was taken up and being amended was agreed to as follows

Whereas there is provision in the Articles of Confederation & perpetual Union for making alterations therein by the Assent of a Congress of the United States and of the legislatures of the several States; And whereas experience hath evinced that there are defects in the present Confederation, as a mean to remedy which several of the states and particularly the state of New York by express instructions to their delegates in Congress have suggested a Convention for the purposes expressed in the following resolution and such Convention appearing to be the most probable mean of establishing in these states a firm national government

Resolved that in the opinion of Congress it is expedient that on the second Monday in May next a Convention of delegates who shall have been appointed by the several states be held at Philadelphia for the sole and express purpose of revising the Articles of Confederation and reporting to Congress and the several legislatures such alterations and

Document 6a. Resolution to convene the Philadelphia
Convention, February 21, 1787. [National Archives]

1787

Feby 21 provisions therein as shall when agreed to in Congress and confirmed by the states under the federal constitution adequate to the exigencies of government & the preservation of the Union

Feby 22   Thursday Feby 22. 1787

Six States only attending namely, Massachusetts New York New Jersey Pensylvania North Carolina & Georgia & from Connecticut Mr S M. Mitchell from Delaware Mr N Mitchell & from Maryland Mr Forrest the chairman adjourned Congress to 10 oclock to morrow. —

23   Friday Feby 23 1787

Six states only attended namely Massachusetts New York New Jersey Pensylvania Virginia & North Carolina & from Connecticut Mr S M Mitchell from Maryland Mr Forrest & from Georgia Mr Few

26   Monday Feby 26. 1787

Congress assembled present Massachusetts New york New Jersey, Pensylvania Virginia, North Carolina & Georgia & from Rhode Island Mr Varnum from Connecticut Mr S M Mitchell from Delaware Mr N Mitchell

March 1   Thursday March 1. 1787

Congress assembled, Present Massachusetts New York Pensylvania, Delaware, Virginia North Carolina & Georgia & from the State of Rhode Island Mr Varnum from Connecticut Mr S M Mitchell & from New Jersey Mr Cadwallader. —

Mr Dyre Kearny a delegate for Delaware attended

The question being taken on the whole of the report from the grand Committee as amended

it passed in the affirmative and is as follows, namely.

Resolved – That in the original formation of the legislature of the United States the first Branch thereof shall consist of sixty five members. of which number

New Hampshire shall send – Three
Massachusetts ——— Eight
Rhode Island ——— One
Connecticut ——— Five
New York ——— Six
New Jersey ——— four
Pennsylvania ——— Eight
Delaware ——— One
Maryland ——— Six
Virginia ——— Ten
North Carolina ——— Five
South Carolina ——— Five
Georgia ——— Three

But as the present situation of the States may probably alter in the number of their inhabitants, the legislature of the United States shall be authorised from time to time to apportion the number of representatives: and in case any of the States shall hereafter be divided, or enlarged by addition of territory, or any two or more States united, or any new States created within the limits of the United States the legislature of the United States shall possess authority to regulate the number of representatives: and in any of the foregoing cases upon the principle of their number of inhabitants,

according

to the provisions hereafter mentioned, namely,

Provided always that representation ought to be proportioned according to direct Taxation; and in order to ascertain the alteration in the direct Taxation, which may be required from time to time by the changes in the relative circumstances of the States. Resolved that a Census be taken within six years from the first meeting of the Legislature of the United States, and once within the term of every Ten years afterwards of all the inhabitants of the United States in the manner and according to the ratio recommended by Congress in their resolution of april 18. 1783 — and that the Legislature of the United States shall proportion the direct Taxation accordingly

Resolved That all Bills for raising or appropriating money, and for fixing the salaries of the Officers of the Government of the United States shall originate in the first Branch of the Legislature of the United States, and shall not be altered or amended by the second Branch — and that no money shall be drawn from the Public Treasury but in pursuance of appropriations to be originated by the first Branch.

Resolved That in the second Branch of the Legislature of the United States each State shall have an equal vote.

It was moved and seconded to agree to the first clause of the sixth resolution reported from the Committee of the whole House namely
"That the national Legislature ought to possess the legislative rights vested in Congress by the confederation"
which passed unanimously in the affirmative

It was moved and seconded to commit the second clause of the sixth resolution reported from the Committee of the whole House
which passed in the negative

And then the House adjourned till to-morrow at 11 oClock . A. M.

WE the People of the States

of New-Hampfhire, Maffachufetts, Rhode-Ifland and Providence Plantations, Connecticut, New-York, New-Jerfey, Pennfylvania, Delaware, Maryland, Virginia, North-Carolina, South-Carolina, and Georgia, do ordain, declare and eftablifh the following Conftitution for the Government of Ourfelves and our Pofterity.

ARTICLE I.

The ftile of this Government fhall be, " The United States of America."

II.

. The Government fhall confift of fupreme legiflative, executive and judicial powers.

III.

The legiflative power fhall be vefted in a Congrefs, to confift of two feparate and diftinct bodies of men, a Houfe of Reprefentatives, and a Senate; ~~each of which fhall, in all cafes, have a negative on the other. The Legiflature fhall meet on the firft Monday in December in every year.~~

The Legiflature fhall meet at least once in every year and that meeting fhall be on the firft Monday in December unless a different day fhall be appointed by law.

IV.

Sect. 1. The Members of the Houfe of Reprefentatives fhall be chofen every fecond year, by the people of the feveral States comprehended within this Union. The qualifications of the electors fhall be the fame, from time to time, as thofe of the electors in the feveral States, of the moft numerous branch of their own legiflatures.

Sect. 2. Every Member of the Houfe of Reprefentatives fhall be of the age of twenty-five years at leaft; fhall have been a citizen ~~in~~ of the United States for at leaft ■■■ years before his election; and fhall be, at the time of his election, ■■■ of the State in which he fhall be chofen.

Sect. 3. The Houfe of Reprefentatives fhall, at its firft formation, and until the number of citizens and inhabitants fhall be taken in the manner herein after defcribed, confift of fixty-five Members, of whom three fhall be chofen in New-Hampfhire, eight in Maffachufetts, one in Rhode-Ifland and Providence Plantations, five in Connecticut, fix in New-York, four in New-Jerfey, eight in Pennfylvania, one in Delaware, fix in Maryland, ten in Virginia, five in North-Carolina, five in South-Carolina, and three in Georgia.

Sect. 4. As the proportions of numbers in the different States will alter from time to time; as fome of the States may hereafter be divided; as others may be enlarged by addition of territory; as two or more States may be united; as new States will be erected within the limits of the United States, the Legiflature fhall, in each of thefe cafes, regulate the number of reprefentatives by the number of inhabitants, according to the ■■■ rate of one for every forty thoufand. *Provided that every State fhall have at leaft One reprefentative.*

Sect. 5. All bills for raifing or appropriating money, and for fixing the falaries of the officers of government, fhall originate in the Houfe of Reprefentatives, and fhall not be altered or amended by the Senate. No money fhall be drawn from the public Treafury, but in purfuance of appropriations that fhall originate in the Houfe of Reprefentatives.

Sect. 6. The Houfe of Reprefentatives fhall have the fole power of impeachment. It fhall choofe its Speaker and other officers.

Sect. 7. Vacancies in the Houfe of Reprefentatives fhall be fupplied by writs of election from the executive authority of the State, in the reprefentation from which they fhall happen.

V.

vacancies happening by refusals to accept, resignation
or otherwise may be supplied by the legislature of the
State in the representation of which such vacancies
shall happen, or by the Executive thereof until the
next meeting of the legislature.

^ of the State, in the representation of
~~which the vacancies~~ | shall happen.

or they shall be assembled in consequence of

V.

Sect. 1. The Senate of the United States shall be chosen by the Legislatures of the several States. Each Legislature shall chuse two members. Vacancies may be supplied by the Executive until the next meeting of the Legislature. Each member shall have one vote.

Sect. 2. The Senators shall be chosen for six years; but immediately after the first election they shall be divided, by lot, into three classes, as nearly as may be, numbered one, two and three. The seats of the members of the first class shall be vacated at the expiration of the second year, of the second class at the expiration of the fourth year, of the third class at the expiration of the sixth year, so that a third part of the members may be chosen every second year.

Sect. 3. Every member of the Senate shall be of the age of thirty years at least; shall have been a citizen of the United States for at least ~~nine~~ years before his election; and shall be, at the time of his election, ~~a resident~~ of the State for which he shall be chosen.

agreed — **Sect. 4.** The Senate shall chuse its own President and other officers.

VI.

agreed **Sect. 1.** The times and places and the manner of holding the elections of the members of each House shall be prescribed by the Legislature of each State; but ~~their provisions concerning them~~ may, at any time, be altered by the Legislature of the United States.

disagreed to — **Sect. 2.** The Legislature of the United States shall have authority to establish such uniform qualifications of the members of each house, with regard to property, as to the said Legislature shall seem expedient.

and may be authorised to compell the attendance
of absent members in such manner and
under such penalties as each House may
provide.

Sect. 3. In each House a majority of the members shall constitute a quorum to do business; but a smaller number may adjourn from day to day.

agreed **Sect. 4.** Each House shall be the judge of the elections, returns and qualifications of its own members.

agreed **Sect. 5.** Freedom of speech and debate in the Legislature shall not be impeached or questioned in any court or place out of the Legislature; and the members of each House shall, in all cases, except treason, felony and breach of the peace, be privileged from arrest during their attendance at Congress, and in going to and returning from it.

agreed **Sect. 6.** Each House may determine the rules of its proceedings; may punish its members for disorderly behaviour; and may expel a member.

agreed **Sect. 7.** The House of Representatives, and the Senate, ~~when it shall be acting in a legislative capacity,~~ shall keep a journal of their proceedings, and shall, from time to time, publish them: and the yeas and nays of the members of each House, on any question, shall, at the desire of one-fifth part of the members present, be entered on the journal. except such parts thereof as in their judgment require secrecy.

Sect. 8. Neither House, without the consent of the other, shall adjourn for more than three days nor to any other place than that at which the two Houses are sitting. ~~But this clause shall not be construed to——~~

Sect. 9 Postponed till
the power of the Senate
shall have been decided on

Sect. 9. The members of each House shall be ineligible to, and incapable of holding any office under the authority of the United States, during the time for which they shall respectively be elected: and the members of the Senate shall be ineligible to, and incapable of holding any such office for one year afterwards.

Sect.

Sect. 10. The members of each House shall receive a compensation for their services, ~~to be ascertained and paid by the State, in which they shall be chosen.~~ *to be paid out of the treasury of the United States; to be ascertained by law.*

Sect. 11. The enacting stile of the laws of the United States shall be. " Be it enacted, ~~and it is hereby enacted by the House of Representatives, and by the Senate of the United States,~~ *by the senate and house of representatives of* in Congress assembled.

Aug. 15 – postponed

Sect. 12. Each House shall possess the right of originating bills, ~~except in the cases beforementioned.~~

Sect. 13. Every bill, which shall have passed the House of Representatives and the Senate, shall, before it become a law, be presented to the President of the United States, for his revision : if, upon such revision, he approve of it, he shall signify his approbation by signing it : But if, upon such revision, it shall appear to him improper for being passed into a law, he shall return it, together with his objections against it, to that House in which it shall have originated, who shall enter the objections at large on their Journal, and proceed to reconsider the bill. But if, after such reconsideration, ~~three fourths~~ of that House shall, notwithstanding the objections of the President, agree to pass it, it shall, together with his objections, be sent to the other House, by which it shall likewise be reconsidered, and, if approved by ~~two thirds~~ *three fourths* of the other House also, it shall become a law. But, in all such cases, the votes of both Houses shall be determined by Yeas and Nays ; and the names of the persons voting for or against the bill shall be entered in the Journal of each House respectively. If any bill shall not be returned by the President within *ten days (Sundays excepted)* after it shall have been presented to him, it shall be a law, unless the Legislature, by their adjournment, prevent its return ; in which case it shall not be a law.

† 12. Section. every order, resolution vote, to which the concurrence of the senate and House of representatives may necessary (except on a question of adjournment, and in the cases herein before mentioned) shall be presented to the President for his revision; and, before the same shall have force, shall be allowed by him, or, being disapproved by him, shall be repassed by the senate and House of representatives, according to the rules and limitations, exercised in the case of a Bill.

VII

Sect. 1. The Legislature ~~of the United States~~ *of the United States shall fulfil the engagements & discharge the debts* shall have the power to lay and collect taxes, duties, imposts and excises ;

To regulate commerce with foreign nations, and among the several States;

To establish an uniform rule of naturalization throughout the United States;

To coin money;

To regulate the value of foreign coin;

To fix the standard of weights and measures ;

To establish post-offices; *& post roads*

To borrow money, ~~and emit bills~~ on the credit of the United States;

To appoint a Treasurer by ballot;

To constitute tribunals inferior to the supreme court ;

To make rules concerning captures on land and water;

To ~~define & punish~~ *define and punish* piracies and felonies committed on the high seas; ~~and the~~ punish ~~ment of~~ counterfeiting the coin of the United States, and ~~of~~ offences against the law of nations;

To subdue a rebellion in any State, on the application of its Legislature; *or without*

To ~~make~~ war; *and reprisals*

To raise armies;

~~To build and equip fleets;~~

To ~~make rules for the government and regulation of the land and naval forces~~ the militia, ~~and~~ to execute the laws of the Union, *provide for calling forth* suppress insurrections, and repel invasions;

And to make all laws that shall be necessary and proper for carrying into execution the foregoing powers, and all other powers vested, by this Constitution, in the government of the United States, or in any department or officer thereof.

Postponed agreed to 23d Aug T

Agreed –

Agreed. –

7 To make laws for organising, arming, and disciplining the militia, and for governing such part of them as may be employed in the service of the United States – reserving to the States respectively, the appointment of the officers, and the authority of training the militia according to the discipline prescribed by the United States. To establish uniform laws on the subject of Bankruptcies

Sect. 2. Treason ~~against the United States~~ shall consist only in levying war against ~~the United States~~ *the United States and convicted* in adhering to the enemies ~~of the United States,~~ The Legislature ~~of the United States~~ shall have power to declare the punishment of treason. No person shall be convicted

or except in cases
to the same overt act [3]

victed of treason, unless on the testimony of two witnesses. No attainder of treason shall work corruption of blood, nor forfeiture, except during the life of the person attainted.

agreed —

Sect. 3. The proportions of direct taxation shall be regulated by the whole number of ▓▓▓▓▓▓▓ free citizens and inhabitants, of every age, sex and condition, including those bound to servitude for a term of years, and three fifths of all other persons not comprehended in the foregoing description, (except Indians not paying taxes) which number shall, within ▓▓ years after the first meeting of the Legislature, and within the term of every ten years afterwards, be taken in such manner as the said Legislature shall direct.

Agreed. —

Sect. 4. No tax or duty shall be laid by the Legislature on articles exported from any State; ▓▓

Referred to a committee.

Sect. 5. No capitation tax shall be laid, unless in proportion to the census herein before directed to be taken. — *agreed*

Struck out, aug. 29th —

Sect. 6. No navigation act shall be passed without the assent of two-thirds of the members present in each House.

agreed — —

Sect. 7. The United States shall not grant any title of nobility.

Agreed.

VIII
This Constitution & the laws [crossed out] of the United States made in pursuance *thereof* ▓▓▓▓▓▓, and all treaties made under the authority of the United States shall be the supreme law of the several States, and of their citizens and inhabitants; and the judges in the several States shall be bound thereby in their decisions; any thing in the constitutions or laws of the several States to the contrary notwithstanding.

VIIII

~~Postponed.~~

Sect. 1. The Senate of the United States shall have power to make treaties, and to appoint ambassadors, and judges of the supreme court.

Struck out

Sect. 2. In all disputes and controversies now subsisting, or that may hereafter subsist between two or more States, respecting jurisdiction or territory, the Senate shall possess the following powers. Whenever the Legislature, or the Executive authority, or the lawful agent of any State, in controversy with another, shall, by memorial to the Senate, state the matter in question, and apply for a hearing; notice of such memorial and application shall be given, by order of the Senate, to the Legislature or the Executive Authority of the other State in controversy. The Senate shall also assign a day for the appearance of the parties, by their agents, before that House. The agents shall be directed to appoint, by joint consent, commissioners or judges to constitute a court for hearing and determining the matter in question. But if the agents cannot agree, the Senate shall name three persons out of each of the several States, and from the list of such persons each party shall alternately strike out one, until the number shall be reduced to thirteen; and from that number not less than seven nor more than nine names, as the Senate shall direct, shall, in their presence, be drawn out by lot; and the persons, whose names shall be so drawn, or any five of them shall be commissioners or judges to hear and finally determine the controversy; provided a majority of the judges, who shall hear the cause, agree in the determination. If either party shall neglect to attend at the day assigned, without shewing sufficient reasons for not attending, or, being present, shall refuse to strike, the Senate shall proceed to nominate three persons out of each State, and the clerk of the Senate shall strike in behalf of the party absent or refusing. If any of the parties shall refuse to submit to the authority of such court; or shall not appear to prosecute or defend their claim

or

Stricken out

or cause, the court shall nevertheless proceed to pronounce judgment. The judgment shall be final and conclusive. The proceedings shall be transmitted to the President of the Senate, and shall be lodged among the public records for the security of the parties concerned. Every commissioner shall, before he sit in judgment, take an oath, to be administered by one of the judges of the supreme or superior court of the State where the cause shall be tried, " well " and truly to hear and determine the matter in question, according to the " best of his judgment, without favour, affection, or hope of reward."

Stricken out.

Sect. 3. All controversies concerning lands claimed under different grants of two or more States, whose jurisdictions, as they respect such lands, shall have been decided or adjusted subsequent to such grants, or any of them, shall, on application to the Senate, be finally determined, as near as may be, in the same manner as is before prescribed for deciding controversies between different States.

X.

Sect. 1. The Executive Power of the United States shall be vested in a single person. His stile shall be, " The President of the United States of America;" and his title shall be, " His Excellency." [He shall be elected by *joint* ballot by the Legislature.† He shall hold his office during the term of seven years; but shall not be elected a second time.

+ to which election a majority of the votes of the members present shall be required

Sect. 2. He shall, from time to time, give information *to the Legislature* ~~to the Legislature~~ of the State of the Union: *and* ~~he may~~ recommend to their consideration such measures as he shall judge necessary, and expedient: he may convene them on extraordinary occasions. In case of disagreement between the two Houses, with regard to the time of adjournment, he may adjourn them to such time as he *shall* think proper: he shall take care that the laws of the United States be duly and faithfully executed: he shall commission all the officers of the United States; and shall appoint ~~*to offices*~~ in all cases not otherwise provided for by this constitution. He shall receive Ambassadors, ~~   ~~ He shall have power to grant reprieves and pardons; ~~but his pardon shall not be pleadable in bar of an impeachment.~~ He shall be Commander in Chief of the Army and Navy of the United States, and of the Militia of the several States. He shall, at stated times, receive for his services, a compensation, which shall neither be encreased nor diminished during his continuance in office. Before he shall enter on the duties of his department, he shall take the following Oath or Affirmation, " I ——— so-" lemnly swear (or affirm) that I will faithfully execute the Office of President" dent of the United States of America." He shall be removed from his office on impeachment by the House of Representatives, and conviction in the Supreme Court, of treason, bribery, or corruption. In case of his removal as aforesaid, death, resignation, or disability to discharge the powers and duties of his office, the President of the Senate shall exercise those powers and duties until another President of the United States be chosen, or until the disability of the President be removed.

Postponed aug. 27

XI

Sect. 1. The Judicial Power of the United States shall be vested in one Supreme Court, and in such Inferior Courts as shall, when necessary, from time to time, be constituted by the Legislature of the United States.

agreed.

Sect. 2. The Judges of the Supreme Court, and of the Inferior courts, shall hold their offices during good behaviour. They shall, at stated times, receive for their services, a compensation, which shall not be diminished during their continuance in office.

Sect. 3. The ~~Jurisdiction of the Supreme Court~~ shall extend to all cases arising under laws ~~   ~~ of the United States; to all cases affecting Ambassadors, other Public Ministers and Consuls; to the trial of impeachment

this clause postp?

peachments of Officers of the United States; to all cases of Admiralty and Maritime Jurisdiction; to Controversies between two or more States ~~between a State and citizens of~~ another State, between citizens of different States, and between a State or the citizens thereof and foreign States, citizens or subjects. In cases of Impeachment, cases affecting Ambassadors, other Public Ministers and Consuls, and those in which a State shall be party, ~~this~~ *the supreme court shall have original* jurisdiction. In all the other cases beforementioned ~~the supreme court shall have appellate jurisdiction~~, *as to law and fact* with such exceptions and under such regulations as the Legislature shall make. ~~The Legislature may assign any part of the jurisdiction abovementioned (except the trial of the President of the United States) in the manner and under the limitations which it shall think proper, to such Inferior Courts as it shall constitute from time to time.~~

Sect. 4. The trial of all crimes (except in cases of impeachment) shall be by jury — and such trial shall be held in the state where the said crimes shall have been committed; but when not committed within any State, then the trial shall be at such place or places as the legislature may direct — The privilege of the writ of Habeas Corpus shall not be suspended: unless where in case of rebellion or invasion the public safety may require it

agreed. —

~~Sect. 4. The trial of all criminal offences (except in cases of impeachment) shall be in the State where they shall be committed; and shall be by jury.~~

Sect. 5. Judgment, in cases of Impeachment, shall not extend further than to removal from office, and disqualification to hold and enjoy any office of honour, trust or profit under the United States. But the party convicted shall nevertheless be liable and subject to indictment, trial, judgment and punishment, according to law.

XII

agreed

~~emit bills of credit~~ No State shall coin money; nor grant letters of marque and reprisal; nor enter into any treaty, alliance, or confederation; nor grant any title of nobility.

XIII

agreed.

No State, without the consent of the Legislature of the United States, shall ~~emit bills of credit, make any thing but gold and silver coin a tender in payment of debts~~ lay imposts or duties on imports; nor keep troops or ships of war in time of peace; nor enter into any agreement or compact with another State, or with any foreign power; nor engage in any war, unless it shall be actually invaded by enemies, or the danger of invasion be so imminent, as not to admit of a delay, until the Legislature of the United States can be consulted.

XIIII

agreed. —

The citizens of each State shall be entitled to all privileges and immunities of citizens in the several States.

XV.

agreed.

Any person charged with treason, felony, or ~~high misdemeanor~~ *other crime* in any State, who shall flee from justice, and shall be found in any other State, shall, on demand of the Executive Power of the State from which he fled, be delivered up and removed to the State having jurisdiction of the offence.

If any Person bound to service or labor in any of the United States shall escape into another State, he or she shall not be discharged from such service or labor in consequence of any regulations subsisting in the State to which they escape; but shall be delivered up to the Person justly claiming their service or labor

referred to the Com. of Eleven. — Amendment Sep 28.

XVI

Full faith shall be given in each State to the *public* acts ~~of the Legislatures, and to the~~ records and judicial proceedings of ~~the courts and magistrates of~~ every other State: *and the legislature may by general laws prescribe the manner in which such acts, records, and proceedings shall be proved and the effect thereof.*

XVII

New States may be admitted by the legislature into this union: but no new State shall be... within the limits of any of the present states...

~~New States lawfully constituted or established within the limits of the United States may be admitted, by the Legislature, into this government; but to such admission the consent of two thirds of the Members present in each House shall be necessary. If a new State shall arise within the limits of any of the present States, the consent of the Legislatures of such States shall be also necessary to its admission.~~

Nor shall any State be formed by the junction of two or more States, or parts thereof, without the consent of the Legislatures of such States as well as of the Legislature of the United States.

Document 8f. George Washington's copy of the Constitution, August 6, 1787. [National Archives]

XVIII

agreed —

The United States fhall guaranty to each State a Republican form of government; and fhall protect each State againft ~~foreign~~ invafions, and, on the application of its Legiflature, againft domeftic violence.

XVIIII

agreed —

On the application of the Legiflatures of two thirds of the States in the Union, for an amendment of this Conftitution, the Legiflature of the United States fhall call a Convention for that purpofe.

XXX.

agreed —

The Members of the Legiflatures, and the executive and judicial officers of the United States, and of the feveral States, fhall be bound by oath to fupport this Conftitution.

XXI

agreed —

The ratification of the Conventions of *nine* States fhall be fufficient for organifing this Conftitution. *between the said states.*

XXII

This Conftitution fhall be laid before the United States in Congrefs affembled, ~~for their approbation~~; and it is the opinion of this Convention that it fhould be afterwards fubmitted to a Convention chofen in each State, under the recommendation of its Legiflature, in order to receive the ratification of fuch Convention.

XXIII

To introduce this government, it is the opinion of this Convention, that each affenting Convention fhould notify its affent and ratification to the United States in Congrefs affembled; that Congrefs, after receiving the affent and ratification of the Conventions of *nine* States, fhould appoint and publifh a day, as early as may be, and appoint a place for commencing proceedings under this Conftitution; that after fuch publication, the Legiflatures of the feveral States fhould elect Members of the Senate, and direct the election of Members of the Houfe of Reprefentatives; and that the Members of the Legiflature fhould meet at the time and place affigned by Congrefs, and fhould, as foon as may be, after their meeting, ~~elect the Prefident of the United States, and~~ proceed to execute this Conftitution.

Document 8g. George Washington's copy of the Constitution, August 6, 1787. [National Archives]

CONGRESS OF THE UNITED STATES.

In the HOUSE *of* REPRESENTATIVES,

Monday, 24th *August*, 1789,

RESOLVED, BY THE SENATE AND HOUSE OF REPRESENTA-
TIVES OF THE UNITED STATES OF AMERICA IN CONGRESS
ASSEMBLED, two thirds of both Houses ~~deeming it necessary~~, That *concurring*
the following Articles be proposed to the Legislature of the several
States, as Amendments to the Constitution of the United States, all
or any of which Articles, when ratified by three fourths of the said
Legislatures, to be valid to all intents and purposes as part of the
said Constitution—Viz.

ARTICLES in addition to, and amendment of, the Constitution of
the United States of America, proposed by Congress, and ratified
by the Legislatures of the several States, pursuant to the fifth Article of the original Constitution.

ARTICLE THE FIRST.

After the first enumeration, required by the first Article of the
Constitution, there shall be one Representative for every thirty thousand, until the number shall amount to one hundred, after which *amendment*
the proportion shall be so regulated by Congress, that there shall
be not less than one hundred Representatives, nor less than one Representative for every forty thousand persons, until the number of
Representatives shall amount to two hundred, after which the proportion shall be so regulated by Congress, that there shall not be less
than two hundred Representatives, nor less than one Representative
for every fifty thousand persons.

ARTICLE THE SECOND.
for the services of the Senators & Representatives ~~of the~~

No law varying the compensation ~~to the members of Congress,~~
shall take effect, until an election of Representatives shall have intervened.
a

ARTICLE THE THIRD.
some religious sect or Society in Prefer

Congress shall make no law establishing ~~religion or prohibiting~~ ~~are to thou~~
~~the free exercise thereof, nor shall the rights of Conscience be infringed.~~ *~~depriving~~*
Articles of Faith or a mode of Worship, or prohibiting the free exercise of Religion.

ARTICLE THE FOURTH.
Congress shall make no law abridging

The Freedom of ~~Speech, or of the Press, and the~~ right of the
People peaceably to assemble, ~~and consult for their common good,~~
petition and to ~~apply to~~ the Government for a redress of grievances, ~~shall~~
~~not be infringed.~~

ARTICLE the FIFTH.

A well regulated militia, composed of the body of the People, being the best security of a free State, the right of the People to keep and bear arms, shall not be infringed, but no one religiously scrupulous of bearing arms, shall be compelled to render military service in person.

amendment

ARTICLE the SIXTH.

No soldier shall, in time of peace, be quartered in any house without the consent of the owner, nor in time of war, but in a manner to be prescribed by law. *a*

ARTICLE the SEVENTH.

The right of the People to be secure in their persons, houses, papers and effects, against unreasonable searches and seizures, shall not be violated, and no warrants shall issue, but upon probable cause supported by oath or affirmation, and particularly describing the place to be searched, and the persons or things to be seized. *a*

Articles of Amendments to the constitution of the U. States

ARTICLE the EIGHTH.

to be twice drawn in jeopardy of life or limb, by any

No person shall be subject, ~~except in case of impeachment, to more than one trial, or one punishment~~ for the same offense, nor shall be compelled in any criminal case, to be a witness against himself, nor be deprived of life, liberty or property, without due process of law; nor shall private property be taken for public use without just compensation. *a*

public Prosecution

8. & 10. united with an amendment

ARTICLE the NINTH.

In all criminal prosecutions, the accused shall enjoy the right to a speedy and public trial, to be informed of the nature and cause of the accusation, to be confronted with the witnesses against him, to have compulsory process for obtaining witnesses in his favor, and to have the assistance of counsel for his defence. *a*

ARTICLE the TENTH.

The trial of all crimes (except in cases of impeachment, and in cases arising in the land or naval forces, or in the militia when in actual service in time of War or public danger) shall be by an Impartial Jury of the Vicinage, ~~with the requisite of unanimity for~~ conviction, the right of challenge, and other accustomed requisites; and no person shall be held to answer for a capital, or otherways infamous crime, unless on a presentment or indictment by a Grand Jury; ~~but if a crime be committed in a place in the possession of an enemy, or in which an insurrection may prevail, the indictment and trial may by law be authorised in some other place within the same state.~~ *a*

10ᵗʰ and 11ᵗʰ incorporated.

ARTICLE the ELEVENTH.

No appeal to the Supreme Court of the United States, shall be allowed, where the value in controversy shall not amount to one thousand dollars, nor shall any fact, triable by a Jury according to the course of the common law, be otherwise re-examinable, than according to the rules of common law. *in any court of the U.S.* *a*

ARTICLE the TWELFTH.

where the value in controversy shall exceed twenty dollars

In suits at common law, the right of trial by Jury shall be preserved. *a*

ARTICLE the THIRTEENTH.

Excessive bail shall not be required, nor excessive fines imposed, nor cruel and unusual punishments inflicted. *a*

ARTICLE the FOURTEENTH.

No State shall infringe the right of trial by Jury in criminal cases, nor the rights of conscience, nor the freedom of speech, or of the press. *dele*

ARTICLE the FIFTEENTH.

The enumeration in the Constitution of certain rights, shall not be construed to deny or disparage others retained by the people. *a*

ARTICLE the SIXTEENTH.

The powers delegated by the Constitution to the government of the United States, shall be exercised as therein appropriated, so that the Legislative shall never exercise the powers vested in the Executive or Judicial; nor the Executive the powers vested in the Legislative or Judicial; nor the Judicial the powers vested in the Legislative or Executive. *dele* *not a*

ARTICLE the SEVENTEENTH.

to the U.S.

The powers not delegated by the Constitution, nor prohibited by it, to the States, are reserved to the States respectively, *or to the People* *it*

Teste,

JOHN BECKLEY, Clerk.

In SENATE, *August* 25, 1789.

Read and ordered to be printed for the consideration of the Senate.

Attest,   SAMUEL A. OTIS, SECRETARY.

S. J. Res. 7

Ninety-second Congress of the United States of America

AT THE FIRST SESSION

Begun and held at the City of Washington on Thursday, the twenty-first day of January, one thousand nine hundred and seventy-one

Joint Resolution

Proposing an amendment to the Constitution of the United States extending the right to vote to citizens eighteen years of age or older.

Resolved by the Senate and House of Representatives of the United States of America in Congress assembled (two-thirds of each House concurring therein), That the following article is proposed as an amendment to the Constitution of the United States, which shall be valid to all intents and purposes as part of the Constitution when ratified by the legislatures of three-fourths of the several States within seven years from the date of its submission by the Congress:

"ARTICLE —

"SECTION 1. The right of citizens of the United States, who are eighteen years of age or older, to vote shall not be denied or abridged by the United States or by any State on account of age.

"SEC. 2. The Congress shall have power to enforce this article by appropriate legislation."

Carl Albert
Speaker of the House of Representatives.

The President of the United States and
President of the Senate Pro Tempore

Document 10. Twenty-sixth Amendment to the Constitution, March 23, 1971. [National Archives]

Oath administered to the President of the U. States.

April 30th 1789.

The Vice President's chair was fixed on right of the President's, Speaker's the left. The Senate did not adjourn — The House did — came up headed by their Speaker and followed by the clerk. The President seated himself, and being informed by the Vice President that the two Houses were ready to attend him to take the oath, The Secretary of the Senate whose seat was inclined to the right of the Vice-President carrying a bible on a cushion, The Chancellor of the State administer-ed the oath, The President laying his hand on the bible and repeating the oath after which the President of the United States kissed the book, and the Chancel-lor proclaimed him President of the United States — The President of the United States returning, and reposing a few minutes on his chair, arose and addressed the two Houses of Congress (as

by

by Journal May 1789.) After the address the procession was formed to S.t Paul's. where prayers being over, the President returned to his own house in a carriage, accompanied by the joint committee of arrangement. The Vice President and Senate returned to the Senate chamber in a body, and the Senate after chusing a committee to answer the speech adjourned. See Journals of Senate April 1789

August 22.d 1789.

President of United States attends personally on treaties.

The President of the United States agreeably to his intimation of yesterday attended the Senate _ and took the Vice Presidents chair. Vice President took Secretary's seat. Secretary to the left. W.G.r doors opened. Doorkeeper only waited at door.. The Vice President, Senate and Secretary arose upon entrance of the President. Secretary at War attended and sat at left hand of the President of the United States without the bar. President of the United

Document 11b. Minutes of the Senate describing George Washington's oath of office ceremony, April 30, 1789. [National Archives].

Philadelphia April 4th 1789.

Dear General

I most sincerely congratulate you upon your election to the most dignified station in the nation, and I pray God to continue your services to your Country for many years.

As you will soon be involved in a multiplicity of Business, I take the liberty to beg the favor of such Testimonial of my Services in the late army as you may think me entitled to. I have with reluctance made this application, but as circumstances may render it necessary, trust I shall be excused.

With most respectfull complements to your Lady I have the Honor to be with the most perfect attachment & esteem Dear General your most

Obd. Servt.

Daniel Brodhead

Sir

Monticello Feb. 14. 1790

I have duly received the letter of the 21st. of January with which you have honored me, and no longer hesitate to undertake the office to which you are pleased to call me. your desire that I should come on as quickly as possible is a sufficient reason for me to postpone every matter of business, however pressing, which admits postponement. still it will be the close of the ensuing week before I can get away, & then I shall have to go by the way of Richmond, which will lengthen my road. I shall not fail however to go on with all the dispatch possible nor to satisfy you, I hope, when I shall have the honor of seeing you at New York, that the circumstances which prevent my immediate departure, are not under my controul. I have now that of being with sentiments of the most perfect respect & attachment, Sir

Your most obedient & most humble servant

Th Jefferson

The President of the U.S.

Document 13. Jefferson's letter to President Washington accepting nomination, February 1, 1790. [National Archives]

To Sen.r Don Francisco Chiappe, agent of the
United States at Morocco.

New York 1.st Dec.r 1789.

Sir,

Both before and since the Arrival of your Letter
of 20.th August 1788 to the President of the late Congress,
the Government of the United States has been in a State
so deranged by the Measures preparatory to the Change
which has lately taken place, that proper Attention could
not be paid to our foreign, and indeed to many other
important Affairs.

It gives me Pleasure to inform you that these
Embarrassments diminish daily. The new Government
has been organized and peaceably established, agreeably
to the Constitution, of which for your Information, I
herewith enclose a Copy.

General Washington, who so gloriously and suc-
-cessfully conducted our military Operations, during the
late War, has, by the unanimous Votes of the States,
been appointed to the supreme executive Authority by
the Title of President of the United States. The
two Houses of the national Legislature have been elected,
and have assembled; but their first Session was wholly
employed in passing such Laws and domestic Regula-
-tions, as the State of the Nation rendered indispensable,
and would not admit of any Delay. They are soon
to assemble again, and then their Attention will be
extended to such Objects as the Situation of our foreign
Affairs may point out; for without their Consent no
Monies can be raised or appropriated.

Document 14a. Jay's letter to U.S. agent at Morocco, December 1, 1789. [National Archives]

The President has appointed Mr. Jefferson to the office of Secretary of State, which now includes the Department of foreign Affairs; but he being still absent, though daily expected, the President has been pleased to direct me to write to you on these Subjects; and to explain to you the Reasons why you have not received more frequent and regular Advices from this Country.

The President has been informed how well you and your Brothers deserve of the United States; and I am persuaded that due Attention will be paid to you and their Services.

I have now the Honor of transmitting to you a Letter from the President to his Imperial Majesty, with a Copy of it for your Information. I also enclose a Letter for your Brother Guiseppe, which I request the Favor of you to forward to him.

I have the Honor to be, &c.

{signed} John Jay.

To Senr. Don Guiseppe Chiappe, agent of the
United States at Mogador.

New York 1st. December 1789.

Sir,

Since the Conclusion of the Treaty between his Imperial Majesty the Emperor of Morocco and the United States of America, a great Revolution and Change in their Government, has peaceably and with general Consent, been made and established.

While these important Measures were preparing and under Consideration, the Attention of the United States to their foreign Affairs necessarily became interrupted;

for

To the President and the Hon'ble the

Congress of the United States of America.—

The Memorial of the Representatives of the people of Kentucky in Convention assembled pursuant to an Act of the Legislature of Virginia passed the 18th day of December 1789, entitled an Act concerning the erection of the District of Kentucky into an Independent State.

Humbly Sheweth, That the Inhabitants of this Country are as warmly devoted to the American Union and as firmly attached to the present happy establishment of the Federal Government as any of the Citizens of the United States.

That migrating from thence, they have with great hazard and difficulty effected their present settlements.—The hope of increasing numbers could alone have supported the early Adventurers under those arduous exertions; they have the satisfaction to find that hope verified. At this day, the population, and strength of this Country, render it fully able, in the opinion of your Memorialists, to form and support an efficient Domestic Government—

The inconveniencies resulting from its local situation as a part of Virginia at first but little felt, have for some time been objects of their most serious attention; & which occasioned application to the Legislature of Virginia for redress.

(Copy)

District of Kentucky (Toaut.)

In Convention July 28th 1790.

Resolved, That it is expedient for, and the will of, the good people of the District of Kentucky that the same be erected into an Independent State on the terms and conditions specified in an Act of the Virginia assembly passed the 18th day of December 1789 entitled an Act concerning the erection of the District of Kentucky into an Independent State

Resolved, That We the Representatives of the people of Kentucky duly elected in pursuance of an Act of the Legislature of Virginia passed the 18th day of December 1789 entitled an Act concerning the erection of the District of Kentucky into an Independent State, and now met in Convention having with full powers maturely investigated the expediency of the proposed seperation on the terms and conditions specified in the above recited Act; do by these presents and in behalf of the people of Kentucky accept the terms and conditions, and do declare that on the first day of June 1792 the said District of Kentucky shall become a State seperate from and independent of the Government of Virginia, and that the said Articles become a solemn compact binding on the said People.

Here your Memorialists would acknowledge with peculiar pleasure the benevolence of Virginia in permitting them to remove the evils arising from that source by assuming upon themselves a State of Independence.

This they have thought expedient to do on the terms and conditions stipulated in the above recited Act, and have fixed on the first day of June 1792 as the period when the said Independence shall commence.

It now remains with the President and the Congress of the United States to sanction these proceedings, by an Act of their Honble Legislature prior to the first day of November 1791 for the purpose of receiving into the faederal Union the people of Kentucky by the name of, THE STATE of KENTUCKY.

Should this determination of your Memorialists meet the approbation of the General Government, they have to call a Convention to form a Constitution, subsequent to the Act of Congress and prior to the day fixed for the Independence of this Country.

When your Memorialists reflect on the present comprehensive system of Federal Government; and when they also recollect the determination of a former Congress on this subject they are left without a doubt that the object of their wishes will be accomplished

And your Memorialists as in duty bound shall forever pray

Attest.
Thomas Todd Clk. C.

(Signed) George Muter Pr.

Document 15c. Petition to make the Kentucky District a state, July 28, 1790. [National Archives]

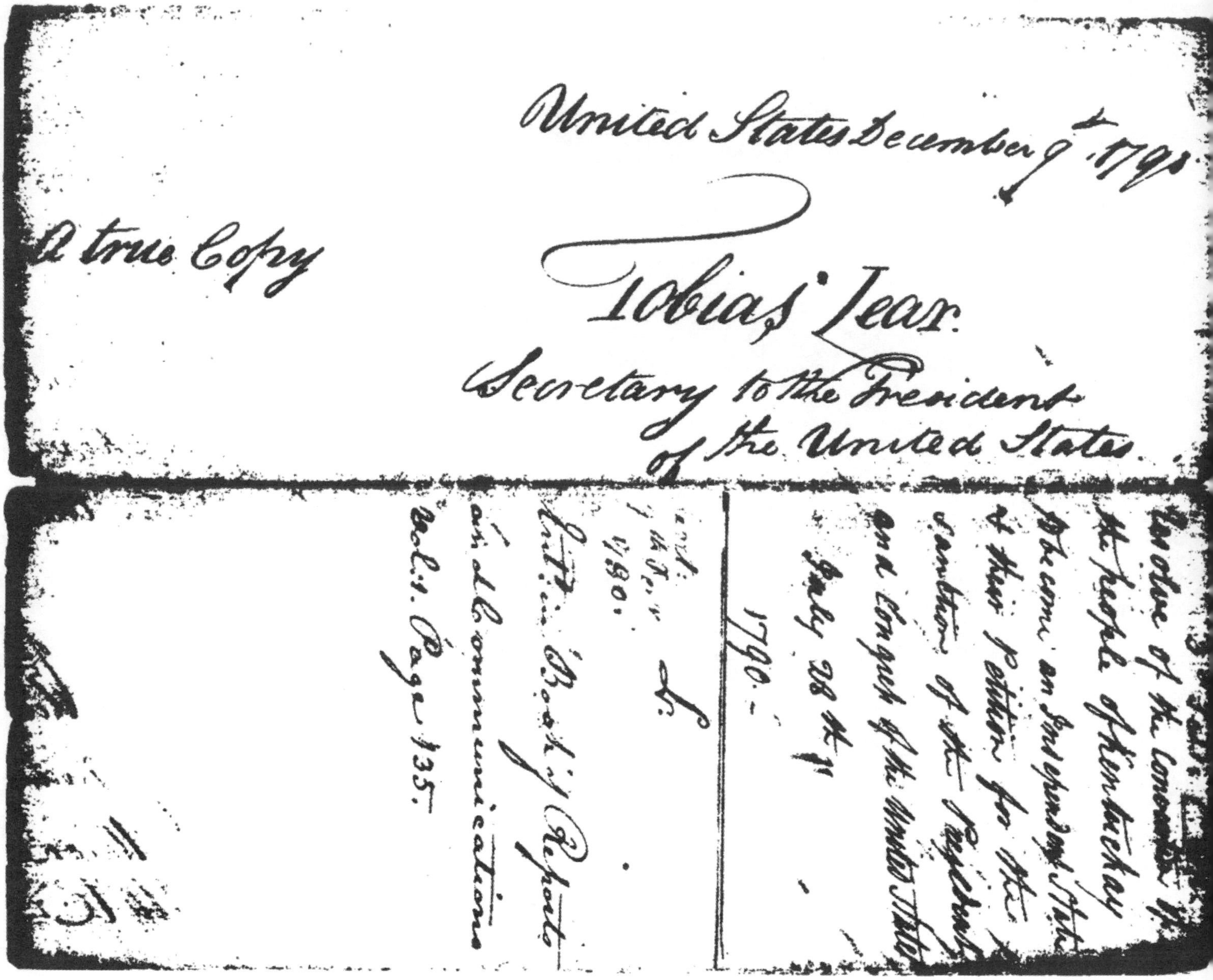

United States December 9. 1790.

A true Copy

Tobias Lear.
Secretary to the President
of the United States

[handwritten docket, rotated:]

Another of the Come....
the People of Kentuckey
District, an Enlargement State
of their Petition for the
Erection of the People...
and Congress of the United States
July 28th 1790. —

ent:
] h.d.n.
1790.
L:
Letter Book, of Reports
and Communications
Vol. 1. Page 135.

United States
vs
William Blount
} Upon Impeachment of the House
of Representatives of the United States
of High Crimes & Misdemeasnors.

In Senate of the United States. Dec.r 24.th 1798.

The aforesaid William Blount saving and reserving to
himself all exceptions to the uncertainty and imperfections of the
articles of Impeachment, by Jared Ingersoll and Alexander James
Dallas, his Attornies, comes and defends the Force and Injury &
says, that he to the Articles of Impeachment preferred against him, by
the house of Representatives of the United States ought not to be
compelled to answer, because he says that the 8th Article of certain
Amendments of the Constitution of the United States, having
been ratified by Nine States, after the same was in a
Constitutional manner proposed to the Consideration of the
several States in the Union, is of equal obligation with the original
Constitution and now forms a part thereof; and that by the same
8th Article it is declared and provided that "In all criminal
"prosecutions the accused shall enjoy the right to a speedy and
"publick trial. by an impartial Jury, of the State and District
. in the crime shall have been committed; which district shall
.have been previously ascertained by law; and to be informed of
"the nature and cause of the accusation; to be confronted with the
"witnesses against him; to have compulsory process for obtaining witnesses
"in his favour; and to have the assistance of counsel for his defence."
That proceedings by Impeachment are provided and permitted by
the Constitution of the United States only on charges of Treason, Bribery, or other High Crimes
and Misdemeasnors, alleged to have been committed by the President, Vice President or any Civil Officer
of the United States in the execution of their Offices held under
the United States; as appears by the 7th Clause of the third Section
of the First Article. and other Articles and Clauses contained in the
Constitution of the United States. That although true it is
that he the said William Blount, was a Senator of the United
States from the State of Tenesee, at the several periods in the
said Articles of Impeachment referred to, yet that he the said William is not now a Senator,
and is not nor was at the several periods so as aforesaid referred
to, a civil Officer of the United States, nor is he the said William
in and by the said articles charged with having committed any crime

or Misdemeanor in the Execution of any civil Office held under the United States, nor with any Mal-conduct in a civil Office or abuse of any Publick Trust in the Execution thereof.

That the Courts of Common Law of a Criminal Jurisdiction of the States wherein the Offences in the said Articles recited are said to have been committed, as well as those of the United States are competent to the cognizance, prosecution & punishment of the said Crimes and Misdemeasnors, if the same have been perpetrated as has been suggested and charged by the said Articles, which however he utterly denies. All which the said William is ready to verify — And prays Judgment whether this High Court will have further Cognizance of this Suit, and of the said impeachment and whether he the said William to the said Articles of Impeachment so as aforesaid preferred by the House of Representatives of the United States, ought to be compelled to answer.

Jared Ingersoll

A. J. Dallas.

1798
Dec 24

Document 16b. Plea to the Court of Impeachment in defense of William Blount, December 24, 1798. [National Archives]

Gentlemen.

Lancaster, March 17th 1789.

The Corporation of this Borough have been instructed by the Inhabitants thereof, and of the adjoining Townships to address You. The New Constitution, to which we anxiously look up as the Means of establishing the Empire of America on the most sure and solid Basis, is 'ere now in Motion, and one of the Objects of Congress will be to fix on a permanent Place of Residence, where their exclusive Jurisdiction can be conveniently and safely exercised. Should the general Interests of the Union point out an Inland Central Situation as preferable to that of a Sea-port for the future Residence of that Honorable Body, We humbly presume to offer ourselves as Candidates for that distinguished Honor. We feel ourselves more emboldened to enter into the Lists, as we find this Borough has been lately put in Nomination by the Honorable Congress under the former Confederation, and we suffer ourselves to be flattered, that the Reasons which then subsisted for such a Choice, exist more strongly at the present Moment. As an Inland Town, we do not perceive ourselves inferior to any within the Dominion of the United States. Our Lands are remarkably fertile and in a high State of Cultivation. Our Country is possessed of every Conveniency for Water Works, as will appear by the Draft herewith sent, and peculiarly healthy; our Water is good. Every necessary Material for Building is to be had in the greatest Quantity desired, and at the most reasonable Rates, and we venture to assert, that there is no Part of the United States which can boast within the Compass of ten Miles the same Number of Waggons and good Teams with ourselves.

We are sensible that Dealing in Generals will have no Effect with dispassionate and temperate Minds. We venture therefore to descend into a more minute Recapitulation & pledge ourselves to you for the Truth and Correctness of the following Statement, which has been made upon the most thorough Examination and in the Carefullest Manner in our Power without Exaggeration. The Borough of Lancaster is a Square encompassing one Mile in Length from the Centre (the Court House) by the Main Streets which intersect it at right Angles. We have five Public Buildings, Including an elegant Court House 58 Feet by 48 Feet. In the second Story thereof is a very handsome Room 44 Feet by 32 Feet in the Clear, and two convenient adjoining Rooms, each being 22 Feet by 16 Feet in the Clear. There are seven Places of Public Worship besides a temporary Synagogue, belonging to the respective Societies of Episcopalians, Presbyterians, Lutherans, Reformed Church of Heidleberg Moravians, Quakers, and Catholics. Within the Compass of the Borough an Enumeration of the Dwelling Houses was actually taken in 1786, and the Number then built was 678, which since

since that Period has considerably increased. Many of the Houses are large, elegant and commodi and would in our Idea accommodate Congress and their Suite at this Period without Inconven =ence. Boarding and Lodgings are to be had at very easy Rates; According to the best Co =putation we can make there are within this Borough about 4200 Souls. A Number of g Roads pass through this Place; — we are a thorough-fare to the 4 Cardinal Points of the Comp. Labour is to be had at 2/. ⅌day. — The Current Prices of Provisions are: Wheat 5/6. R 3/. Indian Corn 2/6. Oats 1/6 ⅌ Bushel, Best Hay £3 ⅌ Ton. Pork and Stall Fed Beef from 2 to 30/ ⅌ Ct. Veal 3 & Mutton 3/2 ⅌ lb. All Kinds of Poultry in great Abundance & reasonabl Shad, Rock & Salmon are plentifully supplied to us from the Susquehanna in their Seaso. The Price of Firewood the last Season has been for Hickory 12/6 & Oak 8/6 ⅌ Cord. —

Within the Distance of 9 & 30 Miles from this Place, we have 6 Furnaces, 7 Forges. Slitting Mills, and 2 Rolling Mills for the Manufacture of Iron. Within a Compass of Miles square we have 18 Merchant Mills, 16 Saw Mills, 1 Fulling Mill, 4 Oil Mills, 5 H Mills, 2 Boring and Grinding Mills for Gun Barrels and 8 Tan Yards. There are a great Nun of convenient Sites for Water Works still unoccupied. Within the Borough alone are the following Manufacturers and Artizans Viz: 14 Hatters, 36 Shoemakers, 4 Tanners, 17 Sadler 25 Taylors, 22 Butchers, 25 Weavers, 3 Stocking Weavers, 25 Blacksmiths & White Smith's, 61 Wrights, 21 Bricklayers & Masons, 12 Bakers, 30 Carpenters, 11 Coopers, 6 Plaisterers, 6 Clock Watch Makers, 6 Tobacconists, 4 Dyers, 1 Brush Maker, 7 Turners, 7 Gun Smiths, 5 Rope Ma 4 Tin Men, 2 Brass Founders, 3 Skin Dressers, 7 Nailers, 5 Silversmiths 3 Potters & 3 Copper Sm besides their respective Journey Men and Apprentices. There are also 3 Breweries, 3 Brick Ya 2 Printing Presses and 40 Houses of Public Entertainment within the Borough. — The Materia for Building, such as Stone Lime, Sand, Clay proper for Brick, Timber, Boards &c are to be in the greatest Abundance, at the most reasonable Rates. We would instance as one Particula that the best Pine Boards from the Susquehanna are delivered here at 5/6 ⅌ hundred Feet

Our Centrical Situation will be best determined by the Consideration of the following =tances, which pursue the Courses of the Roads now occupied but may be shortened, and which we cons as accurately taken Viz. —

From Lancaster to Philadelphia	66 Miles	To Baltimore by McCalls Ferry	60 M.
to Wilmington	50.	To Trenton by the Swedes Ford	90.
to Newport	47.	To Coryell's Ferry on Delaware	87.
to Head of Elk	45	To Reading	31.
to North East	42.	To Easton	83.
to Rock Run	38	To Wrights Ferry on Susquehanna	10.
to Mouth of Susquehanna	42	To Harris's	36.

To Andersons Ferry on Susquehanna . . 13 Miles To Nolands Ferry on Potowmack . . 93 Miles
To McCalls Ferry on do . . . . 16. To Harpers on . . . . do . . . . 110.
To Peach Bottom on . . . do . . . 22.

  We have presumed Gentlemen to make the foregoing Statement, and Address it to You. The general National Interests of America at large, Will We are perswaded be fully considered, when the important Point of the future permanent Residence of Congress is agitated & determined on by that Honorable Body. We have Reason to think that William Hamilton Esqr. who is entitled to the Rent Charges and unoccupied Parts of this Borough would chearfully meet every Wish of Congress, so far as his Property is concerned.

  Permit us only to add that our Citizens are federal & strongly attached to the new System of Government.

    We have the Honor to be with every Sentiment of Respect

      Gentlemen
       Your most faithful
       And Obedient Humble Servts
       In behalf of the Corporation & Citizens

       Edwd Hand Burgess

The Honorable
   Robert Morris & William Maclay Esquires

The Honorable

Robert Morris & William Maclay Esqrs
Senators of the State of Pennsylvania in
the Congress of the United States
at
New York

To the Senate & House of Representatives of the United States—

The Memorial of the Pennsylvania Society for promoting the Abolition of Slavery, the relief of free Negroes unlawfully held in bondage, & the Improvement of the Condition of the African Race—

Respectfully Sheweth,

That from a regard for the happiness of Mankind an Association was formed several years since in this State by a number of her Citizens of various religious denominations for promoting the Abolition of Slavery & for the relief of those unlawfully held in bondage. A just & accurate Conception of the true Principles of liberty, as it spread through the land, produced accessions to their numbers, many friends to their Cause, & a legislative co-operation with their views, which, by the blessing of Divine Providence, have been successfully directed to the relieving from bondage a large number of their fellow Creatures of the African Race— They have also the Satisfaction to observe, that in consequence of that Spirit of Philanthropy & genuine liberty which is generally diffusing its beneficial Influence, such Institutions are gradually forming at home & abroad.

That mankind are all formed by the same Almighty being, alike objects of his Care & equally designed for the Enjoyment of Happiness the Christian Religion teaches us to believe, & the Political Creed of America fully coincides with the Position. Your Memorialists, particularly engaged in attending to the Distresses arising from Slavery, believe it their indispensible Duty to present this Subject to your notice— They have observed with great Satisfaction, that many important & salutary Powers are vested in you for "promoting the Welfare & securing the blessings of liberty to the "People of the United States". And as they conceive, that these blessings ought rightfully to be administered, without distinction of Colour, to all descriptions of People, so they indulge themselves in the pleasing expectation, that nothing, which can be done for the relief of the unhappy objects of their care, will be either omitted or delayed.

From a persuasion that equal liberty was originally the Portion, & is still the Birthright of all men & influenced by the strong ties of Humanity & the Principles of their Institution, your Memorialists conceive themselves

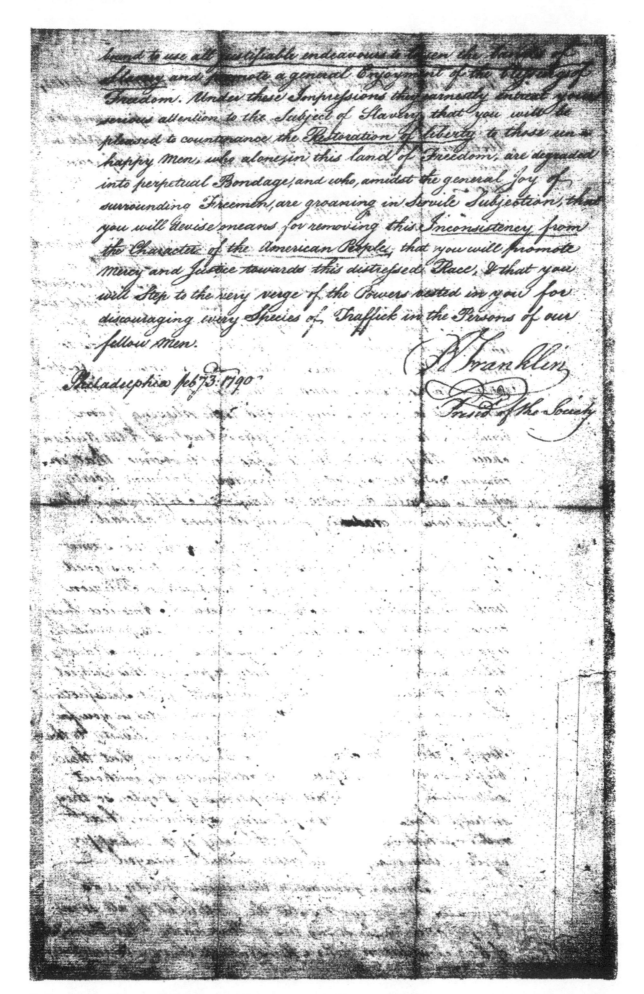

bound to use all justifiable endeavours to loosen the bands of Slavery and promote a general Enjoyment of the blessings of Freedom. Under these Impressions they earnestly intreat your serious attention to the Subject of Slavery, that you will be pleased to countenance the Restoration of liberty to those unhappy Men, who alone in this land of Freedom, are degraded into perpetual Bondage, and who, amidst the general Joy of surrounding Freemen, are groaning in Servile Subjection, that you will devise means for removing this Inconsistency from the Character of the American People, that you will promote mercy and Justice towards this distressed Race, & that you will Step to the very verge of the Powers vested in you for discouraging every Species of Traffick in the Persons of our fellow Men.

Philadelphia feb 3. 1790

B Franklin
Presid of the Society

Document 18b. Franklin's petition to abolish slavery, February 3, 1790. [National Archives]

Honorable Sirs

From the manner in which I was called before this House yesterday, I have reason to suspect an unfavorable disposition in them, towards some parts in my late publications. What the parts are against which they object, or what those objections are, are wholly unknown to me. If any Gentleman has presented any Memorial to this House, which contains any charge against me, or any ways allude in a censurable manner, to my Character or interest, so as to become the ground of any such charge, I request, as a Servant under your Authority, an attested Copy of that charge, and in my personal Character as a freeman of the Country, I demand it. I attended at the bar of this House yesterday, as their Servant, tho' the warrant did not express my official Station, which I conceive it right to have done, otherwise it could not be compulsive unless backed by a Magistrate.—— My hopes were, that I should be made acquainted with the Charges, and admitted to my defence which I am all times ready to make either in writing or personally

I cannot in duty to my Character as a freeman, submit to be censured unheard. I have evidence which I presume will justify me. And I entreat this House to consider how great their reproach will be, when it should be told, that they passed a sentence upon me without hearing me, and that a copy of the charge against me was refused to be me; and likewise, how much that reproach will be aggravated should I afterwards prove the censure of this House to be a Libel, grounded upon a

... which ~~they~~ refused to enquire fully

I make my application to the heart of every Gentleman in this House, that he, before he decides on a point that may affect my reputation, will duly consider his own. Did I covet popular praise I should not ~~send~~ ~~this~~ send this letter: my wish is, that by thus stating my situation to the House, that they may not commit an act they can not Justify.

I have obtained Fame Honor and Credit in this Country. I am Proud of those honors. and as they can be taken from me by any unjust Censure, grounded on a concealed charge, therefore it will become my duty afterwards to do Justice to myself. I have no favor to ask more than to be candidly and honorably dealt by, and such being my right, I ought to have no doubt but this House will proceed accordingly. Should Congress be disposed to hear me, I have to request that they will give me sufficient Time to prepare.

I am Honorable Sirs
Your honors most obt
and dutiful Humble Servant

Thos Paine

Philadelphia
Jan'y 7th 1779

Document 19b. Paine's petition to be informed of charges, January 7, 1779. [National Archives]

By the United States in Congrefs affembled,

October 12, 1785.

WHEREAS it is indifpenfibly neceffary, for the fupport of the federal government, that the ftates fhould fupply their quotas of money, for the purpofes ftated in the eftimates of the fubfifting requifitions of Congrefs.

And whereas certificates for the intereft arifing on loan-office certificates, and other certificates of liquidated debts, previoufly to the laft day of December 1782, from the deficiencies of fome of the ftates to comply with the requifition of the 4th September, 1782, and 27th and 28th of April, 1784, will, in purfuance of the requifition of the 27th of September, 1785, be iffued by the commiffioners of the continental loan-offices in fuch ftates.

And whereas the extra certificates which the faid commiffioners may iffue for the payment of the faid intereft, fhould be called in or redeemed by the deficient ftates in order to compleat their refpective quotas of the intereft of the domeftic debt, fpecified in the faid requifitions of the 4th September, 1782, and 27th and 28th April, 1784.

RESOLVED,

That the feveral ftates be earneftly called on to compleat without delay the whole of their quotas of the requifitions laft mentioned, and that fuch of the ftates as may be deficient in paying their refpective quotas of the intereft of the domeftic debt purfuant to the faid requifitions, be required to collect and pay into the public treafury the amount of fuch deficiencies, either in certificates to be iffued by the commiffioners of the continental loan-offices, purfuant to the requifition of the 27th September, 1785, for the payment of the faid intereft, or in fpecie, to be applied to the redemption of fuch certificates; provided that the fum fo to be paid into the treafury in intereft certificates as part of the requifition of the 27th and 28th April 1784, fhall not at any time exceed the proportion of facilities to be paid into the treafury, agreeably to the requifition laft mentioned.

245

What Plan or System Congress will adopt relative to the hostile Barbary States is not yet decided. The one you suggest has Advantages. The great Question I think is, whether we shall wage War or pay "Tribute". I for my Part prefer War, and consequently am ready for every proper Plan of uniting and multiplying their Enemies.—

Mrs Jay joins with me in requesting the Favor of you to present our Compliments and best Wishes to the Marchioness.—

I have the Honor to be &c:

(signed) John Jay

To the Honorable John Adams Esquire

New York 21st February 1787

Dr Sir

I had the Pleasure of receiving two Days ago your Letter of the 30th November by Mr Mitchel — it was the next Morning laid before Congress.

Nine States are now represented, but as yet little Progress has been made in the Business before them. My Report on the Infractions of the Treaty complained of by Britain, has been referred to a new Committee, and I think a very good one; various opinions

Opinions prevail on the Subject and I cannot conjecture what the ultimate Decision of Congress on it will be. —

The Insurrection in Massachusetts seems to be suppressed, and I herewith enclose the Papers containing the Details we have received since the 6th Instant when I wrote to you by the Packet. Your Sentiments on that Business prove to have been just. I ought to write you fully on many Subjects, but I am not yet enabled — when I shall be cannot be predicted. Our Government is unequal to the Task assigned it, and the People begin also to perceive its Inefficiency. — The Convention gains ground — New York has instructed her Delegates to move in Congress for a Recommendation to the States to form a Convention; for this State dislikes the Idea of a Convention unless countenanced by Congress. I do not promise myself much further immediate Good from the Measure than that it will tend to approximate the public Mind to the Changes which ought to take place. It is hard to say what those Changes should be exactly — there is one however which I think would be much for the better, Vizt. to distribute the federal Sovereignty, into its three proper Departments of executive, legislative and judicial; for that Congress should act in these . . . . different Capacities was I think a great Mistake in our Policy. —

This State in their present Session has greatly moderated

moderated their Severities to the Tories; a Law having been passed to restore a very great Majority of those resident here to the Rights of Citizens. I hope all Discriminations inconsistent with the Treaty of Peace will gradually be abolished, as Resentment gives place to Reason and good Faith. But my Dear Sir, we labor under one sad Evil, the Treasury is empty tho' the Country abounds in Resources, and our People are far more unwilling than unable to pay Taxes. Hence result Disappointment to our Creditors, Disgrace to our Country, and I fear Disinclination in too many to any Mode of Government that can easily and irresistibly open their Purses. Much is to be done, and the Patriots must have Perseverance as well as Patience. —

      I am, Dr Sir &c:

      (signed) John Jay. —

     To the Honorable John Adams Esqr —

     New York 2d April 1787

Dr Sir

   Since my last to you of 25th February I have not been favored with any Letters from you. —

    Congress have made some Progress in my Report on your Letter of 4th March 1786 and the Papers that accompanied it; they lately passed the Resolutions of which you will find a Copy

        here

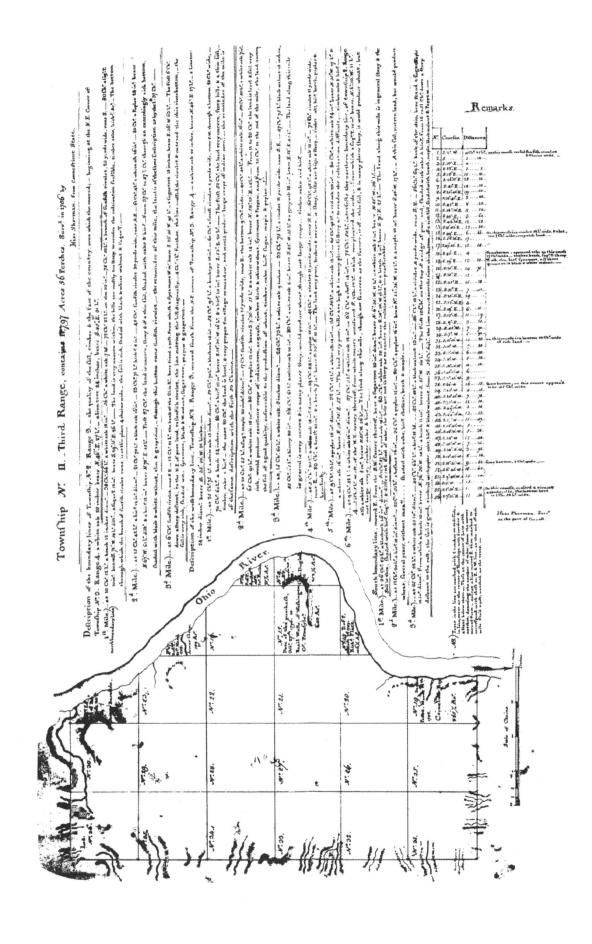

Document 22. Map made in accordance with the
1785 Land Ordinance, 1786. [National Archives]

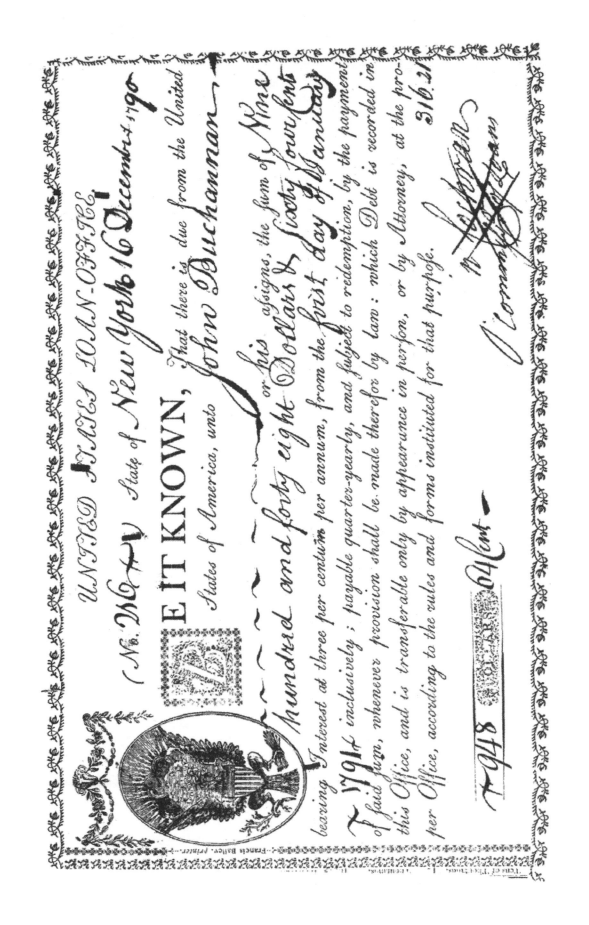

UNITED STATES LOAN-OFFICE,

(No. 266) State of New York 16 December 1790.

BE IT KNOWN, That there is due from the United States of America, unto John Buchannan or his assigns, the sum of Nine hundred and forty eight Dollars & sixty four cents bearing Interest at three per centum per annum, from the first day of January 1791 inclusively; payable quarter-yearly, and subject to redemption, by the payment of said sum, whenever provision shall be made therefor by law: which Debt is recorded in this Office, and is transferable only by appearance in person, or by Attorney, at the pro-per Office, according to the rules and forms instituted for that purpose.

316.21

948 DOLLARS 64 Cent.

—Francis Bailey, Printer.—

Document 23a. U.S. loan certificate, December 16, 1790. [National Archives]

For value received, I assign two thirds of the within Debt to the United States.

New-York, 24 day of Oct. 1832.

Mary Buchanan

Depreciated Loan Office Certificates Cancelled, &
Original Certificates presented & cancelled, & their Specie Value.

Date of old Certificates	In whose favor Issued	N of Certificate	N of Cert Cancelled	Their amount	Partial amount	Amount in Dollars	Rate of Exchange Doll. 90 &	Total Amount Specie Value Doll. 90	Total Amount Specie Doll. &
John Cunningham Jr.									
1778 June 15	Willm. B. Townsend	4190	1	400	400				
"	Do	1459	1	1000	1000	1400	35.44.2	------	496.79
			2.						
David Gilmore									
1778 July 21	David Gilmore	6099	1	200	-----	200	30.17.2	60.34	
1779 May 29	Joshua Prentiss	8746 / 8747	2	400	-----	800	7.47.1	60.17	
Octo 26	David Gilmore	373	1	1000	-----	1000	4.41	44.50	
27	Do	7615	1	500	-----	500	4.39.3	22.16	187.27
			5.						
Hezekiah Broad									
1778 March 18	Joseph Morse	2004	1	600	-----	600	52.84.5	317.57	
1779 Feb 4	Do	4976 / 4977	2	300	-----	600	11.31.3	68.8	385.65
			3.						
John Templeman									
1779 Feb 9	Joseph McLellan	5086	1	300	-----	300	11.5.7	33.17	
March 17	Simeon Mayo	8458	1	400	-----	400	9.45.1	38.	
April 9	John Fox	7450	1	500	-----	500	8.74.4	44.12	115.29
			3.						
William Lambert									
1778 March 6	Jackson Tracy & Tracy	5550	1	200	-----	200	55.78.5	111.67	
April 27	Thomas Chase	5807	1	200	-----	200	44.20.7	88.41	
23	Ebenr Woodward	5789	1	200	-----	200	45.3.1	90.6	
27	Abner Pease	5819	1	200	200				
"	Thomas Chase	4354	1	300	300	500	44.20.7	221.14	
June 5	Ebenr Thayer	1454	1	1000	-----	1000	37.11.0	371.20	
1779 Jan 23	Joseph Tucker	4775	1	300	-----	300	12.5.3	36.16	
25	Elisha Doane	2363 / 2365 / 2399 / 2402	7	600	-----	4200	11.84.3		
28	Do	4856 / 4865	10	400	-----	4000	11.68.2	470.30	
			24.						

Document 24a. Pages from the government Loan Office ledger, January 1, 1788. [National Archives]

Certificates, Issued for their Specie Value.

Specie Loan Office Certificates Issued.

Date of Issuing New Certificates	Their Number	In whose Favor Issued	Date of New Certificate & Commencement of Interest	Denomination of each Certificate Dollars 90th	No. Voucher	Total Amount Issued Dollars 90th
1787 Decemr. 15th	3530	John Cunningham	1st Jany. 1788	. . . .	25.	496.79
"	3531	David Gilmore	— " —	. . . .	26.	187.27
16th	3532	Hezekiah Broad	— " —	. . . .	27.	385.65
20th	3533	John Templeman	— " —	. . . .	28.	715.29
24th	3534	William Lambert	— " —	. . . .	29.	1000.00

Document 24b. Pages from the government Loan Office ledger, January 1, 1788. [National Archives]

be appointed, not only in different States, but in different places of the same State. If commissioners are appointed, for instance, in Charleston, the citizens must attend from the remotest parts of the State, and be worried in travelling backwards and forwards to seek for witnesses, many of whom may be dead, or removed into other countries—not to mention the length of time and the enormous expense which so complicated a business must occasion. He concluded, by declaring it to be his opinion, that the proposition, if agreed to, would throw things into confusion and perplexity, which he could not see the extent of: he should, therefore oppose it.

Mr. MADISON.—If paper, or the honor of statues or medals, can discharge the debts of justice, payable in gold or silver, we cannot only exonerate ourselves from those due to the original holders, but from those of the assignees; so far as paper goes the latter have received the compensation. If honor can discharge the debt, they have received civil honors; look round to the officers of every Government in the Union, and you find them sharing equal honors with those bestowed on the original creditors. But, sir, the debt due in gold and silver is not payable either in honor, appointments, or in paper.

Gentlemen say it will work injustice; but are we not as much bound to repair the injustice done by the United States? Yet I do not believe the assertion has been established by any thing that has been urged in its support. The gentleman from Maryland, (Mr. STONE,) acknowledges that there is a moral obligation to compensate the original holders; how will they get what he admits is their due? He is willing to make an effort by applying the resources of the country to that purpose; but if we are to judge by the sentiments of other gentlemen who have spoken on this occasion, we have little to expect from that quarter. Suppose the debt had depreciated to a mere trifle, and suppose the sale of the Western Territory had extinguished the certificates, let me ask, whether, if the United States had thus exonerated themselves from the obligation to the assignee, whether the claim of the original holder would not still remain in its full force in a moral view? But believing the point of justice to be exhausted, I will just add one remark upon the practicability. The transferred certificates, generally, will show the names of the original holders, and here there is no difficulty. With respect to those granted to the heads of either of the five great departments, the books of the Treasurer of Loans, as well as the accounts of those departments now in the Treasury, will designate with a great degree of accuracy, and this may be followed up by the usual mode of obtaining evidence; and I believe, every security may be provided against fraud in this case that was provided in the case of the commissioners who were sent into the respective States for ascertaining and liquidating the claims of individuals. That there will be some difficulty I admit, but it is enough for me that it is not insuperable; and I trust, with the assistance which the cause of equity and justice will ever obtain

from the members of the National Legislature, they will easily be surmounted.

Mr. WHITE wished to ascertain a fact which had been mentioned. He did not mean to infer that gentlemen had related a fact they did not believe; but supposed they might have been misinformed. He asked, whether foreigners had been induced to purchase in our funds by assurances from the ministers of the United States, residing at Foreign Courts, that no variation would be made in the domestic debt.

Mr. BLAND asked his colleague, (Mr. MADISON,) how long he supposed the settlement which he contemplated would take in its completion? For his part he supposed two or three generations might pass away before that object could be accomplished, considering the dispersed situation of the claimants through America, Europe, Asia, and Africa.

Mr. MADISON said, the claims of individuals were presented and liquidated by the Commissioners throughout the United States in nine months; that was the period fixed for that purpose by Congress; he would not say but it was too short, yet he thought this experiment fairly inferred that the ascertainment he contended for could be effected in a short time.

Mr. BOUDINOT had seen an authentic letter, in which the writer mentioned that the opinion of Mr. JEFFERSON was asked, and obtained. He also had reason to believe the sentiments of the President of the late Congress were given to the same effect.

The committee now rose, and the House adjourned.

MONDAY, February 22.

The House proceeded to consider the amendments of the Senate to the bill providing for the enumeration of the inhabitants of the United States, and agreeing to a part and disagreeing to other parts; a message was sent to the Senate informing them thereof.

PUBLIC CREDIT.

The House then resolved itself into a Committee on the Report of the Secretary of the Treasury, Mr. BALDWIN in the Chair.

Mr. MADISON's proposition still under consideration.

Mr. PAGE.—As the worthy and eloquent member who replied to me did not answer the questions I put to the committee, I suppose he either did not hear them, did not understand me, or could not answer them. I hope, before the committee decide, they will attempt at least to resolve them. I asked, where is the injustice of the States complying with its engagements made to the first holders of certificates, as far as the case admits? Where is the justice of doing more for the assignee than he or his assignor expected could or would be done? Where is the breach of faith in Government, if it paid its whole debt with justice blended with mercy? Where is the interference in contracts, when the proposition is to comply sacredly, as far as the case will admit,

Richmond Supervisors office Aug 13th 1794

Sir

Having necessarily been absent from Town for two mails past, yours of the 8th inst. did not fall into my hands until this morning on my return —

The copy of your letter to the Commissioner of the Revenue as founded upon the intelligence of Mr. Wells, and which you enclosed in the above, communicates your intended conduct when you arrive at Morgan Town on your journey towards Ohio. I feel it my duty to relieve you from the necessity of resting upon a future approbation; in a case where personal danger stands in competition with a duty of office, and have therefore determined to send this immediately by Express to Morgan Town, where I expect you will be found —

The late acts of the people of the country through which you must pass to get to Ohio, renders it certain, that you could not pass in safety, even had you no public money with you, but as you are charged with a considerable sum, that circumstance adds to the necessity for caution — It is also certain that while so extensive an insurrection continues unsuppressed in the powerful counties of Pensylvania which, in a manner, envelope Ohio; it would be folly to attempt measures for executing the laws in the latter, where, even should the people be disposed to comply, their more numerous neighbours would awe them into disobedience, this appearing to be the spirit which actuates those lawless people with regards to the well disposed, who live amongst, or near them. an attempt to enforce the

the laws in Ohio, while the influence of the insurgents is preponderant over that of the Government, could have no probable tendency but to enlist the People of that County, in the cause of the former, and must render the evil greater than it now is.

This Rebellion against Government has now arrived at that degree of atrocity that admits of no longer continuance of that forbearance on the part of Government, which has been practised; decisive measures must, and certainly will, be taken, for apprehending & bringing to condign punishment, the persons who can be ascertained as Actors in the late high Treason which have been committed, and for securing to the Officers of Revenue, their necessary protection in their future operations.

Pending this insurgency in Pennsylvania, it behoves the Officers employed in Virginia, to be vigilant, and as active as possible, to prevent its introduction there. it is not impossible that emissaries will be sent into our Counties of Monogalia, Harrison & Randolph for this purpose; with a view to this circumstance, your remaining at Morgan Town will be extremely proper, and of great public utility. in that situation you will, from time to time, discover whether from any source mischief is to be apprehended, and can take the necessary steps for suppressing the evil. It is unnecessary to mention to you that according to the degree of support which upon any occasion is required in our business, we are to call on the Magistrates and Militia Officers.

How long you shall remain at Morgan Town with a view

to

Document 26b. Supervisor Carrington's letter to U.S. Revenue Inspector Smith about the Whiskey Rebellion, August 13, 1794. [National Archives]

The subjects which I have presented, will depend on your own Judgement, & your proceeding, or not proceeding, to Ohio, must also depend on your intelligence as to the reestablishment of Government in the Counties of Pensylvania, which you in the mean time you will hold such communications with Mr Biggs as you shall judge discreet & proper. write me fully by return of the Express as to such matters as may be passing, and particularly as to the temper of the People in that part of Virginia.

The People of the Monongalia District, even in Ohio, have never shewn any great fondness for joining in the licentious Spirit of their Neighbours in Pensylvania, and I trust, indeed doubt not, that the very unprincipled & base rebellion now raging there, will meet with their decided censure & counteraction ———

I am very respectfully
Sir
your most Obt
Ed Carrington
Supt R.

PS. Herewith you will receive a letter of advice from Mr. Campbell the attorney for the District how you are to act in case of discovery of any emissary from the Insurgents ———

Edward Smith Esq
Inspector of Revenue
now on his way to Morgan Town

Copy Ed Carrington

Document 26c. Supervisor Carrington's letter to U.S. Revenue Inspector Smith about the Whiskey Rebellion, August 13, 1794. [National Archives]

poses;" and the bill, entitled "An act to establish the Treasury Department," for his approbation.

Adjourned to 11 o'clock to-morrow.

WEDNESDAY, SEPTEMBER 2, 1789.

The Senate assembled: present as yesterday.

The bill, entitled "An act to provide for the safe keeping of the acts, records, and seal of the United States, and for other purposes," was read the third time, and

Ordered, That it be committed to Mr. King, Mr. Paterson, and Mr. Read.

The third reading of the bill, entitled "An act for establishing the salaries of the executive officers of government, with their assistants and clerks," was further postponed.

The petition of Harman Stout and others, in behalf of themselves and other clerks in the public offices, was read.

Ordered, That the said petition lie for consideration.

The resolve of the House of Representatives of the 24th of August, one thousand seven hundred and eighty nine, "that certain articles be proposed to the legislatures of the several states, as amendments to the constitution of the United States;" was taken into consideration; and, on motion to amend this clause in the first article, proposed by the House of Representatives, to wit: 'After the first enumeration required by the first article of the constitution, there shall be one representative for every thirty thousand, until the number shall amount to one hundred, by striking out 'one,' and inserting 'two,' between the words 'amount' and 'hundred:'

The yeas and nays being required by one-fifth of the Senators present, the determination was as follows:

YEAS.—Messrs. Dalton, Gunn, Grayson, King, Lee, and Schuyler.—6.

NAYS. Messrs. Bassett, Butler, Carroll, Ellsworth, Elmer, Henry, Johnson, Izard, Morris, Paterson, Read, and Wingate.—12.

So it passed in the negative.

On motion to adopt the first article proposed by the resolve of the House of Representatives, amended as follows: to strike out these words 'after which the proportion shall be so regulated by Congress, that there shall be not less than one hundred representatives, nor less than one representative for every forty thousand persons, until the number of representatives shall amount to two hundred; after which the proportion shall be so regulated by Congress, that there shall not be less than two hundred representatives, nor less than one representative to every fifty thousand persons;' and to substitute the following clause after the words 'one hundred:' to wit, 'to which number one representative shall be added for every subsequent increase of forty thousand, until the representatives shall amount to two hundred, to which one representative shall be added for every subsequent increase of sixty thousand persons:'

It passed in the affirmative.

Adjourned to 11 o'clock to-morrow.

THURSDAY, SEPTEMBER 3, 1789.

The Senate assembled: present as yesterday,

And resumed the consideration of the resolve of the House of Representatives, of the 24th of August, upon the proposed amendments to the constitution of the United States.

A message from the House of Representatives:

Mr. Beckley, their Clerk, informed the Senate, that the President of the United States had affixed his signature to the bill, entitled "An act for registering and clearing of vessels, regulating the coasting trade, and for other purposes;" and to the bill, entitled "An act to establish the Treasury Department;" and had returned them to the House of Representatives;

He also brought up the bill, entitled "An act for allowing compensation to the members of the Senate and House of Representatives of the United States, and to the officers of both Houses;" and informed the Senate, that the House of Representatives had disagreed to the first, second, and third amendments, and had agreed to all the others;

He also brought up the bill, entitled "An act to suspend part of the act, entitled "An act to regulate the collection of the duties imposed by law on the tonnage of ships or vessels, and on goods, wares, and merchandises, imported into the United States." And he withdrew.

The two last mentioned bills were ordered to lie for consideration.

The Senate resumed the consideration of the resolve of the House of Representatives on the amendments to the constitution of the United States.

On motion to adopt the second article proposed in the resolve of the House of Representatives, amended as follows: to strike out these words, 'to the members of Congress,' and insert 'for the service of the Senate and House of Representatives of the United States.'

It passed in the affirmative.

On motion to amend article third, and to strike out these words: 'religion, or prohibiting the free exercise thereof,' and insert 'one religious sect or society in preference to others:'

It passed in the negative.

On motion for reconsideration:

It passed in the affirmative.

On motion that article the third be stricken out:

It passed in the negative.

On motion to adopt the following, in lieu of the third article: 'Congress shall not make any law infringing the rights of conscience, or establishing any religious sect or society:'

It passed in the negative.

On motion to amend the third article, to read thus: 'Congress shall make no law establishing any particular denomination of religion in preference to another, or prohibiting the free exercise thereof, nor shall the rights of conscience be infringed:'

It passed in the negative.

On the question upon the third article as it came from the House of Representatives:

It passed in the negative.

On motion to adopt the third article proposed in the resolve of the House of Representatives, amended by striking out these words, 'nor shall the rights of conscience be infringed:'

It passed in the affirmative.

On the fourth article it was moved to insert these words, ' to instruct their representatives,' after the words ' common good.'

And the yeas and nays being required by one-fifth of the Senators present, the determination was as follows:

YEAS.—Messrs. Grayson, and Lee.—2.

NAYS.—Messrs. Bassett, Carroll, Dalton, Ellsworth, Elmer, Gunn, Henry, Johnson, Izard, King, Morris, Paterson, Read, and Wingate.—14.

So it passed in the negative.

On motion to insert these words after ' press,' ' in as ample a manner as hath at any time been secured by the common law:'

It passed in the negative.

On motion to strike out the words, 'and consult for their common good and:'

It passed in the negative.

And it was agreed, that the further consideration of this article be postponed.

Mr. King, in behalf of the committee appointed on the bill, entitled "An act for allowing compensation to the members of the Senate and House of Representatives of the United States, and to the officers of both Houses," reported amendments: the consideration of which was postponed until to-morrow.

Adjourned to 11 o'clock to-morrow.

FRIDAY, SEPTEMBER 4, 1789.

The Senate assembled: present as yesterday.

The petition of Thomas O'Hara and others, in behalf of themselves and other clerks in the office of the paymaster-general, praying that their compensation may be augmented, was read.

Ordered, That this petition do lie on the table.

The Senate proceeded in the consideration of the resolve of the House of Representatives of the 24th of August, on "Articles to be proposed to the legislatures of the several states, as amendments to the constitution of the United States."

On motion to adopt the fourth article proposed by the resolve of the House of Representatives, to read as followeth: 'That Congress shall make no law, abridging

Eighty-third Congress of the United States of America

AT THE SECOND SESSION

Begun and held at the City of Washington on Wednesday, the sixth day of January, one thousand nine hundred and fifty-four

Joint Resolution

To amend the pledge of allegiance to the flag of the United States of America.

Resolved by the Senate and House of Representatives of the United States of America in Congress assembled, That section 7 of the joint resolution entitled "Joint resolution to codify and emphasize existing rules and customs pertaining to the display and use of the flag of the United States of America", approved June 22, 1942, as amended (36 U. S. C., sec. 172), is amended to read as follows:

"SEC. 7. The following is designated as the pledge of allegiance to the flag: 'I pledge allegiance to the flag of the United States of America and to the Republic for which it stands, one Nation under God, indivisible, with liberty and justice for all'. Such pledge should be rendered by standing with the right hand over the heart. However, civilians will always show full respect to the flag when the pledge is given by merely standing at attention, men removing the headdress. Persons in uniform shall render the military salute."

Speaker of the House of Representatives.

Vice President of the United States and President of the Senate.

APPROVED

JUN 1 4 1954

Document 28. Bill amending the Pledge of Allegiance, June 14, 1954. [National Archives]

ECONOMY STORES

WALTER GOBITAS

Produce, Meats and Groceries

15-17 SUNBURY STREET
MINERSVILLE, PA.

March 7, 1940

Clerk of the Supreme Court
 of the United States
Washington, D.C.

Dear Sir:

In Re: Case of Minersville School District, Appellants,
        vs. Walter Gobitis and others, Plaintiff Appellees

        My chief counsel in this case is

Joseph F. Rutherford of 124 Columbia Heights,

Brooklyn, New York, whom I have substituted in

the place of O. R. Moyle.   I will also be rep-

resented in the case by Mr. H. M. McCaughey of

Philadelphia who is the Attorney of record and

Mr. Hayden C. Covington of Brooklyn, New York.

        Respectfully yours,

        Walter Gobitas

        Walter Gobitas

WG*lg

SUPREME COURT OF THE UNITED STATES

No. 468.—October Term, 1961.

Steven I. Engel et al., Petitioners,
v.
William J. Vitale, Jr., et al.

On Writ of Certiorari to the Court of Appeals of New York.

[June 25, 1962.]

Mr. Justice Black delivered the opinion of the Court.

The respondent Board of Education of Union Free School District No. 9, New Hyde Park, New York, acting in its official capacity under state law, directed the School District's principal to cause the following prayer to be said aloud by each class in the presence of a teacher at the beginning of each school day:

> "Almighty God, we acknowledge our dependence upon Thee, and we beg Thy blessings upon us, our parents, our teachers and our country."

This daily procedure was adopted on the recommendation of the State Board of Regents, a governmental agency created by the State Constitution to which the New York Legislature has granted broad supervisory, executive, and legislative powers over the State's public school system.[1] These state officials composed the prayer which they recommended and published as a part of their "Statement on Moral and Spiritual Training in the Schools," saying: "We believe that this Statement will be subscribed to by all men and women of good will, and we call upon all of them to aid in giving life to our program."

---

[1] See New York Constitution, Art. V, § 4; New York Education Law, §§ 101, 120 *et seq.*, 202, 214–219, 224, 245 *et seq.*, 704, and 801 *et seq.*

PETITION OF WOMEN OF UTAH.

A PETITION

OF

22,626 WOMEN OF UTAH

ASKING FOR

The repeal of certain laws, the enactment of others, and the admission of the Territory of Utah as a State.

JANUARY 13, 1876.—Referred to the Committee on the Judiciary and ordered to be printed without the names.

MEMORIAL OF THE WOMEN OF UTAH TO THE CONGRESS OF THE UNITED STATES.

To the Senate and House of Representatives of the United States of America in Congress assembled :

We, your memorialists, women of Utah, prompted by a due sense of justice, and in consideration of those equal rights so long the proud boast of American citizens, hereby appeal to your honorable body, praying you to grant our petition as shall be herein specified.

We, as a people, are willing to submit to, and do strictly obey, the Constitution and laws of these United States as handed down to us by the fathers of our country ; and we do earnestly pray that you will repeal the anti-polygamy law of 1862 ; also the bill known as the Poland bill ; both being special and unconstitutional measures directed against the people of Utah, holding the peace and happiness of our lives in constant jeopardy by imperiling the safety of our husbands and fathers, by daily and hourly subjecting them to danger of arrest and imprisonment, which would not only deprive us of their society, but also of their support and protection. To you, the executives of a great and powerful nation, we appeal for protection against these cruel and oppressive measures, which have shorn our glorious Constitution of its efficacy and us of every protection but the overruling power of God.

We ask to be relieved from the unjust and law-breaking officials forced upon us by the Government, and that we may have the jurisdiction of our own courts and the selection of our own officers, as we had in the past, when our cities were free from dram-shops, gambling-dens, and houses of infamy. As mothers and sisters, we earnestly appeal to you

Document 31a. Women of Utah petition, December 17, 1875. [National Archives]

for help, that our sons may be saved from drunkenness and vice and our daughters from the power of the seducer; also, that all laws shall be repealed that will restrict us in our religious faith, inasmuch as the Constitution emphatically says: "*Congress shall make no law respecting an establishment of religion, or prohibiting the free exercise thereof;*" also "*No religious test shall ever be required as a qualification to any office o public trust under the United States.*"

And in accordance with our sacred Constitution, which was bequeathed as a protective boon by our forefathers, guaranteeing the right of conscience, we, your memorialists, do humbly pray that no bill or act shall have the sanction of your honorable body that shall in any way conflic or interfere with the belief in and practice of plural marriage as it i practiced by many of the citizens of Utah, and which most of your petitioners have adopted as a portion of their religious faith, in all sincerit believing it to be necessary, not only in remedying evils and producin good in our present existence, but that, without it, man cannot hereafte attain to a fullness of exaltation.

We also ask that each married woman in Utah be granted the righ to homestead or pre-empt one hundred and sixty acres of land in he own name; also, that the citizens of Utah have the right to use for thei own benefit the timber growing on Government land in Utah, which ha been forbidden by the Government officials, to our great detriment thereby depriving us of necessary material for building habitations and otherwise improving our homes.

And, furthermore, we do most earnestly pray that Utah be admitted as a State, with all the rights and privileges guaranteed to every State in this great republic.

That God, in His mercy, will so direct the legislation of your honorable body that we may promptly receive the aid we solicit at your hands, your memorialists will ever pray.

Not one of the 22,626 (twenty-two thousand six hundred and twenty-six) signatures to this memorial has been obtained either by enticement or coercion, and none under twelve years of age have been permitted to sign.

SALT LAKE CITY, *December* 17, 1875.

(Here follow 22,626 signatures.)

○

No. 180

Supreme Court of the United States.

October Term, 1878.

George Reynolds — Plaintiff in Error

vs.

The United States

In Error to the Supreme Court of the ~~State of~~ Territory of Utah.

This cause came on to be heard on the transcript of the record from the Supreme Court of the ~~State of~~ Territory of Utah, and was argued by counsel.

On consideration whereof, It is now here ordered and adjudged by this Court, that the judgment of the said Supreme Court in this cause, be, and the same is hereby, reversed; And that this cause be, and the same is hereby, remanded to the said Supreme Court with instructions to cause the sentence of the district court to be set aside and a new one entered on the verdict in all respects like that before imposed, except so far as it requires the imprisonment to be at hard labor.

per Mr. Chief Justice Waite

5th May 1879

[To be Published October 18th.]

REV. WM. R. CAMPBELL
BOX 1061
Salt Lake City, Utah

October 7, 1899.

MR. EDITOR:- Would you please kindly insert this letter in a prominent place in your valuable paper so as to correct certain false rumors which are afloat in regard to the Roberts case which will come before the next session of Congress. Also please publish the accompanying letter from the Salt Lake Ministerial Association.

1. It is frequently stated in the public prints that the fight which is being made against Mr. Roberts is prompted by partisan motives. The utter falsity of this charge becomes apparent when we remember that his predecessor belonged to the same political party that Mr. Roberts does, and that no fight was ever made to have him expelled from the House. Such a thing was not even thought of in connection with Mr. King.

Moreover, the present political conditions in this State clearly indicate that, if Mr. Roberts is expelled, the man who is elected to fill the vacancy will also be a member of the same party. Hence, neither party has anything to gain or to lose in numerical strength in the present House by the expulsion of Mr. Roberts; but both would gain in prestige before the country and before the whole civilized world by doing their full part in promptly vindicating the historic position of the American Congress in its attitude toward polygamy, the arch-enemy of the home and the greatest foe to our civilization.

The non-partisanship of this movement is further evidenced by the fact that a large percentage, if not the majority, of its staunchest supporters belong to the Democratic party to which Mr. Roberts professes to belong. These men strongly resent the insult offered to the party of Jefferson and Jackson by the proposition that it shall become the champion of the polygamist; and well they may, for as every intelligent person knows, there is nothing in this country which is more anti-democratic, or anti-republican than a polygamous aristocracy, such as Mr. Roberts is seeking to have established upon our American soil.

2. Again, it is frequently stated that we are fighting Mr. Roberts because he is a Mormon, that our campaign is therefore a species of religious persecu-tion. The falsity of this charge is evident from the fact that Mr. King, Mr. Roberts' predecessor, was also a Mormon and a high officer in the said church, the same as Mr. Roberts, though no fight of this kind was ever made upon him because he respected the laws and the covenants made by his people in order to secure amnesty and statehood.

3. Then the apologists of Mr. Roberts in various parts of the country are still industriously asserting that he married all his "wives" before there was any law against polygamy, and they therefore maintain that it is too much to expect a man to put away "wives" whom he married before it was unlawful for him to do so. This is just as false as the other statements referred to. Mr. Roberts married all his "plural wives" long after the law against polygamy had gone into effect; and he married each of them in willful defiance of the laws of his country as well as in defiance of the moral conscience of civilized mankind.

4. Again it is persistently claimed by Mr. Roberts' zealous but ignorant champions that he has obeyed the laws against polygamy and "unlawful cohabita-tion" ever since the manifesto of President Woodruff of the Mormon Church by which the said vicegerent "suspended" the practice of polygamy. There will be abundant evidence presented to Congress to prove that Mr. Roberts has persis-tently defied those laws ever since he was imprisoned for this offense in 1889, and that his case has become very much aggravated since his imprisonment, be-cause he has since that time taken an additional "wife", and because of his continued, willful violation of the solemn pledges which were made by him and the other Mormon leaders in order that they might regain what they had lost by their past defiance of the laws of the land.

These and other falsehoods which are being industriously circulated by the sympathizers of Mr. Roberts cannot do him any possible good. He will not attempt

Document 33a. Campbell's letter to a Salt Lake City newspaper about B. H. Roberts' expulsion from the House of Representatives, October 7, 1899. [National Archives]

to stand by them himself when his case comes before Congress; and the persistent circulation of such glaring misrepresentations cannot fail to react against him when the real facts are made known.

Mr. Roberts is being fought because he is both a covenant-breaker and a law breaker down to date, not excluding the time that has intervened since his election. He is moreover today recognized as the most forcible, most zealous and most persistent advocate and defender of polygamy since the days of Brigham Young, John Taylor and Orson Pratt.

If Mr. Roberts is not expelled it will not be the fault of Congress, for Congress stands ready to do the bidding of the American people, if they will only make known their wishes, so that Congress may understand what they want done in this grave crisis. If Mr. Roberts is permitted to remain in Congress, it will be because the moral sense of the American people has become so dull during the past few years that they no longer resent the insult offered them by the proposition to "force polygamy down the throats of the American Congress", the very body which once, in response to the moral sentiment of the Nation, so nobly stood for the monogamous home, which is the nursery of liberty and the cornerstone of our republican institutions. If Mr. Roberts is permitted to remain in Congress, and we fail to get a constitutional amendment prohibiting the practice of polygamy, this anti-American institution will fasten itself upon this inter-mountain region, whence it will ultimately spread throughout the country, until some day the American people will have to rise in their might and crush it in order to prevent this nation from crumbling into dust. In the meantime thousands of hearts will be broken and multitudes of souls will be sacrificed to the demon of deified lust, while the very name of this fair land will come very near becoming a reproach in the eyes of the civilized world. The developments in the Dreyfus case have demonstrated that no nation in this day can afford to run counter to the moral conscience of Christendom.

In a crisis like this the effort to degrade the campaign into a partisan squabble will utterly fail. The American people are a true and patriotic people. In the face of a deadly foe, all sections, creeds and parties will rally as one man to the defense of their cherished institutions. This campaign will demonstrate that this holds good not only in the presence of a foreign foe, but also when the foe springs up in our midst, especially when the attack is made upon the home, which, to every true American, is the dearest institution on earth.

Feeling sure that you will be glad to give space to correct the misunderstanding which exists in the public mind in regard to the important issues involved in this campaign, and thanking you in advance for the favor, I am,

Yours for the welfare of the land that we love,

Wm. R Campbell

(P. S. Editor will please publish this letter and the accompanying letter of the Salt Lake Ministerial Association in issue for October 18th, or if a weekly or semi-weekly, in the issue which comes nearest to the date of October 18th. This will make its appearance simultaneous in all papers which publish it; and it is sent to a few of the leading papers in every state of the Union. Please send me a copy of the issue in which this letter appears. If you can make some editorial comment, it will be appreciated. I enclose some printed facts which will suggest editorial remarks, if you are not already familiar with these facts. I wish you could start a movement to hold a mass meeting in your county during the week following the last Sunday of October to arrange to have the entire county canvassed to secure the signatures of legal voters to send to each Senator and Representative, and to the President just before Congress meets. I enclose a set of petitions, as a suggestion. Write me, if I can assist the campaign in your vicinity.)

Document 33b. Campbell's letter to a Salt Lake City newspaper about B. H. Roberts' expulsion from the House of Representatives, October 7, 1899. [National Archives]

His Excellency
John Fitzgerald Kennedy
President of the United States of America

On the occasion of the Feast of Christmas, Your Excellency and your gracious wife have thoughtfully sent Us greetings and good wishes, and We acknowledge this kind gesture with warm appreciation and gratitude.

We invoke the choicest blessings of the Infant Saviour upon Your Excellency, upon Mrs Kennedy, your children and family, and upon the people of the United States of America, praying that the New Year may bring true peace and lasting joy to your noble nation and to the world.

From the Vatican, December 31, 1961

Joannes XXIII

Document 34. Pope John XXIII's Christmas greetings to President Kennedy,
December 31, 1961 (John F. Kennedy Presidential Library). [National Archives]

Teaching With Documents Order Form

The Constitution: Evolution of a Government

You may order copies of the following documents in their original size:

Document	Price	Qty.	Total
Document 3. *(17x22, b/w)* Engrossed copy of the Declaration of Independence, August 2, 1776.	$24.00		
Document 22. *(17x22, b/w)* Map made in accordance with the 1785 Land Ordinance, 1786.	$24.00		
Add 5% MD Sales Tax (if applicable)			
Shipping & Handling (Ground Shipping: $10.00, Air Shipping: $22.00)			
Total			

Billing Address:

_____

_____

_____

_____

Shipping Address: (if different from Billing Address)

_____

_____

_____

_____

☐ Check Enclosed payable to Graphic Visions Associates

☐ VISA   ☐ Mastercard   ☐ American Express

_____/_____/_____/_____/   _____/_____/   _____

Credit Card Number   Exp. Date   Authorized Signature

(_____)_____   (_____)_____

Telephone   Fax

Mail Order To: Graphic Visions
640 East Diamond Avenue, Ste. F
Gaithersburg, MD 20877

Thanksgiving Dinner

ALSO BY ANTHONY DIAS BLUE

American Wine
The Buyer's Guide to American Wine

Thanksgiving Dinner

KATHRYN K. BLUE

ANTHONY DIAS BLUE

HarperCollins*Publishers*

Parts of this book originally appeared in slightly different form in *Bon Appétit*.

FIRST EDITION

Designed by Helene Berinsky

Library of Congress Cataloging-in-Publication Data

Blue, Kathryn K., 1943–
   Thanksgiving dinner/Kathryn K. Blue, Anthony Dias Blue.—1st ed.
     p. cm.
   ISBN 0-06-016490-5
   1. Thanksgiving cookery. 2. Entertaining. I. Dias Blue, Anthony. II. Title.
TX739.2.T45B58 1990   89-26961

90 91 92 93 94 DT/RRD 10 9 8 7 6 5 4 3 2 1

For Caitlin, Toby, Jessica, and Amanda,
for whom we give thanks every day

Contents

It has seemed to me fit and proper that they should be solemnly, reverently and gratefully acknowledged as with one heart and one voice by the whole American people. I do, therefor, invite my fellow citizens in every part of the United States, and also those who are at sea and those who are sojourning in foreign lands, to set apart and observe the last Thursday of November next as a day of thanksgiving and praise to our beneficent Father who dwelleth in the heavens.

—Abraham Lincoln, October 3, 1863

Acknowledgments

We started this project because we love Thanksgiving. Now, after more than a year of Thanksgiving dinners, we still do. Not only that, we are still talking to each other and we still like turkey.

What made this such a pleasant experience was the excellent support we received from so many people. First and foremost we want to thank our dear Alice Nolan, who labored long and hard testing and tasting and giving us sound advice, while our administrative assistant, Jack Weiner, manned the phones and ran the office.

Special thanks to Diane Rossen Worthington, an accomplished cook, successful cookbook author, and good friend, who provided guidance and good ideas throughout the process; and to Susan Friedland, our editor, who administered motivation when needed and scoldings when deserved.

Thanks to all those who contributed ideas, recipes, and encouragement: Gertrud Blue, Daniel Boulud, Flo Braker, Daphne Bransten, JoAnn Coffino, Lyn Davis, Fran Deutsch, Patty Dinner, Barbara Folger, Meredith Frederick, Barbara Goldie, Laurie Burrows Grad, Muffie Graham, Paige Healy, Lois Jamart, Maddie Katz, Peggy Knickerbocker, Heidi Insalata Krahling, Martha Kropf, Liz Levy, Susan Lifrieri, Amanda Lyon, Peggi McGlynn, Sirio Maccione, Dinah Malkin, Fran Meiselman, Lee Monfredini, Joan Nathan, Drew Nieporent, Andy Pappas, Jonathan Parker, Cindy Pawlcyn, Debra Ponzac, Mary Powell, Alex Rosenblatt, Caryl Saunders, Bonnie Schmitz, Emmy Smith, Kit Snedaker, James Villas, Martha Pearl Villas, Clark Wolf, Sue Wollack, Sudie Woodson, and Rob Zaborny.

Also we appreciate the help we received from the California Turkey Board, Empire Kosher Poultry, National Turkey Federation, Ocean Spray, and Shady Brook Turkey Farms.

A Little History

The first Thanksgiving feast is reputed to have taken place in 1621 with the Pilgrims and some local Massachusetts Indians in attendance. Some historians give credit to the settlers at Jamestown, Virginia, because they celebrated the Harvest Home Festival, a traditional English autumnal rite, a few years before the Pilgrims.

The traditions of these colonial celebrations go back as long as men have cultivated the earth. In biblical times, the Hebrews celebrated the Feast of the Tabernacles, and a bit later, the Greeks put on an annual party to honor Demeter, the goddess of the harvest. The Romans feted Ceres, the goddess of grain, in a holiday called Cerealia (General Mills take note). In the Middle Ages the French celebrated the Feast of St. Martin of Tours as Martinmas, which featured a gala goose dinner.

The Pilgrims' three-day festival in 1621 is credited by most as the beginning of what Americans know as Thanksgiving. The celebration was proclaimed by Governor William Bradford to commemorate the survival of the colony through its first difficult year. Of the original 102 settlers who arrived at Plymouth in the winter of 1620, only 55 were still alive by the spring of 1621.

Perhaps the entire colony would have perished were it not for the help of the Wampanoag Indians, who taught the colonists how to hunt and fish, as well as how to cultivate corn and other native vegetables. These American crops kept the Pilgrims alive.

The feast of celebration featured venison, game birds (including wild turkeys, we hope), and the bounty of the fields, including pumpkins, squash, and corn. There were games, displays of arms, and general good will between the colonists and the Indians.

Over the next 200 years occasional national days of thanksgiving were celebrated for specific events, such as a victory over the British or the end of the War of 1812. Individual states instituted regular observances, but

there was no regular national Thanksgiving holiday until Sarah Josepha Hale, the author of "Mary Had a Little Lamb" and editor of *Godey's Lady's Book,* an influential magazine, began a movement to have the last Thursday in November established as the permanent day of celebration.

From 1846 until 1863 Mrs. Hale relentlessly lobbied for the holiday. She not only saw it as a patriotic day but also as a day for families and friends. She devoted the November issue of her magazine to the subject, she wrote to congressmen and governors, and she petitioned the president. Finally, on October 3, 1863, President Abraham Lincoln declared Thanksgiving Day a national holiday.

Feasting became a national pastime. The holiday also became a focus for parades and football games. The first big parade was the 1921 Gimbel's procession in Philadelphia, and professional football has been an obsession for decades.

After President Franklin Roosevelt tried to change the date to two weeks earlier to encourage a longer Christmas shopping season, Congress passed a law in 1941 that permanently fixed the date as the fourth Thursday in November.

Thanksgiving Dinner

Planning Ahead

The Thanksgiving dinner requires planning. Each dish must be selected and a shopping list written. Think well in advance about place settings, flowers, wines, tables, chairs, serving dishes, timing, and the guest list. It is important to get started early. Don't wait until the day before or even the week before. Thanksgiving is not a potluck dinner; it is a complex feast that requires organization and considerable precision.

We think about Thanksgiving all year long—discussing and planning, fine tuning the combination of flavors, textures, and colors. But we are obsessed. Normal people need to give the holiday feast some thought by the first of November.

At that time, sit down for a few minutes and sketch out the Thanksgiving meal. Keeping in mind the number of people you expect and who they are, tailor a balanced and appropriate menu.

Become a list maker. Make a list of guests. Make a list of things to do. Make a shopping list. Make a schedule for the days leading up to Thanksgiving.

By the second week of November you should have bought all your staples. Such nonperishables as flour, baking powder, canned goods, onions, potatoes, paper products, wines, spices, and any extra utensils, pans, and dishes should be purchased that week and kept separate from your day-to-day kitchen items. We like to keep the Thanksgiving provisions together in boxes. This way, when it's time to start preparations, everything is already together. Shopping early helps to avoid the last-minute crisis of finding a key item already sold out at your market. It also helps you to bypass the long, slow lines that always develop during the week before Thanksgiving.

Also by the end of the second week of November you should have ordered your fresh turkey. Arrange to pick it up on the Wednesday before Thanksgiving to minimize the time it has to spend in the home refrigerator. If you can reserve other important items—sweet potatoes, Brussels sprouts, persimmons, and so on—do it. Try to avoid as many surprises as possible.

INGREDIENTS

When you shop, here are a few pointers about the ingredients required for the recipes in this book:

BUTTER   We always use unsalted butter. If you use salted butter be sure to reduce the salt in the recipes accordingly. Unsalted is more perishable than salted butter, but it will keep for weeks in the freezer.

FLOUR   We generally use unbleached all-purpose flour.

EGGS   We use large eggs. If you have medium eggs, adjust the recipe by dividing the number of eggs by ¾. This means a recipe that calls for 3 eggs should be changed to 4 eggs.

DRIED HERBS AND SPICES   Most of us keep dried herbs and spices around too long. They lose their potency after six months to a year on the shelf. Unfortunately, most spice companies do not make it easy to determine how old their products are. When in doubt, throw it out. Why let a little tin or jar of lifeless herbs or spices spoil a great dish?

YIELDS

Most of the recipes in this book are for a party of twelve, a typical number for a family Thanksgiving dinner. Using twelve as a basic unit, we like to modularize the holiday feast. We don't feel it is necessary to vary the size of most dishes—other than the turkey—to accommodate a smaller or larger party. Instead, the dinner can be diminished or enlarged by subtracting or adding dishes.

Let us give examples of this kind of planning:

APPETIZERS

Gravlax

Ojai Valley Carrot Soup

MAIN MEAL

12-pound Turkey with Molasses Glaze

Our Favorite Gravy with (or Without) Giblets

Sausage-Crouton Stuffing

Cranberry Chutney

Winter White Purée · Baby Beets with Ginger Glaze

The Ultimate Mashed Potatoes

DESSERTS

Our Favorite Pumpkin Pie

Chocolate-Chestnut Mousse

Philadelphia Vanilla Ice Cream

Thanksgiving Dinner

4

APPETIZERS

Gravlax

Chicken Liver Mousse with Apple and Walnuts

Ojai Valley Carrot Soup

MAIN MEAL

18-pound Turkey with Molasses Glaze

Our Favorite Gravy with (or Without) Giblets

Sausage-Crouton Stuffing

Cranberry Chutney · Meems' Prune Chutney

Baby Beets with Ginger Glaze

Golden Winter Purée · Winter White Purée

Brussels Sprouts with Maple-Mustard Sauce

The Ultimate Mashed Potatoes

DESSERTS

Our Favorite Pumpkin Pie · Pear Mincemeat Pie

Ginger-Applesauce Spice Cake with Ginger Whipped Cream

Chocolate-Chestnut Mousse

Philadelphia Vanilla Ice Cream

Party of Eighteen

APPETIZERS

Cheddar Cheese Crisps

Gravlax · Tuna Pâté

Chicken Liver Mousse with Apple and Walnuts

Ojai Valley Carrot Soup

MAIN MEAL

Two 15-pound Turkeys with Molasses Glaze

Our Favorite Gravy with (or Without) Giblets

Sausage-Crouton Stuffing · Pistachio and Apple Stuffing

Kumquat-Cranberry Compote

Cranberry Chutney · Meems' Prune Chutney

Baby Beets with Ginger Glaze

Garlic, Spinach, and Rice Casserole

Golden Winter Purée · Winter White Purée

Schatze's Corn Pudding

Brussels Sprouts with Maple-Mustard Sauce

The Ultimate Mashed Potatoes

Buttermilk-Sage Biscuits

DESSERTS

Our Favorite Pumpkin Pie · Pear Mincemeat Pie · Apple Pie

Pumpkin-Ginger Cheesecake

Ginger-Applesauce Spice Cake with Ginger Whipped Cream

Chocolate-Chestnut Mousse

Philadelphia Vanilla Ice Cream

As the number of dishes increases, people take a smaller amount of each. For this reason you will see that some recipes show a range of servings. For pies, for example, we have put "Serves 8 to 12." Under normal circumstances, when the pie is the only dessert, cutting it into 8 pieces is proper. When there are four or five different desserts available, smaller servings are much more in order.

Offering a selection of desserts or vegetables also gets people to make choices. Guests at our house decide to take only three or four out of seven vegetables, for instance.

If you choose not to use this modular method, you can make fewer dishes, increasing the amount. Most of the recipes in the book can be doubled easily (or halved, for that matter).

ADVANCE PREPARATION

With very few exceptions, the recipes in this book can be done ahead of time. Most Thanksgiving cooks have at one time or another in their careers learned the cruel lesson that there is nothing more depressing than slaving away in the kitchen while your guests are in the living room enjoying themselves.

Thanksgiving is a family holiday and it should be enjoyed by all—including those who are charged with getting the food on the table.

With this in mind, we have put together a group of recipes that can be made anywhere from Thanksgiving morning to two months before. The few dishes that require last-minute attention are more appropriate for smaller, less pressurized gatherings.

Appetizers and Soups

*A*t our house, we don't worry too much about Thanksgiving appetizers. It doesn't make a great deal of sense to us to spend lots of time on a first course when the dinner that follows it is so ample.

Generally, we like to serve finger foods—spiced nuts, crunchy crisps, and an occasional pâté—things that people can serve for themselves. When you are basting the turkey, warming plates, and finishing the meal, there is no time to serve a fussy appetizer.

Before dinner, we encourage our guests and family to assemble in the living room, where we place dishes and bowls of appetizers to keep them busy. Eventually, everyone drifts into the kitchen.

Our kitchen is big and airy, the focus of our home. When we bought the house twelve years ago, we took out the ancient kitchen and dingy pantries and opened up the whole space. We knew that most of our family moments and all of our parties would take place there. So we designed a room with a central island and lots of space.

At Thanksgiving, when everyone congregates in the kitchen before the meal, we like to serve soup in glass mugs. While the turkey is being carved, everyone stands around sipping and talking. When they finally do sit down, turkey and all the trimmings await them.

Cheddar Cheese Crisps

$\mathcal{I}$t isn't easy finding a good before-dinner munch that is both easy to prepare and not filling. These crackers are simple, quick, and not perishable. You can serve them warm or at room temperature. They can be made well ahead of time and then briefly warmed in a low oven.

Makes about 60 crackers

3 cups all-purpose flour
1½ cups chilled shortening
1 teaspoon salt
¾ cup finely grated sharp
   cheddar cheese

1 egg
1 tablespoon cider vinegar
2 tablespoons ice water

1. In a bowl, mix until crumbly the flour, shortening, salt and ¼ cup of the cheese. In another bowl, beat the egg, vinegar, and water.

2. Combine the flour and egg mixtures, and knead until the dough forms a ball. (This procedure can be done in the work bowl of a food processor fitted with the plastic dough blade. Pulse two or three times; do not overmix.) Wrap in wax paper and refrigerate overnight.

3. Preheat the oven to 350 degrees. Roll the dough out ⅛ inch thick. Cut into 2-inch rounds. (Ovals or rectangles would also be appropriate. In fact, a mixture of shapes is an interesting way to serve these.) Place on a cookie sheet lined with foil. Gather up the scraps, roll out again and cut more crackers.

4. Bake for 8 minutes. Top each cracker with a generous pinch of grated cheese. Bake for 10 to 12 more minutes, or until the cheese is melted and golden brown. Let cool for at least a few minutes before serving.

ADVANCE PREPARATION: Can be prepared 3 days in advance. Store in a covered tin in a cool place. Warm in a 300-degree oven before serving.

Schatze's Cheese Crackers

*A*ndy's mother, affectionately known as Schatze (pronounced Shot-zee), is a talented cook. She makes these crackers for her bridge group, for cocktail parties, and on Thanksgiving. They are always a big hit with guests before dinner.

Makes about 65 crackers

1½ cups grated sharp cheddar
 cheese
1 cup all-purpose flour
½ teaspoon salt
¼ teaspoon cayenne
8 tablespoons (1 stick) unsalted
 butter, frozen and cut into
 pieces

1 teaspoon Worcestershire sauce
1 egg yolk, lightly beaten
Assorted toppings: carraway
 seeds, poppy seeds, sesame
 seeds, slivered almonds, curry
 powder, various seasoning
 mixes

1. Place the cheese, flour, salt, cayenne, butter, and Worcestershire sauce in the bowl of a food processor fitted with a metal blade. Pulse several times until the mixture forms a ball. Remove from the processor and knead on a lightly floured surface by pushing forward with the heel of your hand 6 or 8 times. Divide the dough in half. Wrap the dough in wax paper and refrigerate for 3 hours or overnight.

2. Preheat the oven to 350 degrees. On a well-floured surface, roll out each ball of dough about ⅛ inch thick. Cut into rounds with a cookie cutter, or into squares or triangles with a pizza cutter (one with a fluted edge makes an attractive cracker).

3. Paint the top of each cracker with egg yolk. Top each cracker with one or more of the suggested toppings.

4. Place on a foil-lined cookie sheet, and bake 12 minutes or until golden brown. Cool on paper towels.

ADVANCE PREPARATION: Can be prepared 3 days ahead. Store in a covered tin in the refrigerator. They also can be frozen for several weeks. When ready to serve, warm in a 300-degree oven for 15 minutes.

Herb Crisps

$\mathcal{T}$hese are really simple and very delicious. No matter how many you make, there are never any left.

Makes about 30

1 cup all-purpose flour
1 tablespoon finely minced garlic
1 teaspoon ground cumin
1 teaspoon onion salt
1 teaspoon celery seed
½ teaspoon cayenne
½ teaspoon superfine sugar
8 tablespoons (1 stick) chilled
   unsalted butter, cut into
   pieces

2 tablespoons plus about 1
   teaspoon ice water
1 large egg white, lightly beaten
3 teaspoons herbes de Provence,
   or a mixture of dried thyme,
   basil, savory, and fennel seed

1. Mix the flour, garlic, cumin, onion salt, celery seed, cayenne, and sugar in a medium bowl. Add the butter and cut in until the mixture resembles fine meal. Gradually mix in enough ice water to form a dough that just comes together. Do not overmix. Divide the dough in half; flatten each half into a rectangle. Wrap each piece in plastic wrap and refrigerate for 1 hour.

2. Preheat the oven to 350 degrees. On a lightly floured surface, roll 1 piece of dough at a time to form a thick rectangle 5 inches by ¾ inches by ¼ inch thick. Cut the dough crosswise into ¾-inch strips. Place the strips on an ungreased cookie sheet, spacing evenly. Brush each one with egg white, being careful not to let any drip onto the baking sheet.

3. Sprinkle half the herb mixture over the dough strips. Refrigerate for 15 minutes. Bake for 20 minutes or until puffed and crisp. Transfer to a rack. Repeat with the remaining dough, egg white, and herbs.

ADVANCE PREPARATION: Can be prepared up to 3 days in advance. Cool and store between sheets of wax paper in an airtight container at room temperature. Serve warm or at room temperature.

Spiced Almonds

Makes 3 cups

¾ pound whole blanched almonds
2 tablespoons vegetable oil
2 tablespoons Cointreau
1 tablespoon unsalted butter, melted
¼ cup sugar

1 teaspoon vanilla extract
2 teaspoons ground cinnamon
½ teaspoon freshly grated nutmeg
½ teaspoon ground cloves
Salt

1. In a bowl, whisk together the oil, Cointreau, butter, and sugar. Marinate the nuts in the mixture for 15 minutes.

2. Preheat the oven to 350 degrees. Spread nuts in a single layer on a baking sheet lined with foil. Toast in preheated oven for 25 minutes or until golden.

3. In a bowl, mix the vanilla, cinnamon, nutmeg, and cloves. Toss hot nuts in the spice mixture to coat. Sprinkle with salt. Spread the nuts on paper towels and cool completely.

ADVANCE PREPARATION: These will benefit from being prepared at least 2 days ahead. Store in an airtight tin at room temperature.

Spiced Macadamia Nuts

*T*hese are impossible to resist and don't require much time at all to make. We have settled on cooking them in a wok because it heats oil quickly and makes stirring easy.

Makes 2 cups

12 ounces whole macadamia
   nuts
⅔ cup sugar
¼ cup water
1 whole vanilla bean, split
2 teaspoons ground cinnamon

½ teaspoon freshly grated
   nutmeg
½ teaspoon ground mace
¼ teaspoon ground cloves
1 cup vegetable oil
Salt

1. Spray or brush a baking sheet with cooking oil and set aside.

2. In a small saucepan, bring 2 cups of water to a boil. Add the nuts and cook 1 minute. Strain and turn out on paper towels to dry.

3. In the same saucepan combine sugar and water. Over medium heat, stir to dissolve, brushing any sugar crystals away from the sides of the saucepan with a pastry brush dipped in water. Swirl to melt any crystals while continuing to boil until the sugar forms a thick syrup (248 degrees on a candy thermometer or soft-ball stage). Add the seeds from the vanilla bean and all the spices and stir to combine.

4. In a wok, heat the oil to 375 degrees. It will smoke slightly.

5. Add about one-third of the nuts to the spicy sugar mixture and coat thoroughly. Working quickly, remove the nuts with a slotted spoon, drain off as much sugar syrup as possible, and put the nuts into the hot oil. Stir-fry until they are a mahogany color, about 10 to 15 seconds. Remove from the oil, using the slotted spoon, and place on the greased baking sheet. Separate the nuts with tongs. Repeat until all the nuts are cooked. Salt to taste.

SERVING SUGGESTION: These nuts can be served warm or at room temperature. Other nuts—almonds, walnuts, pecans, or cashews—can be substituted, but mixed nuts are not a good idea. Nuts have such a variety of cooking temperatures that some will burn while others won't be done.

ADVANCE PREPARATION: These will benefit from being prepared at least 2 days ahead. Store in an airtight tin at room temperature.

Spiced Mixed Nuts

Makes 3 cups

1 pound roasted, unsalted mixed nuts	1 tablespoon sugar
2 egg whites	1 tablespoon salt
8 tablespoons (1 stick) unsalted butter, melted	1 tablespoon ground cinnamon
¼ cup Amaretto	1 teaspoon ground mace
	1 teaspoon ground ginger

1. Blanch the nuts by putting them into boiling water and counting 10 seconds after the water returns to a boil. Strain and turn them onto a baking sheet to cool.

2. Preheat the oven to 325 degrees. In a bowl gently beat the egg white until foamy and then add the remaining ingredients. Mix to combine. Add the nuts and stir until coated. Spread the nuts in one layer on the baking sheet lined with foil. Bake them in the preheated oven for 20 minutes, tossing them two or three times during the cooking.

3. Cool the nuts to room temperature before serving.

ADVANCE PREPARATION: These will benefit from being prepared at least 2 days ahead. Store in an airtight tin at room temperature.

Pacbag Tuna Pâté

One of our favorite San Francisco restaurants is the Pacific Heights Bar and Grill or, as it is affectionately known by its regulars, the Pacbag. This recipe of Chef Ellis Casabar has recently become a regular appetizer in our house and it works very nicely as a warm-up to the holiday feast. To heighten its festive appearance, garnish the pâté with extra chopped pistachios, and dress up the crock with an arrangement of seasonal fruits. Serve with rye toast points or toasted rounds of French bread.

This recipe makes enough for a good-sized cocktail party and more than enough for a preamble to a big dinner. You can halve the recipe easily, or leave it as is and eat the extra during the holiday weekend.

Makes 5 cups

1 pound tuna fillet (use ahi, if you can get it), poached (see below) and cooled	½ cup chopped fresh dill
	1 pound cream cheese
	4 hard-boiled eggs, peeled and chopped
¾ cup Cognac or brandy	
1 tablespoon freshly ground pepper	¾ cup chopped pistachio nuts
	Salt

1. In the bowl of a food processor fitted with the metal blade, place the tuna, Cognac, pepper, and dill. Process for 15 seconds or until smooth. Add the cream cheese and eggs. Pulse 3 to 4 times to blend.

2. Pour into a terrine or crock. Line the crock with parchment paper. Fold in the pistachios and salt to taste. Chill well before serving.

Court Bouillon

Makes 3¼ cups

3 cups water	1 bay leaf
¼ cup dry white wine	5 whole peppercorns
1 tablespoon lemon juice	

In a 3-quart saucepan, combine all the ingredients and bring to a boil. Add the fish. Let the liquid come back to a boil, but turn the heat down so the water just barely simmers. Cover and cook until the fish is just done, about 10 minutes. Don't overcook or the fish will be dry.

ADVANCE PREPARATION: Can be prepared 1 day ahead. Cover and refrigerate.

Gravlax

*T*his Swedish method for marinating fresh salmon at home was certainly not served at the first Thanksgiving, but we find it to be a perfect appetizer. We start marinating on Monday and by Thursday we have a delicious and easy-to-serve warm-up for the big dinner.

Serves 12 or more

3½ pounds fresh salmon fillet, cleaned and scaled, center cut, skin on	⅓ cup coarse salt
	⅓ cup sugar
	2 tablespoons white peppercorns, crushed
1 large bunch fresh dill	

1. Examine the fish carefully for bones and use tweezers to remove those that remain.

2. Place half of the fish, skin side down, in a high-sided glass or enamel baking dish that fits it snugly. Chop the dill coarsely and spread it over the fish. Mix the salt, sugar, and peppercorns, and sprinkle them evenly over the fish. Top with the other half of the fish, skin side up.

3. Cover the dish with heavy-duty foil. Try to find a plate, a board, or something else that fits inside the edges of the dish. Then weight down the board with heavy cans, books, or rocks. (We use a foil-wrapped brick.)

4. Refrigerate. Turn the fish over every 12 hours, spooning the liquid in the dish between the two sections of fish each time you do. Continue this procedure for at least 48 hours and preferably for 72 hours.

5. When you are ready to serve the gravlax, remove the fish from the dish. Scrape away the dill and remaining marinade and pat dry with paper towels.

6. Slice the salmon across the grain with a sharp, straight knife, detaching each slice from the skin as you cut. Serve on thin slices of pumpernickel with mustard dill sauce.

Mustard Dill Sauce
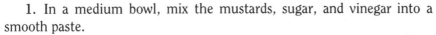

Makes 1½ cups

½ cup dark English mustard
1 tablespoon dry mustard
6 tablespoons sugar

¼ cup white wine vinegar
⅔ cup olive oil
6 tablespoons finely minced dill

1. In a medium bowl, mix the mustards, sugar, and vinegar into a smooth paste.

2. Whisk in the olive oil, drop by drop, until the sauce begins to thicken. Continue whisking while pouring the oil in a thin stream. The sauce should be like mayonnaise. Stir in the dill. Refrigerate until ready to use. Whisk again just before using.

ADVANCE PREPARATION: The gravlax requires three days preparation and it will keep in the refrigerator for a week after being cured. The sauce can be prepared 3 days ahead. It will keep in the refrigerator for a week. However, if making the sauce in advance, omit the chopped dill and add just before serving.

Chicken Liver Mousse
with Apple and Walnuts

*T*his smooth appetizer will keep the hungry hordes at bay until you are ready to serve the turkey. It is based on an idea by Diane Rossen Worthington.

Makes 5 cups

1 cup walnuts, broken into small
    pieces
5 tablespoons unsalted butter
1 medium onion, finely chopped
3 shallots, minced
2 tart green apples such as
    Pippin or Granny Smith,
    cored, peeled, and minced
2 cloves garlic, minced
¼ pound chicken-apple sausage,
    or any mild sausage
1 pound chicken livers

½ cup Calvados
10 ounces cream cheese, at
    room temperature, cut into
    chunks
1 tablespoon chopped fresh
    tarragon, or 1 teaspoon dried
1½ tablespoons chopped fresh
    thyme, or 1½ teaspoon dried
1½ teaspoons freshly ground
    white pepper
1 teaspoon salt

1. Roast the walnuts on a cookie sheet lined with foil in a 350-degree oven for 7 to 10 minutes. Set aside.

2. In a skillet over medium heat, melt 3 tablespoons of butter. Add the onion, shallots, and apples, tossing to coat with butter. Sauté for 10 minutes or until translucent. Add the garlic and sauté about 1 minute. Set aside and cool slightly.

3. Place another skillet over medium heat. Melt 2 tablespoons of butter, and sauté the sausage meat removed from the casing. After about 2 minutes add the chicken livers and sear on each side. Continue cooking for 3 minutes. The chicken livers should be pink inside. Add Calvados, ignite (being careful to avert your eyes), and set aside to cool.

4. Place the onion and apple mixture in the bowl of a food processor fitted with the metal blade. Pulse until the mixture is pastelike but not smooth. Add the cream cheese and process for about 10 seconds. Add the chicken liver mixture and the seasonings. Process to combine, occasionally stopping to scrape down the sides. Add the walnuts, and pulse two or three times, just to incorporate.

5. Put the mixture in a 5- or 6-cup terrine or crock.

VARIATION: Replace half the sausage with ⅛ pound spicy duck sausage, and sauté the two together in step 3. Add ½ teaspoon red pepper flakes with the other seasonings.

SERVING SUGGESTIONS: Remove from the refrigerator about 2 hours before serving to bring to room temperature. Serve with crackers, toast, or slivers of celery.

ADVANCE PREPARATION: Can be prepared 1 day ahead. Cover and refrigerate. Bring to room temperature before serving. Will keep for 3 days. Can also be frozen for up to 2 months.

Yam Soup

The great charm of this thick soup is that it presents the lush, rich flavor of yams with only slight adornment. If you find yams too waxy as a vegetable, you might prefer them as a soup.

Serves 12

6 yams (about 3 pounds)
8 cups Chicken Stock (see page 77)
2 cups heavy cream
½ teaspoon freshly grated nutmeg
¼ teaspoon ground cinnamon
¼ teaspoon ground mace

2 tablespoons lemon juice
½ teaspoon freshly ground white pepper
Salt
Crème fraîche or sour cream (optional)

1. Peel the yams and cut them into 1-inch pieces. Place in a saucepan and cover with the chicken broth. Bring to a boil, cover, and simmer for 45 minutes. Pour into a food processor or food mill and purée.
2. Return the purée to the saucepan and stir in all the other ingredients. Bring to a simmer over moderate heat and serve immediately. If desired, top each serving with a dollop of crème fraîche or sour cream.

ADVANCE PREPARATION: Can be prepared 2 days in advance. Cover and refrigerate.

Turkey Consommé

$\mathcal{T}$his clear soup is elegant yet loaded with flavor. It is a perfect starter for a Thanksgiving party where the main course is something other than turkey. Try the optional dumplings; they add a festive dimension. You can freeze what you don't serve. It will keep 3 months.

Makes 1 gallon

12 egg whites
6 egg shells
1½ cups coarsely chopped celery
1 cup coarsely chopped leeks, whites only
½ cup coarsely chopped onion
½ cup peeled and coarsely chopped carrots
Handful of parsley stems

1 pound ground uncooked turkey
1 teaspoon whole allspice berries
1 teaspoon black peppercorns
1 teaspoon salt
3 quarts poultry stock, at room temperature (see pages 77, 78)

1. In the bowl of a food processor fitted with the metal blade, place all the ingredients except the stock. Pulse to combine.

2. Put the stock in a large pot. Pour in the mixture from the food processor. Stir to mix. Heat slowly, stirring constantly, until the consommé reaches 168 degrees on a thermometer. Stop stirring. A coagulated mass called a *raft* will form. Let the stock come to a boil. Reduce the heat immediately, allowing the stock to simmer. This gentle bubbling action will clarify the stock into a consommé. Check the pot frequently to make sure the stock does not boil violently. This process should take about 1 hour.

3. Turn off the heat. Allow the consommé to cool and the raft to solidify. The challenge is removing the raft and keeping the consommé clear. Using a slotted spoon scoop up spoonfuls of the raft and discard. If the soup didn't clarify, this process can be repeated.

4. To remove any traces of the raft, pass the consommé through thoroughly rinsed cheesecloth. Reheat prior to serving.

SERVING SUGGESTION: The beauty of a consommé is its versatility. A fine dice of vegetables or dumplings adds interest to the soup. Try these almond quenelles.

Creamy Almond Quenelles

Makes about 24 dumplings

1 cup bread crumbs
¼ cup all-purpose flour
2 eggs
2 tablespoons unsalted butter,
    melted

¼ cup ground almonds
Few drops almond extract

1. Combine all ingredients in a food processor fitted with a metal blade. Pulse to blend. The dough should be light and fluffy.

2. In a 1-quart saucepan, bring 2 cups of stock or consommé to a boil, reduce to a simmer. Using two spoons, form quenelles and slide them into the simmering liquid. The quenelles are done when they float to the top and resist a slight pressure when touched. They take about 2 minutes to cook. Serve two in each bowl.

ADVANCE PREPARATION: The consommé can be prepared 2 days ahead. Cover and refrigerate. It will keep in the freezer for several months. The quenelles can be made 1 day ahead. Cover and refrigerate. Reheat in the hot soup.

Ojai Valley Carrot Soup

$\mathcal{T}$his soup may never have been served in the Ojai Valley, a spectacular spot near Santa Barbara, California. Our son Toby was graduated from the Thacher School in Ojai and while we were there for the ceremony, we conceived this recipe.

Makes 8 cups

SOUP

4 leeks, whites only
2 pounds carrots, peeled, tops removed
3 tablespoons olive oil
¼ cup Arborio rice
3 cups Chicken Stock, fresh (see page 77) or canned

1 tablespoon minced crystallized ginger
½ teaspoon sea salt
½ teaspoon freshly ground pepper
¼ cup freshly squeezed lime juice

GARNISH

2 tablespoons crème fraîche
2 tablespoons lime zest

1 tablespoon minced crystallized ginger

1. Slice the leeks lengthwise, then slice into thin half-moon shapes. Cut the carrots into 2-inch lengths.
2. In a stock pot, heat the oil and sauté the leeks until soft. Add the carrots, rice, and stock. Bring to a boil, then simmer for 40 minutes. Add the ginger. Cook for an additional 10 minutes.
3. Purée the mixture in batches in a blender or food processor fitted with a metal blade. Put the purée through the food processor power strainer, if available. Return the soup to the pot and season with salt and pepper.
4. Add the lime juice, thoroughly combining it with the soup. Serve warm with a dollop of crème fraîche and a sprinkling of lime zest and crystallized ginger.

ADVANCE PREPARATION: The soup can be prepared 2 days in advance. Cover and refrigerate. Reheat before serving.

Chestnut Soup

$\mathcal{T}$his is one of the best things we've ever tasted. The two pounds of whole roasted chestnuts are the only problem. If you use the excellent jarred versions imported from France (we use Minerve brand), the cost can be high. If you roast and peel them yourself, the time and effort is substantial. Nevertheless, this is such a delicious soup, it's worth it either way.

Serves 6

8 tablespoons (1 stick) unsalted
   butter
2 pounds roasted and peeled
   chestnuts
1 carrot, peeled and sliced
1 parsnip, peeled and sliced
1 cup peeled and chopped celery
   root
7½ cups Chicken Stock (see
   page 77)

½ cup Madeira
2 fresh parsley sprigs
Pinch of freshly grated nutmeg
½ teaspoon salt
½ teaspoon freshly ground
   pepper
Crème fraîche, sour cream, or
   plain yogurt
Cayenne
2 tablespoons chopped parsley

1. Melt half the butter over medium heat in a large heavy skillet. Add the chestnuts and sauté until heated through, about 5 minutes. Set aside.

2. Melt the remaining butter in a large heavy pot over medium heat. Add the carrot, parsnip, and celery root, and sauté until soft, about 7 minutes.

3. Add the stock to the vegetables and bring to a boil. Reduce heat to low. Add the chestnuts, Madeira, parsley, nutmeg, salt, and pepper. Simmer for 15 minutes.

4. Ladle one-third of the mixture into the work bowl of a food processor fitted with the metal blade. Process for 30 seconds. Pour into a bowl or another stockpot. Repeat this procedure until all the soup has been processed to a smooth texture. (If you want a few small nuggets of chestnut in the final product, cut down on the processing time of the last batch.)

5. Return the soup to a simmer, stirring frequently. Adjust seasoning. Ladle into bowls. Top each with a dollop of crème fraîche, sour cream, or yogurt. Sprinkle with cayenne and chopped parsley.

ADVANCE PREPARATION: Can be prepared up to 2 days ahead. Cover and refrigerate.

Cream of Jerusalem Artichoke Soup

*J*erusalem artichokes are not artichokes at all; they are the tubers of sunflowers. They are also known as *sunchokes* and *girasole*. We love their flavor and this soup is an excellent showcase for this lovely and slightly exotic vegetable.

Serves 12

3 pounds Jerusalem artichokes
8 tablespoons (1 stick) unsalted butter
3 large onions, thinly sliced
3 cloves garlic, minced
12 cups Chicken Stock (see page 77)

2 cups heavy cream
Salt and freshly ground white pepper
4 tablespoons minced fresh parsley
Paprika

1. Wash the Jerusalem artichokes thoroughly. Clean them with a brush under running water. Cut them into chunks.

2. Melt the butter in a 5-quart saucepan. Sauté the artichokes, onions, and garlic for 5 minutes, or until soft. Add the stock and simmer for 45 minutes.

3. Process the soup in a food processor fitted with the metal blade, or pass it through a food mill. Return the purée to the saucepan. Stir in the cream. Season to taste. Garnish each serving with a sprinkling of parsley and paprika.

ADVANCE PREPARATION: Can be prepared 2 days in advance. Cover and refrigerate.

Roasted Butternut Squash and Garlic Soup

Serves 6

1 butternut squash
  (approximately 2 pounds)
3 tablespoons olive oil
1 head garlic, cloves unpeeled
1 cup hot water

2½ cups Chicken Stock (see
  page 77)
1 teaspoon freshly ground white
  pepper
1 teaspoon salt

1. Preheat the oven to 350 degrees. Slice the squash in half lengthwise, and remove the seeds and stringy pulp with a spoon. Rub the flat side with olive oil and place the squash, cut side down, in a glass baking dish; sprinkle the garlic cloves around the squash. Add the water and the rest of the oil. Bake for 1 to 1½ hours, or until the squash is very soft. Remove from the oven and cool slightly.

2. Scoop the squash pulp into the bowl of a food processor fitted with the metal blade. Squeeze the pointed end of each garlic clove, letting its pulp drop into the food processor.

3. Process for 30 seconds, until the mixture is very smooth. Add the chicken stock ½ cup at a time, pulsing the processor after each addition. Add the pepper and salt. Pour the mixture into a 2-quart saucepan and place over medium heat. Bring to a simmer and adjust the seasonings.

VARIATION: Add ¼ cup orange juice with the chicken stock and 1 tablespoon curry powder with the seasonings.

ADVANCE PREPARATION: Can be prepared 2 days in advance. Cover and refrigerate.

November Soup

$\mathcal{L}$ 'Avenue is one of the most innovative new restaurants in San Francisco. This is L'Avenue's Chef Nancy Oakes's version of harvest vegetable soup. It is loaded with flavor and texture, and it has a surprising flash of peppery heat on the palate.

Serves 12

1 medium yellow onion, diced
3 cloves garlic, chopped
3 large leeks, white part only, diced
2 carrots, peeled and diced
3 celery stalks, diced
3 tablespoons virgin olive oil
1 medium perfection squash or 2 acorn squash, peeled and diced
3 zucchini, diced
1 butternut squash, peeled and cubed
2 jalapeno peppers, seeded and diced

1 red bell pepper, diced
Salt and freshly ground pepper
5½ cups good rich Chicken or Turkey stock (see pages 77, 78)
8 small acorn squash (for presentation)
1 cup heavy cream
1 teaspoon fresh (or ½ teaspoon dried) thyme, chopped
3 tablespoons finely diced candied ginger
3 tablespoons finely chopped toasted hazelnuts
Crème fraîche

1. In a large skillet, sauté the onion, garlic, leeks, carrots, and celery in the olive oil until soft. Add all the squash, zucchini, and the peppers. Sauté until blended with the other ingredients. Season to taste and add the chicken stock. Simmer over medium heat until the squash is soft, about 10 minutes.

2. Purée the soup with a blender, food mill, or food processor. Remove 2 cups of the purée and set aside. Pass the remainder through a fine sieve or the power strainer of the food processor. Return the reserved 2 cups to the soup.

3. Preheat the oven to 350 degrees. Cut the tops off the 8 small acorn squash. Scoop out their seeds. Oil their skins and season the inside with salt and pepper. Turn the squash upside down on a baking sheet and bake about 20 minutes in the preheated oven, or until a fork pierces the inner squash meat easily.

4. Flatten the bottom of the squash so that it will sit firmly on a plate. Make sure the shells are intact.

5. Add the cream and thyme to the soup and reheat but do not boil. Add the ginger and hazelnuts. Ladle the hot soup into the prepared squash shells, placing a dollop of crème fraîche in each. Serve.

If you want to forgo using the squash as soup bowls, just skip steps 3 and 4 and go to step 5, using soup bowls.

ADVANCE PREPARATION: Can be prepared 1 day ahead through step 2. Cover and refrigerate.

Celery Celery-Root Soup

S mooth and luscious with lovely, earthy harvest flavors, this soup is easy and quite elegant.

Serves 8

8 tablespoons (1 stick) butter
4 medium onions, thinly sliced
6 cups rich Chicken or Turkey
  Stock (see pages 77, 78)
4 medium celery root bulbs,
  peeled and diced (6 cups)
1 head celery, cleaned, scraped
  of strings, and diced

2 cups heavy cream or milk (for
  a lighter version)
Salt and freshly ground white
  pepper
1 tart apple, peeled, cut into
  ¼-inch dice, sautéed in 1
  tablespoon butter (optional)

1. Melt the butter in a 4-quart saucepan over medium heat. Sauté the onions in the butter until translucent. Add chicken stock. Add the celery root and celery. Simmer over medium heat until the vegetables are tender.

2. Purée the soup in batches in a food processor until it has a creamy texture. Run the puréed soup through a sieve to remove any lumps or fibers. Return to the pot and heat through. Season to taste. Add the cream or milk.

3. Sprinkle 1 tablespoon of diced apple on each serving.

ADVANCE PREPARATION: Can be prepared 2 days ahead. Cover and refrigerate. Warm over medium heat. Do not boil.

Turkey and Other Poultry

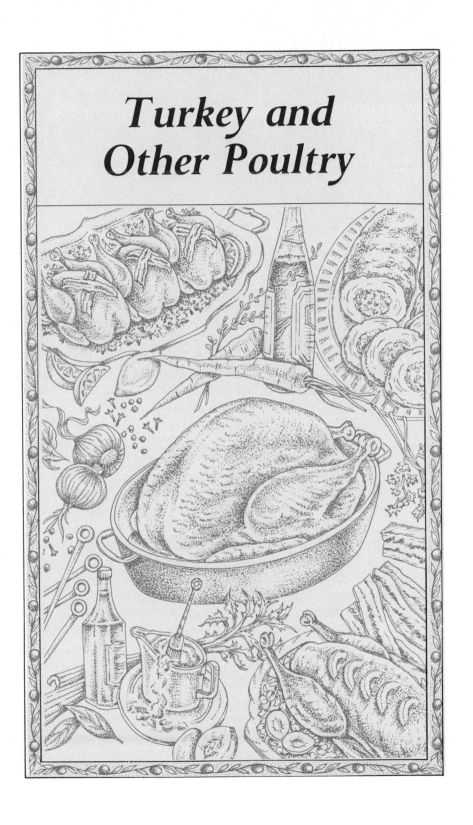

*T*he turkey has been a part of American culture since before the time of Columbus. Actually, this clumsy-looking bird—which some wrongly characterize as dumb—was roaming North America more than eight million years before man made his appearance. Domesticated turkeys were part of the diet of Southwestern Indians at the same time that Julius Caesar ruled Rome.

The value of the turkey as food was discovered immediately by Columbus and Cortez, who gathered up the birds and shipped them back to Europe. By 1530, turkeys were already being raised domestically in France, Italy, and England. Actually the first turkeys raised by the American colonists were not from the native populations, but rather from domesticated stock brought back from Europe. The European stock was crossed with the native wild turkey, and the resultant offspring were the forefathers and mothers of the Bronze turkey, the variety that became the basis of the American turkey industry.

The turkey is America's greatest contribution to the domesticated poultry industry. Benjamin Franklin himself declared the turkey to be the quintessential American avian. In fact, he proposed the turkey as the official United States bird, only to be deeply disappointed when the bald eagle got the nod instead. "I wish the bald eagle had not been chosen as the representative of our country!" he wrote to his daughter. "The turkey is a much more respectable bird, and withal a true original native of America."

The turkey got its name thanks to the same misconception that gave native Americans the title "Indians." Since Columbus thought the New World was connected to India, he assumed that the funny-looking birds were some form of peacock. He called them *tuka,* the Indian name for peacock. (Actually, the turkey is a variety of pheasant with the official scientific name of *Meleagris gallopavo.*)

The India mistake has carried over into some of the names given the bird in other languages. The French word is *dinde,* a contraction of *d'Inde,* meaning "of India," and the Dutch still persist in calling the turkey *calecutische hohn,* the "Calcutta hen."

The diet of early American settlers was dominated by game birds. The North American woodlands were filled with all sorts of delectable flying creatures, and colonists found them to be a ready source of food. The most populous species were passenger pigeons, which in the seventeenth century were estimated to be more than nine billion in number. Wholesale shooting and trapping of these birds brought them to extinction by the early twentieth century.

Luckily the same sad fate did not befall the turkey, which was also plentiful in the early American skies. The wild turkey was a common and noisy part of the natural environment when the first settlers arrived. Great flocks of them were reported in most mid-Atlantic states. In fact, by the 1820s wild turkeys were so common that they were actually disdained by gourmets. Farm chickens cost more. But European connoisseurs, who had been given less opportunity to become blasé about these tasty birds, raved about turkey from the beginning.

M. F. K. Fisher wrote about it in *Serve It Forth:* "French interest in anything from the American colonies ran high, and such dishes as Indian corn pudding and wild roasted turkey made any table smart. Prices for them ran into several figures—almost as expensive as truffles. It took a woman of unlimited income and capricious brain to combine the two whims of the moment, and serve a turkey stuffed with truffles to her admirers."

LOTS OF THEM, AND THEY'RE GOOD FOR YOU

Nearly 250 million turkeys are produced every year in the United States— one for every man, woman, and child in the country. The per capita consumption of turkey in the United States is more than 16 pounds per person, and this figure has been growing steadily since the beginning of the twentieth century. In 1930, per capita consumption was 1.5 pounds, in 1955 it was 5 pounds, in 1968 it was 8 pounds, and it was only 12 pounds as recently as 1985.

The trend toward lighter foods and a good promotional campaign by the National Turkey Federation, a grower association, have spurred consumers to eat turkey at other times besides Thanksgiving and Christmas. In 1987, for instance, only 40 percent of all turkeys consumed were eaten in the fourth quarter of the year.

The heaviest consumption of turkey takes place on the East and West Coasts. California has the highest rate of turkey consumption, averaging more than 23 pounds per person.

Turkey is low in calories and fat. Compared to other popular meats, it

can be considered diet food. Three ounces of pork loin contains 219 calories and 12.7 grams of fat. The same amount of roast beef has 217 calories and 12.9 grams of fat. Lamb chops yield 211 calories and 12.9 grams of fat. Dark turkey meat, on the other hand, has only 143 calories and 4.4 grams of fat, and turkey white meat, lowest of all, 119 calories and just 1 gram of fat. In general, turkey has fewer calories and less fat than chicken, too. Where the Thanksgiving feast becomes fattening is with side dishes—especially stuffing.

In addition to its dietetic charms, the turkey is also very economical. That same three ounces of pork loin mentioned above will cost $.71; the roast beef, $1.65; the lamb chops, $2.57; and even chicken rings in at $.43. Three ounces of turkey will cost only $.37 in 1990 dollars. One of the key reasons for this is the fact that turkey has an exceptionally high percentage of meat in relation to fat and bone. Turkey is 63 percent meat, while chicken is only 47 percent.

PRESENTING THE TURKEY OF THE NINETIES

Modern turkey farming has become a very scientific procedure. Thanks to turkey genetics, farmers are able to produce a pound of meat using a smaller amount of feed in less time than most other domestic meat-yielding animals require. Over the last 30 years or so, genetic scientists have also been able to develop a modern turkey that has a broad, thick breast, thicker thighs, plumper drumsticks, a higher meat-to-bone ratio, and white feathers. Although the turkey's original color was a mottled brown, growers prefer white because it leaves no unsightly pigment under the skin when the bird is plucked.

Today's turkey is raised on one of the more than 2,000 turkey farms in the United States. A typical farm raises 50,000 birds each year. Usually the turkeys are grown in barns that accommodate 7,000 toms (male turkeys) or 10,000 hens (females). In warmer climates the birds are raised outdoors on ranges that hold 5,000 to 10,000.

The turkey industry is completely entrepreneurial and receives no government support or subsidies. Birds are, however, carefully inspected for drug or pesticide residues by the USDA before they are processed. Turkeys are administered medication only when they contract minor diseases. They are not given hormones.

BREEDING IN THE MODERN WORLD

To meet the Thanksgiving demand, extra high quantities of eggs are incubated during April, May, and June. The egg takes 28 days to hatch. After that, a hen requires about 16 weeks to reach market weight and a tom about 19 weeks.

The modern, well-bred turkey is quite different from its wild ancestor. It is much more efficient at converting feed to protein (meat), it is heavier and more compact, and it grows to maturity much faster.

Most domesticated turkeys live on a healthy diet of corn and soybean meal mixed with a supplement of vitamins and minerals. They have a comfortable and pleasant life except for the sad fact that they are unable to mate naturally. Because of his sumo wrestler build, the modern tom turkey is physically incapable of performing his familial duties. As a result, hens are artificially inseminated, a procedure that increases the rate of fertility but certainly must have a negative impact on the turkey's quality of life.

When this problem first became apparent, growers tried all sorts of remedies. The difficulty was that the new-wave tom was too ungainly and clumsy to mount the hen and complete the necessary actions, so some growers devised canvas saddles that were placed on the hens. This helped only so long as the saddles didn't slip or get lost. When that happened the hens had to be caught and resaddled—quite a labor-intensive procedure.

But in the 1950s a technique was developed by Dr. Fred Lorenz and Dr. Frank Ogasawara for an artificial insemination technique that could be used on turkeys. This saved the turkey industry from a rather embarrassing situation and banished the poor, overstuffed tom, once and for all, from the hen coop.

KOSHER POULTRY

In most of the big cities of the United States, kosher turkeys and chickens are readily available. These birds are of high quality and have been raised in a hygienic environment.

Kosher is a very common word, but not that many people really know what it means. The laws of Kashruth are mostly found in the book of Deuteronomy in the Old Testament. They were given to protect the Jewish people from unclean food and to preserve the fair treatment of animals.

Here are the rules: There can be no mixing of meat with milk. Deuteronomy 14 states exactly which animals, poultry, and fish cannot be consumed. Animals without both cuds and cloven hoofs, fish without fins and scales, birds of prey, and insects and crustaceans—are all forbidden.

In addition, all permitted animals must be healthy, and ritually slaughtered and butchered according to a set of rules. Kosher does not refer to a type of food—it only has to do with the way food is treated and in what combinations it can be served.

Many non-Jews regularly buy their turkeys and other poultry from

kosher butchers. These products are of excellent quality and are generally indistinguishable in taste from those sold in better non-kosher shops.

EXPORTS

American turkeys are exported to a number of foreign countries. The biggest customer is Germany, with Venezuela, Japan, Hong Kong, Singapore, Egypt, Saudi Arabia, England, Holland, and Canada also buying significant amounts. The export business is good, but it could be much better except for the fact that some countries, through the use of high tariffs and excessively strict plant requirements, make it uneconomical for American producers to sell their products in some important foreign markets such as Great Britain and Brazil.

BUYING THE TURKEY

The modern turkey industry has made it easy to shop for turkey. The uniformity and high quality of the birds in the butcher shops and supermarkets mean there is really little need to be concerned about such things as freshness, tenderness, and flavor. Just buy from a reliable merchant and you should have no problems. This leaves several other important considerations, and the most important of these is size. How big a turkey should you buy?

Obviously, the size of your turkey is directly related to the number of people you will be feeding at Thanksgiving, but there are other factors that should also influence your choice. Do you want leftovers? Are your guests going to be mostly hungry adults or will there be a substantial number of children, who will eat smaller portions?

We like to estimate the size of the turkey needed by allotting 1 to 1½ pounds of uncooked meat for every person (allow 2 pounds per person if the turkey weighs less than 10 pounds). This leaves a good amount, and it also gives enough white and dark meat to satisfy our guests' preferences. Of course, this doesn't mean that you have to buy just one turkey. If we are having 30 people, instead of bringing home a husky 30-pound tom that will not fit in our oven, we buy two 15-pound birds and roast them side by side.

All turkeys today are classified as *young turkey*. A useful subcategory is *fryer-roaster,* usually a very young bird weighing 6 to 9 pounds and under 16 weeks of age. This size is excellent for a small group and for barbecuing outdoors (see page 48).

HANDLING

If you are selecting a frozen turkey, make sure it is wrapped in tight packaging that is completely free of holes and tears. Also be aware of expiration or "sell by" dates.

Take your fresh or frozen turkey home immediately after purchase and keep it frozen or refrigerated. If you are using a fresh turkey that is not enclosed in a tight plastic wrap, take it out of its wrappings and, after removing the bag containing the giblets, rinse it under cold, running water. Then pat it dry with paper towels, rewrap it in fresh wax paper and place it in a large, tightly sealed plastic bag in the refrigerator. Make the turkey the last thing you pick up before heading home so that it will not be left out of refrigeration for too long.

It is important that the turkey (and other foods) are handled in a clean environment. Make sure that utensils, platters, cutting boards, countertops, and hands are soap-and-hot-water clean. After handling fresh meats you should rinse your hands so as not to transfer bacteria to other foods.

A fresh turkey—and any other uncooked meat, for that matter—should never be left unrefrigerated for more than 2 hours. The key temperatures to remember are 40 degrees and 140 degrees. If you are keeping the turkey (or any other perishable food) cold, it must be at 40 degrees or lower. If you are heating food, it must be 140 degrees or higher. The temperatures in between are ideal for the growth of bacteria and the production of toxins in food.

DEFROSTING

If you are using a frozen turkey, the best way to defrost it is in the refrigerator. This method is slow, but it results in a bird that loses very little of its moisture and will, therefore, cook up moist and tender.

Put the frozen turkey—still in its original wrap—on a platter or tray in the refrigerator. Allow 5 hours per pound of turkey for defrosting. This means that if you are preparing a 15-pound turkey, it will take 75 hours (3 days, 3 hours) to defrost. If you add the cooking time of 4 hours (5 hours stuffed) and 15 minutes resting time, you will know the exact time to start the defrosting procedure. In the case of the 15-pounder, if you want to serve the bird at 5:00 in the afternoon on Thursday, you will have to begin the defrosting at 9:00 A.M. on Monday.

If you need to defrost your turkey a little faster, place the still-wrapped bird in the sink on Wednesday morning and cover with cold water. Change the water frequently during the day and allow about 30 minutes per pound.

Refrigerate immediately. The next morning the turkey will be ready to prepare for cooking.

Although it may seem tempting to avoid the time and work of these two methods, *never defrost a turkey at room temperature.* The bird will become a breeding place for harmful bacteria.

Small turkeys can also be defrosted in the microwave oven. The bird must be unwrapped and placed in the roasting pan you eventually will cook it in. Shield thin or bony areas with small pieces of aluminum foil and rotate the bird several times during defrosting. Consult the oven manufacturer's instructions for thawing times.

Frozen, prestuffed turkeys (which we do not recommend) should *not* be thawed before cooking. Do *not* refreeze turkey unless it still contains ice crystals; otherwise cook the turkey immediately.

FRESHER IS BETTER

Frankly, we much prefer cooking a fresh turkey. As much as modern technology has perfected the flash-freezing method, we have still found a good fresh-killed bird to be superior to its frosty cousin.

Some people like to point to the lower price per pound for frozen turkey, but the difference is not that great. And if you are going to go to all the trouble required to make a Thanksgiving feast, why skimp on the most important part of the whole meal?

On occasions where circumstances required it, we have prepared frozen turkeys, and they have been good. But we always felt they would have been better if they had been fresh.

Go to your butcher or wherever you buy meat and place your order several weeks before Thanksgiving. Most meat departments don't have the room to stockpile a bunch of bulky fresh turkeys in the refrigerator, so they will order from a wholesaler or producer only as many as are spoken for. Don't get caught short.

Do not take delivery of your fresh turkey before Wednesday of Thanksgiving week. Home refrigerators—no matter how fancy they may be—do not offer the right degree of cool or humidity for lengthy storage. When you bring your turkey home, follow the instructions above that call for immediately changing the bird's wrappings.

Before cooking, remove the wrappings, rinse the turkey thoroughly under cold, running water, and pat dry with paper towels. Then you are ready to prepare the bird for cooking. If you want to bring the turkey to room temperature before cooking, drape with wax paper and let sit on a well-ventilated kitchen counter for no more than 1 hour.

ROASTING THE TURKEY

After rinsing and drying, the easiest method for preparing a turkey is to secure the flap of skin over the neck opening with a poultry pin or round wooden toothpick. Place the drumsticks in the precut band of skin, into a hock lock, or tie them together loosely.

Tuck the wing tips back under the shoulders of the bird to allow the turkey to rest more solidly on the roasting rack (this also prevents overbrowning of the wing tips during roasting).

Place the turkey breast side up on an adjustable V-shaped roasting rack set in a shallow roasting pan. The rack should hold the turkey at least ½ inch above the bottom of the pan to allow the oven heat to circulate evenly around the turkey. Roasting pans with high sides inhibit heat circulation, thus increasing roasting time.

We do not recommend the kind of roasting thermometer that stays in the bird during cooking, but if you are using one, insert it into the center part of the thigh next to the body. Make sure it is not touching a bone. Brush the turkey with vegetable oil, butter, or a combination of both to prevent the skin from drying out.

Place the turkey in the center of a preheated 325-degree oven. The relatively low roasting time is the secret to a golden, juicy bird. Drippings will not burn and the meat will shrink less. Higher temperatures may cause the outside of the bird to cook faster than the inside and result in tough, dried-out meat that is difficult to carve.

Set the turkey in the middle of the oven, running lengthwise from side to side, not back to front. Halfway through the roasting process, turn the turkey around, 180 degrees, to ensure even cooking.

If the turkey achieves the proper color before the roasting time is exhausted, cover the bird with lightweight foil, shiny side down, to shield the skin against overbrowning.

HOW LONG?

There is no exact formula for the amount of time a turkey should cook, but there are general guidelines. These times are inexact because there are a number of variables that affect the roasting process. Ovens vary in size, heat distribution can be different for each oven, turkeys have individual physical characteristics, and oven temperature is directly affected by the number of times the oven door is opened. If you are cooking a bird that has been defrosted, the exact degree of thawing will also have an impact.

Thanksgiving Dinner

Here are the approximate roasting times for a turkey in a 325-degree oven:

Weight	Unstuffed	Stuffed
6 pounds	2½ hours	2¾ hours
7 pounds	2¾ hours	3¼ hours
8 pounds	3 hours	3½ hours
9 pounds	3¼ hours	3¾ hours
10 pounds	3½ hours	4 hours
11 pounds	3¾ hours	4¼ hours
12 pounds	3¾ hours	4¼ hours
13 pounds	4 hours	4½ hours
14 pounds	4 hours	4½ hours
15 pounds	4¼ hours	4¾ hours
16 pounds	4¼ hours	4¾ hours
17 pounds	4¼ hours	4¾ hours
18 pounds	4½ hours	5 hours
19 pounds	4½ hours	5 hours
20 pounds	4¾ hours	5¼ hours
21 pounds	4¾ hours	5¼ hours
22 pounds	5 hours	5½ hours
23 pounds	5¼ hours	5¾ hours
24 pounds	5¼ hours	6 hours
25 pounds	5¼ hours	6¼ hours

Remember, these are just approximations. The only way to tell if your turkey is done is to take its temperature by inserting a thermometer—the instant-reading kind—in the upper thigh area. When the internal temperature of the meat is 170 to 175 degrees, the turkey is done.

Another way to tell is to look at the juices that flow from the spot where the thermometer punctures the skin. If they run clear the turkey is done.

If you end up with a turkey that has one of those pop-up gizmos that are supposed to signal when the bird is done, ignore it. We have found that most of the time these things lead to overcooked turkeys. The indicators tend to err on the side of overdone. You can use them, but still take the turkey's temperature at the appropriate times. Frankly, we always remove those things before cooking.

TO STUFF OR NOT TO STUFF?

We have been on both sides of the big stuffing question. For a while we believed strongly that the stuffing should be cooked outside the bird. Then we switched sides and started stuffing our turkeys again.

The arguments on the side of stuffing cooked outside the turkey are (1) the turkey cooks faster and more evenly without stuffing; (2) there is much less chance of bacterial spoilage if the stuffing is kept out of the bird; and (3) the stuffing itself cooks up crisper and can be more easily controlled when it has its own separate casserole.

The arguments on the side of stuffing cooked inside the turkey are (1) this is the traditional method; (2) it is easier to do; (3) it looks great when presented; (4) the stuffing tastes better because it absorbs the flavors of the cooking turkey, and the ingredients of the stuffing flavor the turkey; and (5) the stuffing is moist and always the right temperature.

Frankly, we like it both ways. We love stuffing so much that we always make enough to fill the neck cavity, the large inner cavity, *and* a casserole cooked alongside the turkey. If we are particularly ambitious, we have been known to stuff the neck and the main cavity with two different kinds of stuffing.

There are important rules that must be observed when dealing with stuffing: Make sure the stuffing has been refrigerated or is, at least, cool before putting it into the turkey. Do not stuff a turkey until just before you are ready to cook it. And, be sure to remove the giblet bag from inside the turkey before stuffing.

When stuffing the turkey (or other birds) spoon the stuffing in loosely. Don't overstuff. Stuffing expands during cooking and if it is too firmly packed it is liable to split the turkey.

If you are cooking all the stuffing or some of the stuffing outside of the turkey, put it into a buttered casserole or soufflé dish, being sure to keep it loosely packed. The stuffing should not be cooked as long as you cook the turkey. An hour or less at 325 degrees should be enough to warm the stuffing through.

To keep the stuffing moist, baste the casserole occasionally when basting the turkey, and keep it covered with aluminum foil.

If you have cooked the stuffing inside the turkey, remove all of it from the bird and store the leftovers in a separate container. Leaving stuffing in the turkey carcass is an invitation to bacterial spoilage.

TRUSSING

The classic method for preparing a turkey is to truss it. This involves tying the legs and wings close to the bird's body. The reasons for trussing are

cosmetic: to make the bird look plump and round; practical: to make the turkey easier to carve and to keep it from drying out.

First tie the legs together by looping a long piece of string under the tail. Cross the string over the tail then coil it around the ends of the drumsticks. Bend the second wing joints back. Draw the string tight around the thighs and along the sides of the body and pull it through the notches in the folded wings. Turn the turkey over and tie the string across the back.

If you use a V-shaped rack some of this trussing may be unnecessary. The sides of the rack force the bird into the shape that trussing achieves. It presses the legs and wings against the body and plumps up the breast. The only trussing that may be necessary is the tail-drumstick loop described above.

CLOSING A STUFFED BIRD

One of the most daunting of Thanksgiving tasks may be the securing of the turkey once it is stuffed. Closing the cavity can be a terrifying prospect but it isn't actually that difficult.

The traditional method is to sew the opening closed using kitchen twine and a poultry needle. This is quite effective, but a bit tedious. We have found skewers to be much easier to handle. Most kitchen stores and supermarkets sell poultry skewers made especially for this purpose. They are sharply pointed 4-inch metal pins, two or three of which can easily close a turkey's main cavity.

Place the skin on one side of the cavity over the skin on the other side. Punch the skewer through both thicknesses of skin, press down on the skewer's end, and force its point back through the two pieces of skin. This will efficiently hold the opening closed. Use other skewers whenever needed to completely close off the cavity. Use the same technique on the neck opening.

When the bird is cooked, the skin has lost its elasticity. The skewers can be slipped out of their places and the cavity will remain closed.

BASTING

Keeping the turkey moist while it's cooking is an important consideration. One way to ensure this is to baste the bird. This procedure—occasionally spooning liquid over the turkey—serves several purposes. It keeps the turkey skin moist and tender. It also can help the browning process.

Any number of liquids can be used for basting, but the most common is chicken or turkey stock. As the liquid runs off into the roasting pan, it blends with the rich pan drippings from the turkey. If you use a bulb baster, you can suck up this enriched stock and baste the turkey with it.

The basting liquid in the bottom of the roasting pan helps to keep the oven environment humid (thus keeping the turkey from drying out) and it prevents drippings from burning in the pan and causing unwanted smoke and a burned taste.

Basting is helpful, but don't overdo it. Basting the bird every 20 or 30 minutes or so is plenty. Remember, each time you open the oven door the temperature inside the oven is lowered and cooking time is lengthened.

A method that Andy's mother used frequently was to soak a double thickness of cheesecloth in chicken fat or butter and drape it over the turkey breast. This holds the fat and the basting liquids against the skin of the turkey longer, and basting can be done less frequently. This method is effective, but it is important not to let the cheesecloth dry out. If it does, it will stick to the turkey skin and tear it when removed. If you use this method, remove the cheesecloth 30 minutes before the cooking time is over to brown the breast.

If you end up with a bird that describes itself as "self-basting" this doesn't mean that basting can be given up completely. The "self-basting" turkeys are injected with liquid that keeps the meat moist internally during cooking. But the skin still requires attention, and an occasional baste with stock and pan juices will keep it from drying out.

We are amazed that the government allows the free-wheeling use of the word *butter* applied to some of these self-basters when the liquid used is usually mostly vegetable oil and various chemicals, such as MSG.

TURNING

In a perfect world, the best way to cook a turkey evenly is to turn it over at one point during the process. It makes sense in theory, but just try turning a slippery 16-pounder without dropping it or tearing the skin. Turning a turkey is risky for two people and virtually impossible to do alone.

We do suggest turning the roasting pan about halfway through the cooking process. Whichever way you position the turkey (we like to place it sideways), turn it 180 degrees to roast it evenly.

RESTING

When the turkey is removed from the oven it should not be carved and eaten immediately. The bird needs to rest for 15 or 20 minutes to allow juices to redistribute themselves.

CARVING

There are several methods for carving the turkey and each has its passionate adherents.

Method 1—Traditional

This is the standard way of carving the turkey. It is particularly suited to a presentation at the dinner table in front of the gathered celebrants.

1. First remove the drumstick and thigh on one side by pulling the leg away from the body. Cut the joint near the body with a long, sharp, flexible knife.
2. Separate the drumstick from the thigh by cutting through the tendons at the knee joint.
3. Slice the dark meat off the thigh by cutting even pieces parallel to the bone, ¼-inch thick. Place the cut meat on a warm platter.
4. You can cut off the wing at this point. If you choose to do so, bend it back, away from the body, and cut at the joint.
5. Starting at the ridge at the top of the breast, slice off a slab of meat and skin about ⅛-inch thick. Continue to slice the breast, keeping the knife blade parallel to the turkey's rib cage. Be sure to keep the slices thin.
6. When you finish one side, reverse the bird and repeat the process.

Method 2—In the Kitchen

If you are carving in the kitchen, out of sight of the guests, this is an efficient method.

1.–4. Follow procedures used in Method 1 above.
5. Start at the breastbone ridge—the keel bone—above the breast. Cut down and deep, keeping the blade as close to the rib cage as possible. Following the contour of the bird, remove the entire half breast.
6. Place the half breast on a cutting surface and slice evenly against the grain of the meat. Repeat the procedure with the other half of the breast.

Method 3—The Lateral Cut

This is a clever way to cut clean, regular slices easily. It is also a good method if you are carving in front of a crowd.

1.–4. Cut off the drumstick, thigh, and wings, as in Method 1 above. Make a deep, lateral cut below the breast and parallel with the platter. This allows you to cut straight down instead of following the contour of the turkey.

5. Begin slicing about 2 inches above the cut. Slice off a ⅛-inch-thick piece and continue cutting in the same way, working your way up to the breastbone.

6. Repeat this procedure on the other side of the turkey.

BONED TURKEY

If you work carefully, you can slip off the skin of a chicken just like a glove. Unfortunately, turkeys don't work the same way because they are too big and their bones are too hard. To bone a turkey you must slit the skin down the back, remove the bones, and reattach the two sides.

The ideal size turkey for boning is 12 pounds or so. Do not attempt this on a turkey larger than 15 pounds.

Set the turkey on a flat surface, breast side down, with the neck cavity facing you. Cut the skin down the center of the backbone from the neck to the tail. Using a sharp boning knife and your fingers, peel the meat back on both sides of the cut.

When you reach the wings and legs, dislocate them and sever the tendons that hold them. Slide the knife down the wishbone and remove it. Continue scraping the meat from the rib cage on both sides until you reach the breastbone. Lift out the turkey's whole frame.

To remove the thighbone, slide your knife down the shaft of the bone, then cut the tendons at the knuckle. Leave the drumstick bones and the wings intact.

Lay the turkey skin side down on a flat surface. Place the filling in a line down the center of the turkey. Roll up the skin and sew or skewer it closed at the top.

A boned turkey is usually filled with a dense stuffing called a forcemeat (see page 73).

Turkey with Molasses Glaze

$\mathcal{T}$his is our basic turkey recipe. We have experimented with other temperatures and other glazes, but this has been the most successful! at our table. The glaze gives the bird a deep mahogany color and its adds flavor to the skin. The slow cooking temperature keeps it moist and tender.

Serves 12, with plenty of leftovers

One 16-pound turkey, fresh or
    fully defrosted
Salt and freshly ground pepper
1 recipe Sausage-Crouton Stuffing
    (see page 61)

2 tablespoons molasses
2 tablespoons soy sauce

1. Preheat the oven to 325 degrees. Rinse the turkey inside and out with cold water. Dry thoroughly with paper towels. Sprinkle the cavity with salt and pepper. Stuff loosely (stuffing expands during cooking) and close the opening with metal skewers. Also stuff the neck cavity and skewer it closed. (Place the leftover stuffing in a buttered soufflé dish and bake it alongside the turkey for the last hour of its cooking time, basting the stuffing occasionally with pan juices.)

2. Tie the turkey's legs together and place it on a rack (we use a Teflon-coated V-shaped rack) set in a large roasting pan.

3. Mix the molasses and soy sauce in a small dish. (Variation: Use 2 tablespoons of maple syrup instead of molasses.) With a pastry brush, paint the turkey with the mixture, lifting it up to reach the under side. This method makes the bird very dark, very quickly, so the turkey should either be tented when dark or it could be first painted 2 hours before cooking is done.

4. Place the turkey in the center of the preheated oven and roast, basting occasionally with accumulated pan juices, until a thermometer inserted into the thickest part of the thigh registers 170 degrees and juices run clear. This should take between 4½ and 5 hours. The turkey skin should be quite dark. Check at the 4-hour point and if it isn't, brush again with the molasses mixture.

5. Transfer the turkey to a platter or carving board and let it rest for 20 minutes before carving.

Upside-down Turkey

*T*his is a cumbersome and sometimes exasperating procedure, but the result is worth all the trouble. This may be the moistest and most delicious turkey of all. We do not advise trying this with a turkey any bigger than 12 pounds.

The idea here is to roast the turkey breast side down to make the breast meat very juicy. An hour or so before the end of the cooking time, the bird is reversed so the breast can brown properly. This is the difficult part. We have found that it really requires two people to turn the bird over without damaging the skin.

Serves 12, with leftovers

2 cloves garlic, minced
½ teaspoon chopped fresh
   rosemary
½ teaspoon chopped fresh
   marjoram
½ teaspoon chopped fresh
   thyme
2 tablespoons chopped fresh
   basil
½ teaspoon salt

½ teaspoon freshly ground
   pepper
6 tablespoons unsalted butter,
   softened
One 12-pound fresh turkey
Stuffing of your choice
2 cups dry white wine
Chicken Stock (see page 77) for
   basting

1. In a food processor bowl, combine the garlic, herbs, salt, and pepper with the softened butter. Purée for a few seconds to combine well. Set aside.

2. Preheat the oven to 325 degrees. Starting around the main body cavity, carefully slip your hand under the turkey skin and break the membranes that hold it to the body. With your fingers, smear the herb butter under the skin.

3. Stuff the turkey loosely, in the neck and main cavity, and close the flaps with skewers. Rub the remainder of the herb butter over the skin of the turkey. Set the turkey, breast side down, on a buttered Teflon-coated V-shaped rack set in a shallow roasting pan. Pour the wine in the pan under the turkey.

4. Roast the turkey in the preheated oven for the suggested time (see chart, page 38). Baste occasionally with stock and make sure that the liquid in the pan does not evaporate.

(continued)

5. An hour or so before the turkey is done, slide the roasting pan out of the oven and reverse the turkey. (We have found that using serving spoons is an effective way of doing this, but don't try to do this alone, if you can help it.) Another way sacrifices a clean pair of oven mitts, but seems to be foolproof and reduces the risk of dropping the bird or piercing its skin with objects. Working quickly before juices penetrate the gloves, use heat-proof, heavy gauge oven mitts to pull the pan out of the oven and directly handle the bird.

Turkey Roasted in a Paper Bag

This all-American version of the classic French *papillote* technique helps the bird retain all its moisture. If you hate dried-out turkey (who doesn't?) this is a surefire antidote.

This technique is best suited to a smaller turkey (or a chicken or capon).

NOTE: Some paper bags contain unwanted chemicals. Check at health food stores for all-natural bags.

Serves 8

One 10- or 11-pound turkey, at room temperature	3 carrots, coarsely chopped
Salt and freshly ground pepper	3 stalks celery, coarsely chopped
4 cups any stuffing (see pages 57–73)	2 medium onions, coarsely chopped
2 tablespoons unsalted butter, softened	2 cloves garlic, sliced
	2 bay leaves
	Chicken Stock (see page 77)

1. Preheat the oven to 325 degrees. Rinse the turkey under cold, running water and then pat it dry with paper towels. Sprinkle the neck cavity and main cavity with salt and pepper. Fill each with your choice of stuffing, loosely packed. Seal each with poultry skewers. Tuck the wings under the turkey.

2. Rub the softened butter all over the turkey. Season lightly with salt and pepper. Take a sturdy, clean brown paper bag big enough to hold the turkey, and spray the inside with water. Pour out any excess water. Gently slip the turkey into the bag, facing the neck cavity forward and the legs near the opening. Roll up the opening to seal.

3. Sprinkle the carrots, celery, onions, garlic, and bay leaves evenly over the bottom of a roasting pan that is just big enough to hold the turkey. Put the giblets (except for the liver) in among the vegetables. Add chicken stock to the roasting pan to a depth of ½ inch. Place the closed bag in the roasting pan on top of the vegetables. Make sure the turkey is sitting breast side up.

4. Roast in the preheated oven for 2½ hours. Then gently roll back the bag and insert a meat thermometer into the thickest part of the leg or the thigh. The temperature should read 155 degrees. If it doesn't, roll up the bag and return the turkey to the oven for 15 minutes more. When the temperature registers 155 degrees, tear open the paper bag and raise the oven heat to 425 degrees.

5. Roast the turkey for another 30 minutes, basting occasionally. When done, the turkey should register 170 to 175 degrees on the meat thermometer and the skin should be golden brown.

6. Remove the roasting pan from the oven and transfer the turkey to a platter and cover it loosely with foil. Discard paper bag. Let the turkey sit for 20 minutes before carving.

7. Pour the pan juices through a sieve into a saucepan. Press the solids with a wooden spoon to extract their juices. Place the saucepan over medium heat, and reduce the pan juices until they thicken and form a gravy that coats the spoon. (This can be used as a base for a gravy, or it can be used on its own.)

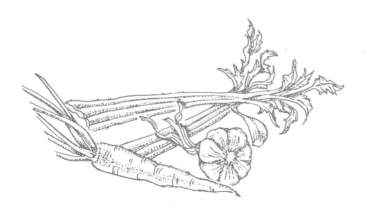

Grilled Turkey

*I*f the weather outside isn't hideous, cooking the turkey on the outdoor barbecue is a good idea. It frees the kitchen oven for other Thanksgiving goodies and it cuts down on cleanup. The grill imparts a delightful smoky nuance to the turkey and to its stuffing.

Our Los Angeles pal Laurie Burrows Grad grills her turkey poolside. Although a quick dip is not necessarily a part of Thanksgiving, temperate weather certainly brings more of the holiday party outside. Her method is simple and logical and the result is really delicious.

Laurie allows 13 to 15 minutes per pound for a stuffed turkey, about 11 minutes per pound for a turkey that is unstuffed. But she notes that outside conditions—wind direction, temperature, and humidity—can affect the timing. So can the nature of your grill. If you are using a gas or electric grill, follow the manufacturer's instructions for the use of indirect heating methods.

Be sure to choose a bird that isn't too big for your grill. You need to allow at least 1 inch between the turkey and the lid and sides of the grill. Actually, a turkey cooked on a grill should not exceed 12 pounds.

If you are using a regular charcoal kettle-style grill, you can get a rich, smoky flavor by soaking about 2 cups of mesquite chips in water for about 1 hour. Put a 12 by 9-inch disposable foil drip pan in the bottom of the grill. Build a fire of about 30 briquettes (not the self-starting kind) on the long sides of the drip pan. Light the coals and let them burn for 30 minutes with the grill uncovered. When the coals are covered with white ash, the fire is ready. Sprinkle the mesquite chips over the coals and start cooking your turkey.

On a gas grill set the heat at moderate around the outside and off in the center.

Prepare the turkey as described in general turkey instructions (pages 35–36).

Place the turkey breast side up in the center of the grill over the drip pan. Cover the grill and cook, adding 9 briquettes to each long side of the drip pan every hour.

The turkey is done when a meat thermometer inserted in the thigh registers 170 to 175 degrees. The center of the stuffing should read at least 160 degrees.

Transfer the turkey to a cutting board and let it stand 20 to 30 minutes before carving.

Roasted Split Turkey

$\mathcal{T}$his is good for a small group. It provides the complete traditional feast —light and dark meat and pan gravy, and very little left over. Split the turkey from the breast bone to the tail and freeze the other half. (If this seems daunting, ask the butcher to do it.)

Serves 4 to 6

½ teaspoon salt
½ teaspoon freshly ground
   pepper
One 7½-pound half turkey

1 tablespoon soy sauce
1 tablespoon maple syrup

1. Preheat the oven to 425 degrees. Salt and pepper the turkey on both sides. Place the stuffing in the breast cavity and place the turkey, cut side down, in a roasting pan.

2. Mix the soy sauce and maple syrup together. Using a pastry brush, paint the turkey skin with the mixture. Bake the turkey for 15 minutes in the preheated oven.

3. Reduce the oven temperature to 350 degrees. Roast for 1 hour, basting every 15 to 20 minutes with turkey stock or melted butter. The turkey is done when a thermometer inserted in the thickest part of the breast or thigh reaches 165 to 170 degrees. Remove from the oven and let rest for 15 minutes before serving.

4. When you lift the turkey out of the roasting pan, the stuffing will remain in the pan. Transfer it to a serving dish and then carve the turkey.

Roast Turkey Thighs
with Corn Bread Stuffing

_T_he Four Seasons Clift Hotel in San Francisco is open every year for Thanksgiving. Since most customers prefer white meat, chef Kelly Mills has developed this recipe for the kitchen staff. By boning out the thigh, a small roast is created that is easy to stuff and even easier to slice.

Serves 8 to 10

1 pound fresh or canned chestnuts
½ cup coarsely chopped dried cranberries
2 cups crumbled Basic Corn Bread (see page 140)
2 beaten eggs
3 tablespoons chopped fresh sage
2 tablespoons chopped fresh parsley
1 cup Chicken Stock (see page 77)

2 turkey thighs (about 3¼ pounds)
Salt and freshly ground pepper
2 tablespoons butter
4 medium shallots, minced
The turkey giblets, minced
½ cup red wine
2 cups reduced Turkey Stock (see page 78)

1. If you are using fresh chestnuts, cut a slit in each one and place in a 2-quart saucepan. Cover with water, bring to a boil over medium heat, and cook for 20 minutes. Let the chestnuts cool in the cooking water until they can be handled. The chestnuts must be moist to be peeled. Remove both outer shell and the brown skin, then chop them coarsely. You should have about 2 cups.

2. In a large bowl, combine the chopped chestnuts, cranberries, corn bread, eggs, sage, parsley, and stock. Toss gently with a fork, being careful to keep the stuffing fluffy. Set aside.

3. With a sharp boning knife, working on each thigh with its skin side down, make a cut along the length of the bone, then peel back the meat from there. Be careful to keep the knife close to the bone. Keep the meat intact and do not pierce the skin. Once the bone is removed, spread out the thigh, making slits in the meat, if necessary, to allow it to lay flat. Place the meat between 2 sheets of wax paper and pound to make them an even thickness.

4. Preheat the oven to 375 degrees. Season the thighs with salt and pepper. Place some stuffing in the middle of each butterflied thigh, in a line running lengthwise. Roll the thighs around the stuffing, and tie them with string in three or four places.

5. Place the thighs side by side (but not touching) in a shallow roasting pan. Roast for about 30 minutes, then transfer to a platter in a warm oven while you prepare the sauce.

6. Place the roasting pan over medium heat. Add the butter, shallots, and giblets to the pan, and sauté for 3 minutes. Add the wine and deglaze the pan, loosening any encrusted bits with a wooden spoon. Reduce the liquid by half and add the stock. Simmer for 20 minutes. Adjust the seasonings.

7. Untie the roasts and slice in rounds about ½ inch thick. Top with sauce and serve.

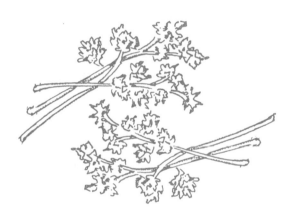

Stuffed Turkey Breast

*T*his is an ideal dish for those who have a fear of carving in front of a crowd but don't mind a bit of preparation.

Serves 6

One 5- to 6-pound turkey breast
½ teaspoon salt
½ teaspoon freshly ground pepper
½ teaspoon ground cinnamon
½ teaspoon ground allspice
1 tablespoon fresh thyme, or 1 teaspoon dried

¼ teaspoon ground cloves
¼ teaspoon ground mace
½ teaspoon ground cardamom
4 cups any stuffing (see pages 57–73)
4 strips bacon

1. The turkey breast must be boned and butterflied. You can ask your butcher to do this for you, or try it yourself. Here's how: First remove the wishbone, which is located at the front of the breast between the wings. Holding the breast in one hand with the small pointed end resting on the cutting board, scrape the meat at the top of the breast with the blade of a boning knife. Once the knife touches bone, use your fingers to loosen the V-shaped end and pull out the bone.

Lay the breast skin side down on the cutting board. Insert the tip of a very sharp boning knife between the meat and the rib cage, about 1 inch down on each side to loosen the muscle. Using your hands, gently pull the breast meat away from the rib cage, toward the center bone.

Turn the breast over and continue loosening the meat from the bone. The meat is firmly attached to the bone by cartilage; to avoid tearing, use the knife to cut the connective tissue as you work your fingers between the meat and bone. This should yield a large, flat piece of meat.

Often the muscle next to the separation in the breast bone will not come off in one piece with the top of the breast. To remove this muscle, slip the tip of the boning knife under the fillet on each side of the bone and pull the section free. If you have to remove this fillet separately, it can be stuffed in the roll or frozen for later use.

To even out the meat, place it skin side down on the cutting board, cover with wax paper, and pound to flatten it.

2. Combine all the seasonings and rub over the surface of the turkey. Refrigerate for at least 2 hours, preferably overnight.

3. When ready to cook, preheat the oven to 400 degrees. Lay the turkey skin side down on a flat surface. Place the stuffing of your choice along the center. Bring both sides of the breast together around the stuffing, forming a long shape about 2 to 3 inches in diameter and 12 to 14 inches long. Tuck one side under the other to form a very tight roll, and either sew, skewer, or tie it with string like a roast. Cut a piece of aluminum foil long enough to cover the roast with a few inches to spare.

4. Butter the foil. Place the strips of bacon the length of the roast on top and wrap tightly. Twist the ends of the foil to secure the wrap. Place the roast seam side up in a baking pan. Bake in the preheated oven for 40 minutes.

5. Reduce the oven temperature to 350 degrees. Peel back the foil and bake for 20 minutes, or until golden brown. If you wish, you can baste the roast once or twice with a combination of stock and butter or oil.

6. Remove from the oven. Let rest 5 to 10 minutes, remove strings or skewers, and cut in slices ¼ inch thick. Serve with the juices that collect in the foil or with a gravy of your choice.

Stuffed Cornish Game Hens with Zinfandel Gravy

*T*here is something appealing about each guest getting his or her own whole bird to feast on. Cornish game hens are another purely American addition to the realm of poultry. In this case, the plump little birds are a result of crossing Plymouth Rock hens with various types of small game birds. They are always available frozen, and frequently you can find them fresh.

Serves 6

6 Rock Cornish game hens
1 lemon, cut into sections
Salt and freshly ground pepper
6 cups Chicken Liver Stuffing
  (see page 69)
6 strips bacon

½ cup (1 stick) unsalted butter, melted
2 cups good Zinfandel
1 cup Chicken Stock (see page 77)
2 tablespoons flour
2 tablespoons water

1. Preheat the oven to 350 degrees. Rinse the birds under cold running water, and dry with paper towels. Rub the cut sections of lemon inside and outside the birds. Sprinkle with salt and pepper inside and out.

2. Loosely stuff each bird with 1 cup of stuffing. Sew or skewer closed.

3. Cut each strip of bacon in half and lay two halves on each bird's breast in an X.

4. Place the birds on a rack in a low-sided roasting pan. Place in the preheated oven and roast for 1 hour. Use a bulb baster to baste frequently with the melted butter and any pan juices.

5. Transfer hens to a warm serving platter. Pour off the fat in the roasting pan.

6. In a saucepan over moderate heat, combine the wine and stock and bring to a boil. Reduce to a simmer.

7. Put flour and water in a container with an airtight lid. Shake vigorously to mix. Strain mixture and then pour into stock and wine mixture. Stir constantly until it begins to thicken.

8. Place roasting pan over heat and pour in the thickened stock. Stir constantly with a wooden spoon, scraping the entire pan to loosen the baked-on juices. Season the sauce to taste. Pour into a gravy boat or spoon over the hens. Serve immediately.

Roast Duck Stuffed with Couscous

$\mathcal{W}$hat to serve for a small Thanksgiving party is always a question. The smallest turkey you can buy will serve 6 or even 8 people. This means you will need something smaller—unless you want to be working on leftovers for a week or so.

If you are just two or perhaps four, you'll need to find something other than turkey. A roast chicken will certainly do the trick, but if you are interested in something a bit more festive, we recommend duck.

Duck is mighty rich, but for this special day it is quite appropriate. The fattiness can be reduced while roasting and cut with the use of a tangy kumquat cranberry compote.

Serves 2 as a full meal, or 4 as part of a big holiday feast

One 5-pound duck	1 tablespoon soy sauce
1 lemon, cut in half	1 tablespoon maple syrup
Salt and freshly ground pepper	
3 cups Couscous Stuffing (see page 68)	

1. Remove the neck and giblets from inside the duck. Reserve them to make stock. Rub the duck inside and out with the lemon halves. Pierce the skin all over with the tines of a fork to speed the loss of fat during cooking. Liberally sprinkle the bird with salt and freshly ground pepper inside and out.

2. Preheat the oven to 400 degrees. Stuff the duck cavity with Couscous Stuffing and close the opening with skewers. Place some stuffing in the neck cavity and close. Tie the legs together with string and place the bird on a rack in a sturdy baking pan.

3. Combine the soy sauce and maple syrup in a small dish and paint the mixture all over the duck with a pastry brush. Roast for 15 minutes, then reduce the heat to 350 degrees. Bake for 1 hour, or until the juices run clear when you pierce the thigh with a skewer. If the duck gets too brown, cover with foil. Serve.

Roast Goose

Serves 6

One 11- to 13-pound goose,
  fresh or frozen
1 tablespoon salt
1 tablespoon freshly ground
  pepper
1 lemon, cut in half

Port, Apricot, and Rice Stuffing
  (page 72)
2 cups Goose (see page 78) or
  Chicken Stock (see page 77)
Port and Currant Jelly Sauce
  (see page 85)

1. If using a frozen goose, thoroughly defrost it by storing in the refrigerator for 38 hours. Remove from the refrigerator, place on a platter, and bring the bird to room temperature (this should take about 4 hours).

2. Three hours before serving, prick the skin all over with a sharp fork and rub the exterior and interior of the goose with the lemon halves. Cut off the wing tips at the second joint. Preheat the oven to 350 degrees.

3. Sprinkle the goose inside and out with salt and pepper. Stuff the bird loosely and leave the cavity open. Put a small amount of stuffing in the neck cavity and skewer it closed. If you have extra stuffing, put it in a baking dish and cook it alongside the bird, basting occasionally. Either tie the legs together or make a slit in the skin above the tail that is large enough to insert the ends of the legs.

4. Set the goose, breast side up, on a rack in a roasting pan. Baste every 20 minutes with stock. Remove fat periodically from the pan with a bulb baster or spoon. Cook for 2½ hours, or until a meat thermometer inserted in the center of the upper thigh registers 180 degrees.

NOTE: It may be necessary to cover the goose with foil to prevent over-browning, but if you use such a cover, take it off for the last 10 minutes of cooking time to give the bird a glossy golden brown finish.

Stuffing

We guess that if a vote were taken in our house for the most popular part of the Thanksgiving feast, stuffing would win hands down. The rich mix of flavors and textures make a good stuffing delicious and make it one leftover that never lasts more than a day.

Stuffing is a self-contained side dish. Its close contact with the turkey (or other poultry) creates a strong bond. The turkey takes on the flavors of the stuffing, and the stuffing absorbs the juices and flavors of the turkey. In fact, stuffing is the ideal vehicle for adding seasonings to the essentially monochromatic turkey.

The American stuffing or, as those nineteenth-century puritans who found the word risqué would have it, "dressing" is loosely packed in the cavities of the poultry. It is served as a vegetable. Most stuffings are usually based on a starch—bread, bread crumbs, rice, potatoes—and they are seasoned with herbs, nuts, fruits, and other interesting items.

The probable ancestor of American stuffing is forcemeat (from the French, *farcir,* "to stuff"), a dense mixture of ground meat, spices, and herbs. The difference between the two is the fact that forcemeat is tightly packed and is usually cut and served as part of the bird. Stuffing is scooped out and served on the side.

The key thing to remember about stuffing is to keep it cool and never stuff a turkey or other poultry in advance. Stuff only when you are ready to put the bird in the oven. If not handled correctly, stuffing can become a ripe medium for bacteria.

STUFFING THE TURKEY

The general rule is to allow ¾ to 1 cup of moistened stuffing per pound of dressed-weight turkey. Another way to arrive at the amount is to multiply the number of servings by ¾ cup.

Stuffing should be kept airy and not compressed when filling the cavities of the turkey or other poultry. The action of heat and moisture during cooking causes stuffing to expand and, in an extreme case, might cause an overstuffed turkey to burst. Keep in mind that extra stuffing can be tucked into the neck cavity.

This table indicates how much stuffing is normally required for birds of certain weights. It is difficult to be exact with these amounts because the size of turkey cavities varies considerably. Nevertheless, this should be a helpful guideline.

Bird Size	Approximate Amount of Stuffing
2 to 4 pounds	2 cups
4 to 6 pounds	4 cups
6 to 8 pounds	5 cups
8 to 10 pounds	6 cups
10 to 12 pounds	8 cups
12 to 15 pounds	10 cups
15 to 20 pounds	12 cups
20 to 25 pounds	16 cups

This should not intimidate stuffing lovers who want to make much more than will fill a bird. They can place the excess stuffing in a covered casserole and bake it alongside the turkey for about 1 hour. Cooked stuffing may be frozen and kept for 3 or 4 weeks.

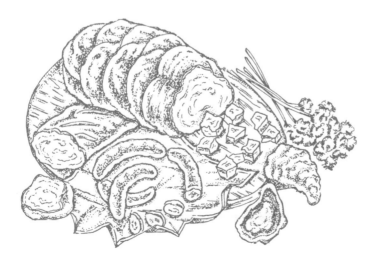

Quick Stuffing

Makes 6 cups

2 tablespoons unsalted butter
1 clove garlic, minced
¼ cup chopped red onion
¼ cup diced celery
1 tablespoon fresh sage, or 1
   teaspoon dried
¼ teaspoon fresh rosemary, or
   pinch of dried

1 cup fresh or frozen peas
1 cup stock
5 cups of crisp, dry bread cubes
   made from white or corn
   bread
1 egg, lightly beaten (optional)
½ cup chestnut halves

1. In a skillet, melt 1 tablespoon butter. Sauté the garlic and onion for 1 minute. Add the celery, seasonings, and peas. Sauté for 2 minutes to warm. Add the stock and bring the mixture to a simmer over medium heat. Cook for 5 minutes.

2. Remove the vegetables from the skillet with a slotted spoon. Reserve. Raise the heat, bring the liquid still in the skillet to a boil, and reduce to ¾ cup.

3. In a large mixing bowl combine the bread and the vegetables. Spoon the reduced liquid over the stuffing and toss gently. The stuffing should hold together. If it doesn't, add an egg and toss with a fork to combine.

4. In a skillet, melt the remaining butter, add the chestnuts and sear. Add to the stuffing mixture and toss again to combine. Refrigerate until ready to use.

ADVANCE PREPARATION: Can be prepared 2 days ahead. Cover and refrigerate. Bring to room temperature before using.

Sausage-Crouton Stuffing

$\mathcal{W}$e developed this stuffing for *Bon Appétit* magazine. Frankly, we thought of the name first, then created the recipe to go with it. This is a rich, earthy, and extremely delicious stuffing with great texture.

Makes 16 cups

1¼ pounds challah or other egg bread, crusts trimmed, cut into ½-inch cubes

1 pound sweet Italian sausage, casings removed

1 medium onion, chopped

4 celery stalks, chopped

½ cup drained canned water chestnuts, quartered

½ cup (about 2 ounces) toasted and coarsely chopped pecans

2 tablespoons chopped fresh parsley

4 teaspoons chopped fresh sage, or 1½ teaspoons ground dried

¼ cup Chicken (see page 77) or Turkey Stock (see page 78)

2 tablespoons unsalted butter, melted

Salt and freshly ground pepper

1. Preheat the oven to 300 degrees. Spread the bread cubes in a single layer on 2 large cookie sheets. Bake until crisp, about 20 minutes. Transfer to a large bowl.

2. Crumble the sausage meat into a large skillet, and sauté over medium heat until cooked through, about 12 minutes. Add to the bread crumbs, using a slotted spoon.

3. In the same skillet, sauté the onion and celery until transparent, about 10 minutes. Add to the bread mixture. Mix in the water chestnuts, pecans, parsley, and sage. Add the stock and butter and toss to combine (the mixture will be dry). Season with salt and freshly ground pepper.

ADVANCE PREPARATION: Can be prepared 1 day ahead. Cover and refrigerate. Bring to room temperature before using.

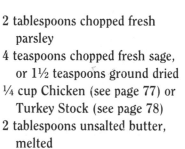

Glazed Chestnut, Apple, and Sausage Stuffing

Makes about 8 cups

4 ounces veal sausage
4 ounces pork sausage
½ onion, chopped
2 celery stalks, chopped
8 slices stale honey wheat berry or whole wheat bread
1 cup Goose (see page 78) or Chicken Stock (see page 77)
5 tablespoons dry white wine
2 teaspoons sugar

1 cup canned chestnuts broken into large pieces
1 cup chopped tart green apple, either Granny Smith or Pippin
1 egg, beaten
2 teaspoons dried ground sage
¼ cup chopped fresh parsley
Salt and freshly ground pepper

1. Crumble sausages in chunks into a medium skillet set over medium heat, and sauté until just brown. Add onion and celery and cook until the celery is bright green, about 5 minutes.

2. Preheat the oven to 250 degrees. Place the bread slices on a cookie sheet and bake until crisp, about 15 minutes. Remove from the oven and cut into 1-inch squares. Combine with sausage mixture and toss gently.

3. In a small sauté pan combine the stock and white wine and reduce by half over moderate heat. Stir in the sugar and simmer for a few minutes longer. Toss the chestnuts in the glaze until completely coated. Remove with a slotted spoon, then repeat the procedure with the apples.

4. Add the chestnuts and apples to the sausage mixture along with the egg, sage, and parsley. Season to taste with salt and pepper, and mix gently with a fork, being careful to keep the stuffing fluffy, not compressed. (If the stuffing is too dry, add a dash of wine or stock to moisten it. If you are using fresh sage, double the amount.)

ADVANCE PREPARATION: Can be prepared 1 day in advance. Cover and refrigerate. Bring to room temperature before using.

Corn Bread Stuffing

There are people in our family who dote on stuffing. We suspect they might even like stuffing better than the turkey itself. One year Andy helped himself and was halfway through dinner, paying special attention to the large pile of stuffing on his plate, when he realized that he had completely forgotten to serve himself some turkey. "I never missed it," he said licking his lips. This was the stuffing in question.

Makes 8 cups

¼ cup chicken or turkey fat or
    butter
3 medium onions, chopped
3 stalks celery, sliced
2 cloves garlic, minced
2 eggs, well-beaten
1 cup Chicken (see page 77) or
    Turkey Stock (see page 78)
½ cup minced fresh parsley

4 cups of crumbled Basic Corn
    Bread (see page 140), dried
    out either in a turned-off oven
    overnight or in the dry air
½ cup chopped walnuts
½ cup chopped water chestnuts
    (optional)
Salt and freshly ground pepper

    1. Melt the fat or butter in a medium skillet. Sauté the onions, celery, and garlic until the vegetables are translucent but not brown. Add the eggs, stock, and parsley. Stir to combine.

    2. Place the corn bread in a large bowl and add the onion and celery mixture. Add the walnuts and water chestnuts, if desired. Season to taste with salt and pepper. Toss to combine, being careful not to compress the stuffing any more than necessary. Keep it fluffy. Cover the bowl and refrigerate until ready to use.

    ADVANCE PREPARATION: Can be prepared 2 days ahead. Cover and refrigerate. Bring to room temperature before using.

Oyster Corn Bread Stuffing

*A*lthough it sounds trendy, oyster stuffing has been traditional Thanksgiving fare for a very long time. We found it in some cookbooks published in the late nineteenth century. This version adds a few twists, including corn bread and Paul Prudhomme's idea of prebaking the stuffing before putting it into the bird. This gives it a deep mahogany color.

Makes 6 cups

Two 10-ounce containers of oysters and their liquor
2 cups cold water
2 teaspoons minced garlic
¾ teaspoon salt
¾ teaspoon cayenne
¾ teaspoon paprika
¾ teaspoon freshly ground pepper
½ teaspoon dried oregano
½ teaspoon dried thyme
2 cups diced onions

1¼ cup finely diced celery
¾ cup chopped red bell pepper
⅔ cup thinly sliced leeks, white only
8 tablespoons (1 stick) unsalted butter
⅔ cup chopped fresh parsley
2 small bay leaves
2 cups crumbled Basic Corn Bread (see page 140)
½ cup chopped scallions

1. In a bowl, combine oysters, their liquor, and cold water. Stir and chill at least 1 hour. Remove the oysters from the liquid and reserve separately; refrigerate until ready to use.

2. In a small bowl, combine 1 teaspoon minced garlic with the seasonings and reserve.

3. In another bowl, combine the onions, celery, bell pepper, and leeks. Toss to mix thoroughly. In a medium sauté pan, over high heat, melt half the butter and add half the vegetables (2⅓ cups), reduce heat to medium, and sauté 30 minutes to brown the onions thoroughly. Stir occasionally.

4. Reduce the temperature to low. Add half of the garlic seasoning mixture and the remaining minced garlic, and sauté 4 minutes, stirring constantly and scraping the bottom of the pan.

5. Add the remaining butter and turn the heat to high. Add the rest of the vegetables, ⅓ cup parsley, and the bay leaves. Sauté for 10 minutes, stirring occasionally.

6. Preheat the oven to 350 degrees. Stir the reserved oyster liquid into the vegetable mixture, and simmer for 15 minutes. Add the remaining

seasonings and stir. The corn bread should be added ½ cup at a time to make a fairly moist stuffing. Remove from the heat. Fold in the oysters, being careful not to break them. Spoon stuffing into an ungreased 8 by 8-inch baking pan. Bake in the oven for 1 hour. After 30 minutes, when a dark crust appears, stir. Scrape from the sides and bottom of the pan. When finished baking, remove bay leaves.

7. Add the rest of the parsley and the scallions, stirring well. Cool the stuffing and refrigerate, being sure to chill it well before it is to be used.

ADVANCE PREPARATION: Can be prepared 1 day ahead. Cover and refrigerate. Bring to room temperature before using.

Sauerkraut Apple Stuffing

K it Snedaker is a great editor and food historian. She found this slightly oddball but quite delicious 1949 stuffing recipe. This stuffing is best with duck or goose.

Makes 12 cups

6 cups coarse, fresh bread
    crumbs
3 cups sauerkraut, drained
2 cups diced apples, (Granny
    Smith or other tart variety
    does best)

1 cup chopped onions
½ teaspoon caraway seed
1 tablespoon grated orange zest

1. Spread the bread crumbs in a jelly-roll pan and bake in a 250-degree oven for 10 minutes.

2. Combine the bread crumbs with the remaining ingredients, and mix well.

ADVANCE PREPARATION: Can be prepared 2 days ahead. Cover and refrigerate. Bring to room temperature before using.

Pistachio and Apple Stuffing

*T*he price of these nuts makes this stuffing almost as decadent as bathing in Dom Perignon. But we present this recipe unashamedly because it is exceptionally delicious.

Makes 12 cups

½ cup currants
¼ cup Calvados or apple jack
¼ cup extra-virgin olive oil
6 cups cubed French bread, crust on
2 cups shelled pistachio nuts
8 tablespoons (1 stick) unsalted butter
3 celery stalks, trimmed and diced
3 medium onions, coarsely chopped
1½ cups sliced mushrooms
3 cloves garlic, minced

½ teaspoon freshly grated nutmeg
½ teaspoon paprika
½ teaspoon dried thyme, or 1 teaspoon fresh
¼ teaspoon cayenne
Salt
2 tart apples, such as Granny Smith, peeled, cored and cut into small chunks
Juice of 1 lemon
½ cup Chicken (see page 77) or Turkey Stock (see page 78) (optional)

1. Place the currants in a small bowl and pour the Calvados or apple jack over them. Let soak 1 hour.

2. In one or two skillets, heat 1 or 2 tablespoons olive oil and brown the bread cubes, turning them several times. Add more olive oil, as needed.

3. Preheat the oven to 350 degrees. Toast the nuts for 8 minutes in a single layer on a baking sheet or a jelly-roll pan lined with foil. Cool and reserve.

4. Melt 4 tablespoons butter in a large skillet over medium heat. Sauté the celery and onions until transparent, about 5 minutes. Add the mushrooms, garlic, and seasonings. Sauté, stirring occasionally, for 3 more minutes. Transfer to a large bowl.

5. In another bowl, moisten the apple chunks with the lemon juice. Add to the onion mixture, and toss to combine. Add the bread cubes and nuts, and toss again to combine.

6. Melt the remaining butter in the skillet and dribble it over the stuffing. If you wish, moisten the mixture with chicken stock, but be careful not to let the stuffing become soggy. Correct seasoning.

ADVANCE PREPARATION: Can be prepared 1 day ahead. Cover and refrigerate. Bring to room temperature before using.

Knickerbocker Corn Bread Stuffing

Peggy Knickerbocker is a successful San Francisco restaurateur and caterer. Her stuffing recipe is a real stunner.

Makes 16 cups

1 pound sliced bacon
2 cups celery, cut into small dice
2 medium yellow onions, finely chopped
1 head garlic, cloves peeled and finely chopped
3 red bell peppers, seeded and cut into small dice
1½ teaspoons dried sage
1½ teaspoons dried marjoram

1½ teaspoons dried thyme
1½ teaspoons dried oregano
Basic Corn Bread (see page 140), dried out either in a turned-off oven overnight or in the dry air
¼ cup Marsala
1 teaspoon salt
Freshly ground pepper

1. Cook the bacon until crisp. Remove from the pan and reserve. Pour off the drippings, leaving ½ cup in the pan. Over medium heat, sauté the vegetables in the fat, but don't let them get too soft. They should retain a little crunch. Add the dried herbs. (If you can get fresh herbs, double the quantities.)

2. In a large bowl crumble the corn bread and bacon. Add the vegetable mixture with its cooking fat, the Marsala, salt, and pepper to taste. Stir to moisten and combine the ingredients.

ADVANCE PREPARATION: Can be prepared 1 day ahead. Cover and refrigerate. Bring to room temperature before using.

Couscous Stuffing

$\mathcal{T}$he combination of couscous, corn, and garlic makes an unforgettable stuffing for small birds. We love it with duck, but it does equally well with chicken, game hens, and small turkeys.

Makes about 5 cups

1½ cups Chicken Stock (see page 77)
2 tablespoons unsalted butter
¼ teaspoon salt
1 cup whole wheat couscous
2 tablespoons olive oil
2 large shallots, finely chopped
2 small celery stalks without leaves, finely chopped (about ¼ cup)
3 baby carrots, finely chopped (about ¼ cup)

1 clove garlic, minced
¼ cup corn kernels, fresh or frozen
¼ cup pine nuts, toasted
½ cup minced fresh parsley
1 tablespoon fresh sage
1 teaspoon Bell's Seasoning, or ½ teaspoon dried oregano and ½ teaspoon dried thyme
Salt and freshly ground pepper

1. In a 1-quart saucepan combine the stock, butter, and salt. Bring to a boil over medium heat. Add the couscous in a steady stream and stir. Reduce to a simmer and cook for 5 minutes. Fluff the couscous with a fork and set pan aside in a warm place.

2. In a medium skillet, heat the oil. Lightly sauté the shallots, celery, and carrots for 2 minutes. Add the garlic and sauté for another minute. Spoon into a medium mixing bowl.

3. Add the couscous, corn, pine nuts, parsley, sage, and Bell's Seasoning to the vegetables. Toss to combine (don't press too hard, try to keep the stuffing fluffy). Add salt and pepper to taste.

ADVANCE PREPARATION: Can be prepared 2 days ahead. Cover and refrigerate. Bring to room temperature before using.

Chicken Liver Stuffing

This rich stuffing is best with small birds, chicken, squab, and game hens. It is loaded with flavor and interesting textures.

Makes about 12 cups

1 pound chicken livers
4 tablespoons unsalted butter
1 medium onion, minced
1 teaspoon salt
½ teaspoon freshly ground
   pepper
1 tablespoon chopped fresh sage,
   or 1 teaspoon dried

2 cups long-grain rice
4 cups Chicken Stock (see
   page 77)
8 ounces baked ham, cut in
   small dice
½ cup shelled pistachio nuts
   (optional)
¼ cup minced fresh parsley

1. In a medium saucepan, sauté the chicken livers in the butter until just barely done, about 5 minutes. Remove the livers from the pan with a slotted spoon. Chop them coarsely and reserve.

2. Add the minced onion to the saucepan. Stir to coat with the butter, cover, and cook over low heat for 8 minutes, stirring occasionally, until translucent. Add salt, pepper, and sage. Add the rice and stir over moderate heat for a few minutes, until the rice becomes translucent.

3. In a separate saucepan, bring the chicken stock to a boil. Pour the stock into the rice mixture, reduce heat to low, and cover. Let simmer for about 20 minutes, until all the liquid has been absorbed and the rice is tender but not mushy.

4. Stir in the chicken livers, ham, nuts, and parsley. Correct the seasonings.

ADVANCE PREPARATION: Can be made 1 day ahead. Cover and refrigerate. Bring to room temperature before using.

Sausage, Prune, and Rice Stuffing

*T*his is a delicious combination that provides harmonious texture and admirable flavor. We like to use this for stuffing smaller turkeys or other birds such as game hen or capon.

Makes about 12 cups

1 pound good quality pork
    sausage
½ cup currants
1 cup best quality soft prunes
2 cups minced onions
3 tablespoons unsalted butter
    (optional)
1 teaspoon salt
½ teaspoon freshly ground
    pepper

1 tablespoon fresh thyme, or 1½
    teaspoons dried
2 cups long-grain rice
4 cups Chicken Stock (see
    page 77)
3 tablespoons chopped fresh
    parsley

1. Prick the sausages all over and place them, with ½ cup of water, in a large saucepan. Cover and simmer over low heat for 5 minutes. Uncover, drain off the water, and sauté the sausages for several minutes, until lightly browned. Remove the sausages, saving the drippings in the pan, and chop them coarsely. Place in a large mixing bowl. (If the sausage casings are too tough, strip them off and crumble the meat into the bowl.)

2. Put the currants and prunes into separate bowls and cover each with very hot water. Let soften for 15 minutes.

3. Over medium heat sauté the minced onion in the sausage drippings in the saucepan. Stir the onion to coat with fat; if there is not enough fat, add the butter. Cover and cook over low heat for 8 minutes, stirring occasionally, until translucent. Add salt, pepper, and thyme. Add the rice and stir over moderate heat for a few minutes, until the rice becomes translucent.

4. In a separate saucepan, bring the chicken stock to a boil. Pour the stock into the rice mixture, reduce heat to low, and cover. Let simmer for about 20 minutes, until all the liquid has been absorbed and the rice is tender but not mushy.

5. Drain the fruits. Squeeze the currants dry in a towel and add to the bowl containing the sausage. Dry the prunes on paper towels, then chop coarsely and add to the sausage mixture. Add the rice and turn the ingre-

dients with a spoon to blend well. Add parsley. Taste for seasoning and correct if necessary. Cover and refrigerate until ready to use.

ADVANCE PREPARATION: Can be prepared 1 day ahead. Cover and refrigerate. Bring to room temperature before using.

Savory Wild Rice Stuffing

*T*his stuffing is wonderful in goose, wild or domesticated turkey, or chicken. It is also a first-class leftover, so make plenty.

Makes 16 cups

8 ounces (2 sticks) unsalted butter	¼ cup chopped fresh parsley
2 cups wild rice	1 tablespoon salt
2 cups long-grain rice	1 tablespoon dried sage
3 large onions, chopped	1 tablespoon dried marjoram
2 cups chopped celery, including leaves	1 tablespoon dried savory
4 cups Chicken Stock (see page 77)	1 tablespoon ground cinnamon
2 cups toasted and coarsely chopped pecans	2 teaspoons celery seed
	1 teaspoon freshly ground white pepper

1. Melt the butter in a large heavy skillet or casserole. Add rices, onions, and celery. Cook over medium heat for 6 minutes, stirring occasionally. Add the stock and bring to a boil. Reduce the heat, cover the pot, and simmer for 25 minutes, or until the stock is completely absorbed and the rice is tender.
2. Stir in the pecans and seasonings, and mix thoroughly.

ADVANCE PREPARATION: Can be prepared 2 days ahead. Cover and refrigerate. Bring to room temperature before using.

Port, Apricot, and Rice Stuffing

$\mathcal{T}$his is an ideal stuffing for such smaller birds as guinea hens, capons, or chickens. It works well with goose also.

Makes 8 cups

1 cup dried apricots, coarsely chopped	2 celery stalks, chopped
½ cup dried currants	2 cups long-grain rice
2 cups ruby port	2 tablespoons minced fresh
4 cups Chicken Stock (see page 77)	thyme, or 2 teaspoons crumbled dried
2 tablespoons unsalted butter	½ cup chopped fresh parsley
2 tablespoons vegetable oil	1 teaspoon salt
1 cup minced onions	½ teaspoon freshly ground pepper

1. Put the apricots and currants into separate bowls and cover each with 1 cup of port. Let soak overnight, or for at least 6 hours, at room temperature.

2. Bring the stock to a boil in a medium saucepan.

3. In a large saucepan melt the butter with the oil over medium heat. Add the onions and celery. Sauté, stirring occasionally, for 5 minutes over medium heat. Add the rice and stir until translucent, about 3 minutes.

4. Add the hot stock to the rice and mix well. Reduce the heat to low and cover. Let simmer for about 20 minutes, until all the liquid has been absorbed and the rice is tender but not mushy. Transfer to a large bowl.

5. Drain the fruits, reserving the port for Port and Currant Jelly Sauce (page 85). Combine the apricots, currants, thyme, parsley, salt, and pepper with the cooked rice. Turn the ingredients with a spoon to blend well. Taste for seasoning and adjust if necessary.

ADVANCE PREPARATION: Can be prepared 2 days ahead. Cover and refrigerate. Bring to room temperature before using.

VARIATION: Substitute a good packaged wild rice and brown rice combination for the long-grain rice.

Herb, Mushroom, and Chestnut Forcemeat

𝒯his is a forcemeat, not a standard poultry stuffing. It should be used with a boned bird—a small turkey (see page 43), a chicken or a capon—and then sliced along with it.

This recipe was suggested by Hubert Keller, a partner and the chef at Fleur de Lys restaurant in San Francisco, one of the country's finest French dining rooms. Mr. Keller is Alsatian and he was trained at the famous Auberge de L'il.

Makes 12 cups

1½ pounds boneless loin of veal
1½ pounds pork fat
10 ounces chicken livers
4 tablespoons olive oil
4 tablespoons chopped shallots
3 cloves of garlic, finely chopped
½ cup finely chopped celery
3 tablespoons port
5 tablespoons cognac
3 eggs
1 tablespoon chopped, fresh rosemary
1½ tablespoons chopped, fresh thyme leaves

2 tablespoons finely cut chives
2 tablespoons finely chopped parsley
Salt and freshly ground pepper
4 tablespoons pistachio nuts
½ pound cooked wild mushrooms (black chanterelles, shiitake, morels, cepes)
1 pound fresh, roasted, peeled chestnuts

1. Finely mince the veal, pork fat, and chicken livers in a meat grinder or in a food processor.

2. Heat the olive oil in a sauté pan. Add the shallots and garlic, sauté until light golden in color, then add the celery. Add the meat and cook for 5 minutes, stirring constantly. Add the port and cognac and transfer the mixture to a bowl. Let cool.

3. Stir in the eggs, herbs, salt and pepper. Check the seasoning. Delicately mix in the pistachios, mushrooms, and the chestnuts without breaking them. Refrigerate for at least 20 minutes before using. Use in a boned turkey (see recipe page 52).

ADVANCE PREPARATION: This can be prepared 1 day ahead. Cover and refrigerate. Bring to room temperature before using.

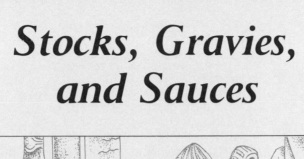

Stocks, Gravies, and Sauces

At young ages and in separate places, we both became gravy lovers. The first time you see someone make an indentation in a snowy mound of mashed potatoes with a gravy ladle, you know.

To both of us, a piece of meat on a plate without gravy or sauce is naked, incomplete. As a result, our Thanksgiving is a gravy festival. We usually have at least two, sometimes three, gravies.

Essentially, a gravy adds texture and flavor depth to the Thanksgiving plate. But a good gravy should broaden and fill out the meal, not overpower it.

The following gravies, stocks, and sauces are the elements that bind the holiday dinner together. Without them, Thanksgiving dinner would be just another meal.

Several of the recipes that follow use butter. The same amount of fat from the roasting pan is more desirable, but then the gravy must be made at the very last minute. The addition of essences from the pan may be worth the extra effort.

Chicken Stock

Chicken stock is an essential ingredient of the Thanksgiving feast (and many other special meals). We start by boiling the chicken alone so that most of the skimming can be done at the beginning of the procedure. After straining the stock, we like to boil it down even more. This makes for a richer, more concentrated stock with a reduced volume that is easier to store and to freeze. You can use it as is, or dilute with water.

Makes 3 quarts

6 pounds chicken (carcasses, feet, necks, backs, hearts, and other parts) cut into small pieces, or use a large stewing hen
5 quarts water
2 stalks celery
3 medium carrots, washed and sliced
2 leeks, most of the green part cut off, washed and split lengthwise
2 garlic cloves, crushed
2 medium onions, quartered
2 teaspoons salt
12 black peppercorns, cracked
1 bay leaf
A sprig of thyme

1. Put the chicken and the water into a large stockpot. Bring to a boil over high heat. Reduce the heat to medium and continue to boil for 20 minutes, skimming the liquid frequently with a spoon.

2. Add the rest of the ingredients. When the liquid returns to a boil reduce the heat and simmer the stock, for about 3 hours, skimming periodically.

3. Strain the stock through a fine sieve or a colander lined with cheesecloth. Return to the stockpot and boil vigorously for another ½ hour.

4. Let cool, cover and refrigerate. When the stock has chilled, use a large spoon to remove and discard the fat from its surface.

ADVANCE PREPARATION: The stock can be made 3 days in advance. Cover and refrigerate. If not using within 3 days, freeze the stock in plastic tubs (it is better to use several smaller containers so that you don't have to defrost the entire batch to use only a few cups).

*Thanksgiving
Dinner*

Turkey Stock

Makes 6 cups

2 pounds turkey parts and giblets	12 crushed peppercorns
1 onion, quartered	4 sprigs fresh thyme, or 1 teaspoon dried
2 carrots, cut in 3-inch pieces	1 bay leaf
2 celery stalks with leaves, cut in half	8 cups cold water
	Salt

1. Place the first seven ingredients in a large stockpot, and add the cold water. Bring to a boil, reduce heat, and simmer. Skim the surface of the stock occasionally during the first 30 minutes.
2. Partially cover and continue to simmer for 3 to 5 hours.
3. Strain and salt to taste.

ADVANCE PREPARATION: Can be made 3 days ahead. Cover and refrigerate. Can be frozen for several months.

Goose Stock

Makes 6 cups

9 cups Chicken Stock (see page 77)	1 celery stalk from the heart, chopped
1 goose neck	1 bouquet garni: 6 peppercorns; 1 celery stalk, cut in half; 2 sprigs fresh thyme; and 1 bay leaf
1 goose gizzard	
1 goose heart	
1 carrot, peeled and chopped	

1. Make a bouquet garni by pressing the peppercorns into one half stalk of celery. Place the thyme and bay leaf on top and tie the other half stalk on top with string to make a tight sandwich.

2. Place all ingredients in a 2-quart saucepan. Bring to a boil, then simmer, uncovered, until the liquid is reduced to 6 cups, about 50 minutes. Strain.

ADVANCE PREPARATION: Can be prepared 2 days ahead. Cover and refrigerate. Can also be frozen for several months.

Basic Pan Gravy

Makes 1½ cups

3 tablespoons fat from the roasting pan	2 cups Turkey (see page 78) or Chicken Stock (see page 77)
3 tablespoons flour	Salt and freshly ground pepper

Blend the fat and flour in the roasting pan, making a smooth roux. Add the stock and bring to a boil over medium heat. Scrape the bottom of the pan with a wooden spoon to loosen baked-on bits. Stir until the sauce thickens. Add salt and pepper to taste, and serve.

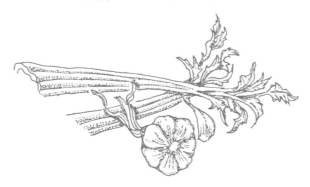

Pan Gravy

Makes 1½ cups

2 cups Turkey (see page 78) or
    Chicken Stock (see page 77)

1 cup red wine
Salt and freshly ground pepper

1. After removing the bird to a warmed platter to rest, pour off the fat from the turkey roasting pan. Place over medium heat and add the stock and wine to the pan.

2. Bring to a boil and use a wooden spoon to scrape up baked-on bits. Continue boiling until the liquid has been reduced by half. Add salt and pepper to taste, and serve.

Goose Pan Gravy

Makes 3 cups

4 cups Goose Stock (see
    page 78)
1 cup dry white wine
2 tablespoons all-purpose flour

4 tablespoons water
Goose roasting-pan drippings
Salt and freshly ground pepper

1. In a saucepan over moderate heat combine the stock and wine and bring to a boil. Reduce to a simmer.

2. Put flour and water in a container with an airtight lid. Shake vigorously to mix. Strain mixture and then pour into stock. Stir stock constantly until it begins to thicken.

3. Place roasting pan over heat and pour in the thickened stock. Stir constantly with a wooden spoon, scraping the entire pan to loosen the baked-on spots. Season to taste with salt and pepper.

Mushroom Gravy

*T*his and most other gravies are greatly enhanced by the addition of defatted and deglazed pan drippings from the turkey.

Makes 4 cups

4 ounces mixed dried wild
    mushrooms or dried porcini
    mushrooms
6 cups Turkey (see page 78)
    or Chicken Stock (see page 77)
4 tablespoons unsalted butter
2 carrots, peeled and diced
1 medium onion, diced

1 celery stalk, chopped
1 pound sliced white
    mushrooms
⅔ cup Madeira
1½ teaspoons chopped fresh
    thyme, or ½ teaspoon dried
Salt and freshly ground pepper

1. In a bowl, cover the dried mushrooms with warm water and let stand 30 minutes. Remove mushroom pieces with a skimmer, then strain liquid through several thicknesses of cheesecloth, a paper towel, or a coffee filter, reserving the liquid.

2. In a 2-quart saucepan, reduce the stock to 3 cups to make a rich base for the gravy.

3. In a medium skillet, melt 3 tablespoons butter and add carrots, onion, and celery. Sauté over low heat until the vegetables are soft, about 15 minutes. Stir occasionally to prevent sticking.

4. Add half the sliced white mushrooms to the skillet. Sauté until tender, about 10 minutes. Add Madeira, reduced stock, and mushroom-soaking liquid. Bring to a boil over medium-high heat, reduce heat, and simmer for 10 minutes.

5. Pour the mixture into a blender and purée until smooth.

6. In the 2-quart saucepan, melt the remaining butter. Add the wild mushrooms and the remainder of the white mushrooms. Sauté until golden brown.

7. Add the purée, thyme, and salt and pepper to taste.

ADVANCE PREPARATION: Can be prepared several days in advance. It will keep, covered and refrigerated, for 3 days. If you are using pan drippings, they must be added at the last minute.

Our Favorite Gravy with (or Without) Giblets

This gravy must be started the day before Thanksgiving, but it's really easy, and we promise you've never tasted anything better. Our children, who have a tendency to be suspicious of sauces, can't get enough of this one.

The recipe allows us the option to finish the sauce with or without the minced giblets. The kids like the gravy without "lumps" and the adults generally like the morsels. We are able to offer two gravies from this one recipe by adding the giblets to only half of the finished product.

Makes about 4 cups

Turkey giblets (neck, gizzard, liver, heart)
1 celery stalk
2 medium carrots, washed and cut into 2 pieces
A few fresh sprigs parsley

3 cups Chicken (see page 77) or Turkey Stock (see page 78)
½ cup chicken fat, turkey fat, or butter
½ cup all-purpose flour
Salt and freshly ground pepper

1. The day before you plan to serve the gravy, simmer the giblets, celery, carrots, and parsley in the stock for about 1½ hours, or until the gizzard is tender.

2. Strain the stock into a bowl. Discard the vegetables. Remove the gristle from the gizzard and discard it. Strip the meat from the neck. Chop the neck meat, the gizzard, and the liver into slivers about ½ inch long. Place the chopped giblets in a bowl with enough broth to cover. Store it overnight, covered, in the refrigerator. Refrigerate the rest of the stock in a separate bowl, covered.

3. The next day, heat the reserved stock in a saucepan.

4. In a medium saucepan, melt the fat or butter over medium heat, add the flour, and stir well to make a smooth, thick roux. Let bubble for a few minutes.

5. Remove the saucepan from the heat, add the heated reserved stock, and simmer for 20 minutes until the sauce coats a spoon and no taste of flour remains. Add salt and pepper to taste.

6. At this point, you can separate the desired amount of gravy and add the reserved giblets to it.

7. When you remove the turkey from the oven, strain the pan drippings into a pitcher or a gravy separator. Defat and add to the gravy. Correct the seasonings. Deglaze the pan with the remaining ½ cup of stock.

VARIATION: For a richer and even more chunky gravy, sauté 8 ounces of chicken livers in 1 tablespoon of fat or butter until they are browned. When they are cool, chop them finely and reserve them in a bowl. Deglaze the pan with ½ cup stock, and reserve the liquid. Add the livers and their liquid to the gravy with the giblets.

Roasted Garlic–Herb Gravy

Makes 1 quart

2 carrots, peeled
2 celery stalks
2 heads garlic, cloves separated
  and peeled
8 cups Turkey (see page 78) or
  Chicken Stock (see page 77)
1 teaspoon salt
½ teaspoon freshly ground
  pepper

4 tablespoons chopped fresh
  Italian parsley
1 tablespoon chopped fresh
  chives
1 teaspoon chopped fresh savory,
  or pinch of dried savory

1. In the last hour of turkey roasting, scatter the carrots, celery, and garlic in the bottom of the roasting pan.
2. In a 3-quart saucepan, bring the stock to a boil over medium heat. Reduce by half.
3. When the turkey comes out of the oven, remove the carrots and celery stalks and place them in a blender or food processor. Add the stock and purée until smooth. Add half the garlic cloves, purée, and taste. (Heads of garlic vary in intensity, so it is necessary to check the strength of the sauce as you go.) Add more garlic to taste, if desired.
4. Stir in the salt and pepper, and just before serving, add the parsley, chives, and savory.

Chestnut Gravy

Makes 1 quart

2 tablespoons unsalted butter
2 carrots, peeled and diced
1 celery stalk, chopped
1 medium white onion, chopped
1½ cups whole peeled and
  cooked chestnuts

2 tablespoons brandy
⅔ cup red wine
6 cups Turkey (see page 78) or
  Chicken Stock (see page 77)

1. In a 3-quart saucepan, melt the butter and sauté the carrots, celery, and onion until tender, about 15 minutes. Add 1¼ cups of chestnuts and continue to cook, stirring frequently, for 1 minute.

2. Add the brandy and wine and deglaze the pan while rolling chestnuts around in the liquid. Add the stock, bring to a simmer, and reduce for 30 minutes.

3. Purée the gravy in a blender or food processor until smooth. Quarter the reserved chestnuts. Stir the remaining chestnuts into the gravy. Serve.

ADVANCE PREPARATION: Can be made 3 days in advance. Refrigerate, covered, until ready to use. Warm in saucepan.

Orange-Port Sauce

Makes 4 cups

8 tablespoons (1 stick) unsalted
  butter
2 carrots, peeled and chopped
1 celery stalk, chopped
2 medium white onions,
  chopped
4 cups Turkey (see page 78) or
  Chicken Stock (see page 77)

1⅓ cups tawny port
1 cup fresh orange juice
1 tablespoon red wine vinegar
2 tablespoons chopped fresh
  thyme, or 2 teaspoons dried
Salt and freshly ground pepper

1. In a 3-quart saucepan, melt 2 tablespoons butter. Sauté carrots, celery, and onions until tender, about 15 minutes.

2. Add the stock, port, and vinegar and reduce by half, about 20 minutes.

3. Meanwhile, in a small saucepan, reduce the orange juice by half, to intensify its flavor. Reserve.

4. Transfer the port mixture to a blender or food processor and purée. Strain back into the saucepan. Over medium heat, add the remaining butter in small pieces, stirring constantly. Do not boil.

5. Add the orange juice, thyme, and salt and pepper, plus any available pan juices from the turkey roasting pan.

ADVANCE PREPARATION: Can be made 3 days in advance. Store, covered, in the refrigerator. Warm in a saucepan.

Port and Currant Jelly Sauce

*T*his sauce is the companion to Roast Goose (page 56) and Port, Apricot, and Rice Stuffing (page 72). If you are using the stuffing, use the port in which you soaked the apricots in this recipe.

Makes 3 cups

2 cups apple cider or sparkling
   apple cider
4 cups Goose (see page 78) or
   Chicken Stock (see page 77)

1 cup port
1 cup currant jelly

In a 2-quart saucepan, boil the cider, reducing it to 1 cup. Add the goose stock and port. Bring to a rolling boil and then lower to a fast simmer for 20 minutes. Add jelly ½ cup at a time. Stir to blend. The sauce should be thick enough to coat the back of a spoon.

ADVANCE PREPARATION: Can be made 3 days in advance. Cover and refrigerate until ready to use. Warm in a saucepan.

Vegetables

*I*f the turkey is the backbone of Thanksgiving dinner, then vegetables are the heart. At our house the feast includes one or two turkeys and anywhere from six to nine vegetable dishes. There are so many wonderful vegetables available at this time of year that choices can be difficult. We generally try to avoid these difficult decisions by making as many vegetables as we can fit on the plate.

Perhaps the best way to choose is to zero in on specific categories. For example, pick one sweet potato dish, one potato dish, one squash, one green vegetable, and one other that you just can't resist. Another important consideration is to make sure that you have several recipes that can be prepared in advance.

Also, think about color. There's nothing worse than four or five dishes all of which are brown or orange. Try to choose things that will complement one another in color and texture.

Thanksgiving is a celebration of the bounty of the harvest and vegetables are the expression of that bounty.

Broccoli au Gratin

*T*his is always a popular dish at our house. It has a lovely color and a good texture. The kids love the crispy cheese crust.

Makes 6 cups (12 ½-cup servings)

3 pounds broccoli, peeled, cut
   into fairly large and relatively
   uniform pieces
3 tablespoons unsalted butter
3 medium shallots, minced
2 cloves garlic, minced
⅔ cup sour cream

1 cup grated Parmesan cheese
½ teaspoon freshly grated
   nutmeg
½ teaspoon freshly ground white
   pepper
½ teaspoon salt

1. In a 4-quart saucepan, bring 4 cups of salted water to a boil. Add the broccoli and boil for 5 minutes. Strain into a colander and spray with cold water to stop the cooking process. Chop coarsely.

2. Melt the butter in a skillet. Sauté the shallots for 3 minutes, stirring frequently. Add the garlic and sauté for another minute.

3. Add the shallot mixture to the bowl of a food processor fitted with the metal blade. Pulse a few times to purée. Add the sour cream and pulse 4 or 5 times to mix. Add the broccoli and ¾ cup of the Parmesan, and pulse 4 or 5 times. The mixture should not be overpuréed. Stir in the nutmeg, pepper, and salt.

4. Preheat the broiler. Spoon the broccoli mixture into a 2-quart au gratin or soufflé dish. Sprinkle the top with the remaining grated Parmesan. Place under the broiler for 2 minutes, or until the cheese is melted and slightly golden. Serve.

ADVANCE PREPARATION: Can be done 1 day in advance through step 2.

Creamed Onions

*T*his traditional dish is controversial. For some, it wouldn't be Thanksgiving without creamed onions; others couldn't care less. One of the problems with the dish is that most recipes for it yield a very bland and uninspiring result. This version is so delectable, thanks to the bechamel sauce, that even confirmed creamed onion haters have been known to have seconds.

Makes 8 cups (16 ½-cup servings)

2 pounds small white onions,
   uniform in size
5 tablespoons unsalted butter
1½ teaspoons fresh thyme, or ½
   teaspoon dried

1 cup Turkey (see page 78) or
   Chicken Stock (see page 77)

BECHAMEL

2 tablespoons unsalted butter
3 tablespoons all-purpose flour
2 cups milk
1 cup heavy cream
½ teaspoon freshly ground white
   pepper
½ teaspoon salt
2 teaspoons freshly squeezed
   lemon juice

½ teaspoon Dijon mustard
¼ teaspoon freshly grated
   nutmeg
⅓ cup freshly ground bread
   crumbs, preferably sourdough
   or egg bread
⅓ cup grated Parmesan cheese

1. Parboil the onions, timing 1 minute after the water comes to a boil. Peel the onions and cut an X in the root end of each to prevent bursting.

2. Melt 2 tablespoons butter in a 12-inch skillet, add the onions and the thyme, and sauté for 5 minutes. Add 1 cup turkey or chicken stock and bring to a boil over medium heat. Reduce the heat, cover, and simmer until the onions are tender, about 20 minutes. Check occasionally to make sure the liquid doesn't boil away.

3. While the onions are braising, make the bechamel. In a 2-quart saucepan set over medium-low heat, melt 2 tablespoons butter and whisk in the flour. Cook for 2 minutes, but don't let the roux brown.

4. In another saucepan, scald the milk and cream. Add a few drops to the flour roux and whisk until smooth. Continue adding the milk-cream mixture in small amounts, whisking after each addition, until all of it is

incorporated and smooth. Continue to stir until the sauce thickens, about 5 minutes. Remove the sauce from the heat and whisk in the pepper, salt, lemon juice, mustard, and nutmeg.

5. Preheat the broiler. Pour one-third of the sauce into a shallow 3-quart casserole or gratin dish. Spoon the onions into the dish and top with the remaining sauce. Mix the crumbs and cheese in a small dish, and sprinkle them over the onions. Dot with 3 tablespoons butter and place under the broiler until the crumbs begin to brown and the cheese melts, about 2 minutes, and serve.

ADVANCE PREPARATION: The bechamel and the onions can each be prepared 2 days in advance. Cover and refrigerate separately. Bring to room temperature before heating in a 300-degree oven, assemble, and begin with step 5.

Green Beans in Hazelnut Butter

$\mathscr{A}$ quick, last-minute recipe.

Serves 12

2 pounds of green beans, preferably small *haricots verts*

8 tablespoons (1 stick) unsalted butter

½ cup hazelnuts, toasted and skinned

Salt and freshly ground pepper

1. Bring 2 quarts of water to a boil in a saucepan. Trim the ends off the beans and add them to the boiling water. Cook over moderate heat for 2 to 5 minutes, or until the beans are just tender. Pour into a colander, and immerse in a large bowl of cold water.

2. Melt the butter in a skillet large enough to accommodate all the beans. Add the beans and sauté for 2 minutes, stirring and tossing frequently. Add the chopped hazelnuts. Stir to combine, and sauté for another minute. Add salt and pepper to taste. Transfer to a warmed serving dish and serve immediately.

ADVANCE PREPARATION: Can be prepared through step 1 one day ahead. Cover and store at room temperature.

The Best Spinach Ever

$\mathcal{W}$e're not kidding about this. We guarantee you have never tasted anything quite as purely delicious. Yes, there happens to be a considerable amount of fat in this spectacular dish, but once or twice a year shouldn't hurt. (Actually, eating this masterpiece is worth any small risk.) The flavor and texture is palate boggling.

This dish, which is attributed to the great French gourmet Brillat-Savarin, takes four days to make, but the actual work time is minimal. In order to prepare for Thanksgiving, you need to start the recipe on the Monday before.

Makes 4 cups (12 ⅓-cup servings)

5 pounds fresh spinach	Freshly ground pepper
1 pound (4 sticks) unsalted butter	Freshly ground nutmeg (optional)
Salt	

1. Rinse the spinach under cold running water. Do not dry. Place a large soup kettle or stockpot over medium heat. Grab a handful of spinach and, after shaking off excess water, put it into the pot. When the first batch has steamed and wilted, push it aside and add another handful. Continue this procedure, pushing all the cooked spinach around the sides and leaving a well in the middle for the cooking of subsequent handfuls.

2. When all the spinach has been cooked, let the spinach cool until you are able to handle it without burning your hands. Then pick it up in handfuls and firmly squeeze out the water. Chop the spinach coarsely.

3. Melt 1 stick of butter in a large skillet. Add the squeezed and chopped spinach, and sauté until all the butter is absorbed. Season with ½ teaspoon salt.

4. Place the spinach in a glass bowl, cover, and refrigerate overnight.

5. The next day, repeat the procedure using another stick of butter. Sauté the spinach until the butter is completely absorbed. Return to the glass bowl, cover, and refrigerate overnight.

6. Repeat the procedure the following day, using the third stick of butter.

7. On the day the spinach is to be served, remove it from the refrigerator 2 hours before dinnertime. Repeat the absorption procedure for the

final stick of butter and add the pepper and optional nutmeg. Taste carefully before adding any more salt. Cover and keep at room temperature until ready to serve.

8. When ready to serve, place the spinach in the skillet one more time, and sauté the spinach briefly to warm through.

Creamed Spinach

$\mathcal{T}$his is so simple we almost didn't include it, but our daughter Amanda brought us to our senses. Go a little easy on the salt because cream intensifies its flavor.

Makes 6 cups (12 ½-cup servings)

8 tablespoons (1 stick) unsalted butter
Four 10-ounce packages frozen spinach, thawed and chopped

2 cups heavy cream
Salt and freshly ground pepper
Freshly grated nutmeg

1. In a large skillet melt the butter over moderate heat, then add the spinach. Toss until all the spinach is coated and no liquid remains.

2. Add 1⅓ cups of the cream. Stir and allow the spinach to absorb the cream before adding more. Repeat until all cream is used. Season to taste with salt and pepper. Just prior to serving, sprinkle with nutmeg.

Garlic, Spinach, and Rice Casserole

*N*atalie Grunewald was a well-known San Francisco decorator in the 1950s. Her rice casserole recipe is still a mainstay in the Thanksgiving menu of her daughter, Ingrid Kornspan. We like to serve this as a vegetable, but it also works well as a stuffing.

Makes 10 cups (20 ½-cup servings)

¼ cup olive oil
2 heads garlic, peeled and finely minced
3 medium onions, finely chopped
2 cups long-grain rice
3 cups Chicken Stock (see page 77)

Two 10-ounce packages chopped spinach, thawed
1 cup grated Parmesan cheese
½ teaspoon freshly ground pepper

1. Warm the olive oil in a large heavy skillet over medium heat. Sauté the garlic and onions until soft. Add the rice and sauté until all the ingredients are lightly browned. Add the stock, bring to a boil, reduce heat, cover, and simmer for 20 minutes, or until the rice has softened and absorbed all the liquid.

2. Preheat the oven to 350 degrees. Take the spinach in handfuls and squeeze out as much water as you can. Put the spinach in a food processor fitted with the metal blade and pulse 4 times to chop finely. Stir the spinach into the rice with ½ cup cheese and the pepper. Sprinkle the remaining cheese over the top of the casserole.

3. Bake for 15 minutes.

VARIATION: If you want to use this as a stuffing, make in the same way, just eliminate the cheese.

ADVANCE PREPARATION: Can be prepared 1 day ahead through step 2. Cover and store at room temperature. Heat at 350 degrees for 30 minutes.

Peas à la Francais

𝒯his is a Thanksgiving vegetable that was a tradition at Kathy's family table for as long as she can remember.

Makes 6 cups (12 ½-cup servings)

4 tablespoons unsalted butter
16 pearl onions, peeled
6 large leaves Boston lettuce,
   shredded
4 cups thawed frozen green peas
¼ teaspoon dried thyme, or
   ½ teaspoon fresh
Pinch of salt and freshly ground
   pepper

2 teaspoons sugar
4 tablespoons chopped fresh
   parsley plus 2 sprigs
½ cup water
2 tablespoons all-purpose flour
Freshly grated nutmeg

1.　In a medium saucepan, melt 2 tablespoons of butter and add the onions, lettuce, peas, thyme, salt and pepper, sugar, 2 tablespoons chopped parsley and the 2 sprigs, and water. Cover and simmer for 20 minutes, stirring occasionally. Remove the parsley stems when the onions are tender.

2.　In a small mixing bowl, cream the remaining 2 tablespoons of butter with the flour and a grating of nutmeg, and mix thoroughly with the peas. Reduce heat to low and gently simmer for 15 minutes, stirring occasionally. Serve in a heated casserole sprinkled with the remaining chopped parsley.

ADVANCE PREPARATION: Can be prepared through the first step 1 day in advance. Cover and refrigerate. When ready to serve, do step 2.

Baby Beets with Ginger Glaze

*T*ry to find baby beets about 1½ inches in diameter. If you have to use full-sized beets, quarter them after baking.

Makes 9 cups (18 ½-cup servings)

4 pounds baby beets
1 cup water
4 tablespoons unsalted butter
2 teaspoons freshly grated
  gingerroot

1 cup Chicken Stock (see page
  77)
2 tablespoons sugar
2 tablespoons chopped fresh
  parsley

1. Preheat the oven to 350 degrees. Place the unpeeled beets in a medium-size pot with the water and cover. Bake in the preheated oven for 40 minutes.

2. Drain the liquid into a small bowl and reserve. Peel the beets as soon as you can handle them.

3. Melt the butter in a saucepan. Sauté the ginger in the butter for 2 minutes. Add the reserved beet liquid, the chicken stock, and the sugar. Bring to a simmer and reduce until the liquid becomes syrupy. Roll the beets in the glaze. Sprinkle with parsley and serve.

VARIATION: If you can find them, use one bunch of golden beets. The contrast between the flavor and color of the two types is very appealing, but be sure to cook the different-colored beets separately as the color of the purple ones will stain the golden variety.

ADVANCE PREPARATION: Can be prepared 1 day ahead. Cover and refrigerate. Bring to room temperature before reheating.

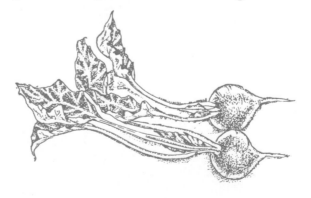

Beet and Pear Purée

$\mathcal{K}$athy loves beets. Over the years we have tried numerous beet recipes and this one is far and away the best of the lot. It has the natural sweetness of the pears, the rich and earthy flavor of beets, and a dazzling magenta color. What more could you ask?

Makes 9 cups (18 ½-cup servings)

8 medium beets
1 pound (4 sticks) unsalted
  butter
1½ cups finely minced Vidalia
  onions (about 4)
4 Bosc pears, peeled, cored, and
  minced

2 tablespoons sugar
½ cup Cranberry Vinegar (see
  page 132) or champagne
  vinegar
1 teaspoon salt

1. Preheat the oven to 375 degrees. Trim the beet tops and scrub the beets clean under running water. Put the beets in a small covered casserole with 1 cup of water. Cover and bake in the oven for 45 minutes, or until tender enough to be pierced with a fork.

2. Rinse the beets with cold water and peel them. Chop coarsely.

3. In a medium skillet melt the butter. Add the onions, pears, sugar, and vinegar. Sauté about 20 minutes or until everything is tender.

4. In a food processor fitted with the metal blade, add the onion mixture and pulse until smooth. Add salt and half of the chopped beets. Pulse again 4 or 5 times. Add the remaining beets and pulse 2 or 3 times. (This leaves some small chunks in the purée for texture.) Correct seasonings and serve.

ADVANCE PREPARATION: Can be prepared 1 day in advance and then reheated in the top of a double boiler.

Golden Winter Purée

*T*his can be served on its own or as a contrast in flavor and color to the Winter White Purée (page 102).

Makes 5 cups (10 ½-cup servings)

1 pound carrots, peeled and cut into 1-inch cubes
1 pound yellow turnips, peeled and cut into 1-inch cubes
1 firm pear, peeled, cored, and cut into 1-inch cubes

6 tablespoons unsalted butter
¾ cup heavy cream
½ teaspoon ground ginger
Salt and freshly ground pepper
1 teaspoon freshly grated nutmeg

1. Bring 4 quarts of salted water to a boil in a stockpot. Add the vegetables and pear, and boil until they are tender enough to be pierced easily with a fork, about 20 minutes. Drain in a colander.

2. Purée the vegetables and pear in a food processor fitted with the metal blade or mash with a potato ricer. Add the butter in small pieces. Add the cream and ginger. Pulse to mix thoroughly. Season to taste with salt and pepper. Spoon into a serving dish, smooth the top, and sprinkle with nutmeg.

ADVANCE PREPARATION: Can be prepared 1 day ahead. Cover and refrigerate. Bring to room temperature before baking at 350 degrees for 20 minutes.

Braised Carrots

*S*imple and delicious, this is a perfect Thanksgiving vegetable. It can be made a day ahead and warmed up in a double boiler. Be careful not to overcook; the carrots should show a bit of resistance.

Mkes 6 cups (12 ½-cup servings)

8 large carrots
4 tablespoons unsalted butter
1 cup Chicken Stock (see page 77)

2 teaspoons sugar
Salt and freshly ground pepper
2 tablespoons chopped fresh chervil or parsley

1. Peel the carrots and cut them into 3-inch-long sections. Split the sections in half lengthwise and cut into sticks. Try to make the pieces uniform by varying the number cut from each piece depending on its size.

2. Melt the butter in a 12-inch skillet. Add the carrots and sauté for about 4 minutes, or until tender.

3. Add half the chicken stock and the sugar and continue to sauté over medium heat, stirring frequently. Add the rest of the stock, and season with salt and pepper to taste. Continue to sautée, stirring frequently, until the liquid has reduced to a glaze. Sprinkle with chopped chervil, correct the seasoning, and serve.

ADVANCE PREPARATION: Can be prepared 1 day ahead. Cover and refrigerate. Bring to room temperature before reheating.

Onion and Carrot Ragout

E asy and incredibly delicious, this combination provides an interesting texture contrast to most other Thanksgiving vegetables.

Makes 9 cups (18 ½-cup servings)

12 medium carrots	12 tablespoons (1½ sticks)
6 medium onions	unsalted butter
	Salt and freshly ground pepper

1. Cut the carrots into slivers 3 inches long and about ¼ inch wide. Slice the onions thinly. You should have about 6 cups of each.

2. In a medium skillet melt 6 tablespoons butter. Add the onions and sauté, stirring frequently, over medium-low heat until caramelized. This should take about 25 minutes.

3. In another skillet melt the remaining 6 tablespoons butter. Add the carrots and sauté, stirring frequently, over low heat until tender. This should take about 10 minutes.

4. Combine the carrots and onions. Toss to mix. Season with salt and pepper to taste and serve.

ADVANCE PREPARATION: Can be prepared 1 day ahead. Cover and refrigerate. Bring to room temperature before reheating.

Carrot Pudding

Our friend Sue Wollack makes this delicious pudding every Thanksgiving and all throughout the year. Her kids love this dish and so do ours.

Makes 10 cups (20 ½-cup servings)

3 egg yolks
½ cup sugar
12 tablespoons (1½ sticks)
   unsalted butter
¾ cup flour

2 pounds carrots, cooked until
   tender, cut into chunks
½ cup grated cheddar cheese
1½ teaspoons baking powder
4 egg whites

TOPPING

2 cups walnut pieces
2 tablespoons unsalted butter

¼ cup sugar

1. Preheat the oven to 300 degrees. In the bowl of a food processor fitted with the metal blade, or an electic mixer fitted with the paddle beater, beat the egg yolks and sugar together until light and fluffy. Alternate additions of small amounts of butter and small amounts of flour, until all are incorporated. Add carrots and cheese. Pulse to blend. Pour into a bowl and fold in baking powder.

2. Beat the egg whites until fluffy. Stir a small amount into the batter with a whisk. Fold in the remaining egg whites.

3. Pour the mixture into a buttered 3-quart soufflé dish or a 9- by 14-inch pan. Bake in the preheated oven for 30 minutes, or until a toothpick inserted in the center of the pudding comes out clean.

4. While the pudding is baking, sauté the walnuts in the butter for about 1 minute, sprinkle with the sugar, and top the pudding. Scoop out helpings and serve.

VARIATION: Top the soufflé with sour cream.

Autumn Vegetable Medley

Makes 5 cups (10 ½ cup servings)

3 large carrots, peeled
2 medium turnips, peeled
2 medium rutabagas, peeled
4 tablespoons unsalted butter
2 tablespoons flour
2 teaspoons Dijon mustard
1 teaspoon whole grain mustard

1½ teaspoons champagne
  vinegar
½ teaspoon salt
½ teaspoon freshly ground
  pepper
2 tablespoons chopped fresh
  chervil, or 1 tablespoon dried

1. Halve the carrots lengthwise and slice them into ¼-inch half moon shapes. Place in a bowl and set aside. Cut the turnips into ¼-inch dice. Cut the rutabagas into a thick julienne. Set these two together aside in another bowl.

2. In a 3-quart saucepan, bring 3 cups of lightly salted water to a boil. Add the carrots and cover. Boil for 3 minutes, until just tender. Add the remaining vegetables, cover, and boil an additional 3 minutes. Strain through a sieve held over a bowl. Reserve the cooking liquid.

3. Return the cooking liquid to the saucepan and bring to a boil. Reduce to 1¼ cups.

4. In another saucepan melt the butter over medium heat. Stir in the flour and cook, stirring constantly, until light brown, about 1 minute. Gradually add the cooking liquid, continuing to stir. Reduce heat. Stir in the mustards, vinegar, salt, and pepper. Cook about 30 seconds more.

5. Add the vegetables and chervil to the mustard sauce. Stir to thoroughly coat the vegetables, cover, and cook over medium heat for 4 minutes. Serve immediately.

ADVANCE PREPARATION: Can be made through third step 2 days in advance. Cover and refrigerate.

Winter White Purée

$\mathcal{T}$his is a rich and luscious purée that transcends its humble ingredients. The apple gives the vegetables the touch of acidity and sweetness that they need. The dish works well on its own or in color and flavor contrast with the Golden Winter Purée (page 98).

Makes 6 cups (12 ½-cup servings)

1 pound white turnips	¾ cup heavy cream
1 pound parsnips	Salt and freshly ground white
1 tart green apple	pepper
½ pound cauliflower	½ cup freshly grated Parmesan
10 tablespoons unsalted butter	cheese

1. Peel the turnips and parsnips, peel and core the apple, and cut them all into 1-inch cubes. Separate the cauliflower florets.

2. Bring 4 quarts of salted water to a boil in a stockpot. Add the vegetables and apple, and boil until they are tender enough to pierce easily with a fork, about 15 minutes. Strain in a colander.

3. Purée the vegetables in a food processor fitted with the metal blade or mash with a potato ricer. Add the butter in small pieces. Add the cream. Pulse to mix thoroughly. Season to taste with salt and pepper.

4. Place the mixture in a buttered 2-quart ovenproof casserole. Smooth the top and sprinkle with the grated Parmesan.

5. Preheat the oven to 350 degrees. Bake for 20 minutes, until lightly browned on top.

ADVANCE PREPARATION: Can be prepared 1 day ahead through step 4. Cover and refrigerate. Bring to room temperature before baking at 350 degrees for 20 minutes.

Creamed Succotash

$\mathcal{A}$ colorful version of a Thanksgiving classic, this should not be made ahead of time.

Makes 5 cups (10 ½-cup servings)

2 cups fresh or frozen lima
    beans
2 cups fresh or frozen corn
    kernels
2½ cups heavy cream
3 tablespoons unsalted butter

½ cup finely diced red bell
    pepper
½ teaspoon salt
½ teaspoon freshly ground
    pepper

1. If using fresh vegetables, bring 6 cups of water and 1 tablespoon salt to a boil. Cook the corn and lima beans until tender but firm, about 5 minutes. Drain, rinse in cold water, and drain again. If using frozen vegetables, thaw thoroughly, rinse, and set aside.

2. In a large saucepan, heat the cream to a boil and reduce to 1¼ cups. This should take about 15 minutes. To prevent the cream from boiling over, place a metal spoon in the pan.

3. In a skillet, melt the butter. Add the bell pepper and sauté for 1 minute, then add the corn and lima beans. Sauté to heat thoroughly. When the cream has reduced, add the vegetables, toss to coat, season with salt and pepper, and serve immediately.

Mill Valley Corn Custard

$\mathcal{L}$iz Levy is a fine Marin County cook and this is one of her greatest creations. It is silky and extremely elegant.

Makes 6 cups (12 ½-cup servings)

1 tablespoon unsalted butter	4 egg yolks
⅔ cup finely chopped red onion	½ teaspoon salt
½ teaspoon cornstarch	¼ teaspoon freshly ground white pepper
1 cup heavy cream	
4 cups fresh or frozen corn kernels	1½ tablespoons chopped fresh chives
2 large eggs	

1. Melt the butter in a skillet and sauté the onion until softened. Cool.

2. In a bowl, combine cornstarch and cream. Stir until the cornstarch is dissolved.

3. Preheat the oven to 350 degrees. Place the onion, the corn, the whole eggs, the egg yolks, and the cream mixture in the bowl of a food processor fitted with the metal blade. Pulse until well blended. Strain the custard through a sieve, pressing down on the solids. Stir in salt, white pepper, and chives.

4. Pour the mixture into a 9½-inch au gratin dish set in a roasting pan filled with ½ inch of hot water. Cook for 25 minutes or until a knife inserted into the center comes out clean. Serve immediately.

Bix's Corn Custard

*O*ne of San Francisco's best restaurants is Bix, a stylish supperclub featuring the creative cooking of Cindy Pawlcyn. Among the appetizers on the menu is this silky corn custard. It has become a favorite. At Bix it is served set on a bed of rich shiitake mushroom sauce. For Thanksgiving the custard without the sauce is more appropriate and, as it turns out, it is excellent on its own. We include the sauce so you can try it both ways.

Serves 6

THE CUSTARD

1 tablespoon unsalted butter, softened

2 eggs

1 cup heavy cream

½ tablespoon Dijon mustard

1½ cups corn kernels (2 ears)

¾ cup grated Monterey Jack cheese

¼ teaspoon salt

⅛ teaspoon freshly ground pepper

1 large scallion, finely sliced

THE SAUCE

6 tablespoons unsalted butter

½ teaspoon finely minced garlic

1 teaspoon chopped shallots

¼ cup chopped fresh fennel

¼ cup sliced shiitake mushrooms

¼ cup champagne vinegar

1 tablespoon white wine

½ cup of reduced Chicken Stock (see page 77)

3 tablespoons minced fennel leaves

Salt and freshly ground pepper

1. Preheat the oven to 325 degrees. In a bowl, combine the eggs, cream, and mustard. When smooth, fold in the remaining ingredients, except the butter. Pour into 6 buttered ½-cup ramekins. Place in a shallow baking dish filled with 1 inch of hot water. Cover with a sheet of heavy-duty foil. Bake for 30 minutes and serve immediately.

2. Melt 2 tablespoons of butter in a skillet. Sauté the garlic and shallots until soft. Do not brown. Add the fennel and mushrooms, and sauté for 2 minutes. Deglaze the pan with vinegar and wine.

3. Add the chicken stock, reduce by half, and add the rest of the butter. When the sauce is thickened, add the fennel leaves and season to taste with salt and pepper.

Schatze's Corn Pudding

*A*ndy's mother, Schatze, has been making this delicious pudding for decades. It is always the children's favorite Thanksgiving vegetable. In fact, this dish is part of nearly every family celebration in the Blue house. The recipe calls for canned creamed corn. Generally, we like to make things from scratch and not use prepared foods, but we have tested this recipe with freshly made creamed corn, and there is no appreciable difference in the final product.

Makes 8 cups (16 ½-cup servings)

8 tablespoons (1 stick) unsalted butter
4 eggs, beaten
Two 17-ounce cans creamed corn
Two 5-ounce cans evaporated milk

1 tablespoon sugar
Pinch of cayenne
6 tablespoons matzo meal
1 tablespoon salt, or to taste

1. Preheat the oven to 350 degrees. Butter a 2-quart casserole.

2. Melt the butter in a saucepan and let cool. In a bowl, combine the rest of the ingredients and add the cooled melted butter. Pour into the casserole.

3. Place the casserole in a pan filled with 1½ inches of hot water. Bake until set, about 1½ hours.

Sagaponack Corn Bread Casserole

*W*hen we first rented a house on Hedges Lane in Sagaponack—a tiny area wedged in between East Hampton and Bridgehampton on the South Fork of Long Island—we used to get our mail and our basic kitchen supplies at the Sagaponack General Store. For fifteen years after that we went to Europe each summer, but eventually we returned to the bucolic charm of the Hamptons.

Among many changes, one of the most noticeable was the metamorphosis of the Sagaponack General Store. It still functions as the town post office and general store, but owners Donald and Mary Spellman have made it much more. The Sagaponack General Store has become one of the most popular caterers in the Hamptons. For exhausted weekenders who would rather pay than cook, Mary turns out anything from tea sandwiches to roasted duck.

Mary's signature dish is this incredible corn bread casserole. While we don't generally use mixes and such, this casserole is so good we happily make an exception.

Makes 8 cups (16 ½-cup servings)

3 tablespoons unsalted butter	2 cups corn muffin mix (We use
1 medium onion, chopped	Flako.)
2 extra-large eggs	1½ cups sour cream
3 cups creamed corn	2½ cups grated cheddar cheese
½ cup flour	

1. Preheat the oven to 400 degrees.
2. Melt the butter in a skillet and sauté the onion until translucent.
3. In a mixing bowl combine the eggs, corn, flour, and muffin mix. Mix well. Add the sautéed onion and mix again.
4. Pour the batter into a well-greased 8 by 11-inch baking dish. Tap to make sure the batter is level, then spread the sour cream on top. Sprinkle the grated cheddar on top of the sour cream.
5. Bake for 25 minutes in the preheated oven. Reduce the temperature to 350 degrees and bake for an additional 25 minutes or until the casserole feels firm in the center.

VARIATION: Add slices of spicy sausage or crisp, crumbled bacon to the batter. If you are making this in the summer add the kernels cut from one fresh ear of corn.

ADVANCE PREPARATION: Can be prepared 2 days ahead. Cover and refrigerate. Bring to room temperature before reheating. This casserole also freezes well.

Corn Fritters

*I*f the corn you are using is very fresh and sweet, cut down slightly on the sugar. As a variation, substitute brown sugar, honey, or maple syrup for the sugar.

Because this can be a time-consuming procedure, make only for a small group or freeze a batch in advance and reheat for 10 minutes at 425 degrees.

Makes about 25

3 cups fresh or frozen corn kernels	1 teaspoon baking powder
2 tablespoons unsalted butter	¼ teaspoon cayenne
2 tablespoons sugar	1½ tablespoons chopped fresh chives
2 eggs, beaten	1¼ teaspoons salt
2 tablespoons heavy cream	Freshly ground pepper
¼ cup all-purpose flour	Corn oil
¼ cup matzo meal or unsalted cracker crumbs	

1. Cook the corn in a saucepan of boiling water until tender, about 5 minutes. Drain well. Melt the butter in a heavy skillet and sauté the corn, stirring frequently, for 3 minutes. Add the sugar and stir for another 2 minutes. Transfer the corn to a small bowl, using a slotted spoon. Set aside.

2. Combine the eggs, cream, flour, matzo meal, baking powder, cayenne, chives, salt, and pepper in a medium-size bowl. Fold in the corn and stir to distribute the kernels throughout the batter.

3. Fill a heavy skillet with corn oil to a depth of 1 inch. Warm over medium heat until a corn kernel dropped into the oil sizzles and floats to the top. With a spoon, scoop heaping tablespoons of the batter and slide them gently into the oil. As the fritters brown on the bottom, turn them with tongs. When golden brown all over, remove the fritters and drain them on paper towels.

ADVANCE PREPARATION: These fritters can be prepared 5 hours ahead. Cool. Place them on a cookie sheet and cover with plastic wrap; let stand at room temperature. Before serving, remove the plastic and bake the fritters in a 350-degree oven until heated through.

Stuffed Acorn Squash

Serves 8

4 acorn squash
Salt
½ butternut squash (about
   1 pound), peeled and cut in
   ¼-inch dice
2 cups whole cranberries

3 tablespoons lingonberry
   preserves (We use Felix Wild
   Lingonberries in Sugar. If you
   can't find this product,
   substitute raspberry
   preserves.)
1 tablespoon honey
2 tablespoons unsalted butter

1. Preheat the oven to 350 degrees. Cut the acorn squash into halves lengthwise. With a spoon scrape out the seeds and fibers. Put halves, face up, into one or more shallow baking dishes and add ¼ inch hot water. Bake for 30 minutes, or until tender.

2. Meanwhile blanch the butternut squash in boiling salted water for 3 minutes. Strain and reserve. In another pot, blanch the cranberries until the berries start to pop, about 5 minutes. Strain and combine with the butternut squash.

3. In a small saucepan, heat the lingonberries and the honey until they bubble. Add the butter. When it melts, add the cranberry-squash mixture and stir to combine—gently so as not to mash the berries. Spoon the filling into the cooked acorn squash.

4. Return the stuffed squash to the oven for 15 minutes. Serve immediately.

ADVANCE PREPARATION: Can be prepared 1 day ahead through step 3. Cover and refrigerate. Bring to room temperature before heating in a 350-degree oven for 15 minutes.

Puréed Butternut Squash

*T*his is extremely easy. It can be made ahead and can be the base for a splendid soup (see page 25).

Makes 12 cups (16 ¾-cup servings)

4 medium butternut squash
   (about 1½ pounds each)
Olive oil
4 cloves garlic, unpeeled

4 tablespoons maple syrup
4 tablespoons unsalted butter
Salt and freshly ground pepper

1. Preheat the oven to 350 degrees. With a sharp knife cut off the stem and split each squash in half from top to bottom. With a pastry brush, paint the cut side of each half with a light coating of olive oil. Place the squash, cut side down, in a roasting pan containing 1 cup of water. Sprinkle the unpeeled garlic cloves around the pan. Bake in the oven for 1 hour, or until the squash is quite soft.

2. When the squash are done, scoop out their seeds and discard. With a spoon, scoop the pulp into the bowl of a food processor or an electric mixer. Squeeze the garlic cloves out of their skins into the squash. Add the maple syrup and butter, and purée. Add salt and pepper to taste, and serve.

ADVANCE PREPARATION: Can be prepared 2 days ahead. Cover and refrigerate. Bring to room temperature before reheating in the top of a double boiler.

Gratin of Squash, Leeks, and Rice

*O*ne of our best friends and favorite cooks is Diane Rossen Worthington. This recipe appears in her excellent book, *The Taste of Summer,* but it works just fine at Thanksgiving.

We have made this many times and adapted it to our cooking style. The only substantive change that has crept into our method is to use Arborio rice instead of long-grain rice.

Makes 9 cups (18 ½-cup servings)

2½ pounds yellow squash and
green zucchini, grated
1½ teaspoons salt
½ cup Arborio rice
¼ cup olive oil
3 medium leeks, well-cleaned
white and light green parts
only, finely chopped (about
3 cups)

2 medium garlic cloves, minced
2 tablespoons finely chopped
fresh Italian parsley
2 tablespoons flour
2 cups half-and-half
¾ cup grated Parmesan cheese
¼ teaspoon freshly ground
pepper

1. Place the grated squash in a colander set over a bowl and add 1 teaspoon salt, tossing to distribute evenly. Allow the juices to drain for 15 to 30 minutes.

2. Squeeze the squash in handfuls or wring it out in a clean dish towel over the bowl to collect the juices. Reserve the juices and dry the squash carefully on paper towels.

3. In a medium saucepan bring 1½ cups of water to a boil and add the rice. Simmer for 10 minutes. Drain and reserve.

4. In a 10-inch ovenproof skillet, heat 1 tablespoon olive oil over medium-high heat. Sauté the leeks until slightly soft, about 5 minutes.

5. Add the remaining olive oil and sauté the shredded squash over medium-high heat until almost tender and all liquid is evaporated, about 4 minutes. Add the garlic and parsley. Sauté for 1 minute.

6. Sprinkle with the flour and stir over medium heat, using a pasta fork, for 2 minutes. Remove from the heat, add the partially cooked rice, ½ cup half-and-half, and ¼ cup vegetable liquid, and stir to combine. Continue cooking, stirring constantly until slightly thickened, about 3 minutes.

7. Continue adding the cream, ½ cup at a time, cooking until thickening begins to occur. After the last of the half-and-half has been added, stir in all but 2 tablespoons of the Parmesan. Add the remaining salt and the pepper.

8. Preheat the oven to 425 degrees. Sprinkle the remaining cheese on top of the dish. Bake until browned and bubbling, about 25 minutes.

ADVANCE PREPARATION: Can be prepared 1 day ahead through step 7. Cover and refrigerate. Bring to room temperature before baking in 425-degree oven.

Baked Pumpkins
with Mascarpone and Sage

*T*his recipe by Heidi Insalata Krahling is an adaptation of a classic French dish in which soup is cooked inside a small pumpkin. Try to get small pumpkins, 6 to 8 inches across, and wider than they are high.

This is a stylish and rather dramatic dish that probably would be best at a small Thanksgiving dinner.

Serves 8

8 miniature pumpkins
1 pound mascarpone cheese
3 eggs
1 teaspoon sugar
½ teaspoon salt

½ teaspoon freshly ground
   pepper
Fresh sage leaves
¾ cup roasted, skinned, and
   chopped hazelnuts

1. Preheat the oven to 350 degrees.

2. With a sharp knife, carefully cut out a lid in each pumpkin. Reserve the lids. Scoop out the seeds and discard. In a shallow baking pan fitted with a wire rack, place the pumpkins and their lids on the rack upside down. Fill the pan with ¼ inch water and bake pumpkins about 30 minutes, or until they are almost cooked but still firm. Let cool to room temperature.

3. Meanwhile, in a bowl whisk the mascarpone, eggs, sugar, salt, and pepper until smooth. Fill the pumpkins three-fourths full, alternating 1 or 2 sage leaves, a spoonful of cheese mixture, and a sprinkling of chopped hazelnuts.

4. Fit the lids back on top. Place the pumpkins back on the rack, and bake until the mascarpone is set—about 20 minutes. Serve hot.

Brussels Sprouts with Maple-Mustard Sauce

*T*he key to this dish is not to overcook the sprouts and to make sure that each and every one of them is well coated with the sauce. This is an eclectic combination of flavors that comes together to make a delectable dish—one that has become quite popular at our house.

Makes 5 cups (10 ½-cup servings)

4 cups (2 pounds) brussels
   sprouts
2 tablespoons champagne
   vinegar
2 tablespoons balsamic vinegar
2 tablespoons maple syrup
2 tablespoons Dijon mustard
1 tablespoon coarse-grain
   mustard

½ teaspoon salt
½ teaspoon freshly ground
   pepper
⅛ teaspoon freshly grated
   nutmeg
½ cup extra-virgin olive oil

1. Trim the brussels sprouts by cutting an X in the stalk end and removing the bitter outer leaves. Drop the sprouts into a large pot containing 7 to 8 quarts of rapidly boiling water. Add 2 teaspoons of salt and bring the water back to a boil. Reduce the heat and simmer slowly for 5 minutes. Remove from the heat and drain thoroughly, letting the sprouts stand for a few minutes.

2. While the sprouts are cooking, mix the vinegars, syrup, mustards, salt, pepper, and nutmeg. Whisk thoroughly. Slowly add oil, a drop or two at a time, then in a thin, steady stream. The mixture will get thicker and lighter in color.

3. Add the brussels sprouts to the bowl containing the sauce. Toss well to coat each sprout. Serve at room temperature.

ADVANCE PREPARATION: Can be made 1 day in advance through step 2. Cover and refrigerate. Bring to room temperature and assemble 2 hours before serving.

Marinated Brussels Sprouts with Pomegranate Seeds and Walnuts

*L*et's face it, brussels sprouts are not the world's most popular vegetable. Some people—especially kids—cringe at the thought of them. But much of the bad reputation these small members of the cabbage family have earned is more a result of poor cooking than anything intrinsically wrong with the vegetable itself.

When not overcooked, brussels sprouts have a charming, subtle flavor. This recipe preserves that flavor and adds the tang of vinegar, the richness of walnuts, and the lovely perfume of pomegranate.

Dealing with the pomegranate takes some skill. The edible seeds, encased in juicy outer flesh, are mounted on a network of waxy membranes. The pomegranate has to be carefully opened and the seeds cautiously removed. The juice can stain, so take steps to protect yourself and your kitchen.

Start by cutting off the blossom end of the fruit and then carefully score the outer skin in quarters, from blossom end to stem. Do not cut into the interior of the fruit; break it carefully to reveal the seeds inside. Separate into quarters, gently remove the seeds, and place them in a bowl.

Makes 6 cups (12 ½-cup servings)

4 cups (2 pounds) brussels sprouts	½ teaspoon salt
1 cup coarsely chopped walnuts	Freshly ground pepper
4 tablespoons raspberry or red wine vinegar	½ cup walnut oil
	The seeds of 1 pomegranate

1. Trim the brussels sprouts by cutting an X in the stalk end and removing the bitter outer leaves. Drop the sprouts into a large pot containing 7 to 8 quarts of rapidly boiling water. Add 1 tablespoon of salt and bring the water back to a boil. Reduce the heat and simmer slowly for 5 minutes. Remove from heat and drain. Rinse the sprouts quickly with cold water to stop the cooking. (If you prefer, you may steam the sprouts for 8 minutes.) Cool.

2. Toast the chopped walnuts in a single layer on a foil-lined cookie sheet for 10 minutes in a 350-degree oven. Cool and reserve.

3. In a small bowl, combine the vinegar, salt, and pepper. Beat rapidly with a wire whisk while adding the walnut oil in a slow, steady stream.

4. When the brussels sprouts are at room temperature, pour the vinaigrette over them and toss to coat thoroughly. Sprinkle the walnuts over the sprouts. Marinate at room temperature for at least 2 hours. When ready to serve, sprinkle the pomegranate seeds decoratively over the brussels sprouts.

ADVANCE PREPARATION: Can be made 1 day ahead through step 3 and refrigerated. The dish can be assembled the morning of Thanksgiving and served at room temperature.

Sweet and Sour Red Cabbage

*A*lthough good with turkey, this is really a perfect accompaniment to goose.

Makes 6 cups (12 ½-cup servings)

4 tablespoons goose fat or unsalted butter	One 2-pound head red cabbage, finely shredded
1 onion, thinly sliced	2 tablespoons dark unsulfured molasses
6 whole cloves	Salt and freshly ground pepper
6 juniper berries	Lemon juice (optional)
½ cup balsamic vinegar	
¼ cup cider vinegar	
2 tablespoons golden brown sugar	

1. Melt the fat or butter in a large skillet and sauté the onion until it is translucent, about 5 minutes. Add cloves, juniper berries, vinegars, and sugar. Bring to a boil, stirring constantly. Mix in cabbage. Reduce to a simmer, cover, and cook until cabbage is very tender and almost no liquid remains in the skillet, about 40 minutes.

2. Add molasses and season to taste with salt and pepper. For a more pungent flavor, add lemon juice to taste.

ADVANCE PREPARATION: Can be made 1 day ahead. Cover and refrigerate. Rewarm over low heat.

The Ultimate Mashed Potatoes

*W*hile our son Toby was at boarding school, he would bring his friend Barrett home for Thanksgiving. For four years Barrett was at our holiday table mainly because of these wonderful, easy-to-make mashed potatoes. We usually had to double this recipe to accommodate Barrett's appetite. These potatoes make a perfect vehicle for gravy.

In the unlikely event there are some of these left over, take a look at the Mashed Potato Pancakes on page 197.

Makes 9 cups (12 ¾-cup servings)

4 pounds medium potatoes	½ cup heavy cream
8 tablespoons (1 stick) unsalted butter	1 tablespoon salt
	6 tablespoons chopped chives

1. Peel the potatoes and drop them into a large pot of boiling water. Boil over medium heat for 25 minutes. Drain into a colander and return to the pan. Shake over high heat to remove excess moisture.

2. Put the potatoes into the bowl of an electric mixer fitted with a paddle. Mix at slow speed. Add the butter and then the cream and salt. If serving immediately, fold the chives into the potatoes, saving some to sprinkle on the top.

VARIATIONS: Sauté the peeled cloves from one head of garlic (about 15) in the butter. Simmer for 20 minutes, making sure that the garlic does not brown. When the garlic is soft, purée it with the butter and mix it into the potatoes.

For fluffier mashed potatoes, put cooked potatoes through a ricer instead of using the mixer.

Mashed Potatoes and Celery Root

Celery root adds deep flavor complexity to the usual mashed potatoes. We thought the kids would riot when we served this, but they actually liked it.

If you have leftovers, this works well in the Mashed Potato Pancakes recipe (see page 197).

Makes 12 cups (16 ¾-cup servings)

2 pounds celery root	1 cup half-and-half
4 pounds potatoes	2 teaspoons salt
½ pound (2 sticks) unsalted butter	Freshly ground white pepper

1. Peel the celery root and cut into ¾-inch cubes. Place in a bowl with cold water to cover and reserve.

2. Put about 2 quarts of water into a medium-size pot. Peel the potatoes and cut them into ¾-inch cubes. As you finish each potato, drop the cubes into the pot. When you have finished, adjust the amount of water so that the potatoes are covered by 2 inches of water. Add 1 teaspoon salt and bring to a boil.

3. Boil the potatoes for 5 minutes, then add the drained celery root. Reduce the heat, cover, and simmer for 12 minutes, or until tender. Drain.

4. Place the vegetables in a food processor fitted with the metal blade and purée for a few seconds, or use a potato ricer. Add the butter, half-and-half, the 2 teaspoons salt, and pepper to taste, then process for a few more seconds.

5. Return the potatoes and celery root to the pot and stir over medium heat. Serve immediately.

Classic Candied Yams

Serves 10

5 yams (about 2½ pounds), scrubbed
2 tablespoons unsalted butter
¼ cup firmly packed brown sugar

1 teaspoon freshly grated gingerroot
1 teaspoon lemon juice

1. Bring 2 cups of water to a rolling boil in the bottom of a large saucepan. Put the yams in a steamer and cover the pot. Cook over moderate heat for 30 minutes, or until a fork can pierce the yams easily.

2. Remove the yams from the steamer and allow to cool while you make the glaze.

3. In a saucepan, melt the butter over medium-low heat and add brown sugar. Stir until dissolved. Add the ginger, simmer for 1 minute, then add the lemon juice.

4. Butter an ovenproof baking dish 7 by 11 by 1½ inches. Peel the yams and slice them in half, lengthwise. Place them flat side down in the dish, and cover with the glaze.

5. Preheat the oven to 350 degrees. Bake for 15 minutes. Serve.

ADVANCE PREPARATION: Can be prepared 1 day ahead through step 4. When ready to serve, remove from the refrigerator and let the dish come to room temperature, then bake at 350 degrees for 15 minutes, or until warmed through.

Maddie's Praline Sweet Potatoes

*M*addie Katz has been making and refining this luscious recipe for nearly thirty years. It is a crowd pleaser and, although it is finished with sugar, it does a good job of showcasing the true sweet potato flavor. The Orange Sauce gives the dish an additional subtlety that is quite appealing. If desired, though, the potatoes can be served without the sauce.

Makes 6 cups (12 ½-cup servings)

4 sweet potatoes
2 eggs
½ cup firmly packed dark brown
   sugar
6 tablespoons unsalted butter,
   melted

2 teaspoons salt, or to taste
½ cup pecan halves
Orange Sauce (see below)

1. Cut a slit in each potato, place on a baking sheet, and bake at 350 degrees for 1 hour, or until soft. Leave the oven on.

2. When done, scoop out the sweet potato pulp and place in a bowl. With a wooden spoon, beat in the 2 eggs, ¼ cup sugar, 2 tablespoons melted butter, and the salt. Pour the mixture into a 2-quart casserole. Arrange the pecan halves on the top in a neat design. Sprinkle with the remaining ¼ cup sugar and drizzle with the remaining butter.

3. Bake for 20 minutes, or until heated through. To complete the dish, place under a hot broiler for 30 seconds to melt the sugar. Serve immediately accompanied by Orange Sauce.

Orange Sauce

Makes 1½ cups

⅓ cup granulated sugar
1 tablespoon cornstarch
Pinch of salt
1 teaspoon grated orange zest
1 cup orange juice, preferably
   freshly squeezed

1 tablespoon freshly squeezed
   lemon juice
2 tablespoons unsalted butter
1 tablespoon Cointreau, or other
   orange liqueur
3 dashes bitters

1. Combine the sugar, cornstarch, and salt in a saucepan. Add the orange zest, and orange and lemon juices. Stir over medium heat until sauce coats the back of a spoon.

2. Remove from the heat and stir in butter, Cointreau, and the bitters.

ADVANCE PREPARATION: The casserole can be prepared 1 day ahead through step 2. Cover and refrigerate. Bring the casserole to room temperature before reheating in a 350-degree oven. The sauce can be prepared 2 days ahead. Cover tightly and refrigerate. Reheat gently before serving.

Caitlin's Potatoes

*T*his is a dazzling, elegant, and extremely simple adaptation of the famous French *Pommes Anna,* the layered potato pancake that has become a classic. We named it for our eldest daughter.

Serves 8

8 tablespoons (1 stick) unsalted butter, melted	1 apple, thinly sliced
	2 tablespoons maple syrup
5 medium sweet potatoes, peeled	Salt and freshly ground pepper

1. Preheat the oven to 400 degrees. Thinly slice the potatoes by hand or use the 3 mm food processor blade. Butter a 9-inch pie pan and arrange a neat layer of overlapped sweet potato slices in it. Dribble a little melted butter over the potatoes. Place a layer of sliced apple, not overlapped, on top of the potatoes. Sprinkle with butter, maple syrup, salt, and pepper.

2. Continue layering the ingredients until the pie plate is filled, finishing with maple syrup, salt, and pepper. (All the potatoes should be used up.)

3. Cover the top with foil and a lid. Bake in the preheated oven for 45 minutes. Remove the lid and the foil and bake until the top is golden, about 15 minutes. Be careful not to overcook.

5. Remove the pan from the oven and let cool for 10 minutes. Invert onto a large round platter and, with the gentle proddings of a narrow spatula, let the crisp pancake drop onto the platter. Serve hot, cut into wedges with a pie knife.

ADVANCE PREPARATION: Can be assembled through step 2 as much as 6 hours ahead. Cover and refrigerate.

Mashed Sweet Potatoes

Makes 5 cups (10 ½-cup servings)

5 sweet potatoes (about 2½ pounds)

4 tablespoons unsalted butter, cut in pieces

¼ cup heavy cream

½ teaspoon freshly grated nutmeg

½ teaspoon freshly ground white pepper

Salt

1 tablespoon chopped fresh parsley

1. Peel the sweet potatoes and place them in a pot. Cover with lightly salted water and place over medium heat. Boil until a fork pierces the potatoes without resistance—about 20 minutes. Drain.

2. At this point, you can mash the potatoes with a potato ricer, or transfer them to a food processor fitted with the metal blade. In either case, alternately add the butter and the cream while beating or processing.

3. When smooth, add the seasonings, garnish with chopped parsley, and serve immediately.

NOTE: If you have leftovers, these potatoes work very nicely in the Mashed Potato Pancakes (page 197).

ADVANCE PREPARATION: Can be prepared 2 days ahead. Cover and refrigerate. Store the parsley separately. Bring to room temperature before reheating in the top of a double boiler.

Wild Rice Ragout

*T*his recipe was suggested by Heidi Insalata Krahling, one of California's most talented young cooks. She is chef at Smith Ranch in San Rafael. Heidi Insalata Krahling's wild rice ragout is very rich and quite extraordinary. It is best served at a smaller, more sophisticated Thanksgiving. It goes beautifully with duck or goose and works well as a stuffing.

Makes 5 cups (10 ½-cup servings)

1½ cups wild rice
3 cloves garlic, peeled
2 bay leaves
5 cups Chicken Stock (see page 77)
2 tablespoons unsalted butter
4 shallots, finely minced
1 large or 2 small heads fennel, thinly sliced
1 tablespoon toasted and ground fennel seed

½ cup brandy
2 cups rich condensed poultry (squab or duck) stock
½ cup orange juice
2 tablespoons chopped fresh chives
¼ cup fresh tarragon leaves, chopped
1 cup chestnuts, preferably freshly roasted and peeled
Salt and freshly ground pepper

COMPOUND BUTTER

6 tablespoons unsalted butter, softened
Grated zest of 1 orange

2 shallots, roasted until golden, then chopped

1. Place the wild rice, garlic, bay leaves, and stock in a saucepan, and bring to a boil over medium heat. Reduce heat to low and simmer until the rice is tender. (Different wild rice brands seem to have different cooking times. Taste a few grains of the rice to make sure that it is soft enough.) Drain the liquid and set the rice aside. Discard the garlic and bay leaves.

2. Melt the 2 tablespoons butter in a sauté pan. Sauté the shallots until softened. Add the sliced fennel and continue to sauté for about 1 minute. Add the ground fennel seed and sauté for 30 seconds more. Deglaze the pan with brandy.

3. Add the rich stock and the orange juice, and reduce the liquid by half. Add the reserved wild rice, the chives, tarragon, chestnuts, and salt and pepper to taste. Stir to mix.

4. Make the compound butter by combining the softened butter, the orange zest, and the chopped roasted shallots. Over low heat, swirl the compound butter into the rice. Season to taste.

ADVANCE PREPARATION: Can be prepared 1 day in advance. Cover and refrigerate. Bring to room temperature before warming in the top of a double boiler.

Spicy Rice

$\mathcal{I}$f you're weary of mashed potatoes or candied yams, this is a dazzling alternative. Earthy, rich, and complex in flavor, this rice is a worthy accompaniment to turkey.

Makes 5 cups (10 ½-cup servings)

2 tablespoons vegetable oil
2 shallots, minced
3 cloves garlic, minced
2 cups long-grain rice
3 cups Chicken Stock (see page 77)

½ cup chopped red onion
1 teaspoon salt
¼ teaspoon cayenne
2 tablespoons chopped fresh parsley

1. In a saucepan, heat the oil over medium-high heat and add the shallots and garlic. Sauté until lightly browned. Remove from the heat and reserve.

2. Rinse the rice quickly and drain for 10 minutes. Add the rice to the saucepan and sauté over medium-high heat for 5 minutes. Add the stock and cover, cook for 7 minutes, stirring only twice. The stock should be completely absorbed.

3. Reduce the heat to low. Add the red onion and cook for 10 minutes longer. Stir in salt and cayenne. Garnish with parsley and serve.

ADVANCE PREPARATION: Can be prepared 4 hours ahead. Cover and store at room temperature. Reheat in the top of a double boiler.

Corn and Tomato Salad with Mustard-Cumin Vinaigrette

*T*his mellow salad brings some new flavors to the Thanksgiving table. The crisp combination of corn, tomatoes, and cumin is a charming contrast to the heavy, rich foods of the season. We also love this for luncheons during the holiday weekend.

Makes 6 cups (8 ¾-cup servings)

4 cups frozen or fresh corn (cut from 8 ears)	1 tablespoon Dijon mustard
1¼ cups chopped red onions	1 tablespoon balsamic vinegar
12 cherry tomatoes, quartered	2 tablespoons red wine vinegar
½ cup chopped fresh parsley	¾ cup extra-virgin olive oil
1½ teaspoons cumin	½ teaspoon salt
	Freshly ground pepper

1. If you are using fresh corn, shuck it partially (let a few of the outer leaves remain), and boil for 8 minutes in a large pot of salted water. Remove from the water and let cool. (You can cook the corn well in advance and refrigerate it until ready to use.) Slice the kernels from each ear. If you are using frozen corn, use the loose kind packed in plastic bags. Allow the corn to defrost.

2. In a large bowl, combine the corn, onions, tomatoes, and parsley. Stir.

3. Combine the remaining ingredients in a screw-top jar or small bowl. Shake vigorously or stir to emulsify.

4. Pour the vinaigrette over the corn mixture and stir to combine. Serve or refrigerate until ready to use. This salad will keep for several days in the refrigerator.

VARIATION: A nontraditional but appealing variation is to add ½ cup of crumbled feta cheese to the salad.

ADVANCE PREPARATION: Can be prepared 2 days ahead, but don't add the tomatoes until ready to serve. Cover and refrigerate.

Condiments

Condiments are a northern European invention. We'd like to think they were created to liven up food that was traditionally bland. Because the colonists who participated in the early Thanksgivings were English, condiments became an important part of the holiday festival and, since they were readily available, cranberries became the condiment of choice.

Cranberries are small, extremely sour berries that grow in sea-level peat bogs, particularly in the New England areas where the Pilgrims settled. They are similar to lingonberries, which are used in Northern Europe as an accompaniment. Because they are so sour, cranberries must be combined with sugar to become palatable. Thus they are ideal for making sweet relishes and sauces.

Cranberries are one of only three native North American fruits (Concord grapes and blueberries are the other two). In fact, long before the settlers arrived in 1620, North American Indians were already combining dried venison with suet and cranberries to make pemmican—a long-lasting convenience food.

The Indians had other uses for cranberries. In addition to their culinary applications, they employed cranberries as dye and they believed that the cranberry had special medicinal properties. Indian women used the bright red juice to color blankets and rugs, and poultices for cleansing infections were brewed from whole cranberries.

In the nineteenth century, American sailors went to sea with barrels of cranberries. The berries were for vitamin C, needed to ward off scurvy (English sailors used limes for the same purpose, thus the nickname *limey).*

The cranberry was named by the colonists. Indians had called it *sassananesh* and *ibimi,* but the Pilgrims thought the bright berry blossom looked like the head of a crane, so they called them *craneberries,* which was eventually contracted to its present form.

Cranberries are grown mainly in bogs or marshes in eastern Massachusetts and Rhode Island. They can also be found in New Jersey, Wisconsin, and along the Pacific coast in Oregon, Washington, and British Columbia.

Cranberry bogs are peat-based swamps that have been drained and topped with a layer of sand. This acid environment is ideal for the trailing vines on which the berries grow. It takes 3 to 5 years for a new plantation to bear a commercial crop, but if care is taken to guard against frost damage, cranberry vines can bear indefinitely. There are some producing bogs that are over one hundred years old.

The vines blossom in the latter part of June or early July and the ripe berries are harvested in September and October. In the past cranberries were painstakingly picked by hand; now they are wet-harvested by flooding the beds. Mechanical harvesters cause the ripe berries to float to the surface where they are scooped up and boxed.

Most cranberries are then delivered to Ocean Spray, a grower cooperative that was formed in 1930. Ocean Spray packages and freezes millions of pounds of the sour little berries. The company also introduced a line of cranberry drinks in 1967 that have become extremely successful.

Fresh cranberries are low in calories. An uncooked half cup has only 25 calories and provides more than 10 percent of the recommended daily allowance of vitamin C.

If you plan to use cranberries at times of the year other than Thanksgiving, buy them in the autumn and freeze; they will keep very well for nine months in the freezer. When using frozen berries, do not thaw.

ADVANCE PREPARATION

The recipes that follow can be made a week or two before Thanksgiving. They should be cooled, jarred, and refrigerated. Most of them actually improve with age. If you want to keep them longer than three weeks, can them in sterilized, airtight jars. In this form, they will keep for several months; they make excellent gifts.

Cranberry Relish

Several years ago Andy was the judge at the National Cranberry Cook-off held in Los Angeles. The winning recipe was for cranberry-cherry relish. The lady who created it, Mrs. Helen Lacina of Grinnell, Iowa, won $1,000 and an engraved silver trophy for her creative efforts.

We have adapted this recipe over the years and it has become a tradition at the Blue house. We found the canned cherries to be a problem so we eliminated them. (The recipe called for 1 cup of pitted cherries, and only the canned version is available at Thanksgiving time. If you were to make this relish during cherry season, by all means add 1 cup of fresh pitted cherries to the blend or use dried cherries, if you can get them.)

Each year Andy gives the recipe on his WCBS radio show in New York and more than 1,000 people write in for a printed copy of it.

This relish can be made well ahead of the Thanksgiving dinner. It will keep nicely in the refrigerator for 2 to 3 weeks, or it can be frozen in plastic containers. It is quite good with ham, chicken, or pork. If you are a guest at someone else's home for Thanksgiving dinner, this relish makes a fine house present.

Makes 6 cups

1 lemon, quartered and seeded
1 orange, quartered and seeded
1½ cups fresh or frozen whole cranberries
2 cups dark brown sugar
1½ cups raisins

½ cup white vinegar
½ teaspoon ground cinnamon
½ teaspoon ground cloves
½ teaspoon freshly grated nutmeg
½ cinnamon stick

Cut the lemon and orange into pieces no bigger than ½ inch. Place them in a large saucepan with all the other ingredients. Bring the mixture to a boil over medium heat, reduce the heat, and simmer for 15 minutes. Remove the cinnamon stick. Cool and refrigerate.

Uncooked Cranberry Relish

*T*his classic condiment offers holiday diners a tangy contrast to cooked cranberry sauce.

Makes 3 cups

1 orange	1 cup sugar
One 12-ounce package (3 cups) fresh or frozen cranberries	

1. With a sharp knife or vegetable peeler remove the outer skin of the orange. Inspect the skin for traces of pith, the bitter white inner skin, and cut off any that you find. Reserve the skin. Remove and discard the white pith from the orange and slice the fruit into sections, cutting off the separating membranes. Remove the seeds.

2. Put the orange slices, the orange skin, and the cranberries into the bowl of a food processor fitted with the metal blade. Pulse 4 or 5 times, or until the fruit is evenly chopped. Put the chopped fruit into a bowl or glass container. Stir in the sugar until dissolved. Refrigerate.

NOTE: This relish, because it is uncooked, will not last as long as some of the other cranberry condiments. Give it a week or two at the most.

VARIATION: Add ½ cup chopped walnuts and pulse with the other ingredients.

Traditional Cranberry Sauce

The traditional sauce—cranberries and sugar—is what most children expect and love. We like to offer a selection of condiments at the Blue holiday table, and this one is usually among them.

We generally serve this sauce along with one or two other condiments. If this is the only one you serve for a party of 8 or more, double the recipe.

Makes 2½ cups

1 cup water	One 12-ounce package (3 cups)
1 cup sugar	fresh or frozen cranberries

1. Combine the water and sugar in a saucepan. Bring to a boil over medium heat, stirring to dissolve the sugar. Add the cranberries, bring to a full boil again, and lower the heat to a simmer. Cook until the cranberry skins begin to pop.

2. Cool completely at room temperature and refrigerate.

VARIATION: Use cranberry juice cocktail instead of water, or try one of the cranberry juice combinations—Cran-Apple, Cran-Raspberry, etc.

Another idea is to add 1 or 2 teaspoons grated orange rind when adding the cranberries.

Cranberry Chutney

This easy-to-make spicy condiment is the brainchild of Susan Friedland, our editor. It not only goes with turkey, it can be used throughout the year with chicken, meatloaf, ribs, or anything else you can think of.

Makes about 1 quart

1 pound cranberries	¾ cup water
Thinly sliced peel of 1 lemon	1 teaspoon salt
1 cup brown sugar	1 teaspoon dry mustard
½ cup raisins	Cayenne
½ cup white vinegar	⅔ cup ginger preserves
1 large onion, sliced	

1. In a large saucepan, combine all ingredients except the ginger preserves. Cook over moderate heat until the mixture thickens and the cranberries pop, 30 to 45 minutes.

2. Remove the saucepan from the heat and stir in the ginger preserves. When the mixture cools, transfer to covered jars and refrigerate. The chutney will keep for months.

Cranberry Cassis Conserve

*T*his is a bright, fruity, condiment with a few interesting flavor twists. It will keep well in the refrigerator for several weeks, or it can be frozen for much longer. You might use the excess for gifts or, if there's just too much, you can cut the recipe in half.

Makes 6 cups

1 thin-skinned juice orange
1 Granny Smith or other firm, tart apple, peeled, cored, and finely minced
2 cups firmly packed dark brown sugar
½ cup raspberry vinegar
½ cup dried currants
1 teaspoon chopped crystallized ginger

¼ teaspoon ground cinnamon
¼ teaspoon almond extract
4 cups (1 pound) cranberries, fresh or frozen
1 tablespoon honey
½ teaspoon lemon juice
2 tablespoons crème de cassis

1. Cut the orange into chunks. In a food processor fitted with the metal blade, chop the orange to a coarse meal texture. Stir in the apple.

2. In a saucepan, combine sugar and vinegar. Over moderate heat, stir to dissolve the sugar. Bring the mixture to a boil and let it bubble for 5 minutes, or until it is a syrupy consistency. Add currants, ginger, cinnamon, and almond extract. Simmer 5 more minutes. Add the cranberries and continue cooking for about another 5 minutes. Remove from the heat when the fruit begins to pop.

3. Add the orange mixture, honey, lemon juice, and cassis. Toss thoroughly to blend. Store in glass containers.

VARIATION: Add ½ cup toasted, slivered almonds and omit the cassis.

Cranberry Jelly

This is a concentrated and intensely flavored natural jelly. Instead of using a jar or other container in step 3, a mold can be used. This makes for a decorative presentation at the holiday table.

Makes 1 cup

Two 12-ounce packages (6 cups) fresh or frozen cranberries

3 cups sparkling apple cider
1 cup sugar

1. In a 3-quart saucepan, combine all ingredients and bring to a boil, stirring to mix thoroughly. Reduce the heat to low and simmer for 1 hour.

2. Line a fine sieve with a double layer of well-rinsed cheesecloth and place over a 2-quart saucepan. Strain the mixture using the back of a ladle to squeeze the juice from the solids. Gather the corners of the cloth and twist hard to extract all the liquid. Discard the solids.

3. Over medium heat, bring the liquid to a boil. Decrease the heat to low, and simmer to reduce the liquid to 1 cup. Pour into a sterile jar or decorative 1-cup mold, cover, cool, and chill.

VARIATION: The juice and zest of one orange can be added at step 3 to make a cranberry-orange jelly. Add two cinnamon sticks (remove at the end of step 3) to add a flavor nuance.

Cranberry Vinegar

This flavored vinegar is useful in many holiday recipes (substitute it anywhere berry vinegar is called for). It adds a unique Thanksgiving character to many dishes.

Makes 3 cups

1 cup cranberries

2 cups champagne vinegar

1. Place the cranberries in a clean, lidded quart bottle. Heat the vine-

gar over moderate heat. When it comes to a boil, pour it over the cranberries.

2. Let the mixture cool and then screw on the lid. Place the jar in a sunny spot and leave it undisturbed for at least a week—preferably several weeks. (We have found the optimum time is about 5 weeks.)

NOTE: This vinegar will keep at room temperature nearly indefinitely if you strain out the berries. If you find the vinegar too tart, stir in 1 or 2 teaspoons of sugar.

Spiced Cranberry Purée

This smooth, thick, spicy, and opulently flavored condiment is excellent with turkey and also is perfect with cold meats such as pork or lamb. This sauce will keep for months in the refrigerator.

Makes about 6 cups

2 pounds (about 8 cups) cranberries, sorted and washed
3 medium onions, coarsely chopped (about 2 cups)
1 cup water
2 cups light brown sugar
½ cup red wine vinegar

½ teaspoon ground ginger
½ teaspoon ground cloves
1 teaspoon ground allspice
1 teaspoon ground cinnamon
¼ teaspoon freshly ground pepper
1 teaspoon salt

1. Put the cranberries, onions, and water into a 5-quart saucepan. Bring to a boil, cover tightly, and boil for 15 minutes. Stir the mixture twice at the end of the cooking time. The berries should have popped and the onions should be tender. Drain the water.

2. In the bowl of a food processor fitted with the metal blade, purée the berries and onions. Add the rest of the ingredients and continue to process for a few seconds.

3. Return the mixture to the saucepan. Over medium heat, bring the sauce to a boil. Remove from the heat and pack at once into 6 or 7 hot, sterilized ½-pint jars, and seal. This will ensure that the sauce will stay fresh for several months.

Ginger-Apple Preserves

*T*his very sweet confection is popular with certain younger people in our house. Frankly, we find it a bit sugary. It does go nicely with duck and goose, however, and it's quite easy to make.

Makes about 4 cups

2 pounds crisp, firm, tart apples (Granny Smiths are perfect), peeled, cored, and coarsely chopped (about 5 cups)	¼ cup freshly squeezed lemon juice
	Zest of 1 lemon
½ cup coarsely chopped crystallized ginger	4 cups sugar
	½ cup water

In a saucepan, bring all the ingredients to a boil. Stir until the sugar is dissolved. Reduce heat and simmer, uncovered, for 1 hour, or until the apples are tender and the preserve is thick. Cool. Refrigerate until ready to use. This keeps for weeks in the refrigerator.

Meems' Prune Chutney

*T*his stuff is just superb. We got the recipe from our friend Mary Powell, who inherited it from her grandmother. Mary serves it with turkey and with the wonderful marinated lamb that her son Alex makes. We make sure that there is a good supply of this magical chutney in our refrigerator at all times, in case of an emergency.

Makes about 5 cups

3½ cups pitted prunes, halved	2 teaspoons mustard seed
1 cup firmly packed dark brown sugar	2 large cloves garlic, thinly sliced
1 cup granulated sugar	¼ cup thinly sliced onion
¾ cup cider vinegar	½ cup thinly sliced preserved ginger
1½ teaspoons crushed red pepper flakes	1 cup seedless white raisins

1. Bring 2 cups of water to a boil. Place the prunes in a bowl. Pour the water over the prunes and soak overnight.

2. The next day, mix the sugars and vinegar and bring them to a boil in a saucepan over medium heat. Add all other ingredients except the prunes. Mix well. Discard the soaking water and stir in the prunes. Simmer over medium-low heat until the mixture is thickened, about 1 hour, stirring gently and frequently. Pour into ½-pint glass jars and refrigerate.

Harvest Fruit Chutney

$\mathcal{T}$his unusual condiment is the creation of Lois Jamart, a talented San Francisco cook. It goes well with turkey and other meats, warm or cold. It keeps for months in the refrigerator.

Makes 5 cups

½ cup raisins
¼ cup brandy
½ cup apricot preserves
½ cup cider vinegar
½ cup firmly packed dark brown
   sugar
2 tablespoons chopped
   crystallized ginger
1 teaspoon curry powder
1 cinnamon stick and 6 whole
   cloves, wrapped in a double
   thickness of cheesecloth and
   tied

1 lime, blanched in boiling
   water for 2 minutes, then
   seeded and chopped
1 firm pear, peeled and seeded
One 12-ounce package (3 cups)
   fresh or frozen cranberries
½ cup chopped walnuts

1. Soak the raisins in the brandy for 2 to 4 hours.

2. In a large saucepan, combine the preserves, vinegar, sugar, ginger, curry powder, and the seasoning bag. Stir until the sugar is dissolved.

3. Add the lime and pear. Simmer over medium heat for 10 minutes. Add the cranberries and brandy-soaked raisins. Simmer, stirring occasionally, for 25 minutes, or until thick.

4. Stir in the walnuts and discard the seasoning bag. Serve immediately or refrigerate until ready to use. Bring to room temperature before serving.

Apple and Cranberry Salad

*T*his crisp and tangy salad, suggested by Martha Kropf, offers an excellent balance to the rich and heavy foods that make up the Thanksgiving feast.

Makes 8 cups

¼ cup freshly squeezed lime juice
1 tablespoon Dijon mustard
1 teaspoon salt
Several grindings of white pepper
¾ cup extra-virgin olive oil
4 tart, crisp apples such as Granny Smiths, cored and cut into ½-inch dice

½ cup thinly sliced scallions
2 cups fresh cranberries, coarsely chopped
4 tablespoons sugar
2 bunches (about 2 cups) watercress

1. In a medium-size glass bowl combine the lime juice, mustard, salt, and pepper. Stir. While beating continuously, add the olive oil in a thin, steady stream. Add the diced apple and sliced scallion. Toss to coat all the ingredients. Cover with plastic wrap. Let stand in the refrigerator for 2 to 3 hours.

2. In another glass bowl, combine the chopped cranberries and the sugar. Stir to combine well. Cover with plastic wrap. Refrigerate for 2 hours.

3. When ready to serve, line each salad plate with well-cleaned and stemmed watercress. Top with a portion of apples and of cranberries. Serve immediately.

NOTE: If you want people to help themselves, line a salad bowl with the watercress. Place the cranberries in the center of the bowl, and arrange the apples around them.

VARIATION: Substitute diced jicama for half the apples.

Onion, Prune, and Chestnut Compote

*H*ere's a real grown-up accompaniment to soothe the more sophisticated palates while the kids are slurping down the mashed potatoes, gravy, and cranberry jelly. This dish, based on an idea by Diane Rossen Worthington, is rich and quite exquisite.

Actually we couldn't quite decide whether this is a condiment or a vegetable, so we decided it's both. In smaller quantities it is an elegant condiment; in larger amounts it is a flavorful vegetable.

Makes about 6 cups

3 tablespoons butter
1 pint pearl onions (2 cups), peeled
1½ cups veal or beef stock
1 cup port
2 cups moist prunes
2 cups whole chestnuts, roasted and peeled

½ teaspoon salt
½ teaspoon freshly ground pepper
2 teaspoons finely chopped fresh thyme (use lemon thyme, if possible), or 1 tsp. dried
Thyme sprigs for garnish

1. In a small saucepan melt 2 tablespoons butter. Add onions and sauté, rolling them on all sides to coat evenly with butter. Add 1 cup stock, bring to a boil, then reduce to a simmer. Cook until the onions are translucent and soft, about 25 minutes. Set aside.

2. In another saucepan, combine ¾ cup port, prunes, and remaining stock, and bring to a boil. Reduce heat and simmer until moderately soft, about 10 minutes. Spoon the prunes into the onions.

3. In a sauté pan, melt the remaining 1 tablespoon butter and add the chestnuts. Add the remaining port and toss chestnuts to coat and lightly glaze. Combine the chestnuts with the onions and prunes. Add salt, pepper, and chopped thyme. Garnish with thyme sprigs. Serve warm or at room temperature.

ADVANCE PREPARATION: Can be prepared 3 days ahead. Cover and refrigerate. Bring to room temperature before warming over low heat.

Kumquat-Cranberry Compote

This tangy concoction can be served either hot or cold.

Makes 3 cups

1 cup fresh kumquats
½ cup dry red wine

¼ cup sugar
1 package (12 ounces) cranberries

1. Slice the kumquats lengthwise. Place them in a 2-quart saucepan and add the wine and sugar. Simmer over moderate heat until the sugar is dissolved and the kumquats slightly softened.

2. Stir in the cranberries and bring to a boil. Reduce heat and simmer, uncovered, for about 10 minutes, or until the berries begin to pop. Remove from the heat. Cool to room temperature and serve or cover and refrigerate.

Breads and Muffins

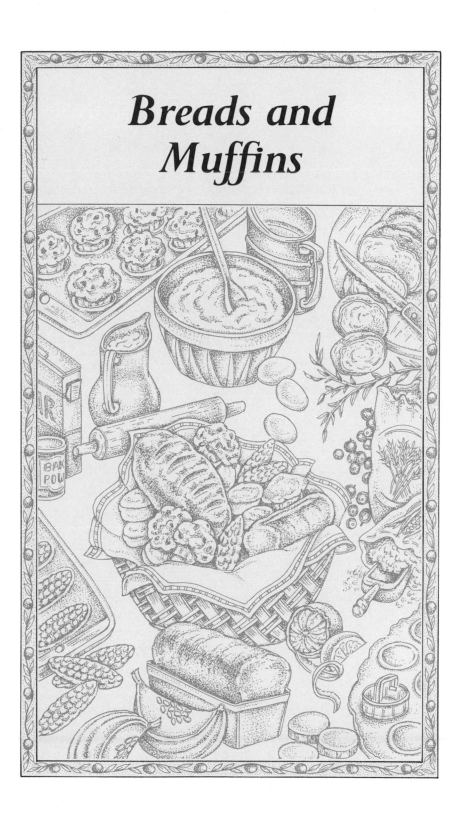

*T*he Thanksgiving feast does not really need bread, but there are a few that are appropriate, especially corn bread, a good accompaniment to turkey and a basis for several stuffings.

Basic Corn Bread

*T*his is a good, moist corn bread that is fine on its own and perfect as an ingredient in various stuffings. The recipe can be doubled. Use a 10 by 15-inch pan for a double recipe.

For stuffing purposes, this recipe makes 6½ cups when crumbled

½ cup all-purpose flour
2½ teaspoons baking powder
1 teaspoon salt
1½ tablespoons sugar
1½ cups yellow cornmeal

3 tablespoons unsalted butter, melted
¾ cup milk or buttermilk
1 egg

1. Preheat the oven to 425 degrees. Sift the flour, baking powder, salt, and sugar together into a large bowl. Add the cornmeal and stir with a fork to combine.

2. In a small bowl, beat the butter, milk, and egg together. Pour into the flour mixture and stir a few times to combine. Do not overbeat.

3 Pour into a well-greased 9 by 9-inch pan. Bake for 25 minutes, or until firm in the center.

Harvest Corn Sticks

*T*hese are made in well-cured, heavy cast-iron molds that are shaped like ears of corn. Traditionally each of these molds makes 7 corn sticks. This recipe makes about 40 corn sticks but since few people own 6 molds, they can be made in shifts. We recommend that you have at least 2 molds, and preferably 3. Keep the corn sticks warm and serve with plenty of soft butter.

Makes 40 corn sticks

2¾ cups all-purpose flour
1 cup yellow cornmeal
2 tablespoons baking powder
2 teaspoons salt
½ cup superfine sugar

3 eggs, beaten
1 cup creamed corn
¼ cup vegetable oil
1½ cups half-and-half

1. Preheat oven to 425 degrees. In a bowl, combine all the dry ingredients. Form a well in the center.

2 In another bowl, mix eggs, creamed corn, vegetable oil, and half-and-half. Pour the mixture into the well, stir just to mix. The mixture will be lumpy.

3. Heat cast-iron corn stick pans in the oven for 5 minutes. Remove the pans and grease them generously with bacon fat or vegetable oil. Fill each mold three-fourths full with the corn mixture. Bake about 20 minutes, until golden brown. Serve warm.

Corn Muffins

$\mathcal{T}$hese are plump, rich, and very delicious. Serve them warm.

Makes 12 muffins

2 cups yellow cornmeal	1 teaspoon salt
¾ cup all-purpose flour	2 eggs
2½ tablespoons sugar	1½ cups milk
2 tablespoons baking powder	½ cup shortening

1. Combine the dry ingredients in a large bowl. Add 1 egg, mix thoroughly, add the second egg, and mix again. Blend in the milk thoroughly. Add the shortening and mix again. Cover and refrigerate for at least 1 hour.

2. Preheat the oven to 350 degrees. Butter or grease the cups (2¾ inches in diameter) of a standard 12-muffin pan. Fill each cup two-thirds full of batter. Bake muffins until their tops are golden brown, about 20 minutes.

Whole Wheat Corn Bread

$\mathcal{T}$his variation is the brainchild of Barbara Folger, who summers on Cape Cod. It works best with a stone ground cornmeal. Barbara gets her ground cornmeal from Leo Manning at Dexter's Grist Mill in Sandwich, Massachusetts.

Makes 1 7 × 1½-inch loaf

2 eggs	1 teaspoon salt
½ cup sugar	1 tablespoon baking powder
1 cup whole wheat flour	1 tablespoon unsalted butter,
1 cup all-purpose flour	melted
1 cup cornmeal	1½ cups milk

1. Preheat the oven to 425 degrees.
2. In a large bowl, beat the eggs and add the sugar. In another bowl,

sift the two flours, cornmeal, salt, and baking powder together. Add the dry ingredients to the egg mixture and stir in the milk and melted butter.

3. Pour the batter into a 7 by 11 by 1½-inch Pyrex baking dish. Bake in the preheated oven until set, about 20 minutes.

ADVANCE PREPARATION: Can be prepared 2 days ahead. Cover and store at room temperature. This corn bread also can be frozen for two months.

Martha Pearl's Buttermilk Biscuits

*M*artha Pearl Villas—food writer Jim Villas's mother—is perhaps the best native Southern cook we have ever met. Her fried chicken is so good that only the hot biscuits that are served alongside can compete.

We like these with Thanksgiving dinner because they are easy to make and are a perfect contrast to the richer textures and flavors of the rest of the meal. The recipe can be doubled.

Makes 20 biscuits

2 cups all-purpose flour	½ teaspoon salt
4 teaspoons baking powder	¼ cup shortening
½ teaspoon baking soda	1 cup buttermilk

1. Preheat the oven to 475 degrees.
2. Sift the dry ingredients together into a medium bowl. Add the shortening in small pieces and mix with your hands until well blended. Add the buttermilk and mix again until soft but—and this is the key—don't over-mix.
3. Turn the dough out onto a lightly floured surface and shape with your hands until smooth. Flatten the dough into a rough rectangle with a ½-inch thickness. Cut out rounds with a floured 2-inch cutter or juice glass. Place the biscuits on a baking sheet. Ball up the scraps of dough and repeat the procedure.
4. Bake the biscuits for 12 minutes, or until they are lightly browned on top.

Buttermilk-Sage Biscuits

Makes about 30 biscuits

½ cup white cornmeal
1½ cups all-purpose flour
2 teaspoons baking powder
½ teaspoon baking soda
2 tablespoons minced fresh sage,
   or 1 tablespoon crumbled
   dried

1½ teaspoons freshly ground
   pepper
½ teaspoon salt
6 tablespoons unsalted butter,
   chilled
⅔ cup buttermilk

1. Preheat the oven to 425 degrees. Grease a baking sheet.
2. In a bowl mix the cornmeal, flour, baking powder, baking soda, sage, pepper, and salt. Toss with a fork to combine. Cut the butter into the bowl and mix with a pastry blender or your fingers.
3. Add the buttermilk and stir just until the dough holds together. Do not overmix.
4. Turn the dough out onto a lightly floured surface. Knead with the heels of your hands a few times. Pat the dough to a ½-inch thickness.
5. With a 1½-inch-diameter round cutter, cut out the biscuits and place them, in a tight formation, on the baking sheet. If you have leftover dough scraps, press them together and cut out more biscuits.
6. Bake the biscuits in the preheated oven for 12 to 15 minutes, until lightly browned.

Cranberry-Orange Muffins

Makes 12 muffins

4 tablespoons unsalted butter
1¼ cups sugar
2 eggs
2 cups all-purpose flour
2 teaspoons baking powder
¼ teaspoon salt

½ cup half-and-half
Zest of 1 orange, chopped
2 cups cranberries, coarsely
   chopped
3 tablespoons orange juice

1. Preheat the oven to 350 degrees. In the bowl of a mixer, cream the butter and sugar together. Continue beating and add the eggs, one at a time.

2. Sift the dry ingredients and add to the butter-sugar mixture, alternating with the cream. Add the orange zest, cranberries, and orange juice.

3. Grease a 12-muffin tin with the softened butter. Spoon the mixture into the cups, filling them three-fourths full. Bake 35 minutes in the preheated oven, or until a toothpick or cake tester inserted in the center of a muffin comes out clean.

Popovers

*C*ommonly served with roast beef, these wonderfully crisp and airy creations are also delicious with turkey.

Makes 18 popovers

1 cup milk	2 eggs
1 cup all-purpose flour	3 tablespoons unsalted butter,
½ teaspoon salt	melted

1. Preheat the oven to 450 degrees.

2. Butter 18 muffin tins or popover cups. In the bowl of a food processor fitted with the metal blade, add the milk, flour, salt, and eggs. Process for 2 minutes.

3. Fill each muffin or popover cup one-third full and pour ½ teaspoon melted butter in the center of each.

4. Bake in preheated oven for 10 minutes, then lower the heat to 400. After 25 additional minutes, poke a small hole in each popover to let out the steam. Leave in the oven 3 minutes to crisp.

ADVANCE PREPARATION: Although popovers are best when fresh from the oven, they can be made a day ahead and reheated. Remove them from the oven before the 3-minute crisping time (step 4). Cover with foil and store at room temperature until ready to use. Then warm in a 250-degree oven for 4 minutes.

Pumpkin-Hazelnut Bread

Makes 18 ½-inch slices

1½ cups all-purpose flour
1 teaspoon baking soda
¼ teaspoon baking powder
¾ teaspoon salt
1 teaspoon ground cinnamon
¼ teaspoon freshly grated
   nutmeg

6 tablespoons butter
1⅓ cups sugar
1 cup puréed or mashed
   pumpkin
2 eggs, lightly beaten
⅓ cup milk
1 cup chopped hazelnuts

1. Preheat the oven to 350 degrees. Grease and flour a 9 by 5-inch loaf pan.

2. In a medium bowl combine the first six ingredients, and stir with a fork to incorporate.

3. In a large bowl blend the butter and sugar with a fork. Add the pumpkin, eggs, and milk, and mix well.

4. Add the dry ingredients to the pumpkin mixture and stir thoroughly. Fold in the nuts and pour into the loaf pan.

5. Bake about 1 hour, or until a cake tester or skewer inserted into the center of the bread comes out clean. Remove from the pan and cool on a rack. This bread freezes well.

Desserts

*I*f Thanksgiving isn't all about desserts, you can't prove it by our family. During the month leading up to the holiday, they freely offer advice about what desserts they think should appear on the dining room sideboard on the big day. Of course, each child has a personal wish list, so we end up making a selection—six or more desserts to satisfy all yearnings.

We feel that Thanksgiving desserts should reflect the bounty of the harvest season. Pumpkins, pears, persimmons, apples, chestnuts, and cranberries are appropriate seasonal ingredients that give a singular flavor to the holiday table. Certain other fruits—bananas, coconut, strawberries among them—just don't seem to fit in. They are representatives of other seasons, other places, and other celebrations.

The desserts that follow have all stood the test of time and diverse palates. These are the sweets that we are proud to serve at our own holiday feast. Most of them are our family favorites, and some are traditions at the tables of friends.

Basic Pumpkin Purée

A number of recipes in the book call for pumpkin purée. Although the canned versions are quite acceptable, there is nothing like doing it all from scratch. A 4-pound pumpkin will yield about 4 cups purée.

Method 1

One 4-pound pumpkin

1. Preheat the oven to 400 degrees. Peel, seed, and cut the pumpkin into 2-inch chunks. Place the pumpkin in a 5-quart ovenproof casserole. Add ¼ inch water. Cover and bake in the oven until tender, about 20 minutes.

2. Pour off any moisture that remains. Purée the pumpkin in a food processor fitted with the metal blade.

Method 2

One 4-pound pumpkin

1. Preheat the oven to 350 degrees. Split and seed the pumpkin, place the 2 halves cut side down in a roasting pan containing 1 cup of water. Bake in the oven until tender, about 90 minutes.

2. Scoop the pulp out of each half and purée in a food processor fitted with the metal blade.

Method 3

One 4-pound pumpkin   5 tablespoons unsalted butter

1. Preheat the oven to 400 degrees. Peel, seed, and cut a 4-pound pumpkin into 2-inch chunks. Melt the butter in a Pyrex baking pan, large enough to fit the pumpkin pieces in one layer, by placing it in the oven for 2 minutes. Put the pumpkin pieces into the baking pan and coat them with the butter. Bake in the oven for 15 minutes. Turn the pieces over and baste. Continue to bake until tender, about 15 more minutes.

2. Purée in a food processor fitted with the metal blade.

Pie Crust

*T*his dough can't miss; it makes a great, flaky crust.

Makes 1 9-inch crust

1 cup all-purpose flour	1 tablespoon beaten egg
Pinch of salt	1 teaspoon vinegar
½ cup vegetable shortening	2 tablespoons water

1. Mix the flour, salt, and shortening in a bowl until crumbly in texture.

2. In another bowl, beat the egg, vinegar, and water until fluffy. Pour this mixture into the bowl with the flour mixture. Mix and knead to combine, but don't overwork the dough. Chill overnight.

NOTE: We generally make this dough in large quantities, usually a triple recipe. The dough keeps well in the freezer. Here are the measurements we use. This makes three 9-inch open-face pies:

3 cups all-purpose flour	1 beaten egg
1 teaspoon salt	1 tablespoon vinegar
1½ cups shortening	6 tablespoons water

Our Favorite Pumpkin Pie

*N*o Thanksgiving is complete without pumpkin pie, but all pumpkin pies are not created equal. There are, of course, various things that can be done with seasonings, crusts, and other ingredients to make a pie unique and memorable. What we have done here is provide our pumpkin pie recipe along with a number of variations. Our favorite invention is among them.

Yes, pumpkin pie can be made without the cream but, to us, it's not as good.

Serves 8 to 12

Pie Crust (see page 150)
2 cups pumpkin purée, fresh
   (see page 148) or canned
3 eggs
1½ cups heavy cream
¾ cup maple syrup

1 teaspoon vanilla extract
1 tablespoon brandy (optional)
½ teaspoon ground allspice
½ teaspoon freshly grated
   nutmeg
½ teaspoon powdered ginger

1. Preheat the oven to 350 degrees. Line a 9-inch pie pan with the pastry, leaving a ½-inch overlap around the top. Fold the upper edge of the crust back, doubling the amount of crust at the rim of the plate. You can decorate the rim by fluting the edge: With your right index finger gently press forward while at the same time press with the other index finger in the opposite direction. You can also use the tines of a serving fork to make a pattern.

2. In a large bowl combine pumpkin, eggs, cream, and maple syrup. Stir in vanilla and the brandy, if you are using it.

3. In a small bowl, combine spices and mix together. Sprinkle over the pumpkin mixture and blend completely.

4. Pour into the prepared pie shell and bake for 1 hour. The pie is done when a knife tip inserted into the center comes away clean. (To avoid the unsightly mark of this test you can also shake the pie slightly. If the center is firm, the pie is done.) Cool on a wire rack.

VARIATIONS: This pie can be completely changed by varying the seasonings. In all of these variations eliminate the brandy, allspice, nutmeg, and powdered ginger and add the following:

1. This is our favorite because it really amplifies the true flavor of pumpkin. Replace the spices with 1 teaspoon freshly ground white pepper.

(continued)

2. Use 1 tablespoon freshly grated nutmeg and 2 teaspoons finely chopped crystallized ginger.

3. Use 1 tablespoon freshly grated nutmeg, 1 tablespoon finely chopped crystallized ginger, and, instead of maple syrup, ¾ cup brown sugar.

4. Use 1 tablespoon freshly grated nutmeg, ½ cup apricot preserves, and, instead of maple syrup, ½ cup brown sugar.

ADVANCE PREPARATION: Can be made 1 day ahead. Cover and refrigerate. Bring to room temperature before serving.

Pumpkin-Ginger Cheesecake

*H*ere is an interesting Thanksgiving idea that became a great dessert. We tried this on a dare and it has become a mainstay of the holiday table.

Serves 10 to 12

CRUST

1½ cups graham cracker crumbs	1 tablespoon sugar
1 teaspoon ground cinnamon	8 tablespoons (1 stick) unsalted
1 teaspoon ground ginger	butter, melted

FILLING

Three 8-ounce packages cream cheese, at room temperature	1 tablespoon vanilla extract
1½ cups sugar	2 tablespoons dark rum
5 eggs	2 tablespoons minced crystallized ginger
One 16-ounce can pumpkin purée, or 2 cups fresh purée (see page 146)	2 teaspoons ground cinnamon
	½ teaspoon freshly grated nutmeg

TOPPING

1½ cups sour cream	½ teaspoon ground cinnamon
½ cup sugar	2 tablespoons dark rum

1. In the bowl of a food processor fitted with the metal blade, combine graham cracker crumbs, cinnamon, ginger, sugar, and the melted butter, pulsing 2 or 3 times to blend evenly. Pour into a buttered 10-inch spring-form pan and press the mixture onto the bottom and one-third up the sides of the pan. Chill for 30 minutes.

2. Preheat the oven to 325 degrees. In the bowl of an electric mixer beat the cheese and sugar with the paddle beater until smooth. Continuing to beat at medium speed, add the eggs one by one, beating well after each addition.

3. In a mixing bowl combine the pumpkin with the vanilla, rum, ginger, cinnamon, and nutmeg. Mix until smooth. Add the pumpkin mixture to the cream cheese in the mixer, and beat to combine.

4. Pour the filling into the crust and bake for 1½ hours, or until set.

5. Whisk the sour cream, sugar, cinnamon, and rum together and spread over the cake. Allow to cool and then chill for at least 5 hours before serving.

ADVANCE PREPARATION: Can be made up to 2 days ahead. Cover and refrigerate.

Pumpkin Praline Pie

$\mathcal{D}$iane Rossen Worthington is one of America's best cookbook authors, and her Pumpkin Praline Pie is a knockout. Diane suggests using a tart pan for an elegant presentation.

Makes 1 9-inch pie or 1 11-inch tart

PASTRY

1½ cups cake flour
Pinch of salt
1 tablespoon coarsely chopped
    pecans

1 tablespoon confectioners' sugar
9 tablespoons unsalted butter,
    frozen, cut into small pieces
¼ cup cold water

FILLING

3 eggs
⅔ cup granulated sugar
2 cups pumpkin purée, fresh (see
    page 146) or canned
½ teaspoon freshly grated nutmeg

½ teaspoon ground ginger
½ teaspoon ground allspice
Salt
¼ cup half-and-half
3 tablespoons bourbon

TOPPING

¾ cup light brown sugar
4 tablespoons unsalted butter,
    melted

2 tablespoons heavy cream
⅔ cup coarsely chopped pecans
½ cup pecan halves

GARNISH

½ cup heavy cream

1 teaspoon vanilla extract

1. Preheat the oven to 400 degrees.

2. For the pastry: Combine flour, salt, pecans, and confectioners' sugar in a food processor fitted with the steel blade. Process a few seconds to blend. Add butter and process until the mixture resembles coarse meal, about 5 to 10 seconds.

3. With the blade of the processor turning, gradually add water until dough is just beginning to come together. It should adhere when pinched.

4. Transfer the dough to a floured pastry board or work surface. Press into a round shape for easy rolling. Roll out the dough large enough to fit an 11-inch flan ring placed on a baking sheet, an 11-inch tart pan with a removable bottom, or a 9-inch pie shell. Drape the dough circle over a rolling pin and fit into the pan. Press into the pan and cut off excess dough with a knife.

5. Place the tart pan or pie plate on a baking sheet. Press the pastry with fingers so that it adheres to the sides of pan. If using a tart pan with straight edges, raise edges of pastry ¼ to ½ inch above top of pan. With your right index finger gently press forward, while at the same time a little to the left, press your left index finger in the opposing direction to make a fluting edge.

6. Cover crust with a sheet of parchment paper or foil and press to fit sides. Pour baking beads, beans, or rice into center of paper and distribute evenly.

7. Bake crust for 8 minutes. Remove from the oven and lift out the paper and beans. Prick the pastry and return it to the oven for 5 minutes. Remove from the oven and let cool 15 minutes.

8. For the filling: Using electric mixer or a food processor fitted with the steel blade, beat eggs and sugar until light, thick, and lemon-colored, about 3 minutes. Add remaining filling ingredients and mix well. Pour into the cooled pie shell.

9. Bake 15 minutes, then reduce oven temperature to 350 degrees. Bake an additional 35 to 40 minutes, or until set. Remove from the oven and let it cool to room temperature.

10. For the topping: Combine sugar, butter, cream, and chopped pecans, and mix well. Spread evenly over the pie. Garnish with pecan halves.

11. Preheat the broiler. Place the pie under the broiler, turning until topping browns evenly. Make sure it doesn't burn. Leaving the door ajar during this procedure is a good idea.

12. For the garnish: Whip the cream with vanilla in a chilled bowl until fairly stiff. Serve the pie warm; pass whipped cream separately.

ADVANCE PREPARATION: This may be prepared up to 8 hours ahead through step 10 and kept in the refrigerator. Bring to room temperature before continuing. Heat before serving.

Perfect Pecan Pie

*P*ecan pie is almost as essential to Thanksgiving as pumpkin pie. The problem we have found with many recipes is that they have an unappealing, gloppy cornstarch filling. We set about developing a pecan pie that is mainly pecans—no filler. The result is a pecan lover's dream: great to look at and packed with nuts.

Serves 8 to 12

Pie Crust (see page 150), ½ recipe for Flaky Pie Crust (see page 151), or the pecan crust from recipe for Pumpkin Praline Pie (see page 156)
4 tablespoons unsalted butter, softened
¾ cup firmly packed dark brown sugar

3 eggs, at room temperature
1 teaspoon maple syrup
1 teaspoon vanilla extract
1½ tablespoons freshly squeezed orange juice
¾ cup dark corn syrup
2½ cups coarsely chopped pecans
1½ cups unbroken pecan halves

1. Preheat the oven to 425 degrees. Roll the pastry into a round on a lightly floured surface. Line a 9-inch pie pan with the pastry, leaving a ½-inch overlap around the top. Fold the upper edge of the crust back, doubling the amount of crust at the rim of the plate. You can decorate the rim by fluting the edge: With your right index finger gently press forward, while at the same time pressing with the left index finger in the opposite direction. You can also use the tines of a serving fork to make a pattern.

2. Cover pan with a sheet of parchment paper or foil and press to fit sides. Pour baking beads, beans, or rice into center of paper and distribute evenly.

3. Bake crust for 10 minutes. Remove from the oven and lift out the paper and beans. Prick the pastry and let it cool 15 minutes.

4. In the bowl of a mixer, cream the butter and sugar until quite light in color, about 7 minutes. Add the eggs, one at a time, beating 2 minutes after each addition.

5. In a small bowl, combine maple syrup, vanilla, and orange juice.

6. With the mixer at medium speed, alternate adding the corn syrup and the vanilla mixture. Fold in the chopped nuts. Pour into the prebaked pie shell.

7. Place the whole pecans in neat concentric circles on top of the filling.

8. Reduce oven temperature to 350 degrees, and bake the pie in the center of the oven until the filling is set, about 50 minutes. If the pecans on top brown too quickly, cover them with foil until the last 5 minutes of baking time.

ADVANCE PREPARATION: The pie shell can be prepared 1 day ahead through step 3. Once finished, the pie will keep in the refrigerator for 2 days.

Chocolate Pecan Pie

$\mathcal{T}$his delectable variation on the traditional pecan pie was suggested to us by Amanda Lyon.

Serves 8 to 12

Pie Crust (see page 150), ½ recipe for Flaky Pie Crust (see page 151), or the pecan crust from recipe for Pumpkin Praline Pie (see page 156)	¼ cup molasses
	¾ cup light corn syrup
	⅓ cup unsalted butter, melted
	1 tablespoon vanilla extract
	¾ cup grated semi-sweet
3 eggs	chocolate
1 cup sugar	1½ cups pecan halves

1. Preheat the oven to 425 degrees. Roll the pastry into a round on a lightly floured surface. Line a 9-inch pie pan with the pastry, leaving a ½-inch overlap around the top. Fold the upper edge of the crust back, doubling the amount of crust at the rim of the plate. You can decorate the rim by fluting the edge: With your right index finger gently press forward, while at the same time pressing with the left index finger in the opposite direction. You can also use the tines of a serving fork to make a pattern.

2. Cover pan with a sheet of parchment paper or foil and press to fit sides. Pour baking beads, beans, or rice into center of paper and distribute evenly.

3. Bake crust for 10 minutes. Remove from the oven and lift out the paper and beans. Prick the pastry and let it cool 15 minutes.

(continued)

4. In the bowl of a mixer, beat the eggs with the sugar until the mixture turns a pale yellow and forms a ribbon when dropped from the beater. Add the molasses, corn syrup, melted butter, and vanilla. Mix to combine. Add the grated chocolate and the pecans.

5. Pour the filling into the pie shell. Reduce oven temperature to 350 degrees, and bake the pie in the center of the oven until the filling is set, about 50 minutes. Test for doneness with a cake tester.

ADVANCE PREPARATION: The pie shell can be prepared 1 day ahead through step 3. Once finished, the pie will keep in the refrigerator for 2 days. Bring to room temperature before serving.

Almond Tart

*T*his is a knockout dessert that offers an elegant alternative to pecan pie. It is buttery, rich, and quite superb.

Serves 8 to 12

CRUST

1½ cups all-purpose flour
Pinch of salt
2 tablespoons sugar
8 tablespoons (1 stick) unsalted butter, chilled

½ teaspoon almond extract
1 egg, separated
2 to 3 tablespoons ice water

FILLING

¾ cup sugar
8 tablespoons (1 stick) unsalted butter
2 tablespoons honey
½ cup heavy cream

1¾ cups sliced blanched almonds (about 8 ounces)
1 tablespoon Grand Marnier, or other orange liqueur
¼ teaspoon almond extract

Sweetened whipped cream (optional)

1. For the crust: Butter a 9-inch tart pan with a removable bottom (it can be fluted or smooth). In the bowl of a food processor fitted with the metal blade, combine flour, salt, and sugar by pulsing on and off for a few seconds. Cut the butter in small pieces and add all to the flour mixture. Add almond extract and the egg yolk. Pulse again for a few seconds, until the mixture resembles coarse meal. Be careful not to overprocess.

2. With the blades of the processor turning, add the water gradually, until the dough is just beginning to come together and will adhere when pinched.

3. Roll out the dough on a lightly floured surface into a ⅛-inch thick round, about 12 inches in diameter. Place the dough in the tart pan by draping it over the rolling pin and gently unrolling it into place. Fold the excess over to give the sides of the crust a double thickness. Press neatly into the sides of the tart pan. Prick the bottom several times with a fork. Refrigerate at least 30 minutes. (Can be prepared 1 day ahead. Cover and refrigerate.)

4. Preheat the oven to 325 degrees. Line the tart shell with foil or parchment and gently press to fit sides. Place enough baking beads, beans, or rice in the crust to fill it. Bake in the preheated oven for 15 minutes. Remove foil or parchment and weights. Lightly brush crust with beaten egg white. Bake until crust is light golden brown, about 15 more minutes. Cool completely on a rack.

5. For the filling: Preheat the oven to 375 degrees. In a heavy 2-quart saucepan cook sugar, butter, and honey over low heat, stirring until the sugar dissolves. Increase the heat to medium and cook until the sugar is golden brown, stirring frequently, about 3 minutes. Remove from the heat.

6. Stir in the cream (the mixture will bubble). Return to the heat and stir until well blended. Mix in the almonds, Grand Marnier, and almond extract. Remove from heat. Let stand 15 minutes. Gently ladle the almond filling into the crust. Bake in the preheated oven until the filling bubbles vigorously all over, about 20 minutes.

7. Cool the tart in the pan on a rack until set, about 4 hours.

8. Remove the tart from the pan. Cut it into wedges and serve topped with dollops of whipped cream, if desired.

ADVANCE PREPARATION: Can be prepared 1 day ahead. When cool, cover with plastic wrap and let stand at room temperature.

Apple Pie

*T*he secret of a great apple pie is the apples. They must be fresh, crisp, hard, and tart. Look for Granny Smiths, Pippins, or Jonathans, and avoid the soft, bland ones, such as Delicious.

Serves 8 to 12

Flaky Pie Crust (see page 151)
½ cup light brown sugar
2 tablespoons flour
1 teaspoon cinnamon
1 teaspoon freshly grated
  nutmeg

6 to 7 large tart apples, peeled,
  cored, and quartered
Juice of 1 orange
2 tablespoons unsalted butter

1. On a lightly floured surface, roll out the dough into 2 rounds, ⅛-inch thick. Use 1 to line the bottom of a 9-inch pie pan. Roll up the second round between 2 pieces of wax paper and refrigerate along with the pie shell.

2. In a small bowl, combine the brown sugar, flour, cinnamon, and nutmeg.

3. Cut each apple quarter into 4 slices. In a large bowl, toss the apples with the orange juice. Combine the brown sugar mixture with the apples. Toss to coat. Let the apples stand, at room temperature, for 1 hour.

4. Preheat the oven to 450 degrees. Using a slotted spoon, fill the pie shell with the apples. They should rise at least 1 inch above the rim. Discard the liquid that collects in the bottom of the apple bowl. Dot the apples with butter. Moisten the rim of the bottom crust with water and cover with the second round of dough, crimping the top to the bottom with your fingers or a serving fork. Cut 4 symmetrical slits in the top crust.

5. Bake in the preheated oven for 15 minutes. Reduce the heat to 350 degrees and bake for an additional 30 minutes more.

ADVANCE PREPARATION: This pie does not improve with age, but it can be prepared 1 day ahead. Store at room temperature. Reheat in a 250-degree oven.

Cranberry Apple Pie

*T*his excellent variation on the traditional apple pie is the brainchild of Peggi McGlynn, one of San Francisco's best cooks.

Serves 8 to 12

Flaky Pie Crust (see page 151)
3 cups fresh or frozen
   cranberries
4 large tart apples, peeled,
   cored, and quartered
1 cup maple syrup

4 teaspoons cornstarch dissolved
   in 2 tablespoons cold water
1 teaspoon freshly grated
   nutmeg
2 tablespoons unsalted butter

1. On a lightly floured surface, roll out the dough into 2 rounds, ⅛-inch thick. Use 1 to line the bottom of a 9-inch pie pan. Roll up the second round between 2 pieces of wax paper and refrigerate along with the pie shell.

2. In a medium saucepan, combine cranberries, apples, and maple syrup. Over medium heat, bring the mixture to a boil. Reduce the heat to a simmer and cook until the cranberries have popped, about 4 minutes. Stir the cornstarch mixture into the fruit and simmer until thickened, about 1 more minute. Grate in the nutmeg.

3. Preheat the oven to 450 degrees. Using a slotted spoon, fill the pie shell with the cranberry-apple mixture. Dot the fruit with butter. Moisten the rim of the bottom crust with water and cover with the second round of dough, crimping the top to the bottom with your fingers or the tines of a serving fork. Cut 4 symmetrical slits in the top crust.

4. Bake in the preheated oven for 15 minutes. Reduce the heat to 350 degrees and bake for 30 minutes more.

VARIATION: Roll out the top crust and cut it in strips with a fluted pastry knife. Refrigerate the strips on a baking sheet for 10 minutes. Once the shell is filled, weave the lattice strips over the fruit in a decorative design.

ADVANCE PREPARATION: This pie does not improve with age, but it can be prepared 1 day ahead. Store at room temperature. Reheat in a 250-degree oven.

Jessica's Caramelized Apple Tart

This easy dessert, based on the French *Tarte Tatin,* goes apple pie one step better—it coats the apples in a toasty caramel syrup. Not only is this wonderfully delicious, but it is remarkably easy. For Thanksgiving we generally try to avoid any dishes that require last-minute preparation, but this is so yummy, and so simple to make, that we made an exception.

Serves 8 to 10

½ recipe Flaky Pie Crust (page 151)
6 tablespoons unsalted butter
¾ cup sugar

5 or 6 hard green apples (such as Granny Smiths), peeled and cut into quarters

1. On a well-floured surface, roll out the dough to a round about 10 inches across. Place the dough between 2 sheets of wax paper, roll into a tube shape, and refrigerate. This can be done the day before.

2. Preheat the oven to 400 degrees. In an ovenproof and nonstick 10-inch skillet, melt the butter. Add the sugar and stir until dissolved. Then add the apples to the skillet, round side down, using just enough apple so that the pieces fit snugly in the pan. Sauté over medium heat until the sugar begins to turn golden brown, indicating that it is caramelizing. Do not stir. This process should take about 20 minutes.

3. Place the skillet in the preheated oven for 5 minutes. Carefully remove it from the oven and unroll the chilled dough over the top, tucking the dough inside the rim of the skillet. Increase the oven temperature to 450 degrees. Return the skillet to the oven and bake for 20 minutes or until the crust is brown and crisp.

4. Remove from the oven and quickly reverse onto a cake plate. Scoop any caramel or apple sections that remain in the bottom of the skillet over the tart and serve immediately.

Apricot-Cranberry Dessert

*T*his started as a condiment, but it turned out to be a great dessert with a refreshingly tangy flavor and a bright color.

Makes 6 cups (12 ½-cup servings)

1¼ cups superfine sugar
1⅓ cups water
1 cup cranberries

12 ounces dried apricots
2 navel oranges

1. In a small saucepan combine half the sugar with ⅔ cup water. Stir to dissolve and bring to a boil. Add the cranberries. Simmer gently for 5 minutes, just until the berries start to pop.

2. Remove from the heat and pour into a small bowl. Allow the berries to come to room temperature before chilling. Cover and chill at least 4 hours; for best results, refrigerate overnight.

3. In another small saucepan combine the remaining sugar and ⅔ cup water and dissolve as before. This time, boil the syrup. Add the apricots and toss to coat in the sugar glaze, but do not stir. Let cook, carefully watching to avoid burning. (Apricots are delightful when caramelized to a very light amber color; if cooked too long the fruit becomes tough. To avoid this, have a bowl of cold water large enough to hold the pan. When you reach the light caramel stage, submerge the pan in the water to stop the process.) When done, transfer the apricots to a bowl immediately.

4. Slice the zest off the oranges, removing all of the white pith. Cut out the segments by slicing down into the center of the fruit next to each membrane separation. Leave the segments in the shape of wedges. Julienne the peel and add to the oranges.

5. Combine the cranberries, apricots, and orange segments. Chill for at least 1 hour before serving.

ADVANCE PREPARATION: Can be made 2 or 3 days ahead. Cover and refrigerate. This dessert improves with time.

**Thanksgiving
Dinner**

Pear Mincemeat Pie

*T*his modern mincemeat foregoes the traditional beef suet and as a result it is considerably more digestible and—we think—better tasting than the heavy and very time-consuming old-style mincemeat.

Serves 8 to 12

1 lemon	1 teaspoon ground cinnamon
½ cup firmly packed dark brown sugar	½ teaspoon freshly grated nutmeg
1 cup coarsely chopped currants	¼ teaspoon ground ginger
½ cup coarsely chopped golden raisins	¼ teaspoon ground allspice
1 cup coarsely chopped cranberries	Pinch of freshly ground pepper
2 pounds firm pears, peeled, cored, and coarsely chopped	1 cup walnuts, toasted and coarsely chopped
¾ cup apple cider	⅓ cup Calvados or apple brandy
2 tablespoons unsulfured molasses	2 tablespoons unsalted butter
1 teaspoon vanilla extract	Pie Crust (see page 150), doubled
	1 egg white, beaten

1. Slice the peel from the lemon with a sharp knife or a vegetable peeler. Cut off any of the white pith from the pieces of peel. Mince the peel. After cutting the pith from the lemon, chop the lemon coarsely. Put the minced peel and the lemon into a 2-quart saucepan with the brown sugar.

2. In the bowl of a food processor fitted with the metal blade, place the currants, raisins, cranberries, pears, apple cider, molasses, vanilla, and spices. Pulse 4 to 5 times. Add to the saucepan containing the lemon peel.

3. Place the saucepan over medium heat and bring to a simmer. Reduce the heat and continue to simmer for 30 minutes, stirring occasionally.

4. Preheat the oven to 350 degrees (or use a toaster oven). Toast the walnuts for 20 minutes. Chop coarsely.

5. Add the brandy to the raisin-cranberry mixture and simmer for an additional 5 minutes. Remove from the heat and stir in the walnuts and butter.

6. Line a 9-inch pie plate with a circle of pie crust dough. Pierce the bottom several times with a fork. Fill—but don't overfill—with the mincemeat. Top with the other circle of dough, crimping the edges and piercing the top several times with a small, sharp knife. Brush the top surface with egg white. Bake until the crust is deep golden brown, about 40 minutes. Cool to room temperature before serving.

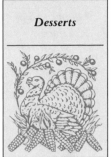

VARIATION: If you don't want to make a pie, this mincemeat is very pleasant as a condiment or as a dessert on its own. Just complete the recipe to the end of step 5. It will make 5 cups of mincemeat.

You can also substitute apples for pears and/or pecans for the walnuts.

ADVANCE PREPARATION: The mincemeat can be made as much as 1 week in advance. The completed pie can be prepared 1 day ahead. Cover and store at room temperature.

Pear Cobbler with Prunes and Armagnac

*H*ere's an easy, all-American dessert from Susan Lifrieri, the pastry chef of the Manhattan Ocean Club in New York City.

Serves 10 to 12

FILLING

1 cup pitted prunes
½ cup Armagnac
8 ripe pears
4 tablespoons unsalted butter

¾ cup granulated sugar
1 tablespoon freshly squeezed
  lemon juice

CRUST

1 cup all-purpose flour
2 tablespoons granulated sugar
¼ teaspoon salt
2 teaspoons baking powder
4 tablespoons unsalted butter
6 tablespoons milk

2 tablespoons unsalted butter,
  melted
2 tablespoons superfine sugar
Crème fraîche or Devonshire
  double cream (optional)

1. For the filling: Marinate the prunes in the Armagnac for 1 or 2 days, or until soft.

(continued)

2. Peel, core, and slice the pears into pieces ¼ inch thick. Heat a skillet over moderate heat and melt 2 tablespoons butter and ¼ cup sugar. Add the pear slices and sauté them until they are glazed with the sugar, about 2 minutes. Add the liquid from the prunes and cook until the liquid is reduced by half. Remove from the heat and cool.

3. Remove the pears from the skillet with a slotted spoon and place them in an 8-inch-square baking dish. Place the skillet over high heat and reduce the liquid in the pan until it becomes a thick syrup.

4. Add the prunes to the pears and stir to distribute evenly. Pour the pan syrup and the lemon juice over the fruit. Sprinkle with the remaining ½ cup sugar. Dot the top with the remaining 2 tablespoons of butter. Set aside.

5. For the crust: Preheat the oven to 425 degrees. Combine all the dry ingredients. Cut in the butter and mix until the dough has an even, crumbly consistency.

6. Add the milk and mix until combined. The dough should be sticky and soft. Place it on a well-floured surface and knead until it holds a shape. (Use no more than ten turns or the dough will be tough.)

7. Roll out the dough about ½ inch thick, until it is large enough to cover the fruit in the baking dish. Trim the edges and tuck the dough around the fruit. Brush the melted butter over the dough and sprinkle with the superfine sugar.

8. Bake in the preheated oven for 40 minutes, or until the crust is golden and the fruit is tender when pierced.

9. Remove from the oven and cool slightly before serving. Serve right from the baking dish. Garnish with crème fraîche or Devonshire double cream.

ADVANCE PREPARATION: Can be prepared 1 day ahead. Cover and refrigerate. Bring to room temperature before baking.

Nana's Walnut Torte

*T*his cake, handed down by Mary Powell's great-grandmother, is an old-fashioned masterpiece. It is big and dramatic and incredibly delicious. This is the cake you would imagine your grandmother making—if your grandmother was a good cook.

Serves 16

THE CAKE

2 cups walnuts
9 eggs
2 cups sugar
Juice of 1 lemon
½ teaspoon salt

¼ teaspoon ground cloves
¾ cup cake flour
2 teaspoons baking powder
Grated zest of 2 lemons

MOCHA FROSTING

½ pound (2 sticks) unsalted
   butter, at room temperature
3 cups confectioners' sugar
1 tablespoon instant espresso
   crystals
1 tablespoon hot water

2 tablespoons all-purpose ground
   chocolate or cocoa
1 teaspoon vanilla extract
½ cup heavy cream
1 cup chopped walnuts

1. For the cake: Preheat the oven to 350 degrees. Butter three 9-inch cake pans and dust with flour.

2. Using a hand nut grinder, finely grind the walnuts. (Do not use the processor for this, it will overprocess the nuts and make them oily. They should be fluffy and dry.)

3. Separate 8 of the eggs. Place the yolks and the 1 remaining whole egg in a mixer bowl. Add 1 cup sugar, the lemon juice, salt, and ground cloves. Combine well in the mixer bowl and, while beating at slow speed, add the remaining sugar. Raise speed to high and beat until the yolk mixture is light and fluffy and almost doubled in bulk, about 7 minutes. Transfer to a large bowl.

4. Sift the cake flour and baking powder together into another bowl.

5. Beat the 8 egg whites in a clean mixer bowl until they are stiff but not dry. Fold one-third of the egg yolk mixture into the egg whites, then add one-third of the flour mixture, nuts, and lemon zest. Repeat until all elements are combined.

(continued)

6. Divide the batter among the three prepared pans. Reduce the oven temperature to 325 degrees and bake for 40 minutes, or until done. Cool on a wire rack.

7. For the frosting: Whip the butter and add the sugar in small amounts. Continue whipping until the mixture is very light and fluffy. Dissolve the instant coffee in the hot water and add, with the chocolate and vanilla, to the butter and sugar mixture. Beat until fluffy.

8. Beat the cream until stiff. Fold in half of the mocha mixture.

9. Smooth the mocha-cream mixture between the three layers of cake. Use the remaining mocha frosting on the top and sides of the cake. Decorate the sides with chopped walnuts.

NOTE: For the mocha frosting, we use Ghirardelli ground chocolate. If you can't find this product, substitute cocoa.

ADVANCE PREPARATION: Can be prepared 1 day ahead. Cover and refrigerate.

Amanda's Chocolate Carrot Torte

A dazzling version of the traditional carrot cake, this is a staple in our kitchen where its life expectancy is about a day or maybe two, at the most. For the holidays, dress it up with a sprinkling of confectioners' sugar and serve it with the Apricot-Cranberry Dessert on page 165.

Serves 8 to 12

¾ cup stale white bread crumbs
2 cups blanched whole almonds
1½ cups sugar
7 ounces bittersweet chocolate, broken in pieces
5 medium carrots, peeled and grated

6 eggs
½ teaspoon almond extract
1 teaspoon vanilla extract
1 teaspoon instant espresso crystals

1. Preheat oven to 350 degrees. Butter a 9-inch bundt pan and refrigerate.

2. In a food processor fitted with the metal blade, place the bread crumbs, almonds, and ½ cup of the sugar. Process for 30 seconds. The mixture should be ground into a coarse meal. Pour into a 3-quart bowl.

3. After wiping out the processor bowl, process the chocolate chunks with ½ cup of sugar until that mixture is the same consistency as the almonds. Combine the chocolate with the almond mixture. Wipe out the food processor again and fit it with a fine grating blade.

4. Cut the carrots in 2-inch lengths. Fit them into the large feed tube and grate. Add the carrots to the chocolate-almond mixture, tossing to mix. Create a well in the center of this mixture.

5. In the bowl of an electric mixer, whip the eggs at medium speed for 3 minutes. Add the final ½ cup of sugar. Turn the mixer to the highest speed, and run for 7 minutes. The eggs should be at a ribbon stage. To test this, remove the beater and hold it over the mixture; it should form a ribbon as it drips from the beater. Add almond and vanilla extracts and coffee crystals.

6. Turn this batter into the center of the well in the chocolate-almond mixture. Using a rubber spatula, fold the egg mixture into the chocolate-almond combination. Continue folding until completely incorporated.

7. Pour into the prepared pan and bake for 1 hour. Test before removing from the oven. This cake makes a crusty surface so you have to press harder than normal to have the cake spring back.

8. When done, allow to cool on a rack for 15 minutes. Then gently unmold and finish cooling on a wire rack.

ADVANCE PREPARATION: Can be prepared 2 days in advance. Cover and store at room temperature.

Ginger-Applesauce Spice Cake
with Ginger Whipped Cream

*T*his delicious moist cake is always popular because it has a texture and flavor that contrasts nicely with some of the dense and rich Thanksgiving desserts.

Serves 8 to 12

2 cups all-purpose flour
1½ teaspoons baking soda
1 teaspoon ground allspice
1 teaspoon ground cinnamon
½ teaspoon ground cloves
½ teaspoon salt
12 tablespoons (1½ sticks) unsalted butter, softened
1 cup firmly packed dark brown sugar
½ cup superfine sugar
2 large eggs, at room temperature

1⅓ cups unsweetened applesauce
⅔ cup sour cream
¾ cup lightly toasted, coarsely chopped walnuts (about 3 ounces)
⅓ cup peeled, minced fresh gingerroot

Confectioners' sugar
Ginger Whipped Cream (see below)

1. Position rack in the center of the oven and preheat the oven to 350 degrees.

2. Butter a 9 x 3-inch springform pan. Dust lightly with flour; tap out the excess.

3. Sift the flour, baking soda, allspice, cinnamon, cloves, and salt into a medium bowl. Using an electric mixer, beat the butter with both sugars in a large bowl until well combined. Add the eggs, one at a time, beating well after each addition.

4. Beat in the applesauce and sour cream (the mixture may appear curdled). Add the dry ingredients, walnuts, and ginger and mix until just combined.

5. Pour the batter into the prepared pan. Place the pan on a cookie sheet in the center of the preheated oven. Bake for 1 hour, or until a toothpick or cake tester inserted into the center of the cake comes out clean.

6. Let the cake cool in its pan on a rack for 15 minutes. Run a small sharp knife around the cake sides to loosen it. Release the pan sides from

the cake. Remove the springform and let the cake cool another 15 minutes or so.

7. When cool, dust the top of the cake with confectioners' sugar, or place a paper doilie on top of the cake and dusk with confectioners' sugar, then remove the doilie and you will have a pretty, lacy design.

8. Serve with a dollop of Ginger Whipped Cream on each piece.

Ginger Whipped Cream

½ cup sugar	1 cup chilled heavy cream
½ cup water	1 tablespoon confectioners'
One 1½-inch piece fresh	sugar
gingerroot, sliced	¼ teaspoon vanilla extract

1. Stir the sugar and water in a heavy medium saucepan over medium heat until the sugar dissolves. Add the ginger and simmer until syrupy, about 8 minutes. Strain into a bowl. Refrigerate the syrup until cold.

2. Using the electric mixer, whip the cream, sugar, and vanilla in a large bowl to soft peaks. Fold in the syrup.

ADVANCE PREPARATION: The cake can be prepared 6 hours in advance. Cool it completely. Cover tightly and let stand at room temperature. The syrup for the whipped cream can be prepared 3 days ahead. After whipping, the finished cream will hold for 5 hours. Cover and refrigerate. If necessary, whisk before using, to stiffen.

Mama Hellman's Date Cake

*T*his is a dark, airy cake that has great chewy texture and plenty of spicy flavor. It is easy to make and keeps well. The recipe comes from Mary Powell's great-great-grandmother.

Makes 1 9-inch cake

1 cup plus 1 tablespoon sugar
5 eggs, separated
½ teaspoon ground cinnamon
½ teaspoon ground allspice
¼ teaspoon ground cloves
2 tablespoons ground chocolate
   or cocoa

⅔ cup finely chopped dates
½ cup plus 1 teaspoon cracker
   meal or matzo meal
Salt
Confectioners' sugar

1. Preheat the oven to 350 degrees. Butter a 9-inch springform pan, then cut a circle of wax paper to fit its bottom. Butter the wax paper, then flour bottom and sides of pan.

2. With an electric mixer fitted with a paddle beater, slowly cream the sugar and the 5 egg yolks. Add the spices, chocolate, and dates. Blend in the cracker meal or matzo meal.

3. In another bowl whip the egg whites and a pinch of salt until stiff. Fold into the date mixture. Pour the batter into the prepared pan.

4. Bake in the preheated oven for 30 minutes. Lower the heat to 325 degrees and bake 50 minutes more, or until done. The center should be moist.

5. Cool on a rack for 1 hour. Unmold and dust the top with confectioners' sugar.

NOTE: We use Ghirardelli for the ground chocolate. If you can't find this product, substitute cocoa.

VARIATION: Spread each serving plate with a bittersweet chocolate sauce. Place a slice of date cake on top. Then top the cake with whipped cream or Ginger Whipped Cream (page 173).

ADVANCE PREPARATION: Can be prepared 2 days ahead. Cover or wrap with plastic and store at room temperature.

A Different Fruitcake

*F*ruitcake is controversial in our house. Andy likes it; Kathy doesn't. We made a number of versions, but we couldn't agree on one, until we tried this recipe by Nancy Oakes of L'Avenue Restaurant in San Francisco.

Serves 10 to 12

3 cups homemade unsweetened
    applesauce
½ pound (2 sticks) unsalted
    butter
1½ cups sugar
⅓ cup honey
1 cup medium sherry
4 eggs, separated
4 cups slivered almonds
1 cup dried tart cherries (not the
    candied or glacéed variety)
1 cup chopped dried apricots

1 cup chopped good-quality
    citron
1 cup chopped good-quality
    candied pineapple
1 cup white raisins
1 cup currants
5 cups all-purpose flour
1 tablespoon plus 1 teaspoon
    baking soda
1 teaspoon salt
½ cup brandy

1. Heat the applesauce in a 2-quart saucepan. Add butter a few pieces at a time and stir until it is melted and the applesauce is bubbling. Add sugar, honey, and sherry. Cook until the sugar dissolves. Cool to room temperature. Add 4 egg yolks and mix well.

2. Preheat the oven to 275 degrees. Butter and flour 10 small loaf pans, 5 by 3 by 2 inches, or use one 3-quart decorative tube pan.

3. In a large bowl combine all fruits and nuts with the applesauce. Sift the flour, baking soda, and salt, then fold them into the applesauce mixture. Beat the egg whites to stiff peaks. Fold them into the mixture.

4. Pour into the prepared pans. Smooth the tops and bake for 60 to 70 minutes for small pans, or 2½ to 3 hours for the larger pan.

5. Remove cake(s) from the pans and brush all sides with brandy while the cake is still warm. Let cool. Wrap tightly in plastic wrap and then foil.

ADVANCE PREPARATION: Must be prepared well in advance, at least 1 week, or up to 3 months. If preparing this cake one to three months in advance, brush with brandy once a month.

Moosehead Gingerbread

*I*f there's a way to improve on this traditional New England cake we haven't found it. This is the gingerbread we all dreamed of as children and have only rarely tasted. It is moist, spicy, and loaded with flavor. Great on its own, this is also a fine base for the Gingerbread Bread Pudding on page 180.

Serves 9 to 12

9 tablespoons butter
¼ cup dry bread crumbs
¼ cup chopped crystallized ginger
¼ cup Cognac or brandy
2½ cups all-purpose flour
2 teaspoons baking soda
½ teaspoon salt
1 teaspoon ground cinnamon
1½ teaspoons ground ginger

¼ teaspoon ground cloves
½ teaspoon dry mustard
½ teaspoon freshly ground pepper
½ cup dark brown sugar
2 eggs
1 cup unsulfured molasses
1 tablespoon instant espresso crystals
1 cup boiling water

1. Preheat the oven to 350 degrees. Grease a 9-inch square pan with 1 tablespoon of butter. Dust with the bread crumbs and tap out any excess.

2. In a small bowl, soak the crystallized ginger in the Cognac. Sift the flour, baking soda, salt, cinnamon, ginger, cloves, mustard, and pepper together into another bowl.

3. In the bowl of an electric mixer, cream the remaining butter until it is light and fluffy. Slowly add the brown sugar. Whip until fluffy. Add the eggs, one at a time, while continuing to beat. Add the molasses.

4. Dissolve the espresso in the boiling water. Add the hot liquid to the butter mixture, ¼ cup at a time, alternating with the flour mixture, until both are fully incorporated. Strain off and discard the liquid from the ginger. Fold the ginger into the batter.

5. Pour the batter into the prepared pan. Smooth the top evenly and bake for 35 minutes, or until a cake tester or skewer inserted in the center of the cake comes out clean. Cool in the pan on a rack for 15 minutes. Invert onto a plate.

ADVANCE PREPARATION: Can be prepared 3 days in advance. Wrap tightly with plastic wrap and refrigerate. If you make the gingerbread 1 day ahead, refrigeration isn't necessary.

Pumpkin Flan

$\mathcal{T}$his is a cool and refreshing dessert that is also richly flavored. It is a fine alternative to pumpkin pie if you want to have a dessert that contrasts with the other pies on your holiday table.

Serves 10 to 12

1¼ cups sugar
½ teaspoon salt
½ teaspoon nutmeg
½ teaspoon ground cinnamon
1 cup cooked and mashed
    pumpkin

5 large eggs, lightly beaten
1½ cups evaporated milk
1½ teaspoons vanilla extract
⅓ cup water

1. In a small saucepan, melt ½ cup sugar over medium-low heat until it caramelizes into an amber syrup. Stir continuously to prevent burning. Pour into a 9-inch pie plate. Pick the plate up and tip it from side to side to coat its bottom with caramel.

2. Preheat the oven to 350 degrees. In a bowl, combine the remaining sugar, salt, spices, pumpkin, and eggs. Mix thoroughly and add the milk, vanilla, and water. Mix again and pour into the pie plate. Set in a pan of hot water that comes 1 inch up the sides of the pie plate, and bake for 1¼ hours.

3. Cool on a rack and then refrigerate. To serve, run a thin knife around the outside of the flan. Jiggle the plate gently to loosen the flan, then invert a platter over the pie plate, and, holding the two plates firmly together, quickly flip them over. Center the flan and serve.

ADVANCE PREPARATION: Can be prepared 1 day ahead. Keep the flan in the pie plate, refrigerated, and remove it only when ready to serve.

Persimmon Pudding

*Y*ear after year this wonderful steamed pudding is the favorite dessert at our house on Thanksgiving. Even the kids come back for seconds. The recipe is fairly straightforward and easy to do—the only problem is getting persimmons that are ripe enough. They begin to appear in the market just around Thanksgiving. Unfortunately, they are often unripe—too firm and tannic. A ripe persimmon should be pillow soft and delicately silky inside.

You can ripen persimmons yourself at home by putting them stem side up in a plastic container. Put a few drops of brandy on their stems and close the container tightly. In 3 or 4 days your persimmons should be ripe. Placing them in a tightly sealed brown paper bag accompanied by a banana works almost as well. As a last resort, you can freeze the unripe persimmons. This will not ripen them but, once defrosted, their texture will be softer.

The following recipe, which came from our friend Paige Healy, is for two 2-quart pudding molds (or four 1-quart molds, or any other combination). We like to make two puddings, one for the Thanksgiving table and another that can either be used as a gift or frozen for Christmas. If you want to make only one mold, halve the recipe—it works fine.

Serves 8 to 12

8 to 10 ripe persimmons
1¼ cups (2½ sticks) unsalted butter, melted
2½ cups sugar
2½ cups all-purpose flour, sifted
¾ teaspoon salt
2½ teaspoons ground cinnamon
3 teaspoons baking soda dissolved in 5 tablespoons hot water

5 tablespoons brandy
2½ teaspoons vanilla extract
1 cup raisins
1 cup currants, soaked in hot water for 30 minutes
2½ teaspoons freshly squeezed lemon juice
¾ cup coarsely chopped walnuts
5 eggs, lightly beaten

1. Spoon the pulp out of the persimmons and purée in a food processor or blender. This should make 4 cups of purée. Reserve.

2. In an electric mixer or a large mixing bowl combine the butter and sugar. Stir in the rest of the ingredients, including the persimmon purée, and combine well.

3. Butter the inside of two 2-quart pudding molds. Fill with the per-

simmon mixture and cover tightly. (Most molds have covers that snap on. If you don't have such a mold, use a ring mold and cover tightly with foil.)

4. Preheat the oven to 350 degrees.

5. In a large kettle or stockpot that contains ¾ inch of water, place each mold on a rack or an inverted Pyrex dish. Don't let the water touch the mold. Over medium heat, bring the water to a boil. Reduce the heat to low and cover the pot tightly.

6. Put the kettle in the preheated oven and steam the puddings for 2½ hours, checking frequently to make sure that the water hasn't boiled away. (If it has, add more by dribbling it down the sides of the pot.)

6. When done, let the puddings rest for 5 minutes. Then remove them from the molds and place on a rack to cool.

NOTES: The puddings can be served warm or at room temperature. A festive touch is to flame the pudding and bring it to the table—after having dimmed the lights. Flaming is dangerous and should be done only by someone who has mastered the technique. Take ¼ cup of brandy (or other spirit) and warm over medium heat in a small saucepan. After about 30 seconds, tip the saucepan away from you and, averting your eyes, light by bringing a match close to the warm liquid, but not too close. Pour the flaming spirit over the pudding and serve immediately with Hard Sauce (page 180) or Foamy Brandy Sauce (see page 185).

If you are freezing your pudding, leave it in the mold so that it may be steamed again (about 30 minutes after defrosting).

VARIATION: If necessary, you may steam the puddings on top of the stove over low heat for 2½ hours. But steaming them in the oven ensures more even heating.

ADVANCE PREPARATION: The pudding can be made 3 days before Thanksgiving and kept unrefrigerated in the mold. When ready to serve, steam for 15 minutes. Unmold onto a platter.

Hard Sauce

A must for steamed puddings.

Makes 1½ cups

8 tablespoons (1 stick) unsalted
    butter

1 cup confectioners' sugar, sifted
3 tablespoons dark rum

In a bowl, cream the butter until soft. Add the sugar ¼ cup at a time, beating it into the butter after each addition. Beat in the rum. Refrigerate to harden. It is helpful to refrigerate the hard sauce in the bowl in which it is to be served.

ADVANCE PREPARATION: Can be prepared up to 3 days in advance. Cover and refrigerate.

Gingerbread Bread Pudding

M eredith Frederick is the talented pastry chef of The Post House, a New York steakhouse. This dish, a regular offering on one of the best dessert carts you've ever seen, is a sensation at the Thanksgiving table.

Serves 9 to 12

1 cup heavy cream
1 quart half-and-half
1 cup golden raisins
5 egg yolks
5 whole eggs

2 cups sugar
¼ cup whiskey
1 tablespoon vanilla extract
1 loaf Moosehead Gingerbread
    (page 176)

1. Preheat the oven to 375 degrees.

2. In a large saucepan, combine the creams and raisins and bring to a boil. Remove from the heat.

3. In a large bowl, combine yolks, whole eggs, sugar, whiskey, and vanilla. Slowly whisk in the cream mixture. Set aside.

4. Layer the bottom of a 9-inch square glass baking dish with thin slices of gingerbread. Ladle enough custard over the gingerbread to cover it. Let it sit for 10 minutes. Continue to layer with custard and gingerbread, allowing 10 minutes resting time in between each layer, until the pan is filled to the brim. Let sit for an additional 10 to 15 minutes.

5. Place the pan inside a larger pan that contains ½ inch of hot water. Bake in the preheated oven for about 40 minutes or until the center tests done by being totally set but not dry.

6. Serve in squares that are warm or at room temperature, accompanied by Whiskey Crème Anglaise.

Whiskey Crème Anglaise

Makes 3 cups

2 cups heavy cream	6 egg yolks
½ cup sugar	¼ cup whiskey

1. Over medium-low heat, scald the cream and ¼ cup of the sugar in a saucepan, whisking constantly.

2. In another saucepan, combine the egg yolks and the remaining sugar. Add the whiskey. Slowly pour the hot cream over the yolk mixture, beating constantly.

3. Stir over medium heat until the sauce thickens just enough to coat the back of a wooden spoon. Remove from the heat immediately and strain through a fine sieve.

4. Chill and serve. (If you want to cool the sauce quickly, place the pan in a larger bowl with crushed ice and stir for a minute or two.)

ADVANCE PREPARATION: The pudding can be prepared 1 day ahead through step 3. Cover and refrigerate the cream mixture. Bring to room temperature before assembling and heating. The whiskey sauce can be made 5 or 6 hours ahead of time.

Philadelphia Vanilla Ice Cream

*T*his eggless ice cream is enormously refreshing. It is similar in texture to the best Italian gelato.

Makes 3 pints (12 ½-cup servings)

5 cups half-and-half
1½ cups sugar
⅛ teaspoon salt

4 vanilla beans (3 inches in length), split lengthwise

1. In the top of a double boiler, combine 3 cups half-and-half, sugar, salt, and vanilla beans. Cook, stirring constantly, for 10 minutes. Remove bean pods, scrape out the pulp, and add back to the half-and-half. Stir well to disperse the tiny seeds, then remove from the heat. Pour into a bowl to cool. Chill overnight.

2. The next day, add the remaining 2 cups of well-chilled half-and-half. Mix well.

3. Freeze in an ice-cream maker, following the manufacturer's instructions.

SERVING SUGGESTION: Top with fruit, syrup, or mix with any number of flavors or ingredients such as chopped chocolate, malt, praline, chopped nuts, or candied fruits.

ADVANCE PREPARATION: Although this ice cream is best when served immediately, it will keep 2 weeks in the freezer. When ready to use, soften at room temperature.

Caramel Ice Cream

*T*his luscious ice cream is a Wolfgang Puck specialty. It is delectable on its own and as an accompaniment to pumpkin or apple pie.

Makes 3 pints (12 ½-cup servings)

1⅔ cups sugar	1 cup milk
½ cup water	1 vanilla bean, split
2½ cups heavy cream	8 egg yolks

1. Combine 1 cup sugar and the water in a small saucepan. Heat to a boil. Using a pastry brush dipped in water, wash down the sides of the pan removing any crystals. Don't stir this mixture with a spoon, simply swirl the pan to blend in any crystals.

2. Cook the syrup to deep golden brown, watching constantly to avoid burning. Remove from the heat and slowly add ⅓ cup cream in a threadlike stream, whisking constantly until the mixture is thoroughly blended. Set aside.

3. In a large saucepan, bring the remaining cream, the milk, and vanilla bean to a boil. In a mixing bowl, whisk the egg yolks and remaining ⅔ cup sugar together.

4. Temper the egg mixture by adding one-third of the hot liquid while whisking constantly, then whisk in the remaining liquid.

5. Return the mixture to the saucepan. Over low heat, stir constantly until the mixture thickens enough to coat the back of a spoon. Stir in the reserved caramel sauce.

4. Strain the custard through a sieve into a bowl placed over ice. Stir as the custard cools. When it is chilled, place in an ice-cream freezer and process according to the manufacturer's instructions. (If you can, chill the custard overnight. The ice cream will be much smoother.)

ADVANCE PREPARATION: Should be made at least 1 day ahead and will keep for 2 weeks in the freezer.

Chocolate-Chestnut Mousse

$\mathcal{W}$e don't ordinarily think that chocolate has a place in the Thanksgiving feast, but the addition of chestnuts makes this rich mousse quite appropriate. We have found that the flavors of this luscious dessert marry more thoroughly if it is refrigerated overnight.

Serves 8

4 tablespoons cocoa	4 tablespoons Amaretto
Two 8¾-ounce cans French chestnut spread	2 cups heavy cream

1. Combine the cocoa and the chestnut spread in a large bowl. Stir in the Amaretto.

2. In another bowl whip the cream until stiff peaks are formed. Fold the cream into the chestnut mixture. Spoon into 8 wineglasses. Refrigerate for at least 3 hours.

NOTE: We use the *crème de marrons* made by Element Faugier, which is widely available, for the canned chestnut spread.

ADVANCE PREPARATION: Should be prepared 1 day ahead. Refrigerate.

Glazed Oranges

$\mathcal{T}$his lively dash of orange brightens up the holiday color scheme.

Serves 12 to 14

12 navel oranges	1 cup sugar
2 cups water	¼ cup crème de cassis

1. Peel the zest of three oranges and chop, making about ¼ cup zest. Cover and reserve in the refrigerator. Peel and cut the pith off all of the oranges with a sharp knife, making sure that none of the white part remains, or the dish will be bitter. The oranges can be left whole or sliced into rounds. If you want to serve this dish immediately, cut into rounds.

2. In a saucepan bring the water and sugar to a boil, then simmer for 5 minutes. Cool for 10 minutes. Add the crème de cassis.

3. Place the oranges in a glass bowl that holds them snugly. Pour the syrup over them and marinate, in the refrigerator, for 4 hours or overnight. (If you have cut the oranges into rounds, the marination can be shortened to 1 hour, but the longer the better.)

4. Before serving sprinkle with the reserved zest.

VARIATIONS: Here are two ways to give the oranges a unique character:

1. Instead of crème de cassis, use 2 tablespoons chopped fresh tarragon and eliminate the 10-minute cooling period in step 2.

2. Add 2 tablespoons grenadine to the crème de cassis syrup to make the fruit look like blood oranges.

ADVANCE PREPARATION: Can be made 1 day ahead. Cover and refrigerate.

Foamy Brandy Sauce

This is a luscious sauce that can add a new dimension to some desserts. We serve it with Persimmon Pudding (see page 178), Jessica's Carmelized Apple Tart (see page 164), Apple Pie (see page 162), or Moosehead Gingerbread (see page 176).

Makes 2½ cups

3 eggs, separated	1 cup heavy cream
¾ cup sugar	1 teaspoon vanilla extract
2 tablespoons unsalted butter, softened	3 tablespoons brandy

1. In a medium bowl, whip the egg yolks and sugar together until thick and light in color. Whisk the butter into the mixture.

2. In another bowl, whip the cream until stiff.

3. In a small bowl, whip the egg whites until stiff but not dry.

4. Fold the egg whites and cream alternately into the egg yolk mixture. Stir in the vanilla and the brandy. Serve chilled.

ADVANCE PREPARATION: Can be kept up to 2 hours in the refrigerator.

Aunt Dink's Penuche Nuts

$\mathcal{A}$ndy's Aunt Dinah (her nickname was "Dink") gave us a container of these nuts every year for Thanksgiving. Dink died in 1989 at the age of 95. She was one of the brightest and sweetest people we have ever known. Her wit and intelligence were an important part of many of our Thanksgiving celebrations.

Makes 3 cups

1 cup firmly packed dark brown
   sugar
½ cup granulated sugar
½ cup sour cream

1 teaspoon vanilla extract
2½ cups walnuts

1. Put the sugars and the sour cream into a saucepan, whisking over low heat. Cook until the mixture starts to boil. Cover and boil for 1 minute.

2. Uncover and cook until a few drops of syrup form a firm ball or a candy thermometer reads 245 degrees.

3. Remove from the heat and add the vanilla and the walnuts. Stir to coat evenly.

4. Empty the contents of the saucepan onto wax paper and, with tongs, separate the nuts. Allow them to cool completely. Store in a closed container in a cool place.

ADVANCE PREPARATION: Can be prepared at least 1 week ahead and stored at room temperature.

Leftovers

*F*or many people leftovers are the best part of the holiday experience. This is especially true for those who actually prepare the Thanksgiving feast. There is so much to think about and so much work to do on the day of, that often the host and hostess don't get much of a chance to sit down, relax, and enjoy the moment.

The next day, when everything is cooked, all the guests are gone, and the cleanup has been done, it's much easier to take the time to really appreciate the work of the days before.

Actually, we generally eat our leftovers "as is," warmed to room temperature on Friday. Most of the ingredients of the Thanksgiving feast are hearty and flavorful enough to taste as good if not better the day after. It is one of our best days of the year, the six of us together around the kitchen table, relaxed and happy.

Turkey, if it was not overcooked on Thursday, is excellent on Friday. It is moist and doesn't pick up secondary flavors like some other meats. Stuffing is excellent on the second day and so are most Thanksgiving vegetables. Things that need to be crisp when served—Caitlin's Potatoes and a few other things in the book—lose texture overnight, but desserts are particularly fine the next day.

But this warm aura around the holiday meal is only good up to a point. After eating the Thanksgiving dinner twice, it's time to magically convert it into something else. In our house, anyway, the same food the third time around is a just cause for mutiny. This chapter is here to save you from mass defections from your dinner table.

What follows are some very clever ways to present the same old food in a completely new format.

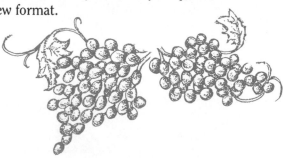

Emmy's Turkey Soup

$\mathcal{E}$mmy Smith was the maid-of-honor at our wedding. She is a talented cook. Emmy, who grew up in Vermont, has enjoyed this delicious post-Thanksgiving soup since she was a little girl. "It's my favorite Thanksgiving dish," she says. This is a "throw together" soup and the ingredients and measurements are only approximate. Let your own leftovers and refrigerator resources dictate the amounts.

Makes enough for 8

1 cut-up turkey carcass
Leftover gravy, stuffing, meat
    and skin scraps (If the neck
    and gizzards haven't been
    used, add them also.)
7 carrots
3 leeks, sliced
2 cups coarsely chopped celery,
    including leaves
4 boiling potatoes
A small handful of fresh parsley

6 crushed peppercorns
Cold water or stock
2 parsnips, peeled and sliced
    into rounds
18 white pearl onions, peeled
    (see step 1, page 90)
12 mushrooms, quartered and
    previously sautéed
3 cups cut-up leftover turkey
1 package frozen peas
Salt and freshly ground pepper

1. Put the carcass, leftovers, 4 coarsely chopped carrots, leeks, celery, 2 peeled and halved potatoes, parsley, and peppercorns in a large soup pot. Cover with cold water (or stock, if you want a richer soup) and bring to a boil. Lower heat and simmer, uncovered, for 3 to 4 hours, skimming frequently.

2. Pour through a strainer into a large bowl. Press down on the solids to extract all liquid. Refrigerate until the fat has risen to the top and solidified enough to remove easily with a spoon.

3. Slice the remaining 3 carrots into rounds, and peel and quarter the remaining 2 potatoes. Return the broth to the soup pot, bring to a simmer, and add the carrots, potatoes, and all remaining ingredients, except the peas.

4. Simmer, uncovered, for 1 hour. Just before serving, add the peas. Adjust seasoning and serve piping hot, accompanied by crusty bread.

Toby's Instant Replay Sandwich

*O*ur son, Toby, loves Thanksgiving dinner so much that he has invented a way to reprise the pleasures of the meal in one quick, no fuss package. This overstuffed (no pun intended) sandwich is one of the greatest pleasures of the holiday weekend.

Makes 1 sandwich

2 ¾-inch slices of brioche, challah, or other egg bread
2 tablespoons leftover gravy
½ cup leftover stuffing

2 or 3 slices cooked turkey breast
¼ cup cranberry condiment

1. Spread both slices of bread with 1 tablespoon of gravy.
2. Evenly distribute the stuffing over one slice of bread. Lay the turkey meat on top and then spread the cranberries evenly on top of the turkey. Top with the other bread slice. Cut in half. Serve.

Open-Face Turkey Sandwich

*H*ere's a quick way to make a dramatic dish out of leftover turkey. We like this for Saturday lunch, when the bird is starting to get a little tired. This saucy preparation will revitalize a sagging turkey.

Makes 1 sandwich

One ¾-inch-thick slice bread from a crusty, round country loaf (We prefer sourdough, if available.)
1 clove garlic
1 tablespoon olive oil
1 shallot, minced
¼ cup white wine

¼ cup leftover gravy
1 small celery stalk, minced
Salt and freshly ground black pepper
3 or 4 slices cooked white turkey meat
Chopped fresh parsley

1. Toast the bread in an oven until hard. Cut the garlic clove in half lengthwise and rub the bread with the cut side.

2. In a skillet, heat the olive oil and sauté the shallot until it is soft, not brown. Add the wine and reduce to 1 tablespoon. Add the gravy and celery. Season to taste, but remember that the gravy is already pretty highly seasoned.

3. When the sauce is heated through, add the turkey slices to warm through, about 1 minute.

4. Place the toast on a plate, top with the turkey slices, and spoon the remaining sauce over the sandwich. Finish with chopped parsley and serve immediately.

Turkey and Rice Casserole

*A*nother kid pleaser, this adaptation of *arroz con pollo* is easy and a real winner.

Serves 6 to 8

5 tablespoons butter	3 tablespoons minced fresh
3 cloves garlic, minced	parsley
2 medium onions, peeled and	½ teaspoon fresh thyme
diced	Salt and freshly ground pepper
3 cups diced cooked turkey	1 cup long-grain rice
1 cup stuffing	2 cups Chicken (see page 77)
	or Turkey Stock (see page 78)

1. Preheat the oven to 375 degrees. In the bottom of a 4-quart oven-proof casserole, melt 4 tablespoons butter over medium heat and sauté the garlic and onions until transparent, about 5 minutes. Add the turkey, stuffing, and herbs, and season to taste with salt and pepper. Stir.

2. In a saucepan, melt the remaining tablespoon of butter. Add the rice and sauté over medium heat until it is transparent.

3. Add the rice to the casserole. Stir to mix. Bring the broth to a boil in a saucepan and pour it over the casserole. Cover and bake for 25 minutes, until the rice is tender. Uncover and bake 15 more minutes. Serve.

Turkey Mornay

*H*ere's an excellent way to convert leftover turkey into a rich and elegant dish.

Serves 4

1½ cups heavy cream
3 cups ½-inch-dice cooked
  turkey meat

½ teaspoon freshly ground white
  pepper

MORNAY SAUCE

2 tablespoons unsalted butter
2 tablespoons all-purpose flour
1 cup hot milk
1 teaspoon salt

1 small onion, thinly sliced
2 egg yolks
5 tablespoons grated Parmesan
  cheese

1. In a medium skillet bring the cream to a boil over medium heat. Reduce heat and simmer, stirring frequently, for 20 minutes, or until the cream is reduced to about 1 cup. Stir in the turkey and the pepper. Continue to simmer for 5 minutes. Set aside.

2. To make the sauce: Melt the butter in a 2-quart saucepan over medium heat and stir in the flour. Continue stirring until the mixture is golden, about 3 minutes.

3. Add the milk, salt, and onion. Stirring constantly, simmer about 5 minutes, or until the sauce begins to bubble. Pour through a fine sieve into a bowl and discard the onion.

4. Return the sauce to the saucepan. Whisk in the egg yolks and 3 tablespoons of Parmesan.

5. Transfer the turkey mixture to an 8½ by 5½ by 1½-inch au gratin dish or an 8-inch glass pie plate. Pour the mornay sauce over the turkey, and sprinkle the top with the remaining Parmesan.

6. Place under the broiler about 5 inches from the heat. Cook until lightly browned, about 45 seconds. Serve immediately.

Killer Turkey Hash

So it's the day after and there you are with a lot of dirty dishes, a cranberry stain on the new rug, and about 10 pounds of leftover turkey. What to do with it? Yes, you can make sandwiches, but then it might take until Christmas to polish off the bird. No, you have to come up with a main course dish that will consume a big chunk of turkey all at once. One excellent suggestion is turkey hash—a delicious dish that everyone loves and a recipe in which you can vary the ingredients at will and still create a culinary triumph.

Serves 6 to 8

2 tablespoons unsalted butter	¾ cup cooked corn
1 onion, chopped	2 tablespoons minced fresh
2 garlic cloves, minced	parsley
3 cups ¼-inch-dice cooked turkey	1 teaspoon salt
	Freshly ground pepper
3 cups crumbled stuffing or ¼-inch-dice boiled potatoes	3 eggs, well beaten
	¾ cup grated Parmesan cheese
1 cup leftover gravy	4 tablespoons bread crumbs

1. Melt the butter in a skillet and sauté the onion and garlic until transparent, stirring frequently with a wooden spoon. Add the turkey and stuffing, stirring to blend. Add the gravy, corn, parsley, salt, and pepper to taste.

2. In a small bowl combine the eggs and cheese. Preheat the broiler.

3. Transfer the turkey mixture to a 2-quart soufflé dish, casserole, or au gratin dish. Add the egg and cheese mixture. Stir to combine all ingredients. Sprinkle the top of the hash with bread crumbs.

4. Place the hash under the broiler until the bread crumbs begin to brown, about 7 minutes. Serve immediately.

VARIATIONS: Substitute or add any combination of the following: walnuts, water chestnuts, pecans, black olives, cooked broccoli or other vegetables, bacon, ham, or pork sausage.

Turkey Tortilla Casserole

A mong a stellar group of leftover creations, this dish is the champion. At least it is a sensation with our kids. The first time we tested this recipe we left it in the kitchen for about 10 minutes and returned to find Jessica, our very fussy 15-year-old, camped over the casserole. Half of it had been eaten.

The recipe came to us by way of Barbara Goldie, one of San Francisco's most charming hostesses.

Serves 12

3 cups ½-inch-dice cooked white turkey meat

1 quart Tamale Sauce

½ cup sliced pitted black olives

¾ cup chunky-style tomato sauce (Use a 15-ounce can and reserve the remainder for Tamale Sauce opposite.)

¼ teaspoon freshly ground pepper

⅛ teaspoon cayenne

1 teaspoon chili powder

1½ cups fresh corn, blanched for 3 minutes, or frozen corn, defrosted

1 red bell pepper, diced and sautéed for 3 minutes in 1 tablespoon olive oil

1 teaspoon sugar

2 teaspoons Worcestershire sauce

1 pound tortilla chips (Use thick and crisp triangular corn chips that are actually made from cut tortillas, not the orange extruded ones made by the big commercial companies.)

½ cup grated Jalisco or Monterey Jack cheese

1. Preheat the oven to 350 degrees. Mix all the ingredients except the chips and cheese in a bowl. Pour into a 15 by 10-inch Pyrex baking dish. Stud the casserole with the chips. Bake in the preheated oven for 30 minutes.

2. Sprinkle the top of the casserole with the cheese. Return to the oven until the cheese is melted. Serve immediately.

Tamale Sauce

Makes 1 quart

1½ cups Mexican-style red chili
   sauce
⅔ cup chunky-style tomato
   sauce
3 cups Chicken Stock (see page
   77)

1 teaspoon chili powder
6 tablespoons unsalted butter
¼ cup masa harina or white
   cornmeal

1. Mix the sauces, chicken stock, and chili powder in a bowl. Reserve.

2. Melt the butter in a large skillet over medium heat and add the cornmeal. Cook for 3 minutes. Mix in the sauce mixture. Stir until thick, about 5 minutes.

NOTE: This sauce can be made a few days in advance of Thanksgiving and refrigerated. The day after, when you are tired, this dish should take only a few minutes to assemble.

Curried Turkey Salad

*T*his is so good that it would be worth cooking an extra turkey just to have it. (In fact, we have been known to cook a whole turkey breast, chill it, and cut it up for the sole purpose of making this salad. It is a perfect warm weather lunch dish.)

Makes 5 cups

2 cups 2-inch-strips cooked white turkey meat
½ cup blanched, slivered almonds
½ cup halved lengthwise white seedless grapes
2 scallions sliced in ⅛-inch rounds

2 stalks of celery, cut into small dice
¼ cup chopped Major Grey chutney
1 tablespoon curry powder
1 cup mayonnaise
Salt and freshly ground pepper

1. In a bowl, combine the turkey, almonds, grapes, scallions, and celery.

2. In another bowl, combine the chutney, curry powder, and mayonnaise. Stir well. Add this mixture to the turkey mixture and toss with two forks to blend. Season. Serve on a bed of lettuce. This is also attractive as a sandwich filling.

Goose Ragout

*Y*ou couldn't ask for a simpler recipe than this, and the result is nothing short of sensational. This ragout is particularly delicious made with goose and Savory Wild Rice Stuffing (page 71), but it would work almost as well with turkey or other poultry. The proportions can be varied.

Makes 6 cups

3 cups goose meat, from the legs, wings, and the carcass, cut into ¾-inch chunks, turkey (preferably dark meat), or chicken

3 cups rice-based stuffing
2 cups Goose Pan Gravy (see page 80)
Salt and freshly ground pepper

Wine and
Other Beverages

*T*he leaves have turned a lovely spectrum of earth colors; there's a crisp, cool stillness to the night air; and in the afternoon you can hear the snap of footballs and the crunch of shoulder pads. The time has come to plan the holiday feast and, once again, to consider that most difficult of gustatory enigmas: What wine should be served with the Thanksgiving turkey?

There are many unanswered questions that puzzle mankind: What is the meaning of life? Who was better, Mays or Mantle? Is there anyone who really likes poi? Among the most troublesome of these questions is the age-old which-wine-with-turkey quandary.

At the first Thanksgiving there was no wine at all. The Pilgrim fathers followed an exigent credo that equated almost everything pleasurable with sin. Thus there was no wine. There also had been no attempt to plant vineyards during the colonists' first months in America. Contemporary Americans have adopted a moderate but far more positive attitude toward pleasure than the Puritans, and wine is near the top of the list of pleasures.

The turkey dinner cries out for wine. Its assertive and complicated flavors need a unifying background, a carefully orchestrated theme that ties all of its diverse elements together. So, the choice of wine moves front and center, and a difficult, complicated choice it is.

"Wait a minute," says the wine maven. "I have the answer. Ever since I was old enough to sit on my father's knee he told me that everything I needed to know in life was summed up in these simple words: 'White with fish and white meat; red with red meat and game.' "

Well, turkey is white meat. So, therefore, if we are being dogmatic, a white wine should be served. Right? Not necessarily. If the Thanksgiving dinner were nothing more than a few slices of breast meat and a nondescript vegetable, then a simple white wine definitely would be the answer.

But Thanksgiving is much more than that. In fact, the turkey may be the blandest and most neutral part of the feast. (Unless, of course, we are talking about dark meat, which changes everything again.) Think about it.

Thanksgiving Dinner

At most Thanksgiving celebrations the turkey is only one element in a parade of aggressively flavored foods.

It is important to think beyond the bird and try to pick the right wine to go with chestnut stuffing, creamed onions, root vegetable purée, sweet potatoes, and three different kinds of cranberry sauce.

This cacophony of intense flavors requires a wine of more than subtle charms. Whatever is chosen to accompany a dinner of such complexity will certainly have to have a balancing, assertive flavor. But it should definitely not be a venerable, aged wine. The nuances of maturity would be obliterated by the pugnacious and uncomplicated flavors of the Thanksgiving feast.

So where does this leave us? If the wine is to be white, it must have intensity, structure, and richness. It has to hold its own against flavors that are alternately salty, fruity, spicy, and rich. If the wine is to be white it should be a husky, barrel-fermented Sauvignon Blanc, a vigorous Gewurztraminer, or America's favorite white—Chardonnay. But it shouldn't be just any Chardonnay. To stand up to the meal it must be a powerful wine with ripe fruit, firm acidity, and rich, toasty oak.

But what about red? Red wines have been gaining in popularity lately as more and more Americans discover their considerable charms. A red might be just the ticket for the holiday repast, but which ones would work? Quite a few. Pinot Noir is ideal, we have found, because it has plenty of fruit and rich flavor, yet it is still a noble wine that is appropriate for an important occasion.

We are such Pinot Noir and Burgundy lovers that we usually look for any small excuse to parade out favorites from Beaune or the Carneros. Actually, we have discovered that these wines are excellent and almost ideal with the harvest feast. Their flavors are forward enough without being coarse and their cherry and plum fruitiness nicely complements all of the predominant Thanksgiving flavors. We have been serving Pinot Noir wines at our Thanksgiving dinners over the past six years and they have been enormously popular with our guests.

Beaujolais wines are another very good solution. The fresh new "Primeur" wines from France are released around November 20, just in time for Thanksgiving. These wines are bright and fruity with lots of charm and plenty of lively acidity. For people who are expecting to drink white wines, these engaging reds are an ideal compromise since they are delicious when served slightly chilled. Frankly, regular Beaujolais wines of recent vintages —those from Fleurie, Julienas, Chiroubles, and Morgon in particular—are even better because they are generally more substantial than the typical "Nouveau" wine.

Another ideal wine for Thanksgiving is Zinfandel. This lush and lively red is a perfect match for cranberry sauce and giblet gravy. A good Zin has smooth, velvety texture and ripe raspberry fruit that complements the big flavors of the holiday feast.

Also appropriate would be Syrah and other Rhone-type wines. These big reds have luscious, broad flavors that wrap themselves around the earthy, rich textures and tastes of Thanksgiving. If you feel strongly that the wines for the most American of holidays should be American, there is a whole new crop of California wines made by some very talented young vintners who call themselves "The Rhone Rangers." These wineries produce fruity red wines from Grenache, Syrah, and Mourvedre, some of the best varieties grown in the Rhone Valley of southeastern France.

If you don't mind being just a little un-American, some crisp Italian reds such as Chianti, Valpolicella, Dolcetto, and certain younger Barbarescos do very well on the Thanksgiving table. These wines have the richness, fruit, and complexity that you would expect from a red wine, but they also have bright, tangy acid that makes them similar to white wines.

You may have noticed that we have not mentioned Cabernet Sauvignon or Merlot. We have found that these wines, with their herbal character, often conflict with the flavors of Thanksgiving. Their subtleties and complexities also tend to get lost in the variety of tones and textures that the holiday feast provides.

Another type of wine that can be appropriate for the holiday fete is "blush" or blanc de noir. These often have a touch more intensity and depth than many white wines, but they still have the fruitiness of whites and can be served chilled. We would caution you to look for blush wines that are crisp and close to dry. Wines that are too sweet will conflict with many of the traditional Thanksgiving flavors.

As you can probably tell, our first choice for a holiday wine would be a red, most likely a Pinot Noir. But there are many other possibilities and some of them are white and some of them are pink.

Actually, we usually start with cold champagne or California sparkling wine with appetizers in the living room. We generally choose a crisp, light blanc de blanc, a wine made entirely from white grapes, in most cases all Chardonnay. Although we think it is important to have American wines at Thanksgiving, we sometimes sneak in a bottle or two of our favorite French champagnes.

One year we poured Chardonnay for the preprandial festivities, and we chose a crisp, lively wine—not a big oaky monster.

At table, guests find a few bottles of red already opened. We like to present wines from various wineries, but we always make the choices

within the type we have selected. For instance, we like Pinot Noir, so we will pick four Pinots, all from the same year but from wineries in four different counties.

With dessert we like to return to sparkling wine, this time choosing a softer wine with a higher *dosage* (sugar content) such as a *cremant* or a luscious rosé.

Most Americans drink white wines too cold and red wines too warm. In warmer weather it is quite acceptable to chill Chardonnays and other whites, but too much cold will shut down their flavor. Keep them at around 55 degrees, no less. A half hour in the refrigerator is time enough to cool your wine; more than that will take the edge off the flavor.

As for reds, it is perfectly okay to pop them into the refrigerator for ten minutes or so. Beaujolais and Zinfandel are particularly good when cooled down to 60 or 65 degrees. A slight chill can add a refreshing dimension to other reds too, but don't get carried away.

But there are other drinks besides wine. For teetotalers at our Thanksgiving table we like to offer sparkling apple cider and sparkling mineral water. Both of these are refreshing and help with the digestion of this rich meal.

Finally there is beer. Actually, beer is quite good with Thanksgiving dinner, but we would suggest a fairly full-flavored beer, perhaps even an ale. Some of the darker, sweeter imports are very compatible with the holiday trimmings.

In any case, the choice of beverages is an important one. Wines and other drinks require some thought and should be an early part of your planning procedure. A good glass of wine can be the thing that turns a good dinner into a great one.

Index